GW00992177

GUIDE TO ENTERPRISE IT ARCHITECTURE

Col Perks
Tony Beveridge

GUIDE TO
ENTERPRISE IT
ARCHITECTURE

 Springer

Col Perks
AMR & Associates
Wellington
New Zealand
col.perks@amr.co.nz

Tony Beveridge
Wellington
New Zealand

Library of Congress Cataloging-in-Publication Data
Perks, Col.
    Guide to enterprise IT architecture / Col Perks, Tony Beveridge.
        p.   cm.
    Includes bibliographical references and index.
    ISBN 0-387-95132-6 (alk. paper)
    1. Electronic data processing.   2. Information technology.   I. Beveridge,
Tony.   II. Title.
QA76 .P4254 2001
004.2′2–dc21

2001048433

Printed on acid-free paper.

Printed in the United States of America.   (EB)

9 8 7 6 5 4 3 2

ISBN 0-387-95132-6

springer.com

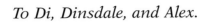

To Di, Dinsdale, and Alex.

Foreword

Because so much of this book is based on The Open Group's Architectural Framework (TOGAF), it is a great pleasure for me, as Director of The Open Group Architecture Forum in which TOGAF evolved, to be asked to write this Foreword.

It is especially pleasurable to be able to recommend this book as a penetrating yet extremely readable account of the key business drivers that, today more than ever, underpin the need for enterprise technical architecture and for a rigorous framework and method for putting enterprise technical architecture into practice.

The authors have drawn on their own in-depth experience of doing technical architecture "at the sharp end"—in an environment where time-to-market is paramount—in order to provide an excellent description of the use of technical architecture in today's highly volatile e-commerce marketplace.

It would be disingenuous of me to pretend that I have no ulterior motive, so I will come clean at the outset. I very much hope that, having read this excellent account of how TOGAF can help the task of enterprise technical architecture, the reader will be motivated to find out more about TOGAF, to use it actively for enterprise technical architecture work, to feed back to The Open Group the experience of its use, and perhaps also to consider joining the Architecture Forum and contributing to the further evolution of TOGAF for the benefit of the architecture community at large.

I realize that I run the risk that what follows will be perceived as simply a "pitch" for TOGAF and The Open Group, and I apologize to any who feel this way.

I hope I need not overdo the apologies, however. If the readers find the content of this book at all compelling and useful, as I very much expect they will, then it will only be natural for them to want to find out more about TOGAF and its ongoing evolution—and that is the need that I intend to address here.

I specifically want to do the following three things.

Firstly, because so much of the book is based on TOGAF, I want to explain to the reader a little about the background of TOGAF—how it was originated and continues to evolve within The Open Group's Architecture Forum, and how the Forum itself operates.

Secondly, because TOGAF is very much a "live" document and continues to be evolved by The Open Group (a newly updated version is published in December each year), I want to point the reader to the latest information on TOGAF and to other resources related to TOGAF that The Open Group makes freely available on its public Web site.

Thirdly, and less charitably, I have a responsibility to make clear to the reader the licensing terms under which The Open Group makes TOGAF publicly available.

I will take these in reverse order and dispense with duty first.

TOGAF Licensing Terms

There are three main groups of people who download TOGAF from The Open Group's Web site:

- Those who are merely curious and interested and wish simply to read TOGAF and possibly evaluate it.
- Those who wish to use TOGAF and its related resources as an architecture tool within their own organization.
- Those who wish to use TOGAF on projects for third parties or in other ways use it for commerical gain (for example, as part of technical architecture tutorial or training materials).

All of these groups are welcome to download TOGAF for their various purposes, including those seeking to use it commercially. However, different terms and conditions apply.

The Open Group makes TOGAF freely available to those seeking merely to read and evaluate it or to use it for internal architecture work. Its use is subject to a license but at no charge.

For those seeking to use TOGAF commercially, there is a license fee associated with its use, which is related to the nature of the using organization using it and the nature of the use. Rather than labor the commercial detail here, I will simply direct the reader to the URL within the TOGAF documentation where the relevant terms and condition are set out: http://www.opengroup.org/architecture/togaf/.

The objectives of this policy are twofold.

Firstly, The Open Group wishes to promote the widespread adoption and use of TOGAF, both for internal technical architecture work and as the basis for commercial services (e.g., consultancy, training, information) in the technical architecture field.

Secondly, The Open Group wishes to ensure that it receives a fair and reasonable return for the use of TOGAF for commercial gain in order to help fund the future development of TOGAF. We owe it to those members who have contributed their time and effort in the past to the work of the Architecture Forum, and to the evolution of TOGAF, to ensure that others make a fair contribution in return.

So much for legal necessities. I turn now to the additional information and resources that I hope the reader will find of interest.

The Development of TOGAF

TOGAF has come a long way since its inception in 1994 at the instigation of The Open Group's User Council (as it then was)—representatives of the computer user community among The Open Group membership.

The original motivations for TOGAF were very much as Tony and Col have expounded so eloquently in the early chapters of this book.

The original development of TOGAF was based on the Technical Architecture Framework for Information Management (TAFIM) developed by the U.S. Department of Defense. The DoD gave The Open Group explicit permission and encouragement to create TOGAF by building on the TAFIM, which itself represented hundreds of person-years of development effort and millions of dollars of U.S. government investment.

Starting from this sound foundation, the members of The Open Group's Architecture Forum have developed successive versions of TOGAF over the years and published them on The Open Group's public Web site.

TOGAF-Related Resources

The Open Group's Architecture Forum portal at http://www.opengroup.org/architecture/ provides a "way in" to the information sources described in the remainder of this Foreword.

The TOGAF documentation can be viewed freely online at http://www.opengroup.org/public/arch/.

The complete TOGAF documentation set, including the Architecture Development Method (ADM), TOGAF Foundation Architecture, and TOGAF Resource Base, can be downloaded under license (free for noncommercial use) from: http://www.opengroup.org/architecture/togaf/.

At http://www.opengroup.org/public/arch/p1/oview, TOGAF provides a business justification for enterprise technical architecture that is aimed specifically at the nontechnical business executive and echoes many of the motivations outlined in this book.

The Standards Information Base (SIB), referenced extensively throughout this book, is at: http://www.opengroup.org/sib/.

Although developed as part of TOGAF, and still forming a part of the TOGAF Foundation Architecture, the SIB is now also a freestanding corporate resource of The Open Group that it makes publicly available.

The Open Group Architecture Forum

The Architecture Forum is one of (currently) nine forums in which the membership of The Open Group comes together to further the goals of The Open Group as a whole. It meets regularly within the ambit of The Open Group quarterly members' conferences.

Details of these conferences, and thereby details of Architecture Forum meetings, can be found at: http://www.opengroup.org/conference/.

Although it is invidious to select individuals for specific mention, I do want to take the opportunity of this book's publication to pay tribute to those past and present members of the Architecture Forum who have served as its officers (Chairs and Vice-Chairs) over the past seven years of its existence. In alphabetical order:

Christer Askerfjord of Sweden Post
Terence Blevins of NCR (now of The Open Group)
Hugh Fisher of the UK National Health Service
Chris Greenslade of Frietuna Consultants
Barry Smith of Mitre Corporation
Walter Stahlecker of Hewlett-Packard
Hal Wilson of Litton PRC

My personal thanks to all of them and to the many other individuals and organizations who have contributed to the development of TOGAF over the years.

Finally, I would like to repeat my welcome to you to this thoroughly enjoyable and rewarding book and to express my thanks to the authors and publisher for bringing TOGAF to a worldwide audience in this way.

John Spencer, Director,
Architecture Forum, The Open Group

Preface

Overview

We dedicate this book to describing the concept, application, development, and maintenance of the enterprise technical architecture. Our overall objectives for this text are as follows:

- Describe what a technical architecture is, how and where it is used within the organization, and what benefits can be derived from its use
- Position technical architecture (compare and contrast) as a discipline and against other forms of architecture (including information architecture, business architecture, and application architecture) and strategic business planning
- The introduction of a significant framework in the area of enterprise technical architecture development—that is The Open Group's Architectural Framework (TOGAF)
- Provide a step-by-step walkthrough of each phase of TOGAF's architecture development method (ADM)
- Introduce the concept of technical architectural governance and the benefits of building a technical architectural capability within the organization

Many organizations enact a strategic view of business, defined through their business strategies and marketing functions, because to survive in business it is critical to understand what the organization is, where it is going, and how it is going to get there. It is obvious, therefore, that most organizations would apply exactly the same disciplines to technology. Unfortunately, we have witnessed many organizations (both large and small) that fully understand the value of business planning but continue to take a remarkably tactical approach to information technology (IT)—many with ingrained cultural "strategies" to adopt "technology du jour", without a reasoned understanding why.

On the other hand, organizations that do apply strategy to their technology are continuing to be frustrated by the pace at which technology is changing. The rapid uptake of the Internet in the mid-1990s has dramatically changed the technology landscape, forcing many organizations to rethink their own technology environments. For many, the speed of change within the industry has forced them to take an increasingly tactical view. The alternative being to use cumbersome and overly prescriptive architectural methodologies. No longer can an organization afford the commitment of time and resources to apply a 6-month (step back and smell the flowers) technical planning window. While such architectural development methods are still common in large organizations, especially government, today, maneuverability is the key.

We assert that an organization can both develop its technology environment based on reasoned planning and strategic incentives and maintain the ability to react quickly to new technical directions. By focusing on key strategic IT principles and adopting rapid and adaptable IT strategic methods, an organization can meet both requirements. An effective enterprise technical architecture provides this framework.

A technical architecture is not a product that can be purchased. It does not have a finite lifetime. It is a capability, a discipline, and an approach used to define, apply, and maintain the technology environment within the organization. It embodies the life cycle of defining the organization's technical strategy, setting and adopting technical standards, and maintaining the technology environment through changes in both business and technology. It can be thought of as the technical equivalent of the business strategy (i.e., the future shape of the business given the current environment).

This book provides the reader with a framework for developing and maintaining an organization's technical architecture. We present tools and approaches for defining the technology architecture, providing direction for the mitigation of some common IT problems. The development of the corporate technical architecture is based on The Open Group's Architectural Framework (TOGAF), an open source framework that embodies significant intellectual property and experience in architectural development. Throughout this book, we use a representative (and fictitious) organization to provide examples of the architectural concepts embodied within the framework.

Organization and Features

This book presents a wide treatment of the development of an organizational technical architecture. The structure of the book is essentially derived from the TOGAF architectural development method (ADM). Although we attempt to provide necessary detail in many areas, the aim of this book is to cover the entire life cycle of architectural development from the realization of the need for technical architecture development to the organizational issues that affect its maintenance. With this objective in mind, the text is clustered into three logical sections.

Section One: Architectural Rationale

This section is targeted as an overview of the concepts of technical architecture development. Its objective is to establish in the minds of the reader the rationale for conducting a technical architecture project. In this section are:

Chapter 1 considers how the term architecture has evolved and how it applies to a considerable number of IT disciplines. We look at a number of different definitions for the term, including technical architecture, application architecture, business systems architecture, and information architecture. We position the technical architecture within this spectrum of enterprise architecture disciplines. This chapter also takes a brief walk through the history of information technology and how it shaped the development of technical architectures.

Chapter 2 reviews a number of real-world IT problems that many readers may find familiar. We introduce some of the issues associated with the explosion of the Internet as a sales and marketing channel and some of the effects the Internet can have on the organization's IT environment. The overall aim of this book is to show how the application of an architectural approach to IT can mitigate the problems identified.

In Chapter 3 we review the many facets of strategic planning and position them in context with the technical architecture. We look in more detail at business (and e-business) strategies, the information systems strategic plan (ISSP), and the information and business systems architecture. Finally, we introduce the fictitious organization that will be used to provide examples of the phases of architectural development.

Chapter 4 analyzes the key criteria to use when selecting a framework for development of an organization's technical architecture. We discuss a number of architectural development alternatives, including government frameworks such as TAFIM and C4ISR. Our chosen development framework, the use of which in defining an enterprise technical architecture will be described in the remainder of this text, is The Open Group's Architectural Framework (TOGAF). We introduce its constituent parts through the concept of the enterprise continuum and include discussion relating to the architectural development method, the technical reference model, and the standards information base.

Chapter 5 details the first major phase of the TOGAF architectural development method—initiation and framework. This is a key phase. It establishes a business basis for the development of the architecture by gathering the relevant strategic information to initiate the architectural program. We discuss artifacts such as the request for architectural work, the scope of work, and the terms of reference. These documents provide the basis for beginning the architectural work and in essence provide a contract between the business and the program.

Section Two: Technical Architecture Development Process

This section delves deeply into the technical aspects of developing the technical architecture. It represents the crux of the TOGAF ADM, and considers the detailed modeling required to build the organization's target architecture. This section has significant technical content.

Chapter 6 investigates the process of discovering the organization's technology baseline. It provides a number of techniques to complete this task. In this chapter, we also introduce in more detail the fundamental TOGAF artifacts including the foundation architecture, the technical reference model, the concept of the TOGAF platform, the standards information base, and architectural views.

Chapter 7 describes a method for slicing through a complicated architecture to support increased understanding and better analysis of both current systems and the target architecture. Using a technique known as architectural views, it is possible to extract specific areas from the architecture and analyze them separately. In this chapter we consider the following views: business process domain, functional, management, security, builders, data management, user, computing, and communications.

Chapter 8 continues with techniques for assessing the current systems environment. In this chapter, however, we provide a method for viewing the current systems in TOGAF terms. We review how aspects such as architectural constraints and principles should be captured and their importance in understanding how the target architecture will be directed. We also view how to translate the current systems into TOGAF services, and we describe their placement in the technical reference model and the standards information base. Finally, we tackle the issue of keeping the architecture on track through the application of requirements traceability and describe artifacts such as the key question list and technology selection criteria.

Chapter 9 demonstrates how TOGAF can be extended due to its framework nature. In this chapter, we present the concept of super services. The standard TOGAF services (defined by the foundation architecture and service taxonomy) employs only limited methods for establishing service hierarchies—services that use lower layer services—yet this is the basic tenet of the life cycle of functionality within the platform. Services begin their lives close to the application. As they become increasingly commoditized, they descend into the platform to be replaced by more contemporary services. This is the basic characterization of a super service.

Chapter 10 considers the development of the organization's target architecture. The efforts applied to understanding the current environment, the enterprise requirements, and the identified issues and gaps are applied to the development of the target architecture. The target architecture is defined in two stages. This chapter discusses the definition of the logical services that will make up the final IT environment. Services are discovered in the journey along the architectural continuum. Beginning at the foundation architecture and finishing with the organizational architecture, we transition through common services and industry architecture discovery.

Chapter 11 scrutinizes techniques necessary to realize the logical service portfolio as physical technologies that will make up the IT environment. This continues the target architecture phase of the ADM. This chapter uses artifacts such as the standards information base, service functionality tables, and service instance maps to define the technological state of the organization's target architecture. Also discussed are industry standards and how they should be treated within the architecture.

Section Three: Project Management and Governance

The last section addresses the project management activities involved with successfully implementing a program that delivers to the target technical architecture. Beyond implementation, the final part of this section looks at the ongoing maintenance of the architecture, how to reduce divergence, and organizational aspects that can effect its success.

Chapter 12 explains the first of TOGAF's implementation phases, opportunity and solution and migration planning. In this chapter we consider the general effects of change on organizations and the specific implications of architectural change. A number of change-management strategies are considered. The implementation of the target architecture is discussed along with techniques for identifying the work packages that will be required to transition to the target architecture. We also take a look at the initiation of the architectural projects. This includes methods for the development of cost-benefit analysis, and processes for project prioritization.

Chapter 13 reviews the final implementation phases of TOGAF, the actual implementation of the architectural projects and the post-implementation maintenance of the architecture. We discuss mechanisms to control and manage the delivery of the architectural projects. The delivered architecture cannot be viewed as a static edifice. From the moment it is delivered, erosion begins. We look at strategies for managing the architecture through the long term, controlling drift, and ensuring that the value of the architecture is maintained.

In Chapter 14, we look at some of the organizational issues that plague architectural initiatives. The concept of architectural drift was introduced in the last chapter. The formalization of an architectural governance structure is critical in controlling drift. We discuss a number of factors that can lead to a failed architecture and mechanisms to avoid such failures.

Audience

This text is targeted at those who are involved with:

- Organizational technology strategic planning
- Technology procurement
- Management of technology projects
- Consulting and advising on technology issues
- The management and planning within technology subject areas
- The management of the total cost of IT ownership

The various organizational roles targeted by this book include IT managers, IT development planners, technical and application architects, project managers, and solutions designers. This book is not exclusively focused on internal organizational roles. It also provides a viable framework for organizations that sell IT products and services such as solutions architects, trainers and educators, and IT consultants.

The definition and adoption of technical architectures is not only the domain of the planners. For it to be successful, anyone working within IT in an organization should have an understanding of what a technical architecture is and why it is important. In many cases, the adoption of architectural "mandates" can be in conflict with other IT imperatives (such as immediate project requirements), and therefore it is important that everyone associated with IT appreciate the importance of its strategic value.

Acknowledgments

We have always felt strongly about the disciplines embodied within the concept of technical architecture and the benefits available to the organization in adopting an architectural approach to its IT environment—perhaps because this is what we do for a living. However, it is also an interesting and dynamic part of the occupation we all call IT. The discipline requires continually keeping abreast of technology and technology advancements, both through research and implementation projects.

We have always considered technical architecture a widely explored field but also felt that its influence had been waning in the face of e-time, especially in New Zealand. We therefore felt an urge to present a paper on the relevance of technical architectures in enabling organizations to support e-business initiatives. The article, titled "Blueprint for a Flexible Enterprise", was published in *Intelligent Enterprise*, and we would like to thank CMP Media for starting us on the long road in the production of this book.

In a typical example of the reach of the Internet, we were contracted by Springer-Verlag. Referring to the article, they inquired whether we had considered writing a book on the subject. We would like to thank Wayne Yuhasz of Springer-Verlag, for considering the article worthy of a book and for his and Wayne Wheeler's support throughout its development.

The model we have used for architectural development within many organizations is The Open Group's Architectural Framework (TOGAF). We have found the model flexible, simple to understand, and effective in producing corporate technical architectures. When planning the book, we felt that TOGAF should be its central theme. We are indebted to The Open Group, and in particular to John Spencer, the Director of Architectures at The Open Group, for allowing us to use TOGAF and for providing us with help and assistance when we were stuck.

Finally, we would like to thank the management team at AMR & Associates, who were required to "ignore" the fact that members of their team stopped work at 5 o'clock to pursue the personal goals of writing this book. We could not have completed the book without their support and constant ribbings of "Is it finished yet?" Special thanks to Darryn Thorn, Ian Miller, Mark Richter, Peter Couper, Phil McCaw, Sharon Weaver, and the rest of the AMR team (including our reviewers, Angela Martin, Clyde Hurley, Dion Woodbury, and Phil Kaye).

Contents

Foreword *vii*

Preface *xi*

Acknowledgments *xvii*

1. **Introduction to Technical Architecture** *1*
   1.1 Background *1*
   1.2 Definition of Architecture *1*
   1.3 A Brief History of Technical Architectures *7*
         The Iron Age *7*
         The Renaissance *9*
         The Industrial Revolution *10*
         Galactic Enlightenment *11*
   1.4 Enterprise Architectures *12*
         Management Checklist *15*
         Information Architecture *18*
         Business Systems Architecture *19*
         Technical Architecture *19*
         Application Architecture *20*
   1.5 Summary *20*

2. **Chaos and Control** *21*
   2.1 Introduction *21*
   2.2 Real-World IT Problems *22*
         Influencing Factors *22*
         Problem Matrix *23*
            The Business / Technical Strategy Gulf *23*
            The Information Inaccuracy and Integrity Problem *24*
            Infrastructure Hell *26*
            The Security Problem *26*
            The Problem of Incompatible Technologies *28*
            The Cost Problem *29*
            Technology Anarchy *32*
            The Problem with the Ongoing Systems
               Management of IT *33*

The Problem with Procurement   *34*
The Collapsing Event Horizon   *34*
2.3   Exacerbating Chaos—The Advent of E-Enablement   *35*
2.4   Control Through Architecture   *37*
2.5   Summary   *40*

**3.   Business Strategy—The Foundation for the
Technical Architecture   *42***
3.1   Introduction   *42*
3.2   Business Strategic Planning   *43*
3.3   Information Systems Strategic Planning   *46*
3.4   Information Architecture   *53*
Common Information Understanding   *55*
Information Needs   *56*
Information Analysis   *57*
3.5   Business Systems Architecture   *58*
Current System Analysis   *58*
Clustering   *60*
Project Definition   *61*
3.6   Architecture Maintenance   *62*
3.7   The Rise of the e-Business Strategy   *63*
3.8   Introduction to the Example Organization   *65*
Key Characteristics   *66*
Introducing Crunchy Frog Ltd.   *66*
CFL Applications   *67*
CFL Infrastructure   *69*
The Architectural Project   *71*
3.9   Summary   *74*

4.   TOGAF and the Architectural Development Method   *76*
4.1   Introduction   *76*
4.2   Architectural Frameworks   *77*
The Notion of a Framework   *77*
The Need for a Framework   *78*
4.3   Introducing TOGAF   *78*
The Enterprise Continuum   *80*
Architectural Continuum   *81*
Solutions Continuum   *84*
Technical Reference Model   *86*
Standards Information Base   *88*
Architectural Development Method   *88*
Expanded Target Architecture Definition   *91*
4.4   Using TOGAF in e-Time   *93*
4.5   Summary   *94*

5. Initiation and Framework   *95*
   5.1   Introduction   *95*
   5.2   Initiation   *96*
         Business Focus   *96*
         What Is a Business or Strategic Driver?   *98*
         TOGAF Process   *99*
         Inputs   *100*
         Steps   *102*
         Outputs   *103*
         Information Gathering   *103*
         Collateral   *104*
         Statement of Architecture Work   *105*
         The Terms of Reference (Corporate)   *106*
   5.3   Warning Signs (or the Semiotics of Dissent)   *108*
         Governance: Ensuring Success   *110*
   5.4   Example   *112*
         Introduction   *112*
         Strategic Plan Input   *113*
         e-business Strategy   *113*
         Architectural Principles   *114*
         Initiation   *114*
   5.5   Summary   *122*

6. Baseline Description   *123*
   6.1   Introduction   *123*
   6.2   Where Is TOGAF Appropriate?   *126*
   6.3   Describing the Current Systems   *130*
         Cataloging Current Systems   *131*
         Obtaining the Information   *132*
         Native Views   *134*
   6.4   TOGAF Terms   *136*
         A Service Portfolio   *136*
            The Technical Reference Model   *137*
            The Application Software   *143*
            The Application Platform   *143*
            Communications Infrastructure   *150*
         Views   *150*
   6.5   Current System Issues   *151*
   6.6   Outputs   *155*
   6.7   Example   *156*
         Introduction   *156*
         Current System Background   *156*
         CFL's Current Systems   *157*
            Network   *157*

Logistics System   *158*
Sales System   *159*
Interfaces   *160*
Regional Systems   *161*
Current System Assessment   *163*
6.8   Summary   *164*

7.   Architectural Views   *166*
7.1   Introduction   *166*
7.2   The Role of Architectural Views   *167*
Recommended Views   *168*
7.3   Business Process Domain View   *169*
Introduction   *169*
Role   *169*
7.4   Functional View   *171*
7.5   Security View   *171*
Basic Concepts   *172*
Generic Security Architecture View   *173*
7.6   Management View   *175*
7.7   Software Engineering View   *175*
Data Intensive versus Information
Intensive Software Systems   *179*
Software Tiers   *180*
7.8   Data Management View   *181*
Database Models   *183*
Data Dictionary/Directory Systems   *185*
Data Security   *186*
7.9   User View   *186*
7.10   System Engineering View   *187*
Client/Server Model   *187*
Master/Slave and Hierarchical Models   *188*
Peer-to-Peer Model   *190*
Distributed Object Management Model   *190*
7.11   Communications View   *191*
Introduction   *191*
Communications Infrastructure   *191*
Communications Models   *193*
Allocation of Services to Components   *195*
7.12   Summary   *195*

**8.   Target Architecture—Baseline Description
in TOGAF Format**   *197*
8.1   Introduction   *197*
8.2   TOGAF Process   *198*

Inputs   *200*
Steps   *200*
Architectural Constraints   *201*
Constraint Satisfaction   *204*
Architecture Principles   *205*
8.3   The Nature of Service-Biased Mapping   *208*
8.4   Reuse Assessment and Requirements Traceability   *215*
Selection Criteria   *222*
Key Questions List   *223*
8.5   Outputs   *227*
8.6   Example   *227*
Gap Analysis   *231*
Requirements Traceability   *237*
8.7   Summary   *238*

9.   **Super Services**   *240*
9.1   Introduction   *240*
9.2   Services and Super Services   *241*
Background   *241*
Application – Service Relationships   *244*
Logical View   *244*
Physical View   *246*
Architectural View—Super Services   *247*
9.3   Example   *251*
9.4   Summary   *254*

10.   **Target Architecture—Selecting Service Portfolios**   *255*
10.1   Introduction   *255*
10.2   Transition   *256*
10.3   The Baseline Description   *257*
10.4   Gap Analysis   *259*
10.5   Services   *262*
10.6   The Enterprise Continuum   *265*
The Foundation Service Portfolio   *268*
The Common Systems Service Portfolio   *272*
The Industry Service Portfolio   *280*
The Organizational Service Portfolio   *285*
Custom Services   *285*
Procured Enterprise-Specific Services   *287*
Iterations   *290*
10.7   The Technical Reference Model   *291*
The TRM Graphic   *291*
Selection Criteria   *293*
The Technical Architecture Document   *295*

10.8   Requirements Traceability   *296*
10.9   Outputs   *299*
10.10   Example   *299*
          Introduction   *299*
          Foundation Service Portfolio   *300*
          Common System Service Portfolio   *300*
          Industry Service Portfolio   *303*
          Organization-Specific Service Portfolio   *304*
          CFL Technical Reference Model   *305*
          Requirements Traceability   *306*
10.11   Summary   *308*

11.   Target Architecture—Architectural Definition   *309*
11.1   Introduction   *309*
11.2   The Solutions Continuum*310*
11.3   The Standards Information Base   *313*
11.4   Service Realization   *313*
          Services and Service Instances   *313*
          Service Instance Relationships   *320*
          Standards and Their Incarnations   *327*
          Architectural Definition   *333*
            Determine Approach   *333*
            Finalize Service Functionality   *340*
            Technology Selection Iterations   *341*
            Instance Mapping   *345*
          Requirements Traceability   *348*
11.5   Output   *350*
11.6   Example   *350*
          Disclaimer   *350*
          Introduction   *350*
          Approach   *351*
          Service Functionality   *351*
          Realization   *355*
11.7   Summary   *358*

12.   Opportunities, Solutions, and Migration Planning   *360*
12.1   Introduction   *360*
12.2   Opportunities and Solutions   *361*
          Background   *361*
          Transition Assessment   *362*
          Change Management   *364*
          Project Identification and Classification   *367*
          Output   *371*

12.3   Migration Planning   *372*
       Background   *372*
       Project Initiation   *374*
       Cost Benefit Analysis   *376*
       Project Prioritization   *382*
       Project Roadmap   *385*
       Output   *386*
12.4   Example   *386*
       Introduction   *386*
       Change Management   *386*
       Work Packages   *387*
       Project Initiation   *387*
12.5   Summary   *390*

13. Implementation and Maintenance   *392*
13.1   Introduction   *392*
13.2   Implementation   *393*
13.3   Maintenance   *399*
       Background   *399*
       The Cyclic Architecture Process   *401*
       Architectural Governance Model   *406*
       Architectural Compliance   *409*
13.4   Example   *413*
       Introduction   *413*
       Architectural Contract   *414*
       Maintenance   *414*
13.5   Summary   *414*

14. A Case for Change   *419*
14.1   Introduction   *419*
14.2   The Ivory Tower Principle   *420*
14.3   Architectural Capability   *422*
14.4   Governance   *425*
14.5   Example   *428*
14.6   Summary   *429*

Bibliography   *431*

Glossary   *435*

Index   *443*

CHAPTER 1

Introduction to Technical Architecture

1.1 Background

This chapter provides an overview of the discipline known as *technical architecture*. In the body of the chapter, we will:

- Introduce and define the concept of technical architecture
- Introduce some of the benefits of a technical architecture approach
- Compare and contrast technical architecture with other types of architecture (information architecture, business systems architecture, and application architecture)
- Position the technical architecture in relation to business strategic planning
- Provide a brief history of how organizations have traditionally developed technical architectures and the form they may take in the future

1.2 Definition of Architecture

The term *architecture* has become increasingly over-used in the context of information technology (IT). It has been applied to a continuum ranging from ethereal concepts in IT management to the physical makeup of a vendor's products, from the structure of information to the delivery of technology, and even the technical management of an IT solution. The term architecture is so wide ranging that all of these uses may indeed be valid. It may be worthwhile to draw on a familiar use for the term—the structuring of physical forms such as buildings. Webster's dictionary defines an architecture as:

> formation or construction as or as if as the result of a conscious act; a unifying or coherent form or structure; the art or science of building

The key components of this definition revolve around a conscious or coherent approach toward something with a defined structure reflecting a certain beauty. The architecting of a building, for instance, is based on solid and coherent reasoning. The architect, the purveyor of the architecture, is charged with considering a wide range of aspects in the development of the architecture. There is the will of the client, the requirements of the site, legal constraints, financial constraints, technology limitations, the building's users, and a host of other considerations that do not immediately appear to be directly related to the formation of the building. In essence, the architect is the conduit through which all of the factors flow in realizing the final structure of the building.

An architecture typically establishes a shared vision. However, simply setting the vision is not enough. It must be communicated to the builders, the clients, and interested third parties alike. It must be maintained throughout the lifecycle of the construction effort, and it must bridge the gap between the requirements of the client, the needs of the builder, and the constraints of the physical world. Figure 1.1 shows some architectural influences.

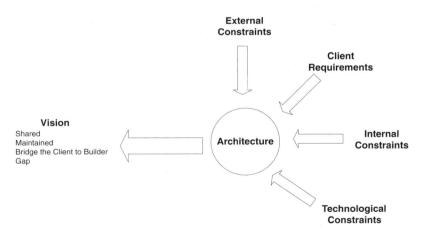

FIGURE 1.1.   Architectural influences.

The term *architecture* was adopted in common usage by the IT industry not that many years ago. It has the same breadth of usage as its meanings in other industries. The eclectic nature of the term bears witness to its application by the industry in many areas within IT. One of the more common uses of the term can be associated with the design of individual systems—called *software or application architecture*. In fact, individual sub-components of systems can represent corresponding architectural practices.

Key Definition: **Architecture.**
A pragmatic, coherent structuring of a collection of components that through these factors supports the vision of the full "user" in an elegant way.

There are a wide variety of definitions for the term software architecture, and there is not as yet a commonly accepted definition. The term has its genesis in the software engineering disciplines. Regardless, the majority of definitions have a number of characteristics in common:

- It is used to define a single "system."
- It describes the functional aspects of the system.
- It concentrates on describing the structure of the system.
- It describes both the intra-system and inter-system relationships.
- It sets in place guidelines, policies, and principles that govern the system's design, development, and evolution over time.

The foundation of contemporary software architecture began with work conducted by Dijkstra[1] in 1968 when he postulated that the design of software should be concerned with structure and viewed in layers. In 1992, Perry and Wolfe[2] put a modern face on Dijkstra's engineering precept. Their definition proposed a set of architectural (or design) elements that have a particular form. In 1999, Booch, Rumbaugh, and Jacobson[3] described an architecture as the set of significant decisions about the organization of a software system, the selection of the structural elements and their interfaces by which the system is composed together with their behavior as specified in the collaborations among those ele-

---

1. Dijkstra, E.W., *The Structure of "THE" Multiprogramming System*, *Communications of the ACM* (1968), Volume 11, Number 5, Pages 345–346.
2. Perry, P., Wolfe, A. Foundation for the Study of Software Architecture, ACM SigSoft Software Engineering Notes, Volume 14, Number 4, October, 1992.
3. Booch, Rumbaugh, and Jacobson, The UML Modeling Language User Guide, Addison-Wesley, Reading, MA, 1999.

ments, the composition of these structural and behavioral elements into progressively larger subsystems, and the architectural style that guides this organization.

There are many streams of work currently active in the industry concerned with software architectures. The Software Engineering Institute (SEI) is preeminent in research and domain knowledge in this area. Other standards organizations, such as the Institute of Electrical and Electronic Engineers (IEEE) and the International Standards Organization (ISO), also provide considerable guidance.

This text does not, however, deal directly with software architectures, although the discipline is referenced at points to provide suitable comparison. It is a major premise of this book that the term *architecture* has a broader meaning than the architecting of individual systems. The use of technology within the entire organization needs to be defined based on a different set of architectural disciplines. In this book, we adopt the term *enterprise information technology architecture* as the possible root for all IT architectural disciplines. At a high level, the enterprise IT architecture consists of a hierarchy of architectural disciplines that can be loosely associated with full IT delivery, as follows:

- The *information architecture* deals with the structure and use of information within the organization, and the alignment of information with the organization's strategic, tactical, and operational needs.
- The *business systems architecture* structures the information needs into a delineation of necessary business systems to meet those needs.
- The *technical architecture* defines the technical environment and infrastructure in which all information systems exist.
- The *software or application architecture* defines the structure of individual systems based on defined technology.

We describe these concepts in more detail later in the chapter, and we dedicate an entire chapter (see Chapter 3) to the concepts surrounding the architectural hierarchy.

However, our specific interest within this text is the technical architecture—the architecture that describes the makeup of the entire technology environment. There are a multitude of ways to describe the makeup of a technical architecture. The organization's view of technical architecture evolves as the architectural maturity of an organization evolves: the greater the emphasis on an overall architectural approach, the more advanced and complete the concept of a technical architecture becomes. Following are a number of technical architecture "motherhood" statements that may help to crystallize a meaning. Importantly, consider how the concepts "coherent," "conscious," and "unifying" from our Webster's definition apply to these statements. A technical architecture:

- describes and defines the structure of the technical environment in which business systems are delivered
- creates and maintains a set of core technology standards with which to measure technology projects
- is an organizational capability—the people within (and outside) the IT organization who provide strategic technical advice
- is a means of resolving organizational technical issues
- sets system (and hence software architecture), project, and corporate technology direction
- establishes a reasoned approach for the integration of technology and business systems
- establishes a framework for technology procurement decisions
- both provides input to and is driven from the IT planning process
- allows the organization to control technology costs
- develops a clear understanding of an organization's critical technical issues
- provides a governance structure to support the ongoing health of the organization's technical environment

In essence, the technical architecture defines the platform on which an organization building and uses information technology for business benefit.

It is important to stress that a technical architecture is not simply a set of standards, an attractively bound strategy, or a glitzy presentation; it is an organizational capability that exists not only in documentation but also in the knowledge and experience of the technical strategists, IT managers, planners, architects, and implementors. It extends the strategic process of the organization through specific governance structures. The collective skills of the entire IT organization aid in its development, its maintenance, and its translation to physical systems.

Key Definition: **Technical Architecture.**
Defines the technical and governance platform on which an organization builds its IT systems to support business benefit.

Without stepping onto the soapbox just yet, we believe that the development and maintenance of an organizational technical architecture builds a well-oiled organization able to react effectively to both business and technology changes, with the ability to assess its strategic requirements, to control the costs associated with IT, and to be successful in the general delivery of technology and specific technology-based projects.

The technical advantages that result from an effective technical architecture also bring the following important business benefits.

A more effective IT operation. Better-defined structure and modularity in the IT environment leads to a much more effective IT operation:

- Lower software development, support, and maintenance costs
- More application portability
- Improved interoperability and easier system and network management
- A better ability to address critical enterprise-wide issues such as security
- Easier upgrade and exchange of system components

Better return on existing investment and reduced risk for future investment. The structure of existing and planned systems is clearly defined, leading to:

- Reduced complexity in IT infrastructure
- Maximum return on investment in existing IT infrastructure
- The flexibility to make, buy, or outsource IT solutions
- Reduced risk overall in new investment and the costs of IT ownership

Faster, simpler, and cheaper procurement. There is a clear strategy for future procurement and migration, with the result that:

- Buying decisions are simpler because the information governing procurement is readily available in a coherent plan
- The procurement process is faster, maximizing procurement speed and flexibility without sacrificing architectural coherence

Flexibility for business growth and restructuring. It is much easier to ensure access to integrated information across the enterprise:

- Maximum flexibility for business growth and restructuring
- Real savings when reengineering business processes following internal consolidations, mergers, and acquisitions

Faster time-to-market. An IT infrastructure much better equipped to support the rapid deployment of mission-critical business applications leads to:

- Faster time-to-market for new products and services, leading to:
- Increased growth and profitability

Now that we have an understanding of what we mean when we use the term *technical architecture*, let us take a brief stroll through the salient phases of IT history highlighting the evolution of architecting technology.

1.3   A Brief History of Technical Architectures

Since the early days of technology, the art of connecting technology components to form complex systems has existed. The concept of the technical architecture existed in the IT industry long before it was even called the IT industry—in fact, even before we called the disciplines of computing *electronic data processing*. As technologies have evolved, as the industry has grown, and as the use of technologies become more sophisticated, the need to architect technology solutions becomes increasingly important. Today, there are literally thousands of products, specifications, standards, guidelines, best practices, and strategies that must be sifted through to enable solutions to be built. The number of different components that go into making a single "system" can be staggering. Given this environment, it is hardly surprising that we continually hear about the "architecting" of IT. The role of the IT architect (and with it, both systems and corporate architectures) is growing. But was it always like this? Have we always had to architect solutions? The answer is yes, it was just different back then.

This is a pertinent point on which to frame our brief view of the history of technology architectures. In many respects, it has always been affected by the technology style of the day, driven not only by the products (and marketing) produced by vendors but also by organizational buying patterns and organizational peer pressure. It is convenient for this discussion to separate the history of architectures (and with it the history of technology itself). We look at the history of IT in four distinct ages. We have colloquially termed them (see Figure 1.2):

- The Iron Age
- The Renaissance
- The Industrial Revolution
- Galactic Enlightenment (maybe)

The Iron Age

The beginning of this era was the genesis of the IT industry as we know it today. This period was characterized by large, proprietary, and above all expensive mainframe technology. Compared with the technology of today, early mainframe systems were cumbersome, complicated, and

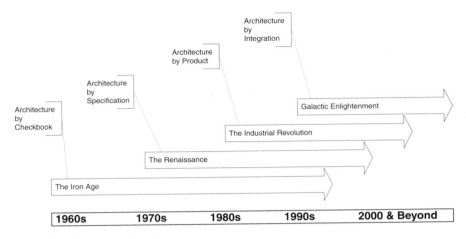

FIGURE 1.2.   The Ages of Architecture.

required a vast array of highly talented and specialized technicians and designers to build even the simplest business systems. During this age, the goal of the technology, which remains relatively unchanged today, was the provision of reliable, robust, unsophisticated, and scalable systems to those with deep enough pockets.

It was during this period that the term *architecture* first came into use. Then architecture was related to the construction of the system itself—predominantly the hardware. It was defined at the time as "the conceptual structure of the system as seen by the programmer" and replaced older, less stylized IBM terms such as "machine organization."[4] This also marked the beginning of the separation of a purely software architectural approach and the architecture of the remainder of the infrastructure and environment.

From the organization's point of view, this was in reality architecture by checkbook. Organizations tended to purchase every component of a business system from a single vendor, such as IBM, and it was seen as the vendor's responsibility to ensure that all parts worked together. This simplistic approach to architecture is one of the primary reasons why this form of technology is still successfully applied in the industry today. Of course, this approach was also driven by the highly proprietary nature of computing components, interoperability not being a mainframes vendor's strong point.

4. Werner Buchholz, Editor, "Comments, Query, and Debate," *IEEE Annals of the History of Computing*, April – May 2000.

The Renaissance

The vendors and architectures of the Iron Age continue to this day, albeit with ever-increasing competition and against an ever-changing technology landscape. The first real mind shift away from "big iron" happened early on. The miniaturization of hardware and a number of new players in the market (among the notables were organizations such as Digital Equipment Corporation) created a cultural shift toward more cost-effective solutions (cost-effective in this sense is relative). The Renaissance was driven by the birth of the minicomputer and the UNIX operating system. Coinciding with the UNIX movement was an increasing focus on open standards. As UNIX moved from academia and metamorphosed into a number of derivatives, it was realized fairly early that UNIX could only "defeat" the mainframe if portability was maintained between the various vendors' platforms. The UNIX world, in essence, began to regulate itself.

UNIX provided a call to arms for interoperable and open computing. As increasing numbers of vendors (including independent software vendors, called ISVs) entered the marketplace, the driving need was for the development of open and standard specifications to aid the integration and interoperability of software products from more than one source.

Standards organizations such as X/Open, Open Software Foundation (OSF), IEEE, and ISO put huge resources into standards development. The problem was that many of the standards bodies began competing—complementary technologies bred rival standards. For organizations, it became critical to understand which standards they should be buying into. Even the supposedly simple act of choosing networking protocols—basic infrastructure choices—was complicated by a variety of competing technologies and vendors.

The best way to summarize the technical architecture approach of this era is architecture through specifications.

This was also the period in which fundamental groundwork on defining an "architectural approach" was completed. Bodies such as IEEE and ISO were the first to begin to describe an instance of a technology landscape in technical reference models (TRMs) and architectural frameworks. The TRM is an important tool in architectural development. The Government Open Systems Interconnection Profile (GOSIP) was an example of an organizational technical architecture based on the Open Systems Interconnection (OSI) group of specifications and aimed primarily at the government domain. X/Open produced its Open System Environment (OSE) TRM targeted principally at the UNIX market. Although these architectures were broad in concept, they were also notoriously difficult to understand and, more importantly, implement. From an organization's point of view, the models were biased towards the technologies defined by specific standards bodies. In short, there was no organizational context.

It is worth noting that during the halcyon days of this age a small American-based network connecting mostly military and academic research institutions called "The Internet" was conceived and was growing slowly.

The Industrial Revolution

The Industrial Revolution was heralded by still cheaper and better performing systems and the arrival of the personal computer. This environmental change provided huge opportunities for all. The market was awash with new vendors, all finding markets in a wide array of technological niches hitherto unknown in the previous ages. Vendors such as Microsoft redefined the industry's approach to IT; the concept of selling small numbers of high-cost technologies was supplanted by dramatic price reductions to push huge volumes. This was the genesis of commodity technologies. Many of the large vendors from the Iron Age struggled during the Industrial Revolution. For them, it was redefine or die.

Curiously enough, although the assumption was that standards and specifications would become even more important, this period was characterized by a small bias back toward proprietary technologies. There were many factors contributing to this. For one, the standard-making process was becoming increasingly cumbersome. Standards and specifications took time to develop. Committees weighted down by greater industry representation led to protracted consensus. Of course, once a standard was agreed upon, vendors still required time to implement it in their products and then sell the products. With the ever-increasing pace of technology advancement, those organizations waiting for standard specifications inevitably lost ground to those choosing proprietary products. Microsoft, Cisco, Oracle, and other vendors began to gain dominance in their particular domains by introducing "proprietary" products (usually thinly masquerading as "industry standard"-based) to market long before standards could be agreed upon and delivered. It was during this time that standards bodies such as ISO, X/Open, and OSF were struggling to maintain their mind share as custodians of open computing. Indeed, many of the OSI specifications were only implemented in very niche situations, and OSI was having less and less impact in organizational environments.

To gain an understanding of the effect of the "committee approach," it is interesting to consider, by way of an example, the OSI directory standards (X.500 – ISO 9594). In the late 1980s, ISO's concept of a global directory was innovative and far ahead of both its time and the technology available from major vendors. Although there were a number of implementations, its complexity (the OSI committees were always charged with developing standards based on the assumption of a global telecommunications environment) and sophistication barred entry for mainstream vendors who, by contrast, were concentrating on solving problems within the workgroup. By the mid-1990s, there was little activity around the X.500 standards. As the Internet began to boom, the X.500 directory was resurrected with an Internet spin by the Internet Engineering Taskforce (IETF) as the LDAP group of technologies, simpler (the L means lightweight) and based upon the now common "good enough" approach. From this point, the global directory concept has grown rapidly.

In architectural terms, this period can be summarized as architecture by product. Organizations were able to make strategic product choices based on alliances with a small number of vendors. The domination of Microsoft at the desktop (and then the server) aided this architectural approach.

Also during this period the Internet exploded—it was finally "discovered." The academic community had been using this tool for decades, but the arrival of the World Wide Web commoditized access, dramatically improving accessibility. This event also began a swing back to industry standards. The IETF had been setting standards for much of the Internet's life—in fact, it was the cornerstone of its success. Without commonly accepted architectures and specifications it would not have been possible to build a global network of this type. The IETF had a different view on standardization that may have helped. Before a specification (known as a Request for Comment or RFC) becomes a standard, it is required that at least two interoperable implementations exist. Also, the IETF collectively took a "good enough" approach to specification— it did not have to be perfect before it was adopted. This may have been a key failing of the OSI approach.

Galactic Enlightenment

The future? Well, there are a number of visions. Certainly we will see the Internet expanding and extending. But will the much-lauded phrase "the network is the computer" be realized? What about web services? Much will depend on infrastructure and capability. The world is becoming so inexorably meshed through Internet technology that economic strength is no longer a factor of single economies. Certainly, we see basic infrastructure consolidation: networks, operating systems, and software architectures will merge into only a small number of key technologies, all necessary to support interoperable Web applications. Still, the Industrial Revolution continues at an ever-increasing pace. This time, however, there will be little or no fighting over "the base platform"; this landscape is clear for the foreseeable future. In this age the battle will rage over the services above the basic platform: knowledge management, entertainment, portals, brokers, and semantics.

Architecturally, the integration of a wide variety of technologies in desired service portfolios will become increasingly important. No longer will systems consist of a few parts. Organizations will not only need to integrate complex internal components into functioning systems, but they will also have to integrate the systems of their suppliers and customers both nationally and internationally. In other words, the corporate architecture will no longer be concerned solely with internal (controllable) aspects but will have to consider the technologies being implemented by its partners, customers, and an ever-increasing collection of anonymous entities, that may mean life or death for the business.

Like much of human history, there is reason to think that IT history will exhibit some form of cyclic behavior. Instead of the perceived inexorable march to galactic enlightenment, maybe the future holds retrenchment, another Iron Age, and an increasing reliance on a number of large vendors pushing proprietary technologies, with increasingly centralized systems. However, regardless of the future, the concept of technical architecture will remain, morphing as the focus shifts.

1.4 Enterprise Architectures

We have already alluded to the various (and more obvious) meanings behind the meaning of *architecture*—typically in the application or system space. The term, also, has many connotations at the strategic level. General architectural disciplines can be applied to the strategic building and sculpting of IT to align to business strategy. For this collection of strategic architectures, we have adopted the term *enterprise IT architecture*.

Key Definition: **Enterprise IT Architecture.**
The collection of strategic and architectural disciplines that encompass the Information, Business System, and Technical Architectures.

In many ways, there is synergy between the Enterprise IT Architecture and the concepts that embodies information systems strategic planning (ISSP). Both provide a medium- to long-term vision and framework within which the IT environment is implemented including people, structure, and technologies. Both the ISSP and enterprise architecture provide guidelines for systems to be implemented, technologies to be considered, and information to be gained. The ISSP, however, considers all of these aspects at a point in time and at a higher (business) level.

We believe that enterprise architecture has two guises. The first is the detailed companion to the ISSP process. The other is a living, breathing entity adapting to its environment in a reasoned way. Some organizations' experience with ISSPs has been less than encouraging. They can be expensive to produce and complicated to implement, and it can be difficult to measure their effectiveness. In some instances, they end up as expensive bookends. On the other hand, the enterprise architecture is never complete and is embodied within every major IT decision made.

This is not to say that the concept of an ISSP is redundant, for there are key areas of an ISSP that the enterprise architecture disciplines avoid such as organizational structure and financial issues. Additionally, the ISSP is a major planning exercise conducted directly in consultation with and totally influenced by the business. However, we are suggesting that the concepts embodied in the ISSP as it stands lack maneuverability and agility in the face of the modern Internet economy. Furthermore, the adoption of an architectural approach to IT removes many of the nonsalient temporally sensitive functions from the ISSP, providing the potential to make it a more responsive and relevant discipline.

At the other end of the architectural spectrum is the structuring of individual systems and applications—software architecture. This book provides some reference to these disciplines insofar as the definition of a technical strategy impacts directly on the architectural philosophy for applications. However, we limit our discussion on this subject area—there are considerable treatments of this topic already in the bookstore.

In this book we are specifically concentrating on the enterprise technical architecture (abbreviated to the technical architecture), and at this point we would like to position this with respect to other architectural disciplines that exist within the enterprise architecture hierarchy. Figure 1.3 provides a high-level view of the planning and architectural processes. In Chapter 3, we provide greater detail both in the architectural disciplines and the strategic planning phases. Notice, however, that the architectural disciplines are driven from the business planning processes. The ISSP lays the groundwork for the (cyclic) enterprise architecture disciplines. The information, business system, and technical architectures, then, exist at an overarching and cooperative level within the IT environment and its governance processes; each feeds off the other. Application (or software) architecture is enacted each time an individual system is procured or built.

The enterprise architecture provides direction to support business ob-

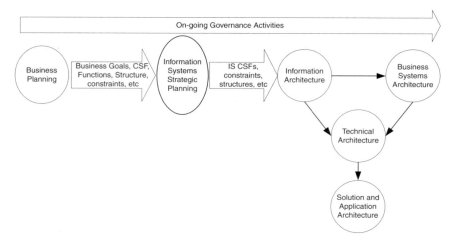

FIGURE 1.3.   Strategic planning and corporate IT architecture process.

jectives through IT. An organization that uses architectural techniques in this manner can satisfy a number of key IT principles:

- The provisioning of business systems and IT can be managed to support business objectives.
- Decisions about the priority and interdependence of business systems, and the opportunities for using IT, are taken on the basis of an agreed formulation of business objectives and information needs.
- The rapid and flexible provision of new and enhanced systems, and information to support business initiatives, is done within a common framework of understanding (i.e., the enterprise architecture).
- The practical evolution of an organization's technology takes into account the organization's current systems and technological situation and the medium- to long-term technology vision.
- The evolution and adoption of technology is driven by business priorities.

In the following, sections we look briefly at the various components of enterprise IT architecture. It is important to note that although Figure 1.3 shows a linear progression through the various architectural stages, this in no way reflects the way it occurs in the real world. Many of the architectural stages will be performed in parallel and in an iterative "good enough" manner, each stage supporting the others in development. There is no point engaging in a 2-year architectural program while the IT organization is continually struggling with tactical imperatives that could (should) have been solved by the architecture.

Importantly—and this is a key basis for this book—the activities of architectural development need not be turned into a long-winded academic exercise resourced by highly skilled (and highly paid) consultants, where the bound volume of work is far more important than the benefits derived from the work. The approach we advocate is one that provides "rapid" architectural development and effective governance (and capability focus) without being overly onerous. Furthermore, it should be resourced from within the organization's current IT structure (possibly with some external guidance). From our perspective, the development and maintenance of the enterprise technical architecture is a core internal IT function. While it is of course possible to outsource much of its development (the leg work, certainly), control and on-going governance must remain internal.

Another point to note is that the linear process shown is not in fact linear but cyclic. Organizations never stand still: their objectives, functions, and structure are continually changing. New market opportunities are continually emerging. New enabling technologies are being recognized and must be acted upon. The objective of the corporate architecture approach is to proactively (and sometimes reactively) manage changing circumstances and redefine the architecture as the business environment changes. As we have already asserted, an architectural approach is critical to the successful use of technology within the organization. Thus, it will fail if it is static and slow-moving. All aspects of the architecture must contain feedback points within itself and other organizational components. It should be continually aligned with changes in the business landscape through interfacing with the changing business direction. If it stands still, or does not evolve in tandem with the business, then it can become a cause of the very problems it is trying to correct.

Information Architecture

Information architecture (IA) views the activities performed by the enterprise and the information required in performing them. This high-level view of activities and data provides a basis for the detailed analysis of business requirements during the development of the business systems architecture. Some of the functions involved in developing the IA are as follows:

- *Identify the organization's information needs*. Establish a set of business facts and express them in terms of the organization's information needs.

- *Define the information architecture.* Architectural definition uses techniques such as parallel decomposition, value chain analysis, and event analysis.
- *Analyze function dependencies.* Verify and refine the function decomposition by identifying the dependencies among functions.
- *Define entities and relationships.* Refine the data portion of the IA—in essence this is a corporate data-modeling exercise.
- *Information needs mapping.* Complete the list of entity types by comparing them with the list of information needs.
- *Analyze entity type use.* Record the expected effects of business functions on entity types, and validate and refine the activity hierarchy diagram and the entity relationship diagram.
- *Map functions and entity types to organizational units.* Relate data to the organization, checking the activity hierarchy and identifying how elements of the IA are used.

Key Definition: **Information Architecture.**
The structure (including interdependencies and relationships) of information required and in use by the organization.

Business Systems Architecture

Business systems architecture (BSA) describes the business systems and principal information stores required to support the IA. The BSA provides an initial prediction of the reuse or enhancement of current (sometimes referred to as "legacy") systems and information and the development of new business systems. During analysis, a more detailed understanding of information requirements determines the content of each business system. The BSA is used to guide the assignment of business activities, business systems, and a macro view of interfaces to current systems and data. As a governance function new system initiatives are considered in the context of the BSA to ensure correct placement.

Key Definition: **Business systems architecture.**
Defines the structure and content (information and function) of all business systems in the organization.

Technical Architecture

Technical architecture describes and maintains the integrity of the hardware, software, and infrastructure environment required to support the

BSA and the IA—that is, in technical architecture speak, The Platform. The delivery of IT solutions, the planning and management of the technical environment, and the reaction to a changing IT landscape depend greatly on the definition of the Technical Architecture. Its responsibility is to ensure that the environment not only functions correctly but to define how the structure functions. This book deals, at a detailed level, with the development of the enterprise Technical Architecture.

Key Definition: **The Platform.**
The platform is central to the concept of architecture and represents a strategic organizational asset. The platform collects all the key services defined in the architecture so that they are available in the infrastructure for use by individual business systems. Services that exist in the platform represent technologies that are proven to be both generic and commodity.

Application Architecture

Application architecture deals specifically with the structure of individual applications and systems. It can be consider the most detailed of the architectural processes and has a functionally-specific focus. There is usually an overlap between the technical architecture and the application architecture. The technical architecture drives standards, techniques, and policy-based aspects of the application architecture. Furthermore, the conceptual foundations and frameworks used in the architecture of applications are delivered by the technical architecture. Allowing individual system projects to produce these artifacts in isolation leads to the chaos we discuss in Chapter 2.

Key Definition: **Application Architecture.**
The set of significant decisions about the organization (structure) of a software system, and the architectural style that guides this organization.

Management Checklist

This simple checklist is a rapid health check of the current state of IT within your organization. It is business, not technically, related, and is designed to zero in on the issues that can be resolved by adopting an enterprise architecture approach. It is by no means complete, but can provide an indicator to the extent of problems within the environment. As the adoption of an architectural approach does not by right guarantee wondrous results this checklist is also applicable to those organizations that already use architectural techniques.

General Subject Area	Indicator Question	Yes / No
Strategy	Is there difficulty measuring the success of the IT environment in meeting the business strategy?	
	Does the cost of the IT environment appear higher than sector competitors?	
	Are you unsure what IT costs?	
	Are the IT systems failing to deliver to all the organization's information needs?	
	Are the IT systems failing to provide all functions required by the organization?	
	Is there a lack of common understanding of key organizational information and business terms?	
	Is it difficult to measure how well the enterprise IT systems meet the needs of the organization?	
	Do you find that a project approach to IT implementation introduces tactical decisions that have a negative effect on the overall IT environment?	
	Is the ability to make in-source out-source decisions hampered by your technology?	
	Is business success hampered (as apposed to enabled) by your information technology?	
Governance	Are IT project prioritization mechanisms limited or non-existent?	
	Do you have difficulty ensuring that projects meet quality requirements?	
	Do projects lack concrete technical quality standards or guidelines?	
	Is it difficult to ensure that the strategic requirements of the organization are maintained by each IT project?	
	Are deviations from the intended strategic IT direction difficult to spot and correct?	
	Do battles ensue (between units) over technology choices? Are there limited mediation mechanisms for these differences of opinion?	

General Subject Area	Indicator Question	Yes / No
Integration	Do your customers complain about your inability to maintain accurate and consistent information about them?	
	Do you find that changes required in one system manifest themselves in costly changes in other systems?	
	Do you find that integrating electronic information from customers and partners is costly and lacks integrity?	
	Do management information reports represent an inconsistent view of the current operational state of the organization?	
	Are there problems with internal business units communicating with each other electronically?	
	Has there been a lack of success in developing a corporate-wide shared knowledge base?	
	Do IT projects sponsored directly by the business exhibit integration and quality problems when introduced into the IT environment?	
	Is the integration between legacy and contemporary systems ineffective and costly?	
Quality	Do you have difficulty measuring how the IT environment supports service levels for IT customers?	
	Do you find that your corporate applications look and behave differently to their users?	
	Do you regularly experience performance difficulties with new and existing systems?	
	Do you find that your systems are difficult and costly to extend?	
	Is the resolution of operational IT problems ineffective and non-timely?	
	Do you feel at the mercy of your technology vendors?	
	Does the delivery of systems into international business units require significant system change?	
	Do systems experience more down-time than is deemed necessary?	
	Does the organization lack a business continuity plan for IT systems?	

General Subject Area	Indicator Question	Yes / No
Procurement	Is the organization continually considering the replacement of existing systems in new technology?	
	Does the procurement process for technology projects require continual re-invention, and appear ad hoc?	
	Is the technology procurement process unnecessarily cumbersome and time consuming?	
	Is there more than one ERP package within the organization?	
Security	Has the organization's IT function been disrupted by a security attach?	
	Does the organization "fear" connecting to the Internet for e-Business?	
	Is there limited or no information that would prove to you that there have been no internal or external security breaches of your IT systems?	
	Do you lack a security policy that sets out how security will be achieved in the organization?	
	Do employees exhibit limited (or no) knowledge of their responsibilities with respect to security?	

While there is no scientific assessment of the answers, a reasonable number of YES answers (say, greater than 10) indicates that the organization should review the way technology is managed. Such a result may mean that you should read on.

1.5 Summary

In this chapter, we introduced the concept of the enterprise information technology architecture and described its constituent parts. We primarily focused on our initial description of the technical architecture, the subject of this text, and compared it with other corporate architecture disciplines. We also described how we view the history and evolution of the technical architecture discipline through the various computing eras.

In the next chapter we look at some key IT problems experienced within most organizations, and we introduce the use of an architectural discipline to mitigate them.

CHAPTER 2

Chaos and Control

2.1 *Introduction*

In this chapter, we consider some of the typical problem areas of an organization's IT environment that suggest the need for architectural control. The intent is to show, both in this chapter and in the rest of the book, how applying architectural principles can aid in tackling many of these problems.

Many of the problems described in this chapter are common to a large number of organizations. However, we also assert that the many facets of e-business not only present further challenges but also can be adept at highlighting any organizational deficiencies.

Until the last few years organizations relied on traditional IT disciplines honed and proven since the "Iron Age." Waterfall-based development cycles stretching into years were not uncommon. Nor were large IT organizations with large budgets and static IT environments to support. The advent of the Internet economy has changed this demographic almost overnight. The ability to react to e-business imperatives and enablers is now being measured in months not years. This impacts IT by altering the way new initiatives must be delivered. Furthermore, the structure of the organization's enterprise technical environment can be put under stress.

The integration of an organization's partners and customers into the internal IT environment is another significant part of the Internet mind shift. This requires the organization to adapt its environment and IT functions to support this shift. The technological demands of the global economy have a tendency to exaggerate any current organizational IT deficiencies.

2.2   *Real-World IT Problems*

Influencing Factors

In no organization is the operation of IT perfect. All IT environments face challenges, both internal and external, in delivering IT capability to themselves and their partners. Many are faced with problems that limit the ability to provide this capability. Although not all problems are solvable using architectural disciplines, a pragmatic approach is to isolate key issues and concentrate effort on their solution. This is a mantra of the technical architecture—isolating and defining problem areas associated with technology, indicating a modified direction, and developing an implementation strategy to reach and maintain that direction.

Organizational IT problems are products of a number of key factors. In general, these factors can be summarized under the broad headings of:

- Technology environment
- IT organizational structure
- Capability
- Industry
- Management philosophy

All are intertwined in some way. The problems defined in this section fall within these categories.

The technology environment within an organization is very much a factor of the organization's history. The types and styles of applications, key to the current functioning of business, provide the context for the current state of the environment. For some IT organizations, technology has been inherited from previous administrations. How an organization uses this technology, and what environments are in place to support it, can generate significant IT problems. Most organizations are cognizant of problems arising from the technology but, due to a number of other factors, are unable to solve them.

The organizational structure of the IT has a significant effect on the ability to support IT. Many organizations have IT departments aligned along traditional horizontals: support, development, and operations. This type of structure does not suit every organization. Problems can appear in such a structure. Processes such as project initiation, architectural governance, vertical application management, and corporate-driven strategic adherence can tax some structures.

Capability is a catchall term relating to an IT organization's skills and resource management. This factor is affected by human resource policies, outsourcing approaches, the type of industry, internal culture, and political factors, among other things. Problems in this area tend to boil down to access to the right people with the right skills at the right time. We have experience with a government body whose policy changed from pro-contract resource to anti-contract resource, almost overnight. The IT organization was fundamentally stripped of its capability because of external influences.

The organization's industry sector influences the application of IT and therefore the likely problem scenarios. Stable industries, such as manufacturing or primary industry, present a problem dynamic that is quite different from highly competitive industries such as telecommunications and technology. The more risk-averse the industry, the more likely that the organization will be faced with problems that have been solved by faster-moving industries elsewhere. Conservative organizations will focus on technology cost of ownership but organizations that must innovate to survive need a different value proposition from IT.

Management philosophy relates to the approach, style, capability, and values of the organization's leading decision-makers, both in IT and in the organization as a whole. The IT environment, like the rest of the organization, must react and embrace management "philosophy." As regimes are replaced, IT approaches can change. As such, many IT organizations tend to find a cyclic pattern emerging in their approaches to technology.

Problem Matrix

The following sections summarize ten real-world IT problems that can be mitigated by adopting an architectural approach. The aim here is to provide the reader with a list of actual problems we have experienced within IT organizations (with names changed to protect the innocent, of course) in the hope that some (if not all) may relate to the reader's own experience. In essence, we would like readers to find themselves thinking, "I've noticed that in my organization."

The Business / Technical Strategy Gulf

- *Problem summary*: The failure of IT environment and planning to be driven by business strategy.
- *Technical architecture to the rescue*: Technical architecture development and maintenance methods demand business requirements traceability in the planning and development of the technical environment.

Most, if not all, organizations embark on regular strategic planning processes with the objective of determining the organization's current position, its desired medium-to long-term position, major issues, and a path to transition from one state to the next. Some organizations carry out strategic IT planning. For most, the strand between the two can be tenuous.

Only the business strategy can effectively control how IT is to be planned, implemented, and managed, yet most organizations do not have a method to support this type of hierarchy. This leads to technically led decision-making and a technology environment that can be out of step with the needs of the business.

An architectural approach provides the connection between business strategy and technical implementation. The approach applies a smooth flow between business and technology planning, driving the technical environment through specific (and strategic) business measures.

The Information Inaccuracy and Integrity Problem

- *Problem summary*: The inability of core systems to support information accuracy due to tactically planned business systems.
- *Technical architecture to the rescue*: The resolution of functional, information, and technology overlap and intersystem integration issues is the focus of the architectural development methods.

In many organizations, the inaccuracy of information, based on the premise that accuracy infers that it is fit for the intended use, is seldom readily apparent. But most organizations suffer from this problem to a greater or lesser degree. It is usually easier to understand the symptoms than to diagnose and fix the problem. Common symptoms that we have seen include:

- Customers complain that their details are not being updated correctly.
- Reconciliation of information (such as financial information) in one system shows different figures than in another system.
- Management information does not appear to represent the actual state of the business.
- Information from external sources (such as order information) results in an incorrect output generated from that information.

As the business systems environment of an organization evolves and systems are added, amended, and replaced, a certain amount of "drift" is experienced. This drift involves the intentional or unintentional duplication of functions and information across multiple systems. This situation is a classic cause of information inaccuracy and the symptoms highlighted previously. Furthermore, it is aggravated by ineffective technical intersystem integration techniques. There are a number of reasons why intersystem duplication can occur.

- Legacy bespoke applications are replaced by package solutions whose function overlaps existing systems. Many organizations that have implemented ERP packages will understand that the functional and information reach of these systems often overlaps with internal systems, either by design or because the extent or existence of the overlap was not truly appreciated during the implementation.
- Legacy systems are traditionally difficult to learn use, modify, and integrate with. Due to these characteristics, they tend to spawn "user friendly" bespoke systems that do not have these characteristics, providing function- or data-specific snapshots. For instance, how many HR or financial databases exist in your organization?
- Corners of the organization—for instance, international offices— may have alternate methods of operation (possibly due to internal or external political forces or judicial or geographic reasons) that dictate different solutions to business requirements. Alternatively, local departments may simply have choices when delivering functional requirements.
- Determining how function and information should be split between systems can be difficult, so they appear in each.
- Technical differences in system architectures have a direct influence on this problem. The greater the degree of technical difference the more likely that duplication will occur. This is especially true with package software; the ability to integrate applications effectively is restricted by the vendor's choice of technology.

It is typical for many organizations to have a large number of bespoke interfaces maintaining system (and hence information) integrity. Inevitably, these interfaces can be quickly compromised through IT operational and functional difficulties. Such difficulties can lead to a lack of information timeliness, data inconsistencies, and possible data corruptions.

An architectural approach can aid in resolving these problems. The development of an information architecture and business systems architecture, described at a high level in this book, identifies function and information overlap and provides for appropriate segmentation. The technical architecture is able to identify areas within the technical environment that restrict effective integration and provide the framework for establishing an effective technical integration environment.

Infrastructure Hell

- *Problem summary*: The tactical manner in which some infrastructure technologies are provided inhibit the ability of the IT environment to cooperate as a whole.
- *Technical architecture to the rescue*: The technical architecture focuses directly on ensuring the effectiveness of the technology environment and supports its continuing health through governance processes.

IT applications are the visible component of the broad web of IT investments. Applications provide the business benefit; they support actual cost savings or revenue generation, for instance. However, applications are merely the tip of a very large iceberg. The infrastructure is the platform on which the applications run. Like other things that affect human existence (such as the road system), if the infrastructure does not operate effectively, the users of the infrastructure will not either. The infrastructure that supports business applications must be in perfect working order.

Organizations will deliberate endlessly on the right applications to buy or build. But the same courtesy is seldom afforded the infrastructure. It tends to be undervalued and under-resourced. In many cases, budgetary and procurement processes make it exceedingly difficult to invest directly in the infrastructure—tangible benefits are difficult to justify. Given such conditions, the infrastructure corrodes. A plethora of product make their way into the environment to support individual application (or business unit) requirements. Interoperability among applications (which is, after all, facilitated by the infrastructure) degrades. Many organizations grow defined, but not interoperable, islands of infrastructure.

Of course, only the symptoms are felt by the organization. However, initiatives such as corporate-wide applications or supply chain integration can show the problems in dramatic ways. The architectural approach considers the infrastructure as a first-class citizen. In fact, infrastructure is a major focus of the technical architecture.

The Security Problem

- *Problem summary*: Many organizations cannot confidently state that their IT environments are secure.
- *Technical architecture to the rescue*: A major service area in the technical architecture's jurisdiction is security. The development of a technical architecture mandates the organization understand its current and future pan-application security needs.

For most organizations that have a mature IT infrastructure, based on mainframe systems, the changing face of information security threats is bewildering. During the Iron Age, the management of security was implicit in the management of centralized mainframe systems. The organization's information was typically housed in a small number of large systems in physically secure sites. Furthermore, users gained access to these systems via "dumb" terminals. Security risks were still apparent, but with adequate user access policies and sufficient system auditing, the risk could be controlled.

The Industrial Revolution brought forth a whole new set of information security difficulties. Physically distributed systems circumvented many of the traditional physical and centralized security countermeasures. Intelligent workstations introduced new security vulnerabilities. Standards-based technologies and networks aided those who wished to violate an organization's security.

As the popularity of the Internet grew, further risks to organizational security quickly became apparent. For most organizations, before the Internet explosion (approximately the mid-1990s), the majority of security threats came from in-house. Only a limited number of high profile organizations needed to concern themselves with external security risks. However, this changed on one summer afternoon in the 1990s. As the number of organizations connecting to the Internet skyrocketed, and interorganizational information transfer increased (e-mail, Web sites, e-business, e-commerce, portals), the accessibility of an organization's systems over the Internet, critical for its reach into the new e-economy, also opened gaping security holes. These holes represented risks that most organizations would not even have identified let alone known how to counter. Email viruses, rogue applets and executables, Trojan Horses, and denial-of-service attacks are merely the public face of realized security threats. What else is happening behind the flimsy corporate security façade that we do not know about?

Of course, many of an organization's security problems are a little more mundane but no less important. There are many symptoms that may be recognized. Here are some that we have uncovered:

- A number of, usually unrelated, mechanisms with which users will identify themselves to the many information systems they need to access. The general complaint from users typically is, "Why do we have to remember so many passwords?"
- Management paranoia over connecting systems to the Internet (or even to other partners over private networks). Generally, this paranoia is an artifact of uncertainty over how information assets will be protected.
- Inability to determine whether attacks have even occurred. This

points to issues with the way systems are audited and the processes for review.

- Individuals who have limited understanding of their responsibilities surrounding information security. Many may not know who to contact about security issues.
- Association of the cost of security measures to the value of the information being protected is seldom understood and rarely taken into account during the design of security systems. Organizations are not sure how much to spend on security measures.
- The obvious symptom of a problem is that of a realized security threat. What type of attack may occur, whether it is the unintentional release of private internal information to an external source, or the spread of an external virus internally, points to deficiencies in the security implementation.

In the same way that information system strategic planning provides the macro technical architecture directions, security policies provide similar direction for architecting security. Many of the symptoms described earlier point in the first instance to an organization that either does not have a workable security policy or has not implemented it accurately. This book does not provide detail on security policy development. It does, however, provide guidance on how the technical architecture, and in particular the architectural development method coupled with the security service definitions, can be used to identify security problems and apply technical direction.

The Problem of Incompatible Technologies

- *Problem summary*: The IT environment does not interoperate effectively to provide support for business processes.
- *Technical architecture to the rescue*: The technical architecture deals directly with the effectiveness of the IT environment.

This is one of the most common problems we come across in organizations. It is certainly reasonably easy to identify. However, combating the problem is by no means easy. Furthermore, understanding the root causes can be difficult. We are referring to the generic problems faced by organizations with incompatible technological components. Generally, we are referring to products (and technologies) that should interoperate to support business processes but do not. This problem is further exacerbated when the organization selects different products to perform the same business function.

Normally, the business processes that overarch technology must continue regardless of technology incompatibilities. Therefore, working around the incompatibilities is common and in many organizations endemic to the point that the technical reasons for the workarounds are often lost. Technical incompatibilities cause greater tactical spending to support the business processes and so lead to a greater cost of IT in general. At an organizational level, technical inefficiencies in the overall business process cause time cost and quality inefficiencies in the processes themselves. This problem has wide-range effects on the success of the organization as a whole.

Typical examples of symptoms of this problem that we have found include:

- Users adopt manual workarounds to conduct a business process which scans incompatible systems.
- Users cannot collaborate effectively with the entire organization. Typically, users within small groups have no difficulty conducting business. However, incompatible collaboration systems thrown about the network can make the task of interacting outside the immediate workgroup difficult.
- The sharing of documents and other information (such as reports, business utilities, or marketing material) is ad hoc and ineffective. Incompatible document-sharing architectures and document-editing applications, and ad hoc methods of distribution, reduce the effectiveness of information transfer.
- The use of new or upgraded "corporate" applications is problematic due to incompatible operating systems and hardware specifications. This tends to lead to islands of application usage.

Generally, the symptoms just described are derived from chaos in the technology selection process. There may be only limited control over technology decisions—business application decisions made only with limited strategic IT involvement can lead to suboptimal technology selections. Some IT departments may even magnify the problem by providing technology advice without holistic focus.

Some organizations inherit this problem. Mergers and acquisitions are a reality of business. Connecting merged organizations from a technical perspective is a huge challenge that must be undertaken with a clear and concise vision of how the IT within the new organization will operate.

The Cost Problem

- *Problem summary*: The cost of IT in organizations is ineffectively controlled or understood.
- *Technical architecture to the rescue*: The technical architecture man-

dates an understanding of the organizational type and takes a reasoned approach to the building of the technical environment that reflects cost drivers.

The cost of IT is the ubiquitous problem. Increasingly it is key that IT be cost-effective and yet be an enabler for the business strategy. Investment is not made in technology for technology's sake but rather as a driver to meet the business strategy and needs. Indeed, the cost of IT must be measured against the gains it provides, and chaos in the IT environment leads to increased IT costs (whether tangible or intangible).

Many of the problems we have discussed in this chapter, and the chaos created by them, have cost implications. Information integrity issues can lead to poor management decisions, inaccurate billing, or lost customers. Problems with security can cripple an organization. Consider the effects of a security attack on an organization's e-business site that brings the site down for days. Lost orders, lost customers, and lost customer mind share and brand awareness are the result. Government organizations are not immune to cost problems either, although costs may have a significant political component also. Is it possible for a major IT problem to have such a significant political influence as to lose a government its power? Possibly.

Most organizations have conflict over their IT spending. There is no magic formula; much will depend on the nature of organization, its view on technology as an enabler, its business strategy, and its historical view on IT spending. One of the most important guides, not only to the degree of IT spending but also to the organization's general attitude toward IT, is the organizational type. Gartner Group[5] classifies organizations into three types in terms of technology adoption, as follows:

- **Type A**. Type A organizations are always considering the risk of adopting new technology against the rewards of competitive advantage. They usually adopt technology long before it is considered stable or commodity and aggressively exploit technology for business-critical processes. Only a small number of organizations fit into this classification.
- **Type B**. Type B organizations focus on the overall value of adopting technology. They may be innovative in some areas and conservative in others. They tend to adopt technology as it becomes mainstream. They are by far the largest group and use IT to improve productivity, product quality, and customer service.

5. Gartner Group Strategic Analysis Report "Advanced Technology Survey: Taking Stock of Technology Management," 7 March 1996.

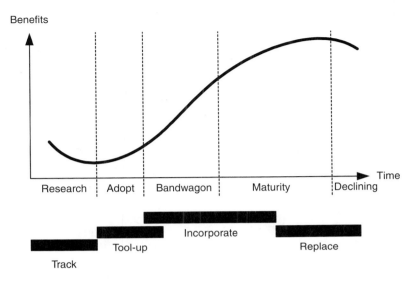

FIGURE 2.1.   The technology maturity curve.

- **Type C**. Type C organizations focus on cost-effectiveness as the major driver for IT. They will wait until technology is commodity, proven, and cost-effective before investing.

This method of organizational classification is straightforward and is highly valuable both as a planning aid for business and technical strategists and for understanding the cost of chaos. The classifications influence the point at which organizations adopt technology along its life cycle, as shown in Figure 2.1. Maturity has a direct relationship to total cost of ownership. Type A organizations will tend to adopt technologies earlier and Type C later.

Type A organizations, by their very nature, will have high IT spending and will live fairly happily in a chaotic environment (typically characterized by adopting technology early in its life cycle). In fact, they expect (and regularly realize) that a cost-effective IT environment can be discarded in the search for innovation.

Type B organizations, with which we deal most often, are inherently value-conscious with respect to IT. They are likely to use technologies in different areas of the business for competitive advantage (much like a Type A organization), but they can also be reasonably conservative in other situations (like a Type C). Hence, there is this dichotomy between expected chaos, brought on in the search for innovation, and the solidity required of a conservative approach to technology. Ultimately, B types usually looks for an effective return on its technology use and will use cost as a driving metric. This type of organization is most likely to experience and suffer the effect of chaos-related cost problems. Generally, it is our experience that government organizations fit between this type and Type C.

Type C organizations are interesting from an architectural perspective because they are totally cost-conscious. Their conservative approach to IT means that it is possible to measure them against established industry cost benchmarks. Implementing technology when it is mature provides an excellent basis for minimizing chaos and therefore controlling cost. Legacy has a different meaning for these organizations.

An architectural approach requires an understanding of the business, its market sector, and its attitude toward IT (derived from the organizational type) before prescribing technologies.

Technology Anarchy

- *Problem summary*: Individuals hold the technology vision for the organization—when they leave, everything changes.
- *Technical architecture to the rescue*: The technical architecture comprises a governance process to ensures that the IT environment is owned and championed by the organization, not the individual.

IT organizations usually operate with the best intentions of supporting a measured (and sometimes architectural) approach to technology. However, it is often the case that reasoned IT decisions, and therefore the stability of the technical environment, are affected by factors that are not technically related:

- Technical advocates leave the organization, resulting in a feeding frenzy as new roles and responsibilities are fought for. This results in dramatic technology changes as advocates in new areas are established.
- Common IT processes, such as tendering, can be enacted a random nature to technology selection.
- Technology vendors can continually remodel their products and services causing confusion, tactical decision-making, and a reliance on "technology du jour" by organizations.
- Autonomous business units make purchasing decisions that make sense for them but not for the IT environment in general.

All of these aspects and many more cause a type of anarchy in the IT environment. Dramatic changes can corrupt an original reasoned approach to IT. IT environments drift between periods of high effectiveness and high dysfunction. Erosion on the IT base can go undetected until a significant breakdown in the IT environment is noted. Adopting an architectural approach provides a solid framework that is not reliant on individual people or business units, and provides a basis for dealing with technology change.

The Problem with the Ongoing Systems Management of IT

- *Problem summary*: IT systems are becoming increasingly less managed.
- *Technical architecture to the rescue*: The technical architecture treats systems management as a key service. Management aspects—known as service qualities—are a fundamental part of the environment.

Many of the systems management disciplines historically associated with IT have been eroded since the 1980s. Traditional IT shops focused on systems management disciplines, processes, and tools. In those "naïve" days, the operationalization of a system was considered as important as its development. IT required specialized skills—in both the vendor and internally—to support systems that typically required detailed interaction at the system level. Applications ran directly on single machines that integrated directly with the management tools tended by hordes of system specialists. Of course, this is a generalization; however the concepts are accurate.

Things have changed. Applications are being deployed in a far more distributed manner. Complex operating environments can be managed by less specialized personnel through simple easy-to-use GUI consoles. Specialists have retrenched into vendor organizations. The market for third-party systems management tools has exploded, and standards bodies provide interoperability standards for managing systems.

Given the major advancements in management technology, we believe that the management of applications has not been in a worse state. Frequently, highly complex distributed applications are designed, developed, and deployed without sufficient consideration of how they will be managed. It is even more critical today that application have a considered approach for providing:

- Availability, including performance, survivability, serviceability, and reliability
- Assurance, including security, integrity, and credibility

- Adaptability, including scalability, interoperability, extensibility, and portability

The overall quality of applications is dependent on their functional and nonfunctional requirements (nonfunctional requirements encapsulate the aspects just listed above and are referred to as service qualities in this text), but the focus is typically applied to functional requirements, whereas service qualities are either ignored or considered late in the life cycle. An architectural approach applies equal importance to both functional and quality aspects of individual systems and the IT environment.

The Problem with Procurement

- *Problem summary*: Procurement processes for IT systems are reinvented for each project.
- *Technical architecture to the rescue*: The technical architecture puts in place a set of standards for procurement.

The number of times IT procurement processes are reinvented can be staggering. We have seen this pattern in a number of organizations. The initial part of a project—the execution of a buy process—sends people scattering throughout the organization looking for tender processes and other collateral required to make product selections. Inevitably there is limited retained knowledge in this area. Therefore, the approach for describing, assessing, and selecting technical components is often ad hoc and ineffective. The quality of the IT procurement process has a direct bearing on the quality of the IT environment.

It is critical that the procurement of technology be aligned with the technical vision and strategy, thus ensuring a robust and maintainable environment. The architecture provides artifacts and processes that input directly into the procurement process to ensure that this occurs.

The Collapsing Event Horizon

- *Problem summary*: Equating rapid delivery with tactical IT decision-making.
- *Technical architecture to the rescue*: The technical architecture provides a set of reasoned artifacts that guide all e-business "tactical" decisions.

As new electronic delivery channels become a key component of a business's selling proposition, most organizations are facing the reduction in time needed to deliver into these new channels. The collapsing technology event horizon has led many to rush headlong into the technology abyss in an effort to reap the potential rewards of on-line selling supply chain integration, information delivery, electronic tendering, business process extension, and so forth.

In some situations the organizations will make the mistake of applying tactical technology implementations to the problem—freeware products have been popular in this arena. In other cases, organizations apply expensive, highly scalable technologies in the hope that e-business will be hugely successful. Both approaches have led to significant problems. Tactical implementation can collapse under the strain of increasing transaction load, integration with backend systems can be problematic, and changes in functionality can affect the stability of the entire environment. On the other hand, highly robust e-business solutions rely on a certain level of commercial success to provide a positive return on investment. Over-investment in e-business infrastructure has led to business failures.

The problem is the lack of a consistent approach for determining how e-business systems should be built and how they should fit into the overall IT environment. All investments in technology should be based on reasoned and structured assessments, taking into account the entire IT environment (while itself being driven by business strategies). Using an architectural approach, the organization can mitigate against the collapsing event horizon by making haste in a pragmatic manner. The architecture provides the necessary processes and artifacts to allow organizations to work smarter.

2.3 Exacerbating Chaos—The Advent of E-Enablement

As always, the problem with chaos is that the organization is far too busy dealing with the tactical problems—firefighting—to step back and deal with the symptoms. There tends to be a feeling of "treading water." There are never enough resources to deal with the day-to-day problems, let alone for management to find the capacity to consider a strategic cure.

This situation is not about to improve anytime soon. Organizations are under increasing pressure in a hyper competitive marketplace. Competitors are becoming progressively hungrier for market share, and they are not afraid to change rapidly to achieve this. Information technology tools provide an excellent enabler for this. More importantly, the maturation of the Internet as a viable carrier for electronic business has changed the playing field on which competition traditionally occurred.

The Internet provides huge benefits in enabling electronic business. The sheer numbers are significant. The number of connected businesses and consumers is growing rapidly. The Internet provides organizations with a truly global customer base.

The Internet's "good enough" mantra is one key reason for its success. As alluded to in Chapter 1, the creation of standards for Internet technology has always been pragmatic, not over endowed with features or overburdened with protracted consensus processes. Also, any interested party can propose technology for standardization. This has given the impression of rapid maneuverability and the ability to keep pace with technology leaps. Organizations can learn from this approach.

The role of vendors in the success of the Internet is critical. In many respects one complements the other. For the Internet to be successful, IT vendors were required to adopt the Internet technology and standards. Of course, once the Internet was successful, vendors had to adopt the "Internet way" or risk marginalizing themselves. The Internet and vendor technology wave has enabled a rapid increase in the number and quality of interoperable technologies. This has given organizations the ability to rapidly construct and deploy e-business applications.

The end user has also played a vital role in the industrial revolution. The technology and infrastructure that make up the Internet are incredibly complex, but typically the end-user interface (for instance, a browser or a mail client) is stunningly simple to use. Therefore, lack of technical knowledge is no longer a barrier for users adopting the Internet, and as such user expectations are continually increasing.

The general approach pervasive in the Internet community—simplicity, rapid change, and interoperability—is setting new expectations within organizations. Business has traditionally accepted long application development times, extended time to market, high IT costs, and failed projects. This is not what they see on the Internet. In fact, generally the contrary is true. Perhaps CEOs witness their children building their own Web sites in a matter of days, or perhaps they see their competitors using this new channel in an innovative way. The outcome is the same; the way IT is delivered must now meet these new expectations. Of course, it is obvious to IT professionals that a static Web site is not e-business. There are many issues that must be resolved before embarking on such systems; however the bar is being re-set.

Most IT groups are burdened with legacy systems, processes, and skills that do not match these new "Internet expectations." The problem therefore is how an organization can react to this new style of delivery while continuing to face internal IT backlogs on legacy platforms. Furthermore, the Internet style of delivery can appear incongruous to a measured "software engineering" approach. It's more reactive, systems may only have a half-life of months, new functionality is consistently required, and most importantly the organization must add new functions faster than its competitors.

If IT delivery is chaotic now, then the Internet has just added a new dimension to the problem. The tendency to focus purely tactically seems to be encouraged. As the Internet style extends into the organization, is firefighting to become the norm?

2.4   *Control Through Architecture*

The manager of an IT group of a large federal organization lamented that he had been asked to develop a strategic plan for his group. His problem was that he was far too busy with current burning issues to even consider planning. To make matters worse, he was not entirely sure how his group's direction should relate to the direction of the rest of the IT Group. His response to the approaching planning deadline was to "cobble" something together as quickly as possible so he could concentrate instead on the current smoldering issues. Although this may appear somewhat contrived, this is actually a true and accurate account.

This is not an uncommon occurrence with IT groups. In fact, the pressure of e-business exaggerates the negative effects of this "approach" to planning. This particular manager could not afford the time to understand where his group should be in the future. Furthermore, his lack of understanding of the objectives and strategies of the overall IT group made it impossible to plan effectively anyway. This is a vicious circle. The less the strategic direction is understood, the more likely the focus will be on immediate problems and the less time available to plan.

Management must focus on immediate problems as they arise. But without a plan, an understanding of where their organization wants to be, and how the planned direction is to be achieved, the more likely it is that tactical problems will occur. In the Internet age, more emphasis on planning is required, not less. Planning is required at all levels from business to technology. Furthermore, the Internet approach to technology (i.e., specifications that put a premium on integration) requires a strong architectural approach to IT. In much the same way as a business or IT strategy sets both the objectives and the method for achieving them, architecture provides the plans that enable business objectives to be achieved through technology. Without such an approach, all new business requirements are delivered via directionless means, corrupting the IT environment as they go. A stable and architectured IT environment can turn to chaos in no more than a year unless architectural disciplines continue to be applied.

IT Project initiation is one of the key processes to tame. We find common themes in IT projects during initiation. Consider how many times you have heard these questions asked as a project begins:

- Should we focus on packages or building?
- Do these requirements already exist (at least partially) within the current systems?
- Where is it logical to implement the requirements? Should they be placed into an existing system or do we need a new system?
- What information do we require, and does it already exist in current systems? If it does, what do we do about it?
- How should the new system integrate with the current systems, and what information should be passed, and in what format?
- What platform[6] should use for delivery?
- How should information be secured, and how should we secure it?
- What about managing the system after delivery?
- How and where should it be deployed?
- What aspects of availability should be considered?
- What tools should we use to build the system?
- What are we doing about reuse?
- How should the application be expected to perform?
- What sort of user interface is required?

Chaos is implied when there are no standard answers to these questions. The absence of answers indicates a lack of technical architecture planning. Most (all?) projects are focused on two overriding mantras—delivery on time and within budget. This is the focus of the project manager and the project team. Unfortunately, this is not necessarily the only focus of the IT Group. For example, the Group is likely to be concerned with controlling IT costs, meeting business strategic aims, ensuring that systems are manageable, ensuring interoperability, and ensuring that change is ordered and responsive. These two focuses can sometimes be contradictory. This is especially the case when the project or the IT Group cannot readily answer the questions defined earlier. If these questions are not answered, a project will establish its own guidelines. It is also likely that these "contrived" guidelines metamorphose and diverge with each new project. The result is IT chaos.

We have encountered organizations in which the security requirements for every new system were different. This is basic stuff, and yet the organization could not even achieve unity in this single area. To extend this example, consider the ramifications of an e-business project

---

6. The platform includes all basic services, such as operating systems, hardware, databases, and transaction management. The Platform is a central concept in this text.

that does not have adequate guidance as to how authentication (or any security requirements, for that matter) should be delivered. Depending on project pressures, the security implementation is likely to have gaps, does not integrate into the organization's security environment, may not protect information fully, may use security technology that is incompatible with current practices, or at worst may be absent altogether. The result can be disastrous.

Security is just one technology area that a project must deal with, and authentication is merely one small component within security. There are countless other technology areas with which a project must either have guidance or be forced to make its own decisions. Each decision taken by the project potentially diverges from the organization's intended technical direction (see Figure 2.2).

We warrant that upfront architectural guidance is the most valid approach to ensure that divergence is kept to a minimum. This guidance should be provided from outside the project, by an architectural approach in general and the enterprise architecture in particular.

The enterprise architecture is the organization's strategy for information, business systems, and technology. In each of these areas, key direction is provided to individual IT projects to ensure that divergence is minimized or eliminated. While we describe the makeup of the information and business systems architecture in Chapter 3, the focus of the text is the technical architecture. The technical architecture provides the technical strategy for the organization and therefore pan-project technical guidance. It defines the platform. The technical architecture must deal with all areas of technology that an organization warrants as critical in meeting its business strategy.

Although we explore in detail the methods for developing the technical architecture, it must be stressed that it is not merely a document

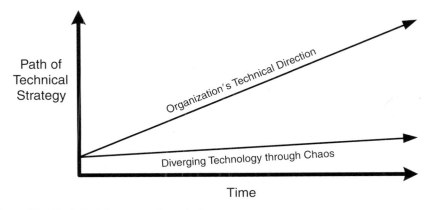

FIGURE 2.2.   Technical divergence through chaos.

or a standard. It must contain such artifacts, of course, but more importantly it is an organizational capability—it is both people and processes. It is whatever is required to keep IT on track. This will differ among organizations. Government organizations (especially Defense departments) can effectively rely on documented standards because this style of guidance is engrained within its culture. Commercial organizations may require "enterprise architects" to provide constant guidance, advice, mentoring, and formal quality assurance. With others a quality management approach may be applicable.

Organizations must understand the concept of architectural governance—the on-going quality management of the technical environment. We provide guidance in this area in the last two chapters. However, research on the successful use of strategic planning techniques has shown that many will adopt an iterative approach to architectural governance and controls, selecting an approach, implementing it, analyzing its success through feedback mechanisms, and adapting it where there are problems—the plan, do, check, correct cycle. Typically, an organization may need to journey through these iterations three or four times before the perfect balance is struck. We have heard IT managers bemoan that enterprise architecture does not work—it takes too long to produce, it does not achieve buy-in, it is just an "intellectual exercise" with no real value, it is corrupted early, it is too expensive, and so on. Perhaps the problem is not that planning for the future is flawed but rather that the current approach must be modified.

Key Definition: **Governance.**
IT governance can be defined as a structure of relationships and processes to direct and control the enterprise in order to achieve the enterprise's goals by adding value while balancing risk versus return over IT and its processes. Specifically, architectural governance provides the processes, policy, and implementation to reduce the instance of architecture drift, ensuring that the organization continues to support and maintain the architectural vision as change occurs.

2.5 Summary

All IT groups will experience problems with IT. These may be related to a lack of integration between business strategy and technical implementation, problems with an ailing infrastructure, problems trying to integrate incompatible technologies, major security issues, or the perennial issue of controlling IT costs. An overarching issue is that the rise of the Internet channel has exacerbated the problems.

We believe that all of the problems described here are symptomatic of the lack of an (or an ineffective) architectural approach to technology. In the rest of this book, we present a framework for architecting an organization's IT environment. Our goal is to demonstrate how the approach presented here can actively aid the resolution of the problems described in this chapter. We begin this journey by positioning technology architecture with respect to other strategic-planning processes.

CHAPTER 3

Business Strategy—The Foundation for the Technical Architecture

3.1 Introduction

The development of a technical architecture cannot be achieved in isolation from the overall business planning process. In fact, a technical architecture is the culmination of a great deal of strategic and architectural planning carried out at the business and IT levels. Development of a technical architecture without considerable direction from both business and IT management is a fundamental flaw of many technical "strategies."

The planning process begins at the highest levels within the organization with strategic management planning. It continues through the formulation of IT strategies. Information system planning represents the alignment of information and business systems to the business strategies. Finally, the technical architecture, drawing from all of the preceding planning stages, details how the organization's technology environment will be structured and maintained. This "hierarchy" was shown in Chapter 1 (see Figure 1.3).

Although the planning hierarchy is shown primarily as a linear flow in Figure 1.3, this is seldom the case. The frequency of each planning activity may not be aligned. Furthermore, the duration between planning cycles differs among planning types. Different imperatives drive each stage in the process, some necessitating shorter or longer planning horizons. Generally, therefore, it is best to consider the entire process as more iterative and overlapping.

This chapter takes a holistic view of the entire planning process, beginning with strategic management planning. We do not delve too deeply into methods but rather provide a background to allow the positioning of the technical architecture. This is the last general chapter before heading boldly into the details of the technical architecture framework. As a precursor to this, we introduce the fictitious organization we will be using to provide examples in the remainder of the book.

3.2 *Business Strategic Planning*

There has been a huge amount written about organizational strategic planning. But although you may consider the concept of strategic planning at an organizational level to be almost as old as the concept of "an organization" itself, it is widely regarded to have had its birth in the 1960s with the works of Chandler,[7] Ansoff,[8] and Andrews.[9]

Strategic planning provides many advantages. In fact, this is true of both business and IT strategic planning, including the development of a technical architecture. Planning avoids chaos by defining a cohesive approach to change. It allows the establishment of an environment to support operational planning and change. It drives resource allocation. It necessitates an organization establish feedback and correction mechanisms, which are critical in measuring the success of a strategy. It provides a common direction for all members of the organization and a framework to ensure that decision-making is aligned to the strategic mission.

It is generally accepted that a strategic plan should contain considerations of the following:

- Mission—"Why do we exist?"
- Vision—"What is the ideal future for us?"
- Guiding Principles—"What principles do we hold that should direct our actions?"
- Planning—"What steps are required to achieve our vision?"
- Direction—"Where do we want to be in the planning horizon?"
- Strategies—"How will we get there?"
- Indicators—"How will we measure our progress?"
- Governance—"What operational processes are required to keep us on track?"

---

7. A.D. Chandler, *Strategy and Structure*, MIT Press, Cambridge, MA, 1962.
8. H.I. Ansoff, *Corporate Strategy*, McGraw Hill, New York, 1965.
9. K.R. Andrews, *The Concept of Corporate Strategy*, Irwin, Homewood, IL, 1971.

The establishment of organizational goals and objectives is an important part of management planning. Goals indicate the long-term success factors, whereas objectives tend to be somewhat shorter-term. A key property of goals and objectives is that they are measurable. Critical success factors (CSFs) are those few goals that must go well to ensure success. Strategies therefore are the plans defined to provide mechanisms for achieving organizational goals. Organizational-level goals then are passed down to individual managers and their staffs. This enables units to understand what must be achieved at a micro, and ultimately an individual, level to ensure that the organization is successful.

Key Definition: **Critical Success Factors.**
CSFs are a subset of an organization's goals and objectives that must go well for success.

Fundamentally, there are a number of high-level tasks that characterize most strategic planning efforts, as described by Finkelstein[10] and shown in Figure 3.1. The key points to understand are firstly, that a strategy considers and is fundamentally derived from the current strategic position; secondly, that the strategy takes into account both internal and external factors (see Porter's model in Figure 3.2); and thirdly, that the strategy considers a number of alternatives before defining a direction. It is interesting to compare this approach with the technical architecture development framework detailed in the remainder of the book. There is a synergy between both methods in structure and intent.

The commonality between these strategic models, in very different domains, in some way highlights what we mean by best practice. Many of the strategic planning methods, and there are a reasonable number of them, have been subjected to considerable trial and scrutiny by a considerable number of organizations over a long period of time. As methods are refined and evolve, successful approaches tend to exhibit common themes and slowly become de facto and generic. Using methods of this type will usually increase the likelihood of success.

Porter's[11] framework of competitive strategy (shown in Figure 3.2) is the most commonly accepted model for the application and understanding of competitive strategy. Porter describes an approach for modeling the competitive forces that influence most organizations. He suggests that identifying the relevant forces and enacting a strategy to weaken them can give an organization a strategic advantage. Most organizations

10. C. Finkelstein, *Strategic Systems Development*, Addison-Wesley, Reading, MA, 1992.
11. M.E. Porter, *Competitive Strategy*, Free Press, New York, 1980.

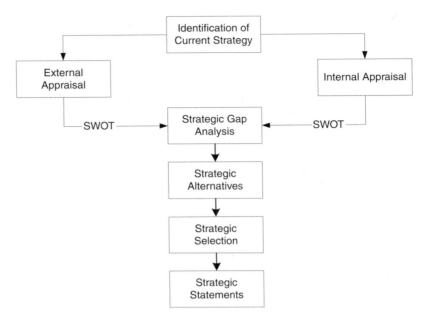

FIGURE 3.1.   General planning framework.

tend to reflect only on the competition in terms of rivals within the same industry. Using this model allows an organization to consider a wider range of factors than typically considered in strategic planning. Approaches for weakening the "Porter forces" can be provided by IT solutions—and hence identified in the information systems plan. For example, IT can support the development of new products that will reduce competitive rivalry or provide business tools that may discourage the entrance of new competitors into the market.

McGee and Prusak[12] suggest, in fact, that the Porter's competitive model is actually more complicated than it first appears. The model in Figure 3.2 can be expanded to include all of the other companies that the organization deals with and their own competitive influences. This concept is a microcosm of the strategic-planning issues that must be faced by organizations integrating their supply chains through e-business.

For IT managers, planners, and strategists to be cognizant of this type of approach to business planning enables a changing focus for IT. IT has traditionally been seen by the business as supporting operational or tactical management requirements. However, IT may act as a strategic en-

12. J. McGee and L Prusak, *Managing Information Strategically*, John Wiley & Sons, New York, 1993.

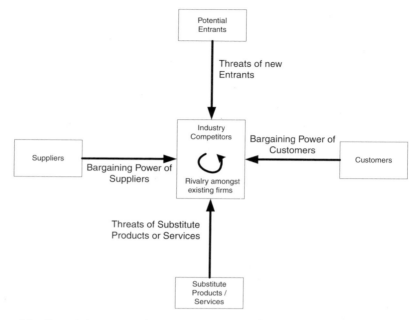

FIGURE 3.2.   Porter's framework of competitive strategy.

abler. To achieve this IT must also be viewed strategically as well. To do this a strategic planning approach to IT is a must. This not only infers the IT strategic plan but also the technology plan, which is the basis for this book.

3.3   *Information Systems Strategic Planning*

IT strategic planning exists in a number of guises; the term "information technology strategic planning (ISSP)" is often used, as is "strategic information systems planning" or even "business technology planning." However, regardless of the terminology the concept is fairly consistent. ISSP is typically the IT unit's version of strategic management planning and is responsible for guiding the use of IT and the IT organization to achieve the organization's business strategy.

Key Definition: **Information System Strategic Planning.**
The ISSP is the organization's strategic plan for IT and the IT group, guiding the direction over a medium to long term period.

ISSP was very much in vogue in the 1980s and early 1990s. We have had experience with a number of organizations (both government and commercial) that undertook lengthy and expensive ISSP projects. Although some were successful in establishing a climate for change, others were not. One government organization attempted to introduce dramatic change within a workforce that, for IT workers, was unusually entrenched. Although some initiatives experienced rapid success, these were short-lived, and many of the changes failed over the medium term.

The most typical criticism leveled at ISSP is its "point in time" perspective, leading to a phenomenon that is not unusual in the strategic-planning area—that of "shelfware." A change of influencing factors, such as those described by Porter, or in technology can quickly lead to the plan becoming out of date and increasingly irrelevant. This is particularly noticeable given the current state of technology and the e-business wave. Ten years ago, it was possible to plan with a 4–6-year horizon; now, this timeframe has contracted. Depending on your organizational type, the planning horizon has more than halved. As with all strategic planning, operational management of the plan—governance—is critical.

This is not to say that ISSP is now irrelevant; we have and will continue to stress in this book the benefits gained from applying a reasoned and planned planning approach. What has become less relevant are the large formal ISSP processes of the past. In today's business and technology climate, ISSP must become increasingly and rapidly predictive and able to support direction changes far more easily. Improved governance and feedback mechanisms are critical to allow the plan to be refined as both business and technology changes occur. ISSPs must become much more adaptive, and therefore planning can no longer be seen as a discrete project but rather a living, ongoing process.

The ISSP is typically used to negate the possibility that information systems and information technology are implemented in a piecemeal or tactical way. Although this may sound like an obvious statement, many lose sight of this premise, continuing to focus on the purely operational aspects of the IT function after the ISSP "is delivered."

In general, ISSP should target the following areas:

- The alignment of IT investment with the business strategy, goals, and objectives
- Opportunities to exploit information and technology for competitive advantage (as described by Porter's competitive model)
- Directing the effective and efficient management of IT resources (people, technology, information, and other assets)
- Directing technical policies and architectures
- Directing on-going strategic governance

There are a huge number of ISSP methods, some commercial and others "home grown" or derived. A number of factors influence the method best suited to an organization. Organizational culture has a huge bearing on strategic planning—how change is accepted, what values and attitudes are preeminent, management attitudes and philosophies on strategic planning, and so forth. The type of organization and the industry are also important (see the discussion on organizational type classification in Chapter 2). How IT is used and viewed for driving competitive advantage also impacts the IT strategy. The organizational approach to innovation, or conversely the approach to process and method is also a factor.

All of these factors and more are important in deciding how to undertake IT planning. Although we do not intend to discuss in detail different planning methods here, we summarize Earl's[13] six generic approaches to IT strategic planning as a way of presenting various flavors.

Earl undertook research within 21 U.K.-based companies in the early 1990s. The objective was to understand the different approaches applied to the IT planning process and the relative strengths and weaknesses of each approach. The organizations Earl selected were leaders in a wide variety of industries including banking, retailing, electronics, IT, and oil. Their annual revenues averaged 4.5 billion pounds. These organizations had a wide range of experience with ISSP—some had almost none, and others had been planning for more than 20 years. Interestingly, Earl discovered that the longer an organization had been using ISSP as a planning tool, the larger the number of methods that had been tried. This was sometimes due to changing organizational behavior (such as the changing philosophies of a new CIO) and sometimes due to limited successes with previous methods.

Earl discovered that a large number of approaches were used for ISSP, but in general he was able to synthesize all of the methods into six generic approaches. These were not necessarily formal or codified techniques.

The Business-Led Approach.

- The assumption is that the business plans are the only plans on which the IT plan can be based.
- The emphasis is on the business leading IT in the formulation of an IT plan.
- Typically, the business strategy does not provide enough detail or is not clear enough to allow IT planners to specify IT needs.

13. M.J. Earl, *Information Management*, Oxford University Press, Oxford, 1996.

- Under this approach, information systems tend to be seen as strategic.

The Method-Driven Approach.

- Derives its approach from the drive to use formal techniques or methodologies.
- Intervention of consultants was common, and this approach typically involved the search for the "best method."
- Most organizations found that the use of formal methods seldom provided total success because the methods were not typically sufficiently robust or comprehensive for the formulation of business strategy.
- The methods tend to be supported by the IT management but do not find much favor with other managers within the organization.

The Administration Approach.

- This approach emphasizes resource planning.
- Typically, it is derived from information systems development proposals from business units.
- It tends to be seen as nonstrategic and bottom-up.
- The entire business has some commitment to the plan.

The Technical Approach.

- Typically it is a formal method for mapping business activities and information flows, the outcome being a business model (such as an information architecture).
- The approach emphasizes the definition of architectures and blueprints.
- Due to its complex technical nature, it tends to be demanding in terms of effort and the skills of resources.
- Usually, technical dependencies tend to displace business priorities.
- It is unlikely to state any business benefits.
- The outcomes of this approach are better at building robust IT infrastructure.

The Competitor-Driven Approach.

- It is driven by the strategy approach of the organization's immediate competitors.
- It can implement in relative safety because the strategy has already been proven.
- It is not innovation driven.

- The organization is likely to become an industry leader, and in some industries not being first may cause disproportionate losses of business.

The Organizational Approach.

- This approach is based on information systems decisions being made through continuous integration between the business and IT units.
- It typically uses more multidimensional and subtle language acceptable by both IT and the business.
- The IS plan tends to concentrate on a small number of important themes, growing the scope over a number of years as organizations realize the benefits of IT.
- The focus is very much on incremental delivery.

The research highlighted a number of general ISSP issues. In analyzing the experiences of the organizations surveyed, common themes emerged with respect to why planning of this nature may not have been successful. Ranked in priority order, these were:

- Resource constraints
- Not fully implemented
- Lack of top management support
- Length of planning cycle
- Poor Business-IS relationship

All of the organizations in this study were therefore asked to rate the various planning approaches against a number of key success factors. Each approach was rated on its strength in method, process, and implementation. Additionally, the organizations were asked to rate each on actual successes in terms of the approach, common concerns, and the ability to deliver competitive advantage applications. In all areas, the organizational approach came out on top.

Based on this research it is possible to understand some of the key factors necessary in a planning approach to increase the chances of success. Thorough IT-business interaction in the process, based on a shared understanding and vocabulary, is key. So is the ability to isolate significant or important aspects and provide incremental benefit, not "big bang" changes. Many of these ISSP themes are carried into the technical architecture planning arena. Readers will not be surprised to note that the stages of IT strategic plan development have much in common with the technical architecture development method described later in this book. This commonality highlights the degree to which successful planning of any type follows common themes.

The various stages in planning will be dependent on the selected approach selected, but a general view of the likely stages is as follows (and is shown in Figure 3.3):

- **Determine Current Position**. During this stage, the current stage of the organization's IT environment is established. An analysis of the IT unit's resources is also undertaken. This stage is also used to understand any issues confronting the organization, highlight strengths, and recognize weaknesses. This is very much an introspective stage.
- **Evaluate Position against the Business Strategy**. This stage is distinctly outward-looking. The organization's strategy directly influences IT planning, and during this stage the business goals, objectives, CSFs, Porter forces, and so forth are factored into the current IT position. This is typically a task undertaken by senior stakeholders.
- **Determine IS Strategy**. Based on the business strategy, and factoring in the current position, the IT strategy is defined. Essential inputs during this process include the opportunities provided by technology to support the business strategy. The outcome of this stage is a strategic plan for IT.
- **Implement Plan**. This stage takes the plan and bundles it into a number of discrete and achievable projects necessary to transition the IT environment to the desired state.
- **Measures and Feedback**. A key aspect of any planning method is to put in place the measures and feedback mechanisms to enable progress to be quantified and corrective actions to be taken if necessary.

It is important to note from Figure 3.3 that the planning stages are cyclic. This is an important characteristic of all planning. The timely assessment of achievement and the application of any necessary corrective action represents successful planning approaches. Implementation problems can be found early and corrected. New business directions (driven from a similar planning process at the business level) can be easily included in the IT planning process without engaging in another full planning cycle. In essence, the process spirals inward, reducing the gap between the current position and the strategic direction.

The architectural approach to planning described in this book has its roots in Earl's Technical Approach. However, we advocate that the derivation of the "architecture and blueprint," as Earl puts it, is not a factor of the IT strategic planning stage itself but rather the next logical (more detailed) step in the formulation of an IT environment that will be driven by the business strategy. Therefore, an important outcome of the IT planning stage is the establishment of an environment within the IT unit

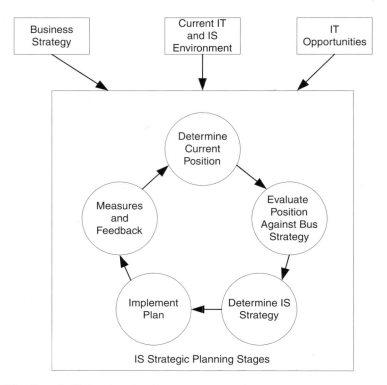

FIGURE 3.3. Generic IS planning stages.

(e.g., culture, resources) that allows more detailed technical planning to become endemic. This means that the IT plan should prescriptively outline how the architectural approach fits into the IT unit and its processes. Without clear direction, there is a gap between the strategy and the operational implementation through IT. The ISSP may consider the following governance mechanisms to achieve this:

- The establishment of an architectural role with custodianship over the implementation of the IS (and business) plans in the IT environment
- The change of IT processes to incorporate architectural and strategic governance in operational processes
- A set of indicators (IT CSFs) with which to measure IT against business metrics
- The establishment of high-level guidelines for the implementation of IT such as buy versus build, the approach to IT standards, and so on
- An indication of the current IT issues and risk and mitigation strategies

The ISSP brings to a close the organizational strategic-planning stages. The next stages of the overall planning process become more architectural. The information, business systems, and technical architectures are responsible for articulating the strategic visions, goals, and objectives established in the organizational and IT planning stages, using technology and information systems as tools.

3.4 *Information Architecture*

The information architecture understands the activities performed by the organization and the information required in performing them. This provides a high-level view of functions and data and forms a basis for the detailed analysis of business and technical requirements.

As the first architectural step following strategic planning the information architecture has two opposing objectives. Firstly, strategic, tactical, and operational information requirements must be aligned with the business and IT strategies. Secondly, it must define information models necessary to define both information system and technical environments.

For an organization to make effective use of information and use it as a competitive tool, an "information culture" must to be present. This culture is an environment whereby information is routinely used to help realize broader corporate goals—hence, the relationship between business strategic planning and the information architecture. In developing this culture, organizations must be cognizant of the Politics of Information, as described by Davenport, Eccles, and Purzak.[14] In fact, as information becomes an increasingly important asset, politics comes into play. For instance, information can become a jealously guarded commodity, not easily given away by its owners.

Davenport et al. conducted a study involving 25 large U.S.-based organizations. The objective of the study was to understand how information was managed in different corporate environments. The outcome of this study was the identification of five information models—or "states"—of politics (see Table 3.1). Far from being discrete states, the research showed that they were regularly overlapped and combined within an organization. Each organization was then asked to rank each of the political states against the following criteria:

- Commonality of vocabulary and meaning
- Degree of access to important information

14. Thomas Davenport, Robert Eccles, and Laurence Prusak, Information Politics, *Sloan Management Review* (Fall 1992).

- Quality of information
- Efficiency in the management of information

This assessment rated the political states in the following descending order of effectiveness in establishing an "information culture" (see Table 3.1):

1. Federalism
2. Monarchy
3. Technocratic Utopianism
4. Anarchy / Feudalism

The focus of the information architecture is to discover the information needs of the organization. This exercise is important when moving to the business systems architecture. The business systems architecture is responsible for mapping the information needs with the organization's information systems, with the objective of determining a mismatch or gap. The definition of information needs sounds simple enough; however, there are a large number of factors to be considered in this process.

Most organizations do not formally undertake information architecture development. Many may have tried but for a number of reasons have not seen the benefits. Typically, problems articulated about information architecture include:

Table 3.1. Models of information politices.

Technocratic Utopianism	A heavy technical approach to information management that stresses categorization and modeling of an organization's full information assets, with a heavy reliance on emerging technology
Anarchy	The absence of any overall information management policy, which leaves individuals to obtain and manage their own
Feudalism	The management of information by individual business units, which define their own information needs and report only limited information to the overall organization
Monarchy	Definition of information categories and reporting structures by the leaders of the organization, who may or may not willingly share the information after collecting it
Federalism	Information management based on consensus and negotiation of key information elements and reporting structures

- Modeling focuses on data elements and entities, the product of which is too granular to be understood by management (the actual owners of the information).
- The data "discovered" are infrequently transformed into usable information.
- Models are cumbersome and complex to maintain.
- Most often, information architecture is considered a "technical exercise."

However, as we have already stated, the information architecture is a critical step in synthesizing an understanding of the organizational strategies and mapping this to the technical (IT) environment. In fact, without an information architecture, there is effectively an unwanted air gap between the technical architecture (and business systems architecture) and the ISSP and business strategy. Such a situation leads to a technology environment that has fundamentally little relationship to the strategic business requirements, and is likely to align only with tactical initiatives.

Just how an organization should tackle the information architecture is dependent on its skills and "information maturity." Organizations that are information-enabled and appropriately skilled may choose to take a full modeling approach, and this may be generally successful. Most do not have the luxury or the patience for such an approach. Therefore, a more pragmatic view of the information architecture may need to be adopted. With this in mind, there are a number of aspects of the information architecture that can be considered as essential to putting in place a solid foundation for the technical architectures that follow. These aspects are discussed in the following sections.

Common Information Understanding

Establishing a common lexicon for information components is key. For instance, the definition of the term "sales" may have vastly different meanings for those who work in Selling and Finance. One of the major objectives of the information architecture is to establish this common vocabulary and to ensure that it is well-communicated to the organization. From an IT perspective, a corporate data model and data dictionary are key tools for maintaining a common lexicon. However, they are not necessarily effective as a communications tool for business people. Note what Davenport et al. said about Technocratic Utopianism, and Earl's comments regarding the technical approach to ISSP. The use of complex technical representations of business concepts is seldom likely to succeed. The use of business or management jargon in the description of information meaning is likely to be more effective.

Information Needs

The information architecture should discover information needs that represent strategic value for senior management, tactical value for middle management, and operational value for those involved in day-to-day operations. Strategic, tactical, and operational entities form an information hierarchy, as shown in Figure 3.4. The number of information entities at the top of the hierarchy is generally small and described by strategic business language. At the bottom, the number of entities can potentially be enormous and have specialized business meaning. It is therefore important not to get bogged down in detailed analysis, especially at the operational level.

The objective is to at least define coarse-grained subject-area views of strategic, tactical, and operational information—detailed attribute analysis may not always be necessary at this stage. The need is to understand what information is needed at all levels within the business so that this can later be aligned with specific business systems. Strategic information needs can be distilled from the organization's strategic plans (business and IS). Tactical information needs can be determined by viewing markets, products, and channels. Operational information needs can be

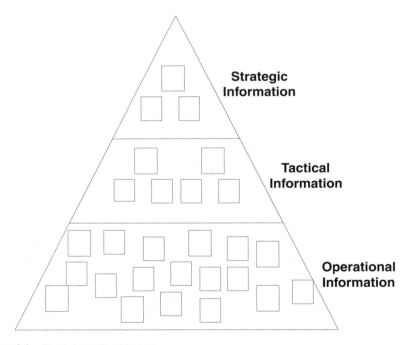

FIGURE 3.4.   The information hierarchy.

understood by studying existing operational systems, procedure documentation, and reports, for example.

Information Analysis

Generally, to understand the information requirements of the organization it is important to study the business functions performed. The functions provide valuable insight into the classes of information required. Typically, to gain an adequate functional understanding, it is necessary to decompose the high-level organizational functions into more primitive functions, using techniques such as functional decomposition. For instance, a product development function may be a subset of the marketing function, which may in turn be decomposed into further lower-level functions. This analysis need not be exhaustive. A point at which key information entities become clear is all that is required. The relationships between functions (or functional dependencies) should also be distilled.

An important tool during the development of the information architecture is the use of matrices. The ability to relate information architecture artifacts with artifacts distilled from other aspects of the strategic-planning process provides both an effective communications tool and a method for highlighting gaps and overlaps. For instance, the following relationships could be considered:

- Map identified information entities against information needs. This aids in proving the models against the strategic, tactical, and operational information needs of the organization. Additionally, this can indirectly aid in identifying functions that satisfy information needs.
- Mapping information entities against business functions provides an indication of the effect of functions on entities.
- Map business functions and entity types to organizational units. This allows information and function to be "assigned," or pigeonholed, against various parts of the organization.

Information analysis allows the business and the architects[15] to model their understanding of the organization based on an information view. This provides valuable information for the next stage, the business systems architecture.

---

15. Throughout this text we will use the term "Architect" to refer to the role responsible for leading and producing the development of the technical architecture. This does not imply a role fulfilled by a single person but rather a specific skill organizational function.

3.5   Business Systems Architecture

The business systems architecture is an activity focused on technical, systems, and application specifics. It is used to describe the business systems and information stores required in supporting the information architecture. Whereas the information architecture needed to be defined in a business-friendly manner, with significant business involvement, the business systems architecture is represented using common systems analysis methods, performed by trained business systems analysts and architects. This is not to say that the amount of business involvement should be small. Requirements gathering and analysis require significant business input. Rather, the methods used during this stage are more likely to produce more technically complex (at least for the business) models. This cannot, and should not be avoided.

The task for this stage of architectural development is to understand how the organization's information needs map to the current business systems environment and whether there are any deficiencies. The identified information needs (more precisely, this will be the "technical" information models defined during the information architecture) are mapped to the current business systems in place, any gaps are identified, information overlaps are determined, and information system problems are uncovered.

The output of this stage is a catalog of business systems required to support the strategic, tactical, and operational requirements of the organization. It is also a good idea to ensure that any new system requirements are prioritized using a suitable method (cost-benefit analysis, for instance). Information on project prioritization is provided in Chapter 13. Additionally, budgets may be obtained and foundation documents for systems replacement/procurement (such as terms of references) may be developed.

Current System Analysis

Understanding how the current business systems meet the information requirements of the organization is a critical first step of the business systems architecture. In analyzing the current systems, the focus must be on the current information needs; however, it is also important to understand the full functional and information support provided by the systems. In some cases, gaps may be found in the information architecture while analyzing the current systems. This analysis then provides the ability either to validate that the missing function / information should be added to the information architecture or that it is now obsolete. Functions and information identified as obsolete provide for an interesting further discussion such as, "Is this business system now also obsolete?"

Coupled with assessing business systems against function and information requirements is the need to understand how effective the system is at providing for these requirements. The effectiveness of a business system is partly qualitative and partly quantitative, but it should at the very least be measurable by some mechanism so that consensus can be reached on any decisions made. We have seen organizations use questionnaires targeted at the business users to measure system effectiveness (questions such as "How would you rate this system against the ease with which it allows you access to information?" are common). Other measures may include ownership cost, strategic value (measured against business strategy), and functional assessments.

The assessment of current systems should be strategically focused, with the objective of determining how the current systems are positioned to meet the (changing) business direction. There are a number of ways to represent current systems findings. We have found that a simple quadrant-based plane, comparing two important factors, can easily communicate the organization's thinking with respect to each system. For instance, plotting business contribution against technical quality can be helpful in balancing strategic business and technical factors. Figure 3.5 shows an example of such a comparison.

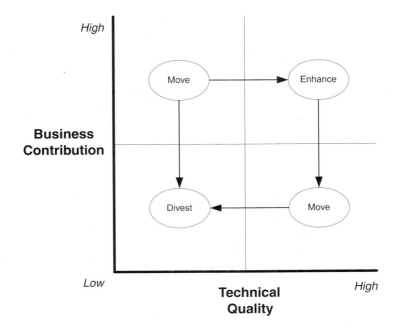

FIGURE 3.5.   System comparison.

Certainly, the information gathering required to plot a system in one of the quadrants can be significant. But its final position can accurately synthesize both opinion and empirical evidence.

The technical quality axis is usually assessed in association with the current technical architecture—or at least an organization should have a technical architecture in place to fully qualify the technical criteria for measuring systems. These factors may include the application architecture of the system, the cost of ownership, supported platforms, integration aspects, adherence to technical architecture directions, ease of use, and any other technical factors considered important to the organization.

Business contribution is derived from a number of business factors that are important to the organization. Combining key strategic factors, such as CSFs, with cost of ownership and information needs can aid in this assessment.

Clustering

Once the information needs have been qualified (usually into entities), the business functions cataloged, and the systems themselves analyzed, all of these factors should be analyzed together. Clustering provides a method for performing this analysis. Typically, clustering is a cross-checking facility.

Comparing entities against functions supports an understanding of how information needs are met by each business function. Entities that are not related to any particular function either indicate a business gap or highlight an error in the information definition. Functions that have no entities assigned may indicate that the function is now irrelevant. Entities that relate to multiple functions may show that the entity is too detailed and that a more generalized information need is required.

Functions and entities should also be mapped to business systems. This is important for a number of reasons.

- It highlights functions and entities that apply to multiple systems. Such a situation demonstrates overlap that will (or already has) led to technical and business integration issues. Maintaining the same entity (or function) in more than one place should ring some alarm bells for the architect.
- It highlights entities and functions that are not being catered to in the current business system portfolio. This is a typical occurrence when an organization has undertaken changes in strategic direction. This gap can indicate that a new system is required (or that an existing system needs augmenting).

■ It highlights systems that are now redundant. Generally if a system is no longer providing current function or information requirements, then that system can be retired. This can occur due to a change in business direction. More typically, the analysis of the system has indicated a need to divest, and its important information and functions have either been moved or assigned to a new system development.

Another useful analysis tool during clustering is to map finalized functions, entities, and systems against business areas (or organizational units). This enables considerable understanding of the distribution of function and entity around the organization. This also provides an indication as to the status of systems (such as corporate-wide or niche). All of this information is useful during the definition of the technical architecture.

Project Definition

The last stage of the business systems architecture is oriented toward project planning. The clustering stage usually highlights gaps in the system inventory. These gaps include the need to enhance, modify, or retire existing systems, while new systems may also be identified.

Changes to existing systems and new system developments must be grouped into manageable projects and then prioritized. The primary factor to consider when prioritizing is the degree of strategic need or benefit. Other factors may include cost, time to market, availability of resources, and alignment with other business initiatives. Prioritization is usually undertaken with key management representation and can (although not always) be facilitated by the IT group.

Prioritization involves identifying thresholds based on resources (typically, cost and the availability of people) and mapping them into the project list. Typically, the list is then separated into three quadrants: "action now," "delay," and "discard." Projects in the "discard" column are fed back into the strategic-planning cycle (the information systems architecture and the business systems architecture) to determine whether the system's functions and entities should be modified in the models.

It is common that a more detailed project schedule be defined for the "action now" projects. The projects are then initiated through whatever process is standard within the organization (note that project initiation is a key IT process and supports maintenance of the architectures). Initiation can include negotiating and assigning final budgets, assigning resources, and moving the project into formal project management mode.

3.6   *Architecture Maintenance*

Architecture maintenance is an important part of the architectural process. The development of business and technology strategies may appear to manifest itself as fixed-term projects; however, the reality is somewhat different. The true nature of a successful strategic project is that it never ends. The strategic process is a continuing cycle of analysis, development, maintenance and control feedback, and reanalysis. In an organization that thinks and acts strategically, there can be no finite end to this process. Changes in business environments (both internal and external) have a continuing effect on the business strategy. Changes in the technology environment coupled with business changes can have significant bearing on the business and technical strategies. Furthermore, success measures and feedback mechanisms set in place as part of the strategic-planning effort provide critical feedback that can alter thinking and direction.

The development and execution of the information, business system, and technology architectures is a considerable undertaking, especially the first time. Such a project can consume a large amount of resources (time, money, and people). There are a couple of issues with such an undertaking. Firstly, the ground can move under the project due to the typical environmental changes an organization experiences. Secondly, the amount of resources consumed can make it difficult to justify further expenditures a few years down the track. These are major problems that face any strategic initiative, increasing the risk of failure and adding to the general level of external (to the project) cynicism that tends to pervade such projects.

Certainly, the risks are high, but so are the benefits. To ensure the ongoing success of strategy development, organizations should incorporate the maintenance of the architectures within the culture of the organization. This means that a strategic IT governance capability needs to be grown within an organization that allows for this cyclic, continuous architectural development. In the final two chapters, we consider this topic in more detail; however suffice it to say that capability is the crux. The IT group must develop people and governance processes that support the maintenance of the architectures.

An architecture that consists purely of a set of documents will not be followed and tends not to be maintained. The organization will be faced with another architectural development project in a few years once it is realized that the current architectural "product" is out-of-date. Furthermore, a document cannot provide advocacy, governance, and the strategic decision-making skills required to ensure that the architectures are maintained. Only trained and knowledgeable people, and the organization as a whole, can provide this service.

Organizations should consider the following responsibilities as important in maintaining an architectural capability:

- Direct interaction with business strategists and key business focus groups/users to understand how the current architecture is processing, and what future plans the organization is considering
- Custodial involvement in the IT project initiation process to ensure that IT initiatives adhere to architectural (and hence strategic) directions
- Involvement in the steering process for IT projects to ensure that internal project decisions are made in line with architectural direction and to provide consultancy and communication of the architectures
- Liaison with executive IT processes such as strategic planning and budgeting
- Managing the feedback processes to understand how the architecture is performing in "real-world" projects and in the operational environment. Fine-tuning of the architectures will always be necessary.
- Understanding how the external factors that affect the architectures are changing (such as technology) and how these changes should be factored into the architectural process

Building this type of capability, and the organizational culture required, will ensure that the architecture remains constantly up-to-date. This will mean that an organization will be able to react more effectively to changes. It will also avoid having large strategic development projects interspersed with periods of inactivity. Major directional changes may require an organization to reevaluate all of its strategies (including its technical strategies), but this should not happen frequently.

3.7 The Rise of the e-Business Strategy

For many years, organizations have allowed technology-driven solutions to augment their business strategies. Porter's competitive model demonstrates how technology-based solutions can be used to counteract competitive forces. This is not IT driving the business as such but rather the business using the tools at its disposal to ensure its continuing success.

The advent of Internet-facilitated consumer and business-to-business interaction has provided organizations with yet another technology-driven weapon. Whether an organization is attempting to reduce the costs of supply chain management, open up new channels for product consumers, or facilitate changes in information interaction, the effect on the business strategy is the same: Internet-based technology is driving organizations to make fundamental changes to their business strategies.

e-business (or e-commerce) is touted as having significant impact on organizational success. For many organizations, e-business represents a paradigm shift, whereas for others it defines their birth. It is the next wave that most organizations will have to ride in some form or other. For these and other reasons, we have seen organizations approach the e-business wave differently from the usual strategic approach. Most have seen it as important enough to warrant a "stand-out" strategy. Some have even adopted e-business as their only strategic direction. Given these approaches, how does an e-business strategy relate to the other strategic activities defined in this chapter?

In many respects, an e-business strategy is fundamentally a mini-strategy. It should consist of all of the strategic planning components already considered and should factor in integration with the current strategies. As shown in Figure 3.6, the e-business strategy is usually driven by the technical opportunities provided by the Internet. As with a normal business strategy, the IT group must provide strategic advice to the business planners as to the state of e-business-based technology and the technical opportunities available. The e-business strategy should feed back into the other key strategies for updating. Considerations of the e-business strategy include:

- The e-business direction needs to be defined, including specific mission, goals, objectives, and priorities. Internal and external constraints affecting e-business should be identified. This analysis should be cross-checked with the business strategy.
- The IT environment must be molded around the e-business business strategy. As with the normal IT strategy, the e-business technical strategy should include objectives, strategies, policies and responsibilities, and budgets.
- The information areas to be tackled by the e-business strategy must be considered. e-business information needs are likely to be already catered to in the current architecture, although new requirements can emerge. Cross-checking is required.
- The functions and business systems affected by the e-business strategy must be identified. New e-business-specific systems are also likely to be required. Typically, e-business initiatives require major systems integration efforts, usually involving interfacing Internet-facing systems with back-end corporate systems. These changes and additions are factored into the normal business system planning cycles.

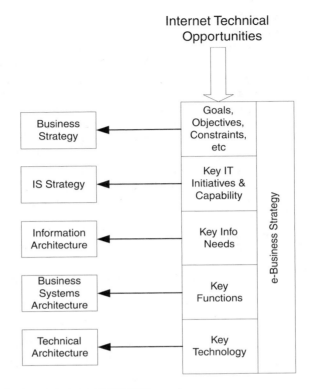

FIGURE 3.6.   e-business strategy relationships.

■ The effect of e-business on the technology environment can be immense. Organizations with predominantly legacy environments will find that the introduction of e-business initiatives requires fundamental shifts in the technical architecture. At the very least, technical services will need enhancement (e.g., security and integration). e-business drives and is driven by the technical architecture.

3.8   Introduction to the Example Organization

Throughout this book, we will be using a fictitious model organization to provide examples of most architecture development steps. It is always difficult to define such an organization in this context while retaining its relevance to all readers. However, the use of a consistent example throughout the book allows us to maintain continuity while describing of the process.

We have attempted to select an organization type that exhibits many of the characteristics that the readers may identify in their own organizations. First and foremost, it is these characteristics that are important rather than the actual industry or specific technologies. The Open Group Architectural Framework (TOGAF) is adaptable to many different organization types: government (both federal and local), large commercial organizations, smaller businesses, and nonprofit organizations. TOGAF's adaptability allows it to be scaled to large architectural projects while still being applicable in small (limited time and budget) architectural ventures. Any organization that takes a strategic view of IT and the way it will support the business can benefit from TOGAF.

Key Characteristics

Our example organization exhibits a number of key characteristics that enable us to highlight architectural development for the reader. These characteristics are:

- The organization has a reliable but increasing legacy computing environment. However, the IT environment has undergone a certain amount of chaotic development over the last few years.
- The organization has a reasonably traditional IT focus, that is, a focus on stable and solid operational computing.
- As with most organizations today, there are a number of both internal and external drivers to adopt new technology in the face of competitors, and the Internet.
- The organization possesses an application portfolio encompassing legacy and contemporary applications developed in-house and a set of common package applications.
- The organization suffers from many of the issues documented in Chapter 2.

Introducing Crunchy Frog Ltd.

Crunchy Frog Ltd. specializes in confections. They manufacture, distribute, and sell their own brands. They have been in business since 1955, just after the Great Chocolate Shortage of 1954. Initially family owned, they have grown rapidly over the last decade to the current point of number 3 in the U.S. market. Their annual turnover is in excess of $50 million. They were publicly listed 10 years ago. CFL is headquartered in New Orleans, which is also the location of their major manufacturing plant. They have 30 distribution and selling centers around the United States. Recently they began selling into Europe and the United Kingdom and have recently opened sales and distribution offices in Germany and England. They employ 10,000 people across the U.S. and 50 people internationally.

CFL's IT group is situated at its New Orleans headquarters. Run by the CIO, she reports directly to the CFL Leadership Team and the CEO. The IT group consists of a number of departments:

- An operational department is responsible for second tier support of the current computing and internal network environment as well as the management of the external vendors (who support the legacy applications and the wide area network).
- A help desk provides the single point of first tier IT support for the business. The help desk is maintained in two locations, on the east and west coasts, allowing for 8 a.m. to 6 p.m. support in all domestic locations. This agreement currently does not include international offices.
- A development group maintains the contemporary custom-developed client/server application suite (but not the legacy applications) as well as providing resources for new application initiatives.

CFL Applications

The following diagram (Figure 3.7) and the remainder of this section provide an overview of the CFL application and infrastructure portfolio.

CFL's core IT system is Logistics, running on four IBM AS/400s at HQ. This system supports inventory, distribution, invoicing, pricing and promotion, and production requirements. It was developed in the 1980s using CICS/COBOL. There are 8000 3270 terminals scattered throughout the organization (including a number at the two international offices), providing access to the system at every CFL location. Originally a package, Logistics has been modified over the years by internal staff. The system interacts with raw material suppliers and customers via printed and batch output. Access to the AS/400s is via green screens attached to an SNA network provided and managed internally. Until recently, the AS/400 also supported the only e-mail system in the organization, a character-based custom-developed application.

The Finance system was originally a custom-developed solution on the AS/400. It was recently replaced by a JDE ERP system. It runs on a Sun UNIX server with NT clients. Managed entirely by the Finance department (including systems management), they have a limited outsourcing agreement with a JDE Integration Partner for support. Used by the 20 people in Finance (and 50 other cost center managers in the various remote offices), it supports accounts receivable, accounts payable, fixed assets, and budgeting. The JDE server is located on a stand-alone departmental LAN managed by NT file servers. They have recently installed Exchange so that they can use Microsoft Outlook e-mail within the department. There is currently a project under way within Finance to extend the JDE system to support both Human Resources and Payroll (Payroll is currently run by a bureau and fed by the Finance system). There are numerous batch transfers between Logistics and JDE to maintain invoicing integrity.

The Marketing department uses Mac-based publishing tools to develop marketing collateral, both for advertising and for regional sales centers. Internal marketing information is file transferred to all distribution locations. The department uses collaboration tools (Microsoft Office, and others) for most marketing functions and is located on a Mac network in Marketing. They have access to both the JDE and Logistics systems and receive regular internal sales information populated into a Microsoft Access database application for analysis. Analysis is aug-

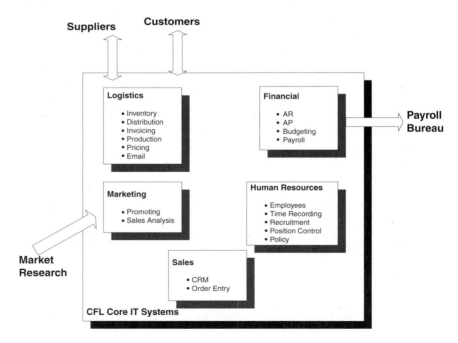

FIGURE 3.7.   Crunchy Frog Limited's core IT systems.

mented by external market research information received regularly over the Internet.

The HR department, working out of HQ, is responsible for all HR functions throughout the organization. The department uses a custom-developed Lotus Notes application that manages employees, recruitment, time recording, and position control. Administrative staff at each regional office have access to the application, primarily for time recording. HR also manages a small Intranet application that provides policy and position information to the organization. Currently, many regional employees do not have access to the Intranet due to network constraints and lack of browser support.

The Sales department manages CFL's regionally distributed salespeople along with all major direct sales customers. The department has recently implemented a custom-developed customer relationship management system (the sales system provided by the IT development group), a two-tier Oracle Forms application running on a small HP UNIX server in the Sales Department at HQ. A Resources module augments the CRM system to allow Sales to track their salespeople's selling targets, bonuses, and so forth (personnel information is provided by the HR system). Regional salespeople, many of whom have laptops, have a stand-alone Oracle application that allows them to capture orders and manage customer contacts. Each salesperson synchronizes this information with the central Oracle system on a regular basis, which in turn integrates with the AS/400 systems.

CFL Infrastructure

The majority of CFL's IT budget is required to support both the AS/400 systems and the SNA network. The SNA network, provided on a telco-supplied X.25 service, reaches all regional locations and provides frame relay access to the German and English offices. OS/2 communications servers (managed by the Operations group) at each location connect to Ethernet LANs. The AS/400s at HQ sit on a Token Ring network.

There are an increasing amount of TCP/IP-based client/server applications emerging within CFL. These are also supported over the X.25 network via software additions to the OS/2 servers. SNA traffic, of course, takes priority.

A number of locations are now using the Internet for various services. The Marketing department receives market analysis via a partner's Web site and has established an initial CFL web site. All CFL executives have personal Internet e-mail access, and sales information is exchanged with external marketing organizations and some customers via PGP encrypted e-mail. The norm is that e-mail accounts are provided through PC dial-up connections from an employee's PC to their chosen ISP (none are based on the CFL domain name). A third-party Web development company hosts CFL's Web site (the CFL domain name is attached to this site). Other Internet usage (such as browsing) is also via dial-ups on individual PCs to various ISPs.

All locations have LANs (either Ethernet or Token Ring) with access to corporate and local systems via PCs and laptops running a variety of operating systems (NT, Windows 95, some DOS, OS/2, and Macintosh). There are still a number of dumb terminals in the manufacturing plant. A number of local file-sharing mechanisms are implemented around the organization. The technology mostly depends on local preferences. In the main, most sites use workgroup file- and print-sharing models (either LAN Server or LAN Manager). The offices in Texas have built a statewide NT-based file- and print-serving environment, whereas the northeastern states have adopted a similar model using a Novell environment.

The AS400 e-mail system remains the de facto intraorganizational e-mail system. All formal messages are sent using this mechanism. Every employee has access to this system. Due in some part to its lack of contemporary style, but mostly due to the inflexibility of the mainframe system, a number of other e-mail (and collaboration) systems have exploded over the last few years. The level of adoption is dependent on the region. At last count, the products in use within CFL included Microsoft Exchange and Outlook, Novell Groupwise, and Netscape Messenger. The Sales department uses Lotus Notes for both the CRM application and e-mail. These systems are not, as a rule, supported by central IT. Most support is either carried out in an ad hoc manner by regional staff or through semiformal regionally managed outsourcing agreements. At this point, there are no e-mail gateways in place to interchange information.

From a security perspective, each of the CFL's major systems has its own methods of authenticating users and checking their access rights. The AS400 systems integrate login via a single menu to the mainframe applications; however, this does not apply to any other systems. An average CFL employee may have 4–10 individual "identities," depending on the number of systems to which they have access. As there is no IT security group (and hence no policy) within CFL, each system has different rules for such attributes as passwords, user registration, and so forth.

The central operations group manages the AS400 environment using standard IBM tools. Netview is used to manage the SNA network and the TCP/IP links. There are service level agreements (SLAs) in place with IBM and the network provider to support these services. The distributed help desk provides first-tier assistance for the AS400 applications plus the network. Other aspects of systems management, outside the AS400 platform, such as software distribution, operations management, and fault management, are either not formally provided or are done so in an ad hoc manner with various external providers. The help desk tracks all faults (and calls) using a custom-developed Visual Basic application front-ending an SQL-Server database. Currently, there is no integration between the systems at each help desk location or to any of the other management tools.

There are an increasing number of systems being developed for local use within the regions. Mostly, these have cropped up either to fulfill local specific requirements or to work around current corporate systems that do not provide easy access to the right information. At this point, the IT group does not have a clear idea of how many of these systems exist and the requirements they are meeting.

The Architectural Project

Although CFL has experienced steady, but not spectacular, growth over the last ten years, there have been a number of internal and external indicators that are of concern to the CFL Leadership Team. A number of well-known international companies are now actively targeting the lucrative U.S. market, some with reasonable success. Domestic competitors have been actively pursuing cost reduction in all aspects of their businesses (especially in the supply chain) to drive production costs down. In addition competitors are now aiming aggressively at alternate distribution and direct sales mechanisms to increase market share. Without exception, this is leading the industry toward the adoption of Internet technology and e-business solutions.

Due to these pressures, the CFL Leadership Team commissioned a business strategy to look first at the current organization and then forecast a three- and six-year direction and provide business imperatives that would lead the organization along a chosen strategic path. The strategy confirmed that IT was a key business enabler in meeting many of the strategic objectives. It was the recommendation of the Leadership Team that an IT strategic plan be undertaken with the objective of providing a technical strategy to support the business direction.

The IT strategic plan, conducted by an external consultancy group, identified the following problem areas:

- A number of key IT processes, including project initialization and procurement, were ad hoc and did not exhibit any alignment to business or IT strategy.
- IT could not measure its success in relation to business goals and objectives.
- A Total Cost of Ownership (TCO) analysis highlighted the high cost associated with the CFL IT environment when compared with in-

dustry benchmarks. Issues contributing to this assessment included inefficient systems management procedures (especially software distribution and user support), non-IT employees supporting key departmental systems, and complex systems-integration techniques.

- The level of support provided for key applications was deemed insufficient or nonexistent.
- The legacy systems (especially on the AS400) were becoming increasingly difficult to maintain and enhance.
- Chaos reigned in the selection and implementation of business systems. There was no defined process to determine the informational, functional, nonfunctional, and technology fit of new applications into the organization. Hence, in many instances, information and function are duplicated across systems, causing information integrity problems and complicating intersystem integration. Furthermore, regional systems have blossomed, causing even greater TCO and integrity problems.
- Technology overlap, in such areas as organizational e-mail and communications, contributes significantly to high environment costs, insufficient support, information duplication, and integration problems.
- There is little technology coordination or management infrastructure evident to enable the strategic use of the Internet. As a key business enabler, the current Internet environment does not have the level of maturity necessary to support CFL business initiatives.
- Reporting (both tactical and strategic) is only provided formally at HQ. Typically, any reports needed by the regions are posted, and usually they are inaccurate or out of date when they arrive. Furthermore, the current reports from the core systems do not provide the level of management information to support strategic decision-making.
- No consistent software development philosophy and delivery mechanism is present.

The ISSP attempted to align CFL's strategic goals and objectives with the goals and objectives for the IT Group. The IT goals are summarized below:

- Support the development of high-value and differentiated products for continued growth.
- Be a best-cost producer.
- Manage the business globally.
- Support identification of target growth opportunities, particularly in international markets.
- Deliver outstanding customer service and support.
- Merge to a common architecture.

The ISSP proposed a number of strategies to meet both the business and IT objectives. In summary, these were

- *Corporate architecture.* Establish an architectural capability, and define and maintain the corporate architecture as an overriding technology policy direction.
- *Business partnership.* Implement IT and IT solutions in partnership with the business by applying a robust project initiation and governance framework.
- *TCO.* Reduce/control TCO by the smarter implementation of technology through a holistic and architectural approach to IT rather than regional or project-by-project.
- *Interface quality.* Ensure the quality (both information and reliability) of interfaces between systems.
- *International coverage.* Extend the CFL IT environment to the International offices in a seamless way.
- *Systems management.* Centralize and streamline systems management tools and processes to increase user satisfaction.
- *Change.* Increase responsiveness with respect to business system changes.
- *Best of breed.* Implement only best-of-breed (but not necessarily open), medium- to low-risk technology; do not play on the hype curve.
- *Vendor partnerships.* Reduce the number of vendors providing services and products for CFL.
- *Usability.* Reduce the effort users apply when interfacing with business systems.
- *Packages.* Implement packaged solutions when requirements exhibit common functionality with industry solutions. Only build if the system is strategic and totally unique to CFL.
- *Internet.* Establish an Internet infrastructure to support e-business.
- *Security.* Ensure that the integrity and availability of CFL information and the IT environment is assured.
- *Software development.* Develop a consistent set of conceptual foundations and frameworks that supports all of CFL's software development.

One of the recommendations of the IT strategic plan was to undertake an architectural exercise with the objective of addressing the problem areas defined. The deliverables from the architectural project were defined as follows:

- Establish set of CSFs that can be traced to the business goals.
- Catalog the information needs of the organization.

- Map the information needs to business systems, and define areas of gaps and duplication. Additionally, understand the scope of the regional systems and determine their drivers.
- Define a portfolio of business applications that allows the organization to meet its strategic, tactical, and operational needs.
- Define a target technology environment that supports the business strategic plan.
- Detail a list of projects to support alignment.
- Update IT processes, especially project initialization, to include strategic assessment.

Among the recommendations of the IT Strategic plan were a number of IT group structural changes to aid the architectural process. A corporate architecture capability was suggested. This capability would be responsible for aligning IT with business strategy, acting across IT functional groups, and providing and maintaining architectural direction through the IT group. The physical realization of the capability into an actual structure was not defined. Meanwhile, an Architectural Steering Group was established to act as the owners of the architectural program.

This book tracks CFL through the development of its technical architecture. The other components of the architectural exercise—the information architecture and business systems architecture—have already been completed and provide input into the technical architecture. The Architectural Steering Group decided on The Open Group Architectural Framework (TOGAF) to support the development of the technical architecture.

3.9   *Summary*

In this chapter, we positioned the concept of technical architecture planning with the other strategic-planning processes used within an organization; namely, business strategy and information systems strategy. Additionally, we segmented the concept of architecture into the notions of information architecture, business systems architecture, technical architecture, and application architecture.

We also discussed some important concepts related to the maintenance of the organization's architectures. These will be described in more detail in later chapters.

We looked at the need for an e-business strategy and where that would fit in relation to the already described strategic processes.

Finally, we introduced the fictitious organization, CFL. We will trace CFL through the development of its technical architecture. It will be used to provide pertinent examples during the major stages of architectural development.

In the next chapter, we take our first look at TOGAF and its architectural development method.

CHAPTER 4

TOGAF and the Architectural Development Method

4.1 Introduction

We have considered the concepts of strategic planning and the relationship between strategic planning and enterprise architectures. Furthermore, we have positioned the various types of architectures that an organization may use to support detailed IT planning. Our focus in this book is on the enterprise technical architecture. The technical architecture describes the technical structure and components of the organization's IT environment. It is concerned with components such as applications at a macro level and is responsible for driving the strategic direction (both business and IT) into the technology environment.

Our treatment of technical architecture has been of a generic nature to this point. As intellectually appealing as an abstract (one might say meta) treatment of technical architectures might be, the focus of the text is ultimately a practical one. Therefore, it is timely that we introduce The Open Group's Architectural Framework (TOGAF) and its associated development method (we decry the use of *methodology* in this text due to its inaccurate application to what are more properly known as *methods*).

4.2   Architectural Frameworks

The Notion of a Framework

Before dwelling on the nature and features of TOGAF, it is interesting to ponder the notion of a framework in the context of architecture and understand the ramifications of adopting a framework.

Initially, what do we really mean by framework? Ostensibly, a framework in the space of architecture is a conceptual skeleton within which one may facilitate the discovery, design, and evolution of a technical architecture. We thus categorize a framework in the following manner, considering that it must be:

- *Reasoned*. A reasoned framework allows one to craft an architecture that behaves deterministically when constraints change (a distinct asset in the e-business theatre) and retains integrity even in the face of unprecedented business or technological change and demands.
- *Cohesive*. A cohesive framework has an appropriate grouping of behavior, being balanced in its outlook and scope.
- *Adaptable*. Each organization in which a framework can be applied may be subtly or radically different and therefore we require of a framework that it may undergo adaptation without losing integrity (of course, this will require additionally a combination of taste, style, and experience on the side of the practitioner).
- *Vendor-independent*. A framework that is dependent on a particular vendor may fail to fully realize benefits for the organization.
- *Technology-independent*. A framework that has a parochial technology focus may limit the agility of the business in situations that oblige a direct, rapid response. Of course, this characteristic may have more than a passing tension with *vendor independence*.
- *Domain-neutral*. Domain neutrality is an essential attribute for a framework that would purport to nurture our organization's aims
- *Scalable*. A desirable framework must operate effectively at departmental, business unit, government, and corporate levels without loss of focus and applicability.

Key Definition: **Architecture framework.**
A reasoned, cohesive, adaptable, vendor-independent, technology-independent, domain-neutral, and scalable conceptual foundation for detailed architecture representation.

Without these qualities, we contend that a framework will be unbalanced and potentially deficient and possibly engendering a limited view of technical architecture development (in its widest sense), to the detriment of the organization's fiscal and human resource investment.

The Need for a Framework

Although we have some key criteria against which we can measure an architectural framework to ascertain its integrity and usefulness, this does not answer the question of why we might actually require a framework. If one considers this question more deeply, it becomes apparent that any useful framework would provide enough rigor, captured expertise, guidance, and a logical method to safeguard our architectural endeavors so that they bear well-designed fruit (to stretch a metaphor). In seeking this coverage, it is apparent that a consensus-driven, standards-based, eclectic framework will meet these criteria, and, as we discuss, The Open Group's Architectural Framework (TOGAF) is that framework.

4.3   Introducing TOGAF[16]

As we noted in Chapter 3, the directed forward momentum of organizations is captured by business strategic plans. The strategic plan captures the fundamental vision of the organization and outlines the preferred future from a macro perspective. As we have also described, an IT strategic plan, connected to the business strategy and supporting known and measurable outcomes, is essential in order to avoid a tactical approach to information technology that ultimately degrades and devalues the worth of IT (and in this instance, technical architectures specifically).

However, the IT strategic plan has as its strength and weakness the fact that it is *just* a strategic plan. To realize and support the strategic vision, it is necessary to support, endorse and devise an IT architecture (also referred to as *enterprise architecture* in this text).

Over the years, government organizations have succeeded in developing and executing targeted, as well as enterprise, architectures. The U.S. Department of Defense (DoD) has placed a version of its architecture, the Technical Architecture Framework for Information Management (TAFIM), in the public domain. This document essentially dictates

---

16. Portions of this text appeared in *Intelligent Enterprise*, 1st March 2000 issue.

procurement, development, and deployment of information technology across the DoD. TAFIM is a verbose framework published in eight volumes (including a Technical Reference Model, Architecture Concepts and Design Guidance, Program Manager's Guide for Open Systems, DoD Goal Security Architecture and Adopted Information Technology Standards). TAFIM most certainly required a large investment of both time and money.

The approach characterized by initiatives such as TAFIM has certainly been the de facto means by which technical architectures are defined but unfortunately labors under some notable flaws:

- The elapsed time required to produce the architecture makes it close to obsolete before completion.
- Architectures of such complexity require specialized and reasonably uncommon IT expertise to complete. The end result is normally incomprehensible to a business-oriented audience and is harder to trace to the business strategy.
- Although an architecture like that produced by DoD is available in the public domain, no specific method is available to guide its development. Hence, ad hoc, piecemeal, or fragmented methods are occasionally misapplied in the name of development.

Perhaps in part due to some of these flaws, the TAFIM was abruptly cancelled, and no public reason has yet been announced for this. Instead, we are led to believe that the Command and Control, Communication, and Computers Intelligence, Surveillance, and Reconnaissance Model (C4ISR) has usurped TAFIM and has been adopted as the new "standard." C4ISR operates under the general aegis of the DISA (Defense Information Systems Agency).

Addressing these flaws would seem to require a framework and associated method that exhibits the characteristics we deemed desirable in our idealized framework at the beginning of this chapter (reasoned, cohesive, adaptable, vendor-independent, technology-independent, domain-neutral, and scalable). It should not be prescriptive, rigidly formal, or brittle.

Another important virtue in our opinion is that the method must provide a "shared vision" among a variety of organizational personnel that collectively possess a diverse range of skills, understanding, influence and motivation.

The Open Group Architectural Framework (TOGAF) is both the framework and accompanying method we espouse in this text as that which is most likely to meet our criteria. It is interesting to note that TOGAF is most definitely a branch of TAFIM and given TAFIM's status, extremely unlikely to be merged into the main development stream.

When one compares the extant TAFIM documentation with earlier versions of TOGAF, there is almost a palpable isomorphism between them.

Notwithstanding this historical link, we have applied TOGAF with notable success in a number of organizations, ranging from corporate through government. TOGAF is ultimately rooted in the open systems movement and (therefore) championed by The Open Group. This meets the criterion of *vendor-independence*. This open systems embrace allows TOGAF to display strength in the development of technical architectures that support interoperability, scalability, and portability (common and unsurprisingly also TAFIM important goals). More importantly, these characteristics of a technical environment are critical in supporting e-business and e-commerce solutions. The Internet and its millions of attached organizations are an eclectic mixture of technology, products, and services. The primary enabler for the e-economy is the integration of this diversity into a connected whole. An architectural framework must embody this enabler.

TOGAF is prescriptive in at least one sense: it observes and opines that enterprise architectures must be driven top-down from a business standpoint instead of being IT-driven and potentially irrelevant, misguided, or just plain wrong in the longer term. The method (which is described in moderate detail in this chapter) requires (or at least strongly advises) that you reflect on and periodically measure alignment of architectural components with business objectives and goals. The implication is that one should not be remiss in understanding and accepting that a technical architecture must be a solution to a *business* problem, and occasionally revisiting that problem(s) will help to ensure IT and business benefit. Certainly, in an e-time or other temporally constrained undertaking, the penalty for a lax attitude can be severe (one only has to study some simple Standish Group or Gartner Group papers to understand that "IT" and "success" do not always sit in easy juxtaposition).

The Enterprise Continuum

TOGAF focuses on the production of a valid, reasoned, deployable, and maintainable architecture for an organization. TOGAF provides the necessary tools with which to produce an IT architecture, including:

- A theoretical base (the continuum we describe here)
- A technical reference model (TRM)
- Standards information base (SIB)
- An architectural development method (ADM)

The tools provided by TOGAF exist within an overarching context that TOGAF defines as the *enterprise continuum*. The enterprise continuum is the "cornerstone" of TOGAF, and, in our opinion, a fundamental tenet of successful architecture creation in a business-driven context. We may view the continuum as a succinct depiction of the evolution of architectural planning and realization.

Applying TOGAF ultimately yields an IT architecture that is specific to an organization and its business needs and goals. The resultant architecture attains the status of the strategic blueprint for solution implementation. In essence, we seek to derive a specific "city plan" for the IT architecture. This noble goal begins by stating "architectural concerns" at a generic (almost abstract) level and gradually and deterministically evolving them to organizationally specific components under the guidance of TOGAF. This approach illustrates the adaptability of TOGAF (and directly meets another of our key framework criteria) in that it provides the core generic pieces to construct a foundation architecture but allows (in fact, encourages) latitude in the process so that a domain specific architecture results.

In TOGAF, the enterprise continuum provides a common "architectural vocabulary" when discussing and considering architectural concerns and options. For example, when discussing an industry-specific reference model (such as an industry consortium's e-commerce portal model, a vendor-specific EAI product architecture, or Web–legacy integration technique) with vendors, consultants and internal personnel, showing the model in the continuum can be most illuminating.

The enterprise continuum aggregates two essential continua, the *architectural continuum* and the *solutions continuum*. Simply put, the architectural continuum describes the generalization/specialization of architectural components, whereas the solutions continuum illustrates the actual implementation of the components.

Key definition: **Enterprise continuum.**
The TOGAF enterprise continuum collects together the architectural and solutions continua.

Architectural Continuum

The architectural continuum (see Figure 4.1) represents an architectural development progression. Development begins at the logical level and at this point is generically focused on IT technology. As a result, there should initially be a lack of consideration for specific implementation concerns, enabling architects to focus on the services required for the solution. As development of the architecture continues, the logical architecture is implemented by a physical architecture that deals with the specific technology and service requirements of the organization or particular system. As the architecture progresses toward the physical, it

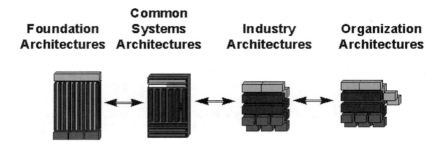

FIGURE 4.1. Architectural continuum.

becomes increasingly focused on business needs and organizational constraints.

Key Definition: **Architectural continuum.**
TOGAF-specific, it presents a linear (in presentation, although not in usage) roadmap in the definition of the technical architecture. The generic end of the continuum denotes re-useable architectural assets for building an individual organization's IT environment. The continuum's specific end evolves the foundation architecture with organizational-specific architectural input.

Although not prescriptive, the architectural continuum begins at the foundation level, moves through common systems architectures, industry-specific architectures, and then culminates in one that is specific to your organization. Note, however, that the "information" connection between each stage is bidirectional, *implying* the existence of a rudimentary feedback loop. For example, it is possible to recognize the need for an additional industry architectural component after completing a gap analysis of the organizational architecture and business requirements. The architectural continuum aids this process also by providing a common understanding that has as a side effect the tendency to minimize redundancy. In travelling along the architectural continuum, the architect is collecting architectural intellectual property (in the form of models) from a variety of sources represented by the continuum point.

Key definition: **Foundation architecture.**
The foundation architecture is a key part of TOGAF. The foundation architecture contributes a reference model, a service taxonomy, and a list of compliant products and technologies (personified in the standards information base). It essentially represents the generic IT environment.

The various levels of the architectural continuum and their relationship to the final product are:

- *Foundation architecture.* The TOGAF model architecture is an excellent and comprehensible way to initiate an organization's architectural work. The TOGAF model is generic as well as reasonably comprehensive and is an intelligible way to describe (at a conceptual level) the architectural components of IT systems. TOGAF allows a focus on the use of technology services to meet business and system requirements. The fundamental pillars of the TOGAF foundation architecture are the technical reference model (TRM) and the standards information base (SIB). Figure 4.2 shows these constructs, and includes the concept of building blocks, which will be discussed in Chapter 6.

- *Common systems architecture.* Common systems architectures are still reasonably generic (and therefore incomplete with respect to solution domains requirements) but tend to focus on a specific technology subject area (distributed computing, security, or management, for example); they are common across the IT industry (e.g., horizontal). An example of a common architecture would be the CORBA (Common Object Request Broker Architecture) model, which itself sits within the Object Management Architecture of the Object Management Group (OMG). In addition, vendors such as IBM, EDS, and Microsoft are possible sources for common systems architectures that can be adapted or applied to an organization. As a counterpoint to CORBA, for example, Microsoft would counter

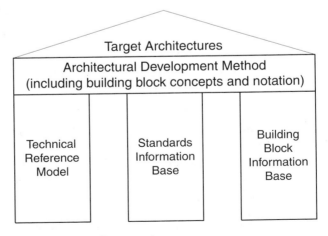

FIGURE 4.2.   TOGAF Foundation Components.

with COM+, whereas IBM might counter with SOM (but is more likely to proffer COM+ or J2EE at the time of writing).

- *Industry-specific architecture.* Industry architectures are more specific than common systems architectures and are more closely aligned with the industry or the domain in which one is working. The petrochemical industry publishes a number of key architectures that may need to be applied or considered when operating in this rather demanding problem space. Likewise, the government environment has a number of extant architectures available for consideration. In addition, one may adopt specific subject area architectures such as enterprise application integration (EAI) or e-commerce/e-business. Examples of these include Information Management Associates (IMA) Inc.'s Internet Component Architecture, which supports demand chain management; the Analytical Solution Forum's Multidimensional APIs; the Open Buying on the Internet (OBI) Consortium's technical specifications; or Dialogic's CT-Server and CT-Media specifications. Interestingly, the OMG has a range of special-interest groups that are tasked with creating industry specific architectures (in OMG terminology, *domain architectures*) including electronic commerce, finance, telecommunications, and health care.

- *Organizational Architecture.* The organizational architecture is the most visible and pertinent to the organization, and it guides the final implementation of systems. Leveraging the architectures developed along the continuum, this step is aggressive in its consideration of business needs, capabilities, and requirements. Arguably, it is at this point that the architecture provides the most value to the organization; the direct effect of unique and/or strategic constraints will be most in evidence here. It is somewhat unusual to apply architectural planning at each step, and with the advent of e-business pressure, commercial imperatives often cannot pause for the amount of time required for "purity." However, we tend always to start with the foundation architecture, and, if available, take "high-profile" or easily discernible components from the common systems architectures and industry architectures. The greatest intellectual effort is applied when developing the organization-specific architecture from information gained in the previous steps. Additionally, significant input from specific business drivers guides the architect's hand, and this is balanced with the omnipresent obligation to assure that the organizational architecture will enjoy an appropriate life span as the travails of business agility alter or intensify tensions.

Solutions Continuum

The solutions continuum parallels the architectural continuum in its presentation. Again, the continuum progresses from left to right, generic to specific, with bidirectional links between each stage in the continuum. Essentially, each stage in the solutions continuum can be logically connected to the corresponding stage in the architectural continuum. Figure 4.3 illustrates the solutions continuum.

The stages of the solutions continuum are:

- *Products and services*. Products are distinct, procurable entities that provide capability, value, and/or a solution and may be represented by hardware, software, and services. Services relate to any activity that enhances, provides capability, or supports the deployment and use or maintenance of solutions.
- *Systems solutions*. A systems solution corresponds to a horizontal (cross domain) solution. Such solutions are typically standards-based and open (although this is not essential to the definition). Systems solutions are typically supplied by vendors and may display a certification or accreditation. Systems solutions include TP monitors, CORBA- or J2EE-based middleware, systems management products (SNMP/WBEM-based), and security services. Hence, systems solutions may contribute to the quality and/or functional characteristics of an architecture.
- *Industry solutions*. These are instances of industry architectures and are domain-focused. It is common for industry solutions to be provided across a range of systems solutions due to the requirement to accommodate a range of possible deployment options.
- *Organizational solutions*. This is the most specific entity in the solutions continuum. Organizational solutions represent unique or strategic investments made by the organization to satisfy specific business needs or support a strategic vision. Such solutions will ordinarily build upon the foundation of the three preceding stages to provide value.

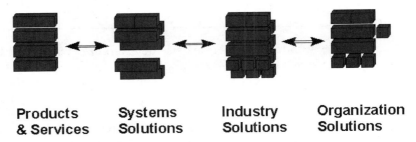

**Products   Systems   Industry   Organization
& Services   Solutions   Solutions   Solutions**

FIGURE 4.3. The TOGAF solutions continuum.

Key Definition: **Solutions continuum.**
The Solutions Continuum represents the physical implementations of the architectures at the corresponding levels of the Architecture Continuum. At each level, the Solutions Continuum populates the architecture with purchased products, or built components, that represent a solution to the organization's business need expressed at that level.

Technical Reference Model

The seminal concepts of the *technical reference model* (TRM) and the *standards information base* (SIB) are crucial guides in the architectural development method (ADM) process and, as noted, are the fundamental pillars of the foundation architecture. Figure 4.4 illustrates the standard TOGAF TRM, referred to in the text as the base or foundation architecture.

The TRM describes, among other things, the taxonomy of logical services to be provided in support of business or infrastructure applications. The TOGAF TRM prescribes a relatively simple taxonomy to facilitate effective partitioning of necessary services so that one may describe, for example, services that reside in the application software layer (specific application software) and application platform—a cohesive, typically functional set of logical services for the application software layer. The reader should recognize that most business applications will use the majority of platform services defined in the foundation TRM. In this sense, the TRM is reasonably complete but without organizational bias.

Key Definition: **Technical reference model.**
The TRM simply provides a visual classification of all the technical functions (or services) of the "foundation"—in a TOGAF sense—IT environment.

In addition, there exists the *external environment* layer (entities and systems external to the application platform known to the architecture) and the interfaces among the layers. Surrounding the TRM are the quality attributes (which we touched on briefly before) that provide for various nonfunctional constraints. An excellent example of a quality attribute that has intra- and extra-enterprise effects is a security service. For a security service to be effective, all platform services must support its implemented policy and intent—such a service behaves in a way that is

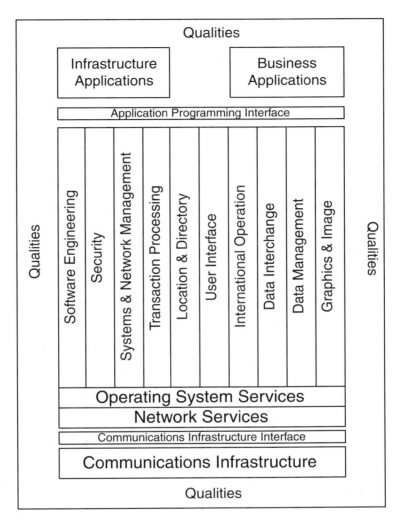

FIGURE 4.4. The TOGAF technical reference model.

orthogonal to that of "ordinary" platform services, for example. It may be illuminating to consider a service that represents, implements, or supports a quality attribute in the same way that one might compare a common systems architecture with an industry architecture in the architectural continuum. As one can see, assurance of mutually reinforcing services in an overall quality "blanket" has the potential to be complex and compromising if not undertaken with an appropriate methodical approach.

Standards Information Base

The SIB is effectively a standards reference that provides input to, and is generated from, the architectural development process, specifically in the latter stages of development when more abstract notions must be mapped to concrete, reliable organizational standards. An organizational SIB represents those standards that have been specifically adopted or replaced with an organization's IT architecture. Aside from technical architecture considerations, the SIB provides value in the technology procurement guidelines and activities (considered part of architectural governance). The Open Group has a comprehensive SIB available on-line,[17] and this is a useful foundation for many organizations.

Key Definition: **Standards information base.**
The SIB collects the organization's technology standards within the TOGAF service taxonomy.

Architectural Development Method

TOGAF possesses a most adequate theoretical base, but we have yet to address the key issue of architectural development. We have already noted that a framework should provide a reasonably general method according to which it may be applied. TOGAF provides such a methodical, logical method—the *architectural development method* (ADM).

With the supporting concepts of the TRM and SIB in place, we now outline the ADM. It is important to note that the ADM is cyclic (see Figure 4.5)—the development of the architecture, to achieve greatest benefit, must be an ongoing process. This concept does not imply that the architecture is in a state of flux; rather, it implies that it must be actively tended rather than neglected. It is a truism that the grandest, most elegant architecture will erode and decay if not maintained. Additionally, the rate of change of technology (which is beginning to outpace the decades-old Moore's Law[18] and the increasing feasibility of computationally intensive tasks (online analytic processing queries, for example) mandate a periodic review of the state of the "architectural nation." One may no longer rest easy in the knowledge that an architecture is "complete," for it will never be so! This is one of the tenets recognized and endorsed by the ADM.

---

17. See: http://www.opengroup.org.
18. Moore's Law refers to the fact that the amount of information storable on a given amount of silicon doubles roughly every year.

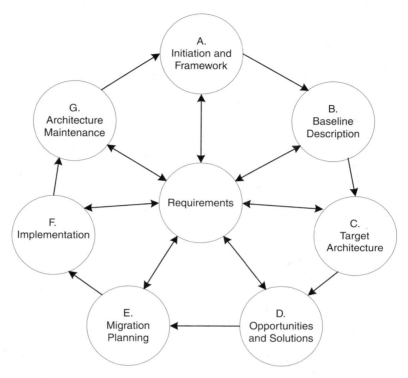

FIGURE 4.5. The cyclic directed graph of the ADM.

Key Definition: **Architectural development method.**
The ADM is a TOGAF-specific process, consisting of seven major phases for the development and maintenance of an organization's technical architecture.

Each stage of the ADM presages the arrival of the next, with the outputs of one stage being connected to the inputs of the next. Each phase of the ADM is described in greater detail in the following chapters, and so we concern ourselves with only an overview of each.

- *Initiation and framework*. We use key stakeholder requirements, business drivers and objectives, and organizational context in this phase to build a vision for the architecture. Agreement at this stage, primarily affected in our experience by factors such as executive management buy-in, realistic and definable business objectives, and reasoned business and information technology strategic planning, is essential for crystallizing the essence of the development. With such an understanding in place, you can confidently enter the next phase.

- *Baseline description.* Typically, legacy information or IT assets will already exist in an organization. Therefore, it is necessary to discover and document the scope and nature of already extant services, facilities, and architectural mechanisms so that they may be reengineered, exposed, or otherwise provided by the new architecture. By ensuring that you possess a clear description of the present environment, you can craft a fledgling mapping from the currently considered architecture to the **TOGAF TRM**, which then feeds directly into the next stage.

- *Target architecture definition.* This stage is the pivotal and most demanding one of the ADM, where you will be tasked with formulating, using various projections (views), the nature of the architecture that will support critical business drivers, strategy, and requirements and embrace or otherwise support the existing model of business services and IT platforms and technologies. The more detailed stages (which form some of the chapter decomposition of this text) are covered in the next section to first give an overall impression of the ADM.

- *Opportunities and solutions.* This phase identifies the dimensions of change. A first cut of the top-level projects required in moving from the current environment to the target architecture is created. The gap analysis from the preceding stage is typically the richest source of initial input, followed by brainstorming techniques and technical architect style and taste. This stage represents the strategy (if you will) precursor of the implementation because it is more concerned with what will need to transpire to implement the target. The issue of managing change is paramount in this step. The refinement of this stage is the basis of the implementation plan.

- *Migration planning.* Here we sort projects by both dependency and priority. For example, there is little point in commencing a security architecture design process if the security policy is not defined! One may also note that certain projects would seem more suited to purchased rather than bespoke solutions. If the scale of change is just too great, then one might consider an iterative approach, requiring a stepped and dependency-aware (and possibly risk-aware) approach.

- *Implementation.* This phase is often highly organization- or possibly vendor-specific, as one defines artifacts that impact the commencement of each project. TOGAF recommends that one formulate recommendations for each implementation project and construct an architecture contract to govern the system implementation and deployment. This sort of activity is sometimes split across a terms of reference (TOR) document and any associated governance input. We have only occasionally had the luxury of time to create a custom architecture contract or the equivalent of it, tending to rely on existing, more general IT strategic documents (for example, publishing the technical architecture principles of the organization, noting conformance and compliance requirements, publishing the SIB and so on). Of course, this phase sees the system implemented and deployed.

- *Architecture maintenance.* As we alluded to earlier, without some (even rudimentary) maintenance procedure for the new baseline (that is the result of the implementation phase), it is likely that our technical architecture will grow stale or erode and drift over time. We like to regard this phase as supporting a periodic technology architecture "refresh," where one considers changes in business strategy, IT strategy, or adopted technology (although an IT-driven refresh may suffer from tunnel vision). This refresh cycle is used to decide when a new phase of architecture evolution should commence (which often requires a request for funding). The processes endemic in the refresh cycle are those of architecture governance. Most readers will identify with the suggestion that the refresh cycle is contracting.

Expanded Target Architecture Definition

It is informative and useful to consider the target architecture phase in greater detail before summarizing and continuing with a journey into phase one of the ADM.

Initially, it is useful to represent the information discovered from the baseline phase in TRM terms and populate a relevant and contemporary (to the organization) SIB. These two items are of crucial importance, allowing one to apply foundation architecture-specific (i.e., TRM and SIB) approaches to the target architecture design and to trace TOGAF activities directly to an IT architecture design undertaking, cementing one's understanding of TOGAF. Remember that the baseline is typically couched in organization-specific terms, and so this phase normalizes that information, creating an agreed-on vocabulary.

To ensure that the various facets of business and technical requirements are adequately fulfilled by a design, TOGAF suggests that you consider the target architecture from a number of perspectives, or *views*. TOGAF introduces functional, implementation and physical views; each of which contains sub-views. For example, the top-level implementation view includes, among others, data management, security, and management views. As an aside, we have found that views are also useful in the baseline description phase, allowing one to partition activities and present information in intellectually comprehensible "chunks." This allows consensus to be achieved with respect to the completeness of the information.

Key Definition: **Architectural views.**
Views are different slices through an architecture, each type embodying a different perspective, therefore allowing for a complete architectural analysis. Views are used as a method of cross-checking and tradeoff assessment.

Our multiperspective (view-based) investigation of the baseline and target services is applied at this stage to formulate a general model of how functional business needs will be satisfied by the technical services (the platform services) to be defined by the technical architecture. In TOGAF terms, the abstract architectural model consists (on a simple level) of several interdependent, crisply defined, and replaceable services, with defined interfaces. You could consider these services as the technical architecture equivalent of software components.

Ultimately, the architecture must help realize the deployment of a range of services that are identified from the existing system or noted as new business requirements, perhaps as a result of some environmental shift in response to a changed or new business driver. For example, we have found that a resurgence of interest in customer intimacy systems has introduced more exotic architectural services, such as neural networks. In a recent engagement, we noted that such an element is not classified by TOGAF, leading us to introduce a new (admittedly more abstract) TRM service, artificial intelligence. This deliberately broad classification lets us allocate other AI domain facilities to this service as they enter the mainstream.

A (perhaps *the*) significant litmus test for the target architecture is its satisfaction of business objectives and goals and hence its ability to support functional business systems. We see as an absolute necessity what we call the practice of *objective (or requirements) traceability*, realized as a diaphanous link between the business drivers, business objectives, and architectural (technical) objectives. This link represents a sacrosanct contract between the IT architecture and the business and encapsulates the integrity of the mapping from the business system to the technical implementation.

In order to select a specification or set of specifications, it is usual to determine and capture the criteria by which specifications can be selected. Of course, this is very much an open systems viewpoint, and you may find that this stage is not required depending on an organization's IT history and focus. If one has a considerable Microsoft infrastructure, it would not be unusual to continue building on that rather than attempting to integrate a best-of-breed technology approach, for example.

For those organizations with a more eclectic focus, one should consider the more detailed architectural requirements and business objectives. Often these are quite well-known and in turn eclectic: mature, standards based, stable, industry standard, few or known limitations, free, and so on.

Of course, we still must define the architecture at an appropriate level of detail. This stage is the embodiment of top-down, service-oriented decomposition; we design and capture the relationships between platform service groups of the architecture and the nature of the services themselves (in greater detail). Note that as this typically iterative process proceeds, you transition from the architectural continuum to the solutions continuum. This transition manifests itself in an ever more concrete (in the best sense of the word!) architecture on which you may initiate planning and implementation activities.

A gap analysis is a simple illustrative device that enables one to easily and simply detect omissions or areas of deficiency if one can depict the area of interest as a simple two-dimensional grid. The technique is used in the target architecture definition phase to identify any missing functionality. This activity therefore also complements objective traceability. TOGAF recommends a rudimentary gap analysis that measures the veracity of the target architecture in supporting all identified business-processing needs. As we recently decided in a legacy migration project, complete coverage of business-system needs is not always necessary or desirable.

4.4   Using TOGAF in e-Time

As we begin to consider in depth the transition required by our fictional organization (CFL), it will be noted that TOGAF does indeed provide us with a conceptual framework that can respond in e-time to business imperatives. What one must consider, however, is that even though architectural "agility" is required, this does not equate to slap-dash approaches and cursory consideration. It is necessary to reason about the architectural effects of (in our case) e-enablement. It is necessary to consider a number of perspectives before proceeding in a certain direction— and it is necessary to ensure a certain, shall we say, orthonormality and integrity in our decisions. We, of course, contend that TOGAF does indeed provide us with some of these tools, and the purpose of this text is in part to demonstrate how they may be applied under rather more severe constraints than frameworks such as TAFIM originally were.

The crux of the matter is that decisions effected in e-time are no different from decisions made in ordinary time. The frame of reference does not in effect alter, and the gravity of a poor architectural choice will be just as apparent. In fact, one may assume that poor IT architecture planning may be *more* (or more quickly) apparent in the epoch of e-time. This means that technical architects, now perhaps more than ever, are required to exercise technical agility with controlled rigor, the rigor in this case being the application of a framework. Interestingly, one may consider this as a spin on an age-old psychology poser: "Is quick thought better than deep thought?" Our stance is that when driven by business imperatives, our answer should be that there is no palpable difference.

4.5   *Summary*

This chapter saw us introduce the notion of a framework, list the desirable qualities of such an entity and consider why we might employ one. Our framework under consideration, TOGAF, was introduced via a brief historical sidebar that traced its roots from the TAFIM initiative of the U.S. Department of Defense.

Examining TOGAF more closely, we described the enterprise continuum and the discrete points that TOGAF notes along the two complementary sub-continua of which the enterprise continuum is composed—the architectural and solutions continua. Classifying TOGAF as a foundation architecture, we noted briefly (they will be covered in much greater depth in later chapters) the seminal concepts of the technical reference model and the standards information base. Then we examined the value and composition of the architectural development method (ADM) that is part of the TOGAF tool set. Each distinct phase was introduced and briefly described. As we noted the structure of the ADM is mirrored to a certain extent in the following chapters as we apply the method to our fictional organization.

In the next chapter, we begin our journey through the ADM by considering the structure of the initiation and framework phase.

CHAPTER 5

Initiation and Framework

5.1   Introduction

The initial, and arguably most important (from a business perspective), phase of the architectural development method (ADM) is that of *initiation and framework*, as depicted in Figure 5.1.

In this phase, we seek to set the stage of architectural analysis and design by capturing, understanding, and verifying the strategic and business drivers for the architecture program. It is important to note that any program[19] that has as its goal the design and implementation of a technical architecture is typically both demanding and complex, requiring careful analysis, experience, and tradeoffs to arrive at a satisfactory outcome. The use of the term *outcome* is deliberate—it is an ever-popular phrase in both business strategy and architecture program initiation documents. Using this term in the initial ADM phase is especially relevant because the end result of our endeavors must support a technical and business outcome. Without the ability to trace architectural objectives to business outcomes (from which we can derive business drivers and critical success factors as well), a program may find itself in the invidious position of not being able to ultimately justify its implementation. On occasion, we have encountered programs that suffer from this malaise, which we have termed *IT-driven* or alternately *technology-driven*. Although such programs may at times be extremely exciting, with one in the position of implementing technology for technology's sake, it

---

19. We use the term *program* to stress that the development of a technical architecture is a coordinated program of work that can be made up of separate programs.

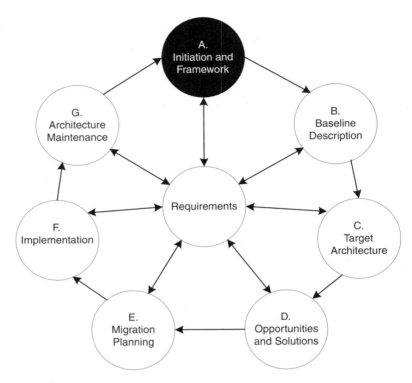

FIGURE 5.1. ADM, with initiation and framework highlighted.

is our experience that such programs will languish if not fail. Although IT is increasingly seen as an important adjunct to business armory, accountability will be required for any significant undertaking, and the support of business objectives will help provide this.

In this chapter, we review the initiation of the architectural program. We consider the factors that will ensure success, business and strategic drivers, and the specific steps enumerated by the TOGAF initiation and framework phase.

5.2 Initiation

Business Focus

It is a critical responsibility of the architect to ensure that this accountability exists. The days of the purely technically focused architect are in decline, and we foresee a great need for architects to understand their (at times) pivotal role in an organization's future. With this understanding, they must then ensure that *they* understand the actual business need for an architecture iteration (which, as we will see, the ADM most definitely represents). Additionally, it has always been true in any field that an incomplete understanding of business requirements may lead one to proffer a square wheel in place of the desired result! Of course, on a micro level (such as software application development, for example) the ramifications of such a situation may range from minor to severe in effect. However, at a technical (or enterprise) architecture level, the implications of a misunderstanding or misinterpretation can be astounding and may severely compromise an organization's ability to compete, thrive, or even exist. It is also a truism that the cost of addressing flaws in the translation of requirements grows exponentially with the stage at which corrective action is suggested.

In a now very well-known market research paper created by the Standish Group (www.standishgroup.com) and entitled simply "Chaos," projects were classified as follows (see Figure 5.2):

Resolution Type 1, or project success: The project is completed on time and on budget, with all features and functions as initially specified.

Resolution Type 2, or project challenged: The project is completed and operational but over budget, over the time estimate, and offers fewer features and functions than originally specified.

Resolution Type 3, or project impaired: The project is canceled at some point during the development cycle.

The report summarized the analysis of responses from 365 organizations and involving over 8000 (software) applications:

Overall, the success rate was only 16.2%, while challenged projects accounted for 52.7% and impaired (canceled) for 31.1%.

Importantly, two of the most popular reasons for failure were lack of executive sponsorship and incomplete or incorrect requirements. Without these, and at an application level, the probability of failure or curtailment is approximately 0.84. We contend that with today's electronic business focus, and businesses requiring even greater agility in the face of a vociferous demand or value chain, the role of understood, captured, and traceable business requirements is greater than ever before. With appropriately presented requirements, business sign-off can be secured (admittedly this is often easier said than done), with a real sense of

Project Resolution by Type

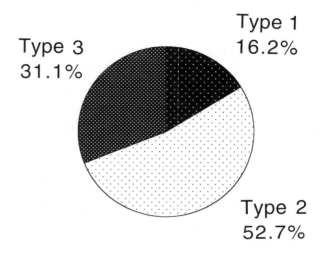

FIGURE 5.2.   Program resolution, Standish Group report.

ownership being evident once that signoff has occurred. Even though the requirements stage may have been preceded by a business case, it is frequently the position that the requirements noted in the business case have undergone some alteration by the time an architecture program commences. This is becoming increasingly true as the business case itself becomes an exploration document, with options being enunciated and SWOT (strengths, weaknesses, opportunities, and threats) analyses being presented.

What Is a Business or Strategic Driver?

It is timely to recapitulate some of the concepts presented in Chapter 3, where we introduced key strategic concepts and identified their relation to architectural or technical objectives.

Essentially, a business or strategic driver is an external, internal or environmental (legislative, economic or domain-specific) force or tension that requires a response from the organization upon which the force acts. The following sources of drivers are common in our experience:

- *Economic*. A quantifiable, positive financial benefit will accrue from the program.

- *Legislative*. Typically, but of course not limited to government or publicly owned organizations, a change in existing legislation or introduction of new legislation will elicit a response.
- *Competitive*. Closely related to a domain driver, a competition-rooted driver exists when a certain outcome would engender a competitive advantage for the organization.
- *Domain*. A domain driver is classified as one that exists within a particular domain and may not actually be quantifiable or tangible but is seen as recognizing the need for the organization to respond to a common theme within its industry or domain.
- *Internal or internal/strategic*. A driver that would allow internal streamlining, cost reduction, or greater efficiency.
- *Reactive*. The weakest driver of those identified; a reactive driver is indicative of an "after the fact" response by the organization. Such drivers are often accompanied by the smallest budget and most compressed time frame (often described with a euphemism of "challenging").
- *Demand or supply chain*. Consumer and demand or supply chain participants may "force" a change in operation perhaps in the name of greater convenience (electronic commerce/business channels), ubiquitous access (electronic commerce/business channels again), reduction in cost, or even the "me too" syndrome.

A particular program will rarely be limited to a single type of driver, and we typically see a spread of at least three types, with reactive, demand and internal, and legislative and economic being the most common.

As we will discover, one of the most important aspects of TOGAF is its tacit encouragement of a connection between business drivers and IT drivers.

TOGAF Process

TOGAF employs a standard and simple format to describe processes (phases and stages[20]) within the ADM, with each one possessing an objective, approach, inputs, steps, and outputs. Reproduced below is the objective of the initiation and framework phase:

> The objective of this phase is to define the relevant business requirements that apply to this evolution of the architecture, based

---

20. A phase is a major step defined in the ADM, such as initiation and framework. Each phase can have a number of stages (or steps).

on the business goals and strategic drivers of the organization, and to define an architectural vision that demonstrates a response to those requirements.

Throughout the text, we will use a simple wiring-diagram symbology to summarize the major inputs and outputs for each TOGAF phase (and, in some cases, stage). The inputs and outputs are guidelines only. TOGAF is not wholly specific with respect to generated documents; in fact, it provides very little in the way of prescriptive document templates— merely guidelines for inputs and outputs. This is also its strength. The ability to tailor the framework to fit a particular organization is enhanced. Such an approach relies on quality and experienced architects and sponsors applying their knowledge and experience to the problem. To enable a successful outcome, this is a reasonable assumption.

Figure 5.3 shows the inputs and outputs wiring diagram for the initiation and framework phase.

Inputs

The catalyst for the commencement of this phase is, according to TOGAF, the receipt of a request for architecture work, directed from the (abstract) "sponsoring organization" to the (abstract) "architecture organization." Of course, in many instances these organizations will in fact be business units, departments, or identical; rarely will they be legally or physically separate organizations.

We have yet to be engaged upon a program that was driven from a request for architecture work! This term is reasonably euphemistic. Typically, the initiating stimulus, event, or document will be any of these:

- *Request for proposal (RFP).* The RFP process typically generates a range of concerns, admission or identification of deficiencies, or demonstrably new or unaddressed requirements.
- *Enterprise architecture maintenance.* Farsighted, organized, or effi-

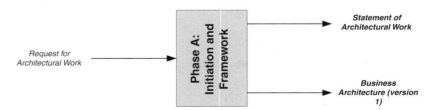

FIGURE 5.3.   Initiation and framework wiring diagram.

cient IT units often generate work requests as part of the maintenance or enhancement process for an enterprise (IT) architecture.

- *Terms of reference (TOR)*. A TOR may often arise as the result of identified architectural work, or may be the output from a general program undertaking.
- *Ad hoc*. A random event, that occasionally leads to a successful outcome.

The Open Group sees the request for architecture work capturing the "architectural vision," a vision that is often captured in other documents within the organization. However, for the sake of argument it is acceptable to view the statement of work logically as opposed to physically, and note that the intent of this document will be represented by or able to be assembled from some source within the organization. It is important to note that if this vision cannot be secured, agreed upon, and remain stable, the program itself is most likely doomed to fail or, at best, languish.

However, one must not be too quick to dismiss the request for architecture work. In its basic **TOGAF** form, this composite input contains a selection from the following:

- *Organization sponsors*—those that will foot the bill!
- *Organization's mission statement*—often discerned from the business strategic plan or founding document.
- *Business goals (and changes)*—the goals that will be supported by the requested work.
- *Strategic plans of the business*—these are not necessarily limited to the classic business strategic plans but may also include the IT strategic plan or, on occasion, an IT business unit plan.
- *Time limits*—temporal constraints are an omnipresent constraint on architectural creativity (or excess, depending on your viewpoint).
- *Changes in the business environment*—most easily related to the domain business driver as described in this chapter.
- *Organizational constraints*—aspects of the organization that affect the program, including resources, political, and so on.
- *Budget information and financial constraints*—again, a very effective filter with respect to architectural excess. On a more serious note, a cost–benefit analysis may have been performed or a return on investment (ROI) exercise undertaken that led to certain constraints being identified.
- *External and business constraints*—refer to the business or strategic driver section in this chapter.
- *Current business system description*—of course, unless one has the good fortune to find oneself engaged in a "green field" scenario, a

business system description, architecture description or similar depiction is likely to exist. However, such documents (even if informal) often provide a valuable context.

- *Current architecture/IT system description*—again, many organizations have such documentation available. Architecture documents range from practically useless ("blocks and lines"), to notional (physical) to formal (UML, formal capture through special purpose languages and so on).
- *Description of developing organization*—a more obscure TOGAF conception, often related to the mission and vision of the organization itself, which may be in a state of flux.

Steps

The procedural nature of this section of each TOGAF ADM phase should not lead one to believe that a "recipe" for architecture is being espoused. It is important to note that one must apply good taste and experience with a method such as TOGAF. Failure to do so will often lead to an inflexible result or an inability to adapt to unusual or complex domains.

The noted tasks for this phase are:

1. Identify, document, and rank the problems that drive the program. This is often called a problem statement. An inability to document a clear problem or requirement is a sign of premature engagement of the architecture team.
2. Identify environment and document, as business architecture models, the business and technical environment where the problem situation is occurring. Although this can be formally represented, it is often useful enough to capture these models with simple graphical tools such as Visio or Microsoft Word pictures (for example).
3. Identify and document desired objectives, the results of handling the problems successfully.
4. Identify human actors and their place in the business model, the human participants, and their roles.
5. Identify computer actors and their place in the technology model, the computing elements, and their roles.
6. Identify and document roles, responsibilities, and measures of success per actor, the required scripts per actor, and the desired results of handling the situation properly.
7. Document the statement of architecture work.
8. Check the original motivation for the program against the Statement of Architecture Work and Business Architecture and refine it only if necessary.

   This fairly prescriptive list of simple tasks appears as a rather uneasy juxtaposition of contemporary approaches (note the use of the term *actor*) and standard ideas (business and architecture models). However, each step adds a valuable justification to the initial process. We cannot stress enough that this initial phase if not formally governance should at the very least be viewed as a valuable management and control process adjunct.

Outputs

The TOGAF process defining the outputs from this phase is two fold: the statement of architecture work (SOW) and an initial version of the business architecture. The SOW is described later in this chapter, and this initial iteration of the business architecture will consist of not much more than gathered collateral or the creation of a skeletal business systems architecture derived from identified requirements. The example illustrates an opening attempt at a business systems architecture.

Information Gathering

The output from this phase is critical because it places a frame of reference around the remainder of the program. The framework statements provided here will be quoted often in later stages of the program: ". . . but the overriding business driver was this." Therefore, it is important that the correct people are involved and that the information described is accurate and stable. Changes to this information at a later stage could have drastic effects on the entire architectural program.

   During this phase, it is most important to interview the key stakeholders. The architectural program sponsor (most likely to be the CIO) should be driven to provide the necessary conduit to the right people. Furthermore, these people should take some form of ownership in the final outcome and the information they provide. Considering that the necessary information revolves around business and technical strategy and drivers, organizational constraints, and key business process descriptions, it is important to elicit information for people at the relevant level within the organization.

   Interviewing members of the organization's strategic management team would be a good start, including financial and operational areas. Key business users (of all core corporate systems) should also provide input. Furthermore, it is possible to obtain information from company reports and business unit strategic documents.

It is important not to gloss over this phase. The architect must have the information necessary to continue the process. Test the information provided using key, strategically derived questions such as:

- Have the key financial, organizational, and architectural constraints been identified?
- Have key performance measures been described for the IT environment?
- Does the architectural program have (measurable) acceptance criteria?
- Has the architectural vision (or principles) been described in a manner that can be understood and delivered to?
- Do the sponsors know what is required of them during and after the program?

Finally, ensure the quality of the outputs by revalidating them with the key stakeholders and sponsors.

Collateral

A range of collateral exists in most organizations that can provide valuable input into the initiation phase. Specifically, we seek out at least the following documents:

- The ISSP (information systems strategic plan)
- Business case (if the architecture program is being driven from or associated with a business unit or organization program)
- Business strategy (this may be e-business or general business strategy)
- Previous architecture work (this may include an information and business systems architecture)

The absence of any of these documents (except for previous architecture work) can indicate that the organization is not in fact ready for the architecture work being proposed. For example, if there is no vision for IT and/or the business, exactly what is the architecture supposed to support, given its relation to strategic intent? It is important to consider the role of the technical architecture in the development of organizational business (and IT) strategy. The technical architecture draws from other strategic plans to guide the development of the technology plan. It should not be used to make strategic decisions that should have been founded in "higher-level" plans. Gaps in these plans must be noted at this stage and the sponsor and steering group be required to determine how these gaps will be filled.

Statement of Architecture Work

The statement of architecture work captures essentially the intent, scope, structure and vision of the architectural engagement to be undertaken or that is being proposed. Although a relatively simple document, it represents a key milestone in the progress of an architecture endeavor in that the inability to capture and present this information should trigger either a degree of apprehension or questions with respect to the likely success of the program.

The essential elements of the SOW (note that some are trivial enough not to be commented on) are defined by TOGAF as follows:

- *Statement of work title*
- *Program request and background*
- *Program description and scope.* Often just as critical as those elements not included are those that are excluded. It is important to note this clearly and without fear of contradiction or misinterpretation because statements of work may often form part of a legal contract.
- *Architecture vision.* A crisp, IT-strategy-aligned vision sets the scene, so to speak, for an appropriate outcome. It cannot be stated too many times that a lack of vision indicates a flawed, incomplete, or mistaken program.
- *Architectural principles.* These are the major architectural values held as paramount by the organization. These will include statements of direction with respect to technology, high-level technology selection criteria, styles of application delivery, and other principles that may also be described in the information systems strategic plan. The principles establish the vision for the forthcoming architecture development. As such they must be tested aggressively for validity, the rationale for the principle stated. In our experience many organizations establish principles that actually represent implied truths or unsubstantiated corporate lore—"We must implement open systems" is a typical directionless doctrine. Thoroughly explore the "whys" of each principle to ensure its robustness.
- *Managerial approach.* This describes the governance structure and approach for the program.
- *Change of scope procedures.* These are often just a summary reiteration of the sponsoring organization's change-control procedures.
- *Responsibilities and deliverables.* Less commonly, responsibilities of participants or roles within the program will be defined. Almost invariably, deliverables will be noted along with a brief description of their nature.
- *Acceptance criteria and procedures.* Again, these are less common because the sponsoring organization will typically provide or require conformance to stated acceptance criteria. However, for unusual or

advanced programs, acceptance criteria may be agreed upon with the architecture team (organization) to ensure early agreement.

- *Program plan and schedule.* This is another standard inclusion, typically limited to a high-level or summary plan and an indication of resources as opposed to a detailed program plan, which is fully resource-leveled with program financials included.
- *Support of the enterprise continuum.* This section is obviously entrenched deep within TOGAF philosophical territory! The enterprise continuum (composed of the two inter-related and connected continua of *solutions* and *architecture* as described in Chapter 4) represents the core of TOGAF, and an indication of the architectural works support and positioning within this continuum aligns it with TOGAF in a readily understandable and logical manner.
- *Signature approvals*

These sections then comprise the basic SOW. Used properly, this document forms a valuable auditing tool to ensure that the original vision and requirements can be traced through to implementation.

Key definition: **Architectural principles.**
Architectural principles set the high-level vision and goals for the architectural development and the entire IT environment. They are typically derived from organizational business and IT strategic outputs have a defined rationale and considered implications.

The Terms of Reference (Corporate)

The corporate corollary of the statement of architecture work is the terms of reference (TOR), produced as the initial instrument in an engagement to demonstrate that one party (the "doers") understands the requirements of the other party (the "clients"). Again, this document will often form part of the contract between both parties, either in total, formally or as an attachment. The TOR is typically composed of the following sections:

- *Introduction.* This is a brief description of the program background and main stimuli.
- *Objectives.* This is a list of the objectives of the assignment.
- *Scope.* This can be the most contentious (for the client) or (for the vendor) most important part of the TOR in that it presents those tasks and deliverables that are included and explicitly those that are excluded with respect to the program. We do not develop a TOR in the

example of this chapter, but the following table illustrates a common presentation format. As is obvious, every included task is not necessarily paired with an excluded task.

IS TO	IS NOT TO
Document identifiable nonfunctional and functional requirements.	Implement technology or solutions.
Document proposed/existing entry points and internal systems.	Negotiate or broker agreements with third parties.
Confirm existing business drivers and objectives from the e-business strategic plan.	Critique the strategic plan.
Review relevant recent initiatives or issues and apply them during architectural design.	Document in detail related programs or constraints.
Design a risk-mitigating, standardized set of target architectures.	Create or modify the technical reference model; produce analysis or object models, implementations or tests.
Produce appropriate architecture documents and presentations.	Produce detailed program plans.
Create a program plan that outlines in interim detail the major iterations, tasks, and milestones.	

- *Approach*. This is a partially ordered set of tasks and/or activities that the vendor will undertake (at a high level) to use as the procedural approach to the program.
- *Deliverables*. This is a simple list of those artifacts that the vendor elects or is required to produce for the client.
- *Program sponsor*
- *Program staffing*. This is a list of staff and abridged CV's.
- *Program rates and cost estimates*
- *Agreement*
- *Terms of business*. Most TORs will include a terms of business section that will list, in legal terms, such items as warranties, liability, termination, and intellectual property issues.

5.3   Warning Signs (or the Semiotics of Dissent)

Throughout this chapter, we have alluded to the various warning signs that one must be aware of in order that a program may be guided, reconsidered, or rejected (for example, if one is in the position of consulting for a vendor contracted to a client). In a fashion similar to the software engineering argument that requirements omissions are best detected early in the program cycle (to avoid the exponential increase of cost to fix as the program proceeds), we advocate that all forces, tensions, objectives, and constraints (or at least 80–85% of them) must be known before any serious architectural work commences.

Our experience leads us to suggest that the following categories of symptoms exist and may be detected reasonably early. Each category includes some common manifestations and possible mitigation.

- *Program sponsor.* For nearly all architecture-centric work, a strong, consistent, and well-placed program sponsor is essential. A sponsor who can achieve the appropriate degree of executive management coverage will be required to ensure that competing forces do not overwhelm an architecture program. Such programs are often targets for trimming, scope reduction, or redesign, mostly because the impacts of a poorly thought out or designed architecture may take some time to be observed and even longer to impact other concerns, such as revenue, IT spending, and TCO.
- *Financial.* Another common category of program woe is the perennial financial constraint. The detection of this category of risk may sometimes be entirely due to the expertise of the architect and other times is stunningly, almost painfully, obvious to all those involved. We have found that strange boundary conditions also occur when the buy versus build battle has been waged, leaving one in the position where either option would be (financially) feasible. Most often though, you will encounter the project that simply has not allocated sufficient funds to execute appropriately. Many projects can be traced to a business case that has outlined a cost–benefit analysis or return on investment, and the budget for the project has been derived from that. When faced with such a conundrum, it may be inordinately difficult to achieve a resolution, especially when one considers a specter such as capital release.
- *Temporal constraints.* Another old "friend" is the temporal constraint. This is typically couched in phrases such as "the legislative process demands. . ." or "in order to compete, we must. . . ." Faced with an argument that depends on rhetoric or business imperative, it can be extremely difficult for an architect to mount a successful defense.

Indeed, it requires a strong consultant to stand against this form of resistance because it is unfortunately true that there will nearly always be someone (be that an individual or company) else who is willing to step forward and assume the role of architect. The only heuristic in this situation is whether one is willing to retain one's integrity or is prepared to compromise and potentially damage one's integrity in the process. Of course, you should ensure that every avenue is explored in order to secure further funding, and many times the strength of the sponsor can have a significant bearing in this area. As a last resort, the scope of the program can be reduced, but one must be careful to ensure that the architectural vision that remains is sound.

- *Scope.* A hardly rare constraint is that of scope in that the scope may be too extensive for the budget, time allowed, or organizational readiness. As for the financial symptom, the only viable approach here may be to reduce the scope and revalidate the architectural vision.

- *Organizational.* On one of our recent projects, we encountered a large organization that apparently required the deployment of an architecture and set of infrastructural services to support an e-business endeavor. However, after a few question-and-answer sessions, it became apparent that the organization itself was not actually ready to embrace e-business in any way, shape, or form, mainly because the extant IT architecture was flawed and would not reliably support extension or integration with e-business technologies. The precursor to the e-business architecture (or e-service architecture) had been ignored, leaving the organization in the rather unenviable position of trying to graft electronic business services onto a barely stable façade.

- *Governance.* The popularity of governance waxes and wanes periodically. The basic premise of governance is the control, risk management, and processes associated with information technology and its deployment within an organization. It is our contention that the application of IT, unless on a small scale, requires a degree of governance to ensure that resources are deployed appropriately within programs that fulfill the organization's IT objectives (and transitively, the business objectives). We discuss governance in the next section.

- *Business process.* Much more difficult to discern, and therefore the most insidious, is the symptom of business process flaw or lack of readiness. By this, we mean when the business processes that we seek to support or enable via the program are in fact candidates for reengineering or should not be considered within the scope of the program. This is of course most common in contemporary IT when a business rushes to embrace electronic commerce or electronic business and finds for example that the process to be electronically mounted requires several instances of human intervention or (at best) heuristic-driven approaches to a solution. This can lead to severely suboptimal approaches to e-enablement. One site we visited had made available an electronic form to provide clients with the ability to apply for loans over the Internet. The form itself presented no great difficulty for use through a Web browser, the security was comparatively simple to design and arrange, and the capacity of the system was sufficient to support program growth. However, a single field on the form, required for internal use, could not be derived from any of the information provided on the form. The solution was "obvious" to the architects: instead of attempting to redesign the process, examine heuristic methods to reach a solution, or interpose a "middle man" system to enable intervention (all requiring high cost and time commitments), it was decided that the scope of the program would be altered. The alteration was thus: instead of transferring information electronically from the Internet-submitted form to the main back-end system, the form instead would be printed off, the missing field completed, and the form then *manually* typed into the back end system. As one might expect, Web-based users were somewhat surprised when responses to applications sometimes stated the wrong or misspelled names as a consequence of the rekeying effort that occurred behind the scenes!

The message here is that one should be aware of the traps and pitfalls in the early stages of a program. One might find that a keen eye and critical approach could be the salvation of a well-intentioned program or the appropriate death knell for a flawed one. All that one requires is foresight, vision, experience, and courage!

Governance: Ensuring Success

An additional warning sign that is easily overlooked is the lack of a formal means of IT governance within the organization. Although this is covered in greater detail in Chapters 13 and 14, we touch on the subject here by way of introduction.

According to the IT Governance Institute (www.itgovernance.org), one may define IT governance thus:

IT governance helps ensure achievement of this critical success factor [Information Technology] by efficiently and effectively deploying secure, reliable information and applied technology. IT governance is a structure of relationships and processes to direct and control the enterprise in order to achieve the enterprise's goals by adding value while balancing risk versus return over IT and its processes. The relationships are between management and its governing body. The processes cover setting objectives, giving direction on how to attain them and measuring performance.

As is plainly obvious, the place of technical architecture within a well-reasoned governance structure cannot be underestimated. In our experience, architecture without governance suffers the same drawbacks as the silo business unit model; that is, excellence can be achieved but only at a local or restricted level. The effects of this excellence are also localized, and the overall and ongoing benefits erode over time because an overarching control is not exercised.

The Open Group suggests that in order to support governance, two key concepts should exist to support the IT architecture. Firstly, an architecture board should be formed that has as its mandate the oversight of the implementation of the IT governance strategy. Secondly, an IT architecture compliance strategy should be created so that the compliance of new solutions, products and architectural extensions can be measured and, to a certain extent, certified. Obviously, The Open Group espouses a narrower view of IT governance than the IT Governance Institute, due to their general focus on the process to govern all of IT.

The architecture board is the most interesting of these governance devices. The board is typically comprised of architecture group personnel, a sponsor from executive management, a program director (if applicable), and a representative of the organization—often, less than ten people are required. To a certain extent, the architecture board resembles a steering committee, and its charter is generally similar. The primary responsibilities of this group include:

- Consistency between subarchitectures
- Identifying reusable components
- Flexibility of enterprise architecture
- Meeting changing business needs
- Leveraging new technologies
- Enforcement of architecture compliance
- Improving the maturity level of architecture discipline within the organization

The crucial nature of these responsibilities becomes apparent when one examines a program that has suffered architecture compromise or (sometimes willful) ignorance, where the glittering architecture mutates into a tarnished, complex and unmaintainable entity. One area that is overlooked is the actual need for an independently funded architectural stream of development. Although it is true that the board may ensure that new or proposed projects comply with the enterprise architecture, projects driven from a business unit perspective often do not want the overhead and financial burden that architectural extension can imply. This is especially true when budgets are decentralized; that is, each business unit controls its own IT budget, as opposed to a more "command and control" structure, where a central IT unit maintains the majority of IT project budgets. For example, a project that in actuality requires an addition to the architecture in terms of services (take integration brokering as an example) may not have the budget or inclination to support that addition. Also, the project itself may only require a subset of the behavior provided by the service. That being the case, and if the project is important enough from the perspective of the business, it can be observed that the project will be completed with a suboptimal service being introduced (for example, simple message-oriented middleware instead of an integration broker). The danger of this approach is that the new "service" may in fact assume the status of de facto standard and be used by a subsequent project. Even if this "reuse" does not occur, the cost of retrofitting a valid and acceptable service may prove prohibitive and/or unpalatable for the organization. The tradeoff among budget, purity, and governance is difficult to solve in commercial and even government environments. Hence, unless one is careful or astute in these matters, the architecture board may find itself tagged with terms such as ineffectual or even toothless!

The solution to this quandary is simple when distilled to its essence but often eludes organizations due to the collaborative nature that the solution implies. We posit that the solution consists of an architecture budget, controlled and allocated centrally, that exists solely to be applied to a project before or at its inception. This architecture budget is applied at the board's discretion to ensure that architecture services are developed appropriately, in a timely fashion, and without penalizing business units whose projects place them at the forefront of technology or business leadership or challenge the architecture's ability to support new business needs.

5.4   Example

Introduction

This section documents a partial exemplar of the initiation and framework phase of TOGAF as applied to our example organization, CFL.

A series of interviews was conducted at CFL with the intention of eliciting as much relevant information as possible. The terms of reference for this work, as supplied by CFL, are not documented here.

After ascertaining and contacting the key stakeholders and scheduling a series of interviews, the following existing information was discovered:

- ISSP (information systems strategic plan)
- Business strategic plan
- e-business strategic plan
- Cursory business systems architecture

Strategic Plan Input

On examination, both the ISSP and business strategic plan appeared to be reasoned documents, with all of the major elements one would expect in such plans and with (for the ISSP) an appropriate planning horizon. The e-business strategy was a little naïve and perhaps too ambitious in scope (see the following sections). The business systems architecture (BSA) was little more than a simple "blocks and lines diagram" and not particularly worthy of the term BSA.

The ISSP was examined and provided detailed IT goals to achieve the business objectives noted (and described in some detail in the business strategic plan). These goals are:

- Support the development of high-value and differentiated products for continued growth.
- Be a best-cost producer.
- Manage the business globally.
- Support identification of target growth opportunities, particularly in international markets.
- Deliver outstanding customer service and support.
- Merge to a common architecture.

e-business Strategy

The e-business strategy for CFL is supposed to deliver the following outcomes:

- Support global operations.
- Reduce the cost of transactions.
- Provide CFL with the capability to develop faster solutions for future business problems.
- Improve customer convenience.

The e-business strategy also suggested a number of prioritized projects to support the organization's strategy. It was suggested by the business that the technology required to implement these projects should be considered as part of the architectural program. At this point in the process, neither the business nor IT could accurately describe the current readiness of the technical environment to support the e-business projects and what effort would be required to put it in place. Therefore, the strategy lacked detailed implementation costs associated with technology (making the overall cost–benefit analysis a trifle tenuous). The key programs are as follows:

- Electronically integrate the supply chain with CFL's two leading raw material suppliers.
- Offer a catalog browsing service to customers.
- Offer electronic ordering for key (yet to be identified) customers.

Architectural Principles

The CIO was also able to provide us with a number of architectural principles (derived from the ISSP) that CFL was using to guide the development of its IT environment. The CIO stressed that the principles had not been updated for a "number" of years and that no indicators were in place to determine conformance. It was suggested that they be used merely as a basis, and further work applied to update them during the architectural program. They are summarized as follows:

- Implement best-of-breed (not "bleeding-edge") technology.
- Centralize processing and data at HQ where possible.
- Computer technology must be widely employed.
- All computers must be networked together with a consistent architecture.
- Computing and networking resources must be reliable, secure, and capable of delivering accurate information in a timely and consistent manner.
- Information must be within reach of all users, regardless of location.
- The mechanisms required to locate, access, and communicate data required by users must be transparent.
- Applications must be designed to allow users to work with data in ways most productive for them.
- Applications must work together.

Initiation

The approach to developing the strategy involved two phases of work. Firstly, to understand the possible opportunities and overall context for e-business within CFL, interviews were held with business representatives and key stakeholders. These interviews covered the following topics: key concepts; the role of each business area within CFL; the flows and types of information exchanged to and from the business unit of the interviewee; and previous process and technology initiatives that the interviewee had experienced.

Based on the results of the interviews, the consultants employed to create a strategic plan constructed a framework within which the e-business opportunities available to CFL could be discussed. The framework broke the CFL business processes and stakeholders into four major categories:

- Manufacturing
- Sales and order entry
- Mobile operations
- Internal business

From this information, we understand the following critical success factors (CSFs):

- The most convenient delivery channels are available for use by the CFL demographic.
- Services delivered are relevant and timely.
- Delivery channels are available 24 hours a day, 7 days a week.
- Information is delivered within a secure and/or private environment.
- The delivery channels are publicized and based on open technology (low barrier to entry).

To increase the usefulness of the BSA, further interviews were conducted to enable the discovery and documentation of a reasonable artifact. The current CFL attempt at a BSA is summarized in Figure 5.4.

Of course, the lack of an information architecture (Chapter 3) somewhat limits the usefulness of this depiction because no appeal is made to the information needs of the organization. The interviews helped to shape the *basis* of an information architecture and allow us ultimately to augment the BSA. The following tables (Tables 5.1–5.3) outline the basic information needs of CFL, with each need categorized by department and noted as either strategic, tactical, or operational in nature (see Chapter 3).

Table 5.4 introduces the Finance department's information needs, which are primarily disjointed from most of the organizational units in CFL. Note the spread of both tactical and strategic needs.

Table 5.5 includes the needs of the Logistics organizational units.

Of course, as Chapter 3 noted, information needs represent only a portion of the information required to aid in building the BSA. Realistically, an information architecture is necessary, but it is beyond the

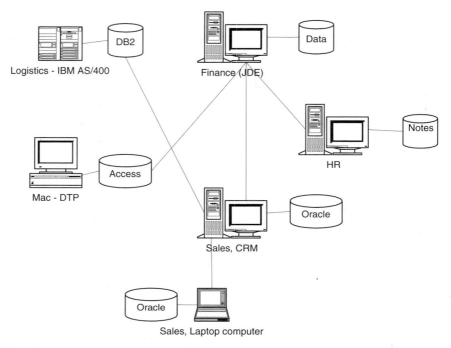

Figure 5.4.   Cursory BSA for CFL.

scope of this text to offer the development of an information architecture. However, we can outline partially the business functions discovered for the Financial, Sales, and Logistics departments of our example organization and note the various systems to which they apply. Based on this information, we are able to produce a BSA, a partial view of which is offered here.

Firstly, we present the business functions identified for each of the three systems we are currently examining (Table 5.6).

During the course of the interviews, we also asked the users to rate each system in terms of effectiveness, stability, and usability. Their comments are presented in Table 5.7.

There are some points worth noting from the users' comments, qualitative though they might be:

- All classes of user complain about the reliability of batch updates between the systems, a classic systems integration problem.
- The Logistics team highlights supplier invoicing issues, as does the financial unit; these obviously are to the detriment of supplier relations and transaction costs.

Table 5.1. Marketing information needs.

Information Need	Type (Strategic, Tactical or Operations)
Sales by zone, region, customer, product	T
Market share by type	T
Gross profit	T
Competitor Analysis	S
Forecast	S
Revenue by product class	T
Trends in market share	S
Average product life	S
Average incarnations of product	T

Table 5.2. Sales information needs.

Information Need	Type
Sales by zone, region, salesperson	T
Forecast by salesperson	T
Commission by salesperson	T
Total Commissions	T
Cost of sale by product, salesperson	T
Lead time, order to delivery	T

- The Sales team requires easier and simpler access to sales analysis to enable appropriate targeting of customers appropriately.
- All users complain about fragmentation of behavior across systems, maintaining a customer being a pertinent example.

Another analysis tool of note is the creation of simple matrices that capture dimensions of information, a sort of simplified data-mining function. Table 5.8 identifies whether all information needs are currently met by the business systems.

Table 5.9 aids in the identification of redundant or duplicate business functions, and Table 5.10 highlights create, read, update, and delete considerations that (as Chapter 3 intones) provide insight into information store placement and function duplication.[21]

21. Actually, in the interest of brevity, only a few pertinent information needs are shown.

Table 5.3. General business information needs.

Information Need	Type
Number of complaints or recalls and trend	S
Defection rate	S
Gross margin and trend	S
Market share and trend	S
Fixed assets and trend	S
Net revenue and trend	S

Table 5.4. Finance department information needs.

Information Need	Type
Budget	T
Forecast	S
Gross income	T
Gross margin	S
Capital commitment	S
Operational expenditure	S
Cash flow	T
Debt servicing	T
Debtors, total current	T
Bad debts	T
Creditors, total current	T
Profit by customer	T
Profit-and-loss sheet	T
Depreciation	T
Fixed assets	S

As noted, Table 5.9 will allow us to deduce certain facts with respect to business functions.

Even from the simple example, we can observe that, for example, the view customer history business function is not related to an identified information need, and the maintain forecast and maintain fixed assets functions are present in both the Logistics and Finance systems. Of course, it may be that this is perfectly acceptable, but it does provide one with possible avenues of investigation.

Table 5.5. Logistics information needs.

Information Need	Type
Scrap (product changes)	T
Fixed costs	T
Inventory (on hand)	T
Direct material cost	T
Labor cost	T
Fixed assets	S
Capacity	O
Down time	O
Supplier costs	S
Volume by commodity	T
Forecast versus actual	S
Order to inventory	T
Transport as % of wholesale cost	T
Distribution centers by inventory	T

Table 5.6. Finance, logistics, and sales functions.

Finance	Logistics	Sales
Maintain accounts payable	Transfer batch (automated)	Transfer batch (automated)
Maintain accounts receivable	Receive batch (automated)	Receive batch (automated)
Write off debt	Maintain invoicing	Maintain salesperson
Maintain invoice	Maintain purchase order	Generate commission sheet
Generate balance sheet	Maintain labor costs	Maintain forecasts
Maintain fixed assets	Maintain bill Of materials	Maintain budget
Maintain depreciation schedule	Print invoice	Upload order
Maintain forecast	Print purchase order	Maintain order
Transfer batch (automated)	Maintain supplier	View customer history
Receive batch (automated)	Maintain fixed assets	Generate trends by criteria
Maintain customer	Maintain overheads	Maintain customer
	Reconcile	
	Maintain customer	

Table 5.7. User comments, business system.

Sales	Logistics	Finance
Batch updates do not always work	Performs well	Good interface
Mostly usable	Batch failures observed	Some hand analysis is required because the system not easily extended
Variable performance	Reliable	Overnight updates sometimes fail
Too easy to forget password—too many to remember	User interface dated, unable to innovate with business process	Batch functions (profit/loss, reconciliation) can take too long, impacting operational window
On the road salespersons find the sales package interface too cumbersome and slow	Suppliers dislike paper handling; errors and omissions occur	Information not always timely
Sales teams need easier access to timely information to help target customers	Lead time from product design to implementation is too long by industry standards	Suppliers have difficulty reconciling some invoices
Business functions are distributed across too many systems	Customer must be updated in too many systems	Entities are spread across business units

We introduce Table 5.10, to provide the CRUD analysis. We can note from Table 5.10 that there are indeed areas of overlap but of differing types. For example, the maintain budget business task appears duplicated in Sales and Finance; however, on further investigation, we found that the actual type of budget was in fact quite different and no information sharing or duplication was occurring. However, for tasks such as maintain product and maintain fixed asset, there is indeed duplication and an opportunity for rationalization. A pattern of duplication is not unusual in organizations where systems have grown independently of others in the business; however, they do compromise a standard architectural principle of information being maintained in only one place.

Table 5.8. Information need by business system.

Information Need	Sales	Logistics	Finance
Trends in market share	X		
Number of complaints or recalls			
Fixed assets and trends	X	X	X
Competitor analysis	X		
Forecast	X	X	X
Capital commitment			X
Gross margin			X
Supplier cost		X	X
Labor cost		X	X
Fixed costs		X	X
Defection rate			

Table 5.9. Business function by business system.

Information Need	Function	Sales	Logistics	Finance
Trends in market share	Generate trends by criteria	X		
Fixed assets	Maintain fixed assets		X	X
Competitor analysis	Generate analysis by criteria	X		
Forecast	Maintain forecast	X		X
	View customer history	X		

Table 5.10. Business function by business system by CRUD attributes.

Business Function	Sales	Logistics	Finance
Maintain invoice	CR--	CRUD	CR--
Maintain forecast	CRUD	CRUD	CRUD
Maintain budget	CRUD		CRUD
Transfer batch	CRU-	CRU-	CRU-
Maintain fixed asset		CRUD	CRUD
Maintain supplier	-R--	CRUD	CRUD
Maintain bill of materials		CRUD	
Maintain labor costs		CRUD	-R--
Maintain product	CR--	CRUD	CRUD
Maintain Customer	CRUD	CRUD	CRUD

5.5 *Summary*

This chapter saw us introduce the first and possibly most important phase of The Open Group's Architectural Framework, that of initiation and framework.

By describing some of the principles and ideas behind business and strategic drivers, and the importance of traceability between strategic plans and any architectural endeavor, we provided a pertinent introduction before delving into the TOGAF process and activities for this phase. An appeal to the Standish Group's famous paper on project failures sounded a telling note, and, cautious as ever, we noted several common distress signals that may issue from a program and suggested ways in which they may be overcome, minimized, or accepted. Finally, we documented a view of the initiation and framework phase for our example organization, CFL. This initial foray into CFL commences the threading of a comprehensive illustration of TOGAF in action.

With a firm business basis defined for the architectural program, we can now move to the next phase—a more detailed understanding of the organization's current IT environment.

CHAPTER 6

Baseline Description

6.1 *Introduction*

As we have already seen in Chapter 3, the internal processes of most strategic methods (such as the business strategy, the ISSP, and so on) involve a baseline phase. This is a key activity in providing the foundation for further strategic work. Without a good knowledge of the current state of affairs, it is impossible to determine a reasoned direction. You may remember that later phases in most strategic methods include a migration assessment—the TOGAF architectural development method (ADM) has the migration planning phase. This migration phase requires that the organization understand the current (or baseline) state, the end state, and the gaps between the two that represent the migration.

This chapter takes a look at the TOGAF ADM baseline description phase. As shown in Figure 6.1, this is the second major ADM phase. In this chapter, we describe the properties of this phase and conclude with the baseline description for our example organization to demonstrate the concepts.

The baseline description phase is the second major phase in the TOGAF ADM. As stated in TOGAF, its objective is to:

> Build a high level description of the characteristics of the current environment. This is necessary as the description documents the starting point for architectural development, and lists the interoperability issues that the final architecture will have to take into account.

It is key for the architect to develop a solid understanding of the current technology environment. This establishes the necessary basis for the next phase (the target architecture). The TOGAF inputs and outputs for this phase are shown in Figure 6.2. The inputs have been generated

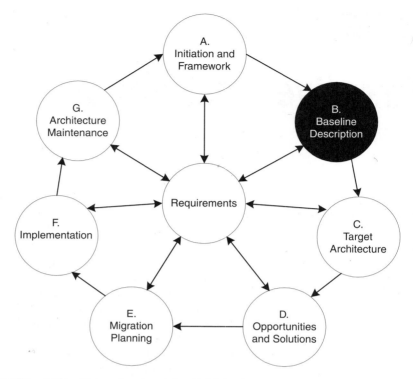

Figure 6.1. ADM, with baseline description highlighted.

from the initiation and framework phase, while the outputs are required for the target architecture phase.

The initiation and framework phase will have delivered a full context for the architectural project. This will include both organizational and project contexts. This phase will gather information from various sources so that the current environment (systems, technologies, and processes) can be described. Sources may include

- IT operational documentation
- Individual business systems design documents
- Environmental (e.g., network, security) documentation
- Interviews with development and operational staff
- Interviews with key users and management

The output of this phase is version 2 of the business architecture that

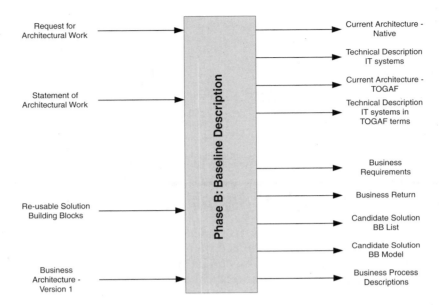

FIGURE 6.2.   Baseline description wiring diagram.

extends on the initiation documentation collected during the previous
phase.

We do not intend to use fully the TOGAF concept of building blocks
(see the next section), yet TOGAF calls for initial building-block specification during this phase. In their place we intend to introduce a concept we call "super services." As we descend further into this chapter, the
notion of services will be introduced more fully, and Chapter 9 is dedicated to a full description of super services. In short, a super service is
a clustering of technical (typically not business) functionality that collects and extends the base TOGAF foundation platform services. During
this phase the architect may note that higher-layer technology services
are being developed within business systems. Additionally, strategic
business requirements may dictate technology services that blur the line
between platform and business system. These technical functions should
be captured, and their placement considered. Figure 6.3 shows a slightly
altered view of the standard TOGAF inputs and outputs. Here, we show
the information-gathering inputs to this phase. Also, the building blocks
have been removed and are instead replaced by an initial view of the
service portfolio.

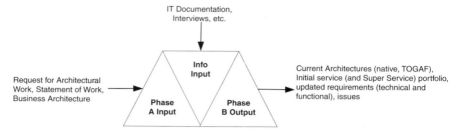

FIGURE 6.3.   Phase B – adjusted inputs and outputs.

6.2   Where Is TOGAF Appropriate?

It is important to understand how TOGAF is holistically positioned against the various different types of architecture. Due to its framework structure, TOGAF can be used as an architectural development tool at a number of architectural levels, as follows (Figure 6.4 summarizes the characteristics of using TOGAF at differing levels):

- TOGAF can be used at an enterprise architectural level. Using TOGAF, we can define the organization's enterprise technical architecture. This represents the high-level use of TOGAF and is the subject of this text.
- TOGAF can be used to describe architectures that represent the specification and integration of various systems. This is a medium-level treatment of TOGAF.
- TOGAF can be used to architect individual business systems. This is the lowest-level, most specific use of TOGAF.

TOGAF competes with an increasing number of other approaches as the described architecture becomes increasingly solution-specific. Due to its structure and defined artifacts, we believe that TOGAF is most effective at the enterprise level and that this was its original intent.

There are a wide variety of methodology choices when the desire is the architecting of individual systems (or even components). Methods such as Rational Unified Process™ (RUP) combined with Unified Modeling Language (UML) provide detailed approaches, notions, artifacts, and tools for the description of application architectures. In this area, TOGAF does not provide a specific or detailed enough framework to currently compete.

The relationship between TOGAF and application architectures is important in the success of enterprise architectures. We believe that TOGAF-produced enterprise architectures provide the necessary tech-

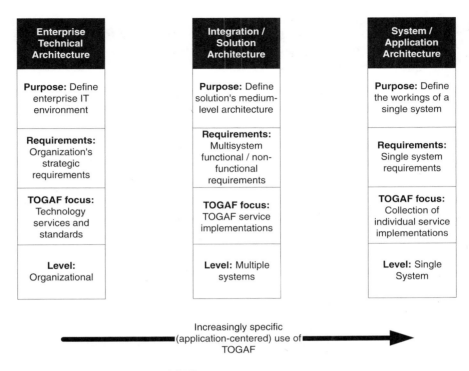

Enterprise Technical Architecture	Integration / Solution Architecture	System / Application Architecture
Purpose: Define enterprise IT environment	**Purpose:** Define solution's medium-level architecture	**Purpose:** Define the workings of a single system
Requirements: Organization's strategic requirements	**Requirements:** Multisystem functional / non-functional requirements	**Requirements:** Single system requirements
TOGAF focus: Technology services and standards	**TOGAF focus:** TOGAF service implementations	**TOGAF focus:** Collection of individual service implementations
Level: Organizational	**Level:** Multiple systems	**Level:** Single System

Increasingly specific (application-centered) use of TOGAF

FIGURE 6.4.   Characteristics of TOGAF use.

nology governance and base constructs (such as the standards information base) with which to architect individual business system projects. Furthermore, applications may use TOGAF service notations to describe system-wide features such as interoperability, scalability, and manageability (known as the –abilities). Ensuring that individual systems accurately follow the organization's technical architecture is essential. However, we do not believe TOGAF will compete with other methods in the architecting of individual systems.

With the advent of e-business, the pressure is now for organizations to consider not only the Internet-facing systems themselves but also the entire back-end integration required to extend business processes to external parties (e.g., customers, partners, suppliers). This increases the requirement to describe and architect the integration environment fully before embarking on individual e-business systems projects. Describing the (medium-level) components of this integrated environment suits a TOGAF approach. Using the concept of services, it can be valid for the architect to map out the integration environment in full TOGAF terms. Such a use is analogous to a "mini enterprise-wide" approach. Using

TOGAF artifacts at this level allows the effective description of the essential interface implementations, the technologies adopted for these interfaces, and the platform-quality aspects to be achieved by the final deliverables. TOGAF provides a complete approach for capturing the overall business requirements for the integrated environment and ensuring that they are met. Used in this way, TOGAF essentially describes the solution architecture. We have used a TOGAF approach effectively in a number of organizations at this level.

The third potential use of TOGAF is for the definition of the corporate technical architecture; that is, the technology framework within which the organization will deliver its technology. In this book we concentrate specifically on this use of TOGAF. The technical architecture is a component of the strategic-planning cycle, as discussed in Chapter 3, and defines the organization's strategic technology direction, the platform on which business functions sit. At this level, architectural development is more general and increasingly high-level. Development is impacted less by the requirements of individual systems and more by the overarching requirements of IT and the business. Indeed, architectural development is less about defining the architecture for an individual system but is more focused on the architecture to be applied in a general corporate sense.

One of the contemporary components of TOGAF is the concept of building blocks. Defined in TOGAF, building blocks are characterized as follows:

- A building block is a package of functionality defined to meet the business needs across an organization.
- A building block has published interfaces to access the functionality.
- A building block may interoperate with other, interdependent building blocks.
- A good Building block has the following characteristics:
    - It considers implementation and usage and evolves to exploit technology and standards.
    - It may be assembled from other building blocks.
    - It may be a subassembly of other building blocks.
    - Ideally, a building block is reusable, replaceable, and well-specified.
- A building block may have multiple implementations but with different interdependent building blocks.

A building block is therefore simply a package of functionality defined to meet business needs. The way in which functionality, products and custom developments are assembled into building blocks will vary widely across organizations and business applications. Every organization must decide for itself what arrangement of building blocks works best for it. Systems (in the wider sense) are built up from collections of building blocks, so building blocks must interoperate. Wherever that is true, it is important that the interfaces to a building block be published and reasonably stable.

TOGAF suggests that building blocks can be defined at various levels of detail, depending on the current stage of the architecture development method. For instance, at an early stage, a building block can simply consist of a collection of functionality such as a customer database and some retrieval tools. Building blocks at this functional level of definition are described in TOGAF as architecture building blocks (ABBs). Later, real products or specific custom developments replace these simple definitions of functionality, and the building blocks are then described as solution building blocks (SBBs).

The Open Group is continuing to develop the concept of building blocks in TOGAF. In its current state, we have found that using TOGAF building blocks for enterprise technical architecture development can be somewhat confusing in intent. In their current state, it is difficult to rationalize how building blocks can be put to use in defining an organization-wide architecture, where we are not concerned as much with the functional make-up of business systems, rather the technology makeup of the platform they will operate on. At this level of architectural work, the finest grain of functionality (both business and infrastructural) considered tends to be the business system (note that in some cases more detailed analysis may be required to understand core subsystems for service reuse) and services. Typically, business systems are defined in the business system architecture and augmented with domain-specific application models. Services are already a major facet of TOGAF. It therefore does not appear necessary, or correct, to describe these aspects again in the technical architecture with building blocks. Viewing business systems with the aim of identifying reusable functionality that can be migrated to "the platform" (i.e., into a technical service) is a key objective of the technical architecture; however, building blocks may not necessarily be the best method of achieving this aim.

TOGAF also suggests ". . . applying the architectural building block method introduces application space into the architectural process. This is the means of linking the services view, which addresses functionality that must be considered on an enterprise basis, with the applications view, which may or may not address global functionality." Certainly, this approach has some merit, especially at a more detailed architectural level. However, at the enterprise level we are less concerned with application functionality and more concerned with the technology environment in which the applications operate (i.e., the platform and its services).

At the enterprise technical level, we are particularly interested in the technology services either provided by or used by the business systems. This form of technical functionality is readily encapsulated in the TOGAF concept of *services*—there is no need to describe them as building blocks. In fact, it is possible to consider a service as having the same characteristics ascribed to building blocks. Services have a greater level of synergy with the development of the technical architecture than do building blocks. Services describe the *platform* or infrastructure components of the corporate technical environment; for instance, network, integration, or transaction management typifies platform services. One of the primary focuses of the enterprise technical architecture is to define and describe all the key technical services that make up the IT environment. Services (and the actual technologies or standards that implement them) provide the platform on which business systems are implemented.

As described earlier, the concept of building blocks is a reasonably new introduction to TOGAF. It is our opinion that as they evolve their use will become clearer. The reader is encouraged to follow their development. However, we have chosen to make only limited reference to building blocks within the text. This does not corrupt the way we are using TOGAF to define the organization's technical architecture, it merely demonstrates its flexibility. TOGAF is a framework, and as such it can be molded in many ways to achieve the goal of producing a technical architecture; it need not be applied prescriptively. Architects are encouraged to extend or subtract from the framework to ensure that it fits the requirements of the organization and the architectural program. In this way, TOGAF is equally suitable for a medium-sized organization wishing to carry out a two-week "architectural" exercise or a large corporate or government department requiring a detailed technical architecture.

Our relegation of building blocks does have an impact on our description of the phases of the TOGAF ADM. The development of architectural and solutions building blocks forms parts of the ADM phase outputs. We will continue to faithfully present the TOGAF inputs and outputs for each phase (and in some cases this may include building blocks).

6.3 Describing the Current Systems

The main objective of this phase is to form an understanding of the organization's current IT environment. We do this for a number of reasons:

- An architectural project is rarely based on a "green fields" situation. There are always "legacy" systems and technologies. The target architecture (defined in the next phase) will have to augment, replace, or maintain aspects of the current environment. The validity of the target architecture will depend on just how the current environment is treated.

- To understand the issues with the current environment. The target architecture is a product of the current environment, identified issues, and the gaps between the target and the current environment. The current environment may never have been put under an "architectural microscope." Stepping back and viewing the individual systems holistically against the rest of the IT environment—not to mention the business strategies—can throw new light on system issues not apparent at first.
- To catalog the technologies, standards, and products that make up the individual systems. This allows the architect to understand areas of technology overlap, where multiple technologies provide the same service, and technology gap.
- To understand how business systems are integrated.

There are a number of ways to describe the current systems. The first, and most intuitive (to the organization, that is), is in a native form. This means that current system descriptions are based on the notations that already exist in the organization. Most organizations will have voluminous documentation describing systems. This material can be easily summarized to provide the necessary baseline descriptions.

A second method is to view the current system structures in TOGAF terms. This means translating the documentation already held on the current systems using techniques that are native to TOGAF, such as services and reference models. This approach has some value as well because it means the artifacts produced can transition smoothly into the next ADM phases, which use a pure TOGAF style.

Cataloging Current Systems

Business systems (and infrastructure) consist of a wide variety of complex interworking components that make up the whole. In analyzing the architecture of a system, it can be difficult to appreciate its full extent. However, understanding its breadth and depth are key to the architectural process. That is not to say that the system needs analysis of the detail of every subsystem or interface but rather that the key components—or to put it another way, the significant architectural components—are well-understood.

It can sometimes be difficult to operate at a level above system detail. For instance, application architects will wish to develop an in-depth understanding of an application's internal stuctures. The job of the technical architect is to understand some aspects of this detail but not to spend endless hours descending into system design minutiae. The aim is to consider aspects of the system that have bearing on the enterprise view of technology. In essence, extract the TOGAF artifact components from systems, which includes:

- Technologies, such as specifications
- Standards adopted either by the system independently or through a more holistic organizational mandate
- Interfaces (such as APIs and exchange formats) that may be both industry-provided or proprietary
- Products, particularly infrastructure or service-related ones
- Quality aspects, such as scalability, availability, and security
- Policy and procedures

As an example, an application architect may be interested in the functionality of a Web portal component that transforms XML via XSL into a device-specific delivery channel (such as HTML or WAP). The Technical Architect is interested in XML, XSL, HTML, and WAP as key standards (technologies and interfaces) used within the application, and will wish to understand what products have been used to implement them and the conceptual frameworks under which they will be implemented. This is a recurring mantra for describing the technical architecture—standards, frameworks, and governance. It is therefore critical to be able to separate the significant components that are relevant to the technical architecture without delving into unnecessary detail.

Obtaining the Information

The cataloging of current systems can be a time-consuming and laborious process. It is therefore important to ensure that the scope of the assessment is fully understood and that only pertinent information is gathered.

Obtaining the necessary information requires that the correct people be approached. Normally it is a good idea to understand the IT group's hierarchy, including key positions and personnel. Furthermore, IT management (such as the CIO or departmental managers) will be able to list the "people in the know." Establishing an informal communications web with subject matter experts will speed the process. Note the members of all IT steering groups, including the IT strategy group (the strategy group may, of course, be the steering group for the technical architecture work). These key people are not only necessary for information gathering purposes but are important quality-assurance resources, architectural advocates, and change agents.

There are a number of strategies that can be used to obtain the necessary information, including:

- Interviews
- Library or documentation research
- Surveys

We find that the most productive method of gathering information on the current systems is through direct interviews. Although identifying the subject matter experts can be difficult, generally the detailed knowledge they can bring to the assessment will be invaluable (documentation can seldom provide the level of information gained through these interviews). Consider approaching the application architects, the network specialists, infrastructure support personnel, and help desk personnel. Also, implementation project managers can have reasonably detailed technical knowledge of the entire solution.

Regardless of how the information will be finally described (e.g., native or TOGAF), it is important to prepare a template of sorts, listing the areas of prime interest, to keep information gathering from being sidetracked.

As an interview technique, it can be worthwhile to predetermine key questions that delve into as many facets of the system as possible. For instance, use:

- *Fact finding* questions such as "How does that work?" or "What does that component do?"
- *Leading* questions such as "Did you consider any alternate technologies here?" or "What quality aspects do you consider important?"
- *Exploring* questions such as "Why was that used?" or "Was integration a problem?"
- *Perception* questions such as "Did you all agree with that architecture?" or "What do you think about the way the system is managed?"

Always close by summarizing the important facts extracted from the interview. Use language such as "My understanding is that . . ." or "I think that . . . is this correct?"

Most IT groups have a large amount of documentation describing their current systems. Although the quantity may be high, extracting useful information of a strategic architecture nature may be somewhat of a challenge. Always search out the original design documents. If possible discover the methodology applied to the implementation. This can tell the architect the types of design documentation that may be available. For example, an object-oriented project will inevitably provide some sort of software architecture document. When viewing documentation, it is important not to be focused entirely on one subject—say the application architecture or the network design—even if this is the most readily accessible. Always attempt to gather a cross section of information affecting all of the services provided by the application. Operational documentation, such as service-level agreements, can also provide a valuable insight into the quality aspects of the application platform such as performance, capacity, and availability.

Surveys are another approach to gathering information about the current systems. Compared with face-to-face contact, this can sometimes be a suboptimal approach. However, it may be unavoidable where the people with the information are more inaccessible (e.g., the international offices of a large corporation or from remote vendor organizations). Additionally, surveying can be less time-consuming for the architect, and can lend an air of formality. The structure of the survey is critical because there is seldom an opportunity to clarify answers. Structure the survey to match the selection method of describing the systems. Using a TOGAF approach can be more beneficial in this respect because it defines formal technology taxonomy. Always test the survey on a readily accessible system specialist before submission.

Native Views

One of the most effective ways of describing the current system is in native terms. This means that the architect will use the vocabulary and taxonomy already used by the IT group to describe the current environment. By their very nature, native views are embodied in the current system documentation and culture of the group. Using a native vocabulary, the architect can easily extract relevant information without the need to transform it into a neutral or common industry format (such as TOGAF). The advantage of native views is that they should be instantly recognizable and understandable by the organization.

The business (and infrastructure) systems are the very reason the IT environment exists. Large organizations will have countless systems, and it is important to understand the scope of the assessment before starting. This would be defined in Phase A: Initiation and Framework. The business systems architecture, if available, should also provide a list of all of the major systems and may have also prioritized them in order of importance. Begin with the core systems. Understand as much as possible about the structure of these systems. Consider the technologies used both to build and deploy the systems. Describe the physical topology of the systems, including the placement of clients, servers, and other important physical components. Attempt to collect any capacity, performance, and scalability information; the support teams will be a principal source of information here.

It is also imperative to view how business systems interoperate. Most major corporate systems will exchange information in many ways. Even the lowly batch-generated flat file (or even manual data re-entry) is an interchange, and its details should be captured. Consider all methods of integration, such as component-to-component interfaces, asynchronous message passing, or flat files on removable storage. Understand the communications protocols used to support information exchange and the format of information exchanged (i.e., how the syntax of the information is described); some may use comma-separated values whereas others are described in XML or EDIFACT. Understand, also, libraries that provide integration support and any applicable ADIs.

The infrastructure should not be forgotten. This consists of the technology that supports the business systems while being reasonably isolated from them. Areas to consider include:

- The network. Include both the wide area and local area networks in the assessment. Consider any external or partner networks that are significant (e.g., the Internet or any extranets). Understand structure or topology, the protocols supported, and current and future capacity assessments. Also catalog significant network equipment, such as routers and switches.

- The systems and network management environment. This includes all of the components used to manage the business systems and the infrastructure. Organizations without a discernable systems management implementation are likely to still have components in the field that need cataloging. Areas to look for include management protocols and information formats, products, application instrumentation techniques, and the overall capability (including the physical reach of management).

- E-mail, directory, file sharing, and other infrastructure applications. Most organizations have a significant investment in these infrastructure applications. They are important to the integrity of the entire environment and support vital user-productivity functions. Consider products, protocols, formats, and physical topologies.

- Security environment. Typically, security is implemented within individual business systems. However, an organization may also have an enterprise-wide solution supporting a number of systems. Consider the protocols, technologies, cryptography algorithms, and products used to implement this service. Also define how the individual systems integrate with the security environment.

One other aspect that may be interesting is the opinion of the IT professionals and other business users. During interviews, this sort of opinion will be voiced. Whether it is perception or whether there is some quantifiable justification, anecdotal comments may prove invaluable later when assessing the current environment. Always attempt to substantiate key evidence, especially if it will be used later to provide input into target architecture decisions.

6.4 TOGAF Terms

Using TOGAF terms to describe the current systems can be more time-consuming if the organization (and architect) is not familiar with its structure and vocabulary. We provide a brief, generic discussion on what constitutes "TOGAF terms" in this section. Without TOGAF experience, it is unlikely that any systems within the organization will be fully described in TOGAF (or proto-TOGAF) terms, so the architect would need to translate native terminology into the TOGAF taxonomy.

As the organization becomes more familiar with TOGAF terminology—after all, the final technical architecture will be described in this way—it will be increasingly likely that new business systems projects will begin using TOGAF vocabulary for describing structure at the high level. The same goes for the enterprise architect. The greater use made of TOGAF, the more likely it will be that system descriptions will be easily seen in TOGAF terms. In fact, the TOGAF way is not in any way exceptional, or wildly academic, but rather it uses a nomenclature that should be immediately familiar to most in IT.

Sooner or later the current system assessment will be translated into TOGAF terms. This translation could occur during this phase of the ADM because it will be required as an initial input into the target architecture phase, or a translation can be applied during target architecture development. However, it is best that it occurs at this point, and therefore we would encourage architects to migrate their thinking into TOGAF mode during the description of the current systems.

Chapter 8 takes a detailed look at the processes involved in converting the organization's current system view in TOGAF terms, a key step in moving into the target architecture development stages. In this section, we provide some of the base constructs of the TOGAF way.

A Service Portfolio

What TOGAF components can be used to describe the current systems? As has already been described, TOGAF is an architectural framework, and as such it can be applied in any number of ways to the description of the enterprise architecture. TOGAF is constructed from a number of important parts, some of which have already been presented and others that will come to light in more detail in the chapters to come. Primarily, the main components of TOGAF are:

- The architectural continuum
- The architectural development method (ADM)
- The foundation architecture
- A standards information base (SIB)

- A taxonomy of views
- A governance framework

Applicable TOGAF components at this stage include the foundation architecture (specifically, the generic services), the concept of the SIB (rather than its TOGAF implementation), and architectural views. We provide an initial description of these in the remainder of this section.

The Technical Reference Model

The technical reference model (TRM) is a component of the TOGAF foundation architecture (this exists at the left-most end of the architectural continuum; see Chapter 4). The foundation architecture is a collection of generic technology services, defined by The Open Group, that provides the basis for refining the organizational services. The services described are intentionally generic so that they can be used as a basis for further, organization-specific, work. Some organizations will find that the generic services completely describe their technical architecture, whereas others will need to augment, replace, add, or delete services. The process of evolving the TRM services follows the architectural continuum (moving from left to right, from generic to organization-specific). The process for controlling this evolution is the architectural development method (ADM).

The TRM simply provides a catalog of all of the technical functions (or services, to use the TOGAF vocabulary) required to support business systems. It presents this in a visual representation (i.e., a reference model) and as a taxonomy, thus providing a method of describing the collection of technologies required to support the organization's business (and infrastructure) systems.

Key definition: **TOGAF taxonomy.**
Defines TOGAF-specific terminology and provides a coherent description of the components and conceptual structure of an IT environment and its set of services. The TOGAF taxonomy is depicted graphically through the Technical Reference Model.

An important concept for understanding exactly how the enterprise technical architecture differs from, say, an application architecture, is the *application platform*. The TRM—its catalogue of services—exists within the application platform. The platform defines the set of services required to support all custom-developed and package applications. The technical architecture is primarily interested in the platform, for it is the crux of the organization's IT environment and therefore represents its technical strategy. Using this basis, the definition of the platform comes before the definition of individual applications; that is, applications plug into, and use the services of, the platform, not the other way around.

For instance, the application will require data management services (most likely via a database of some type). The contents of the database (i.e., the tables, attributes, rows, and columns) and the data model are application-specific; these exist in the TOGAF notion of an application. However, the database access mechanisms (such as the SQL API) and the formats of requests and responses transacted between the database and the application exist in the platform. At a foundation level, such database mechanisms exist as part of the data management services service. The fact that, once in the platform, they represent non application-specific services is the reason why they would affect the organization's technical direction. Generally, the organization will mandate to the application designers just what technologies will be used by the application to gain access to data management services.

The technical architecture is all about setting and controlling platform standards. But what about all those negative aspects associated with standards, in particular the affect on application architect and developer innovation? It is true that one of the central themes behind the enterprise services is commoditization and standardization. But standardization in this context has noble aims—the tackling of the endemic concept of "not invented here." How many security services does an organization need? Certainly not one per application. It is no secret that the more technologies delivering the same function the greater the total cost of IT to the organization. Regardless IT persists in reinventing technical functions because the existing functions were not built by the current faction. At some times this may be perfectly justifiable; however, in many circumstances it is merely a whim of the project team. Application development is all about business function, not building technical infrastructure.

Certainly, standardization can stifle innovation. However, the technical architecture is not targeted at the areas of an application architecture that respond to innovative practices—the domain-specific parts. The technical architecture attempts to identify those functions (or services) that exist within applications that can be considered commodity and not specific to an individual application (i.e., cross-domain). We believe that extracting such services from applications and standardizing these in the platform enables the application architects to continue to innovate and ensures the IT environment to meet its own strategic goals.

Figure 6.5 provides a high-level view of the TOGAF TRM and the application platform. Notice that the application uses the functionality within services of the platform via an interface (actually, a number of interfaces) of some type. Additionally, the application platform inter-

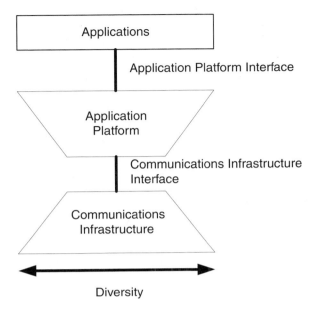

FIGURE 6.5. High-level view of the TRM.

faces directly with the communications infrastructure. The communications infrastructure consists of the physical elements that make up the networking environment, including network hardware and software and physical communications links. Note the fact that the application is sheltered from the physical network implementation by the services provided in the platform. This is a key strategy of the technical architecture.

The platform and service approach stress key architectural goals for the organization's technical architecture:

- *Portability.* Although a change in business requirements will necessitate some change to the application (possibly replacement), if the interface between the application and the platform service is standardized in some way, it is perfectly possible to replace a platform service without a major effect on the application.
- *Interoperability.* The ability of applications to interoperate through the use of common services and common interface semantics is a key driver for any organization wishing to use IT effectively.
- *Commonality.* The ability to recognize common functions within the IT environment, possibly derived from individual business systems, which should be "promoted" to the platform and used by all systems.
- *Architectural gap.* Understanding what platform services an organization should have and what they currently possess provides for a

robust gap-analysis process. Additionally, determining areas of technology overlap is easily described using this service approach.

- *Isolation*. It is increasingly important for contemporary applications to be isolated from the machinery of the IT environment. "Engines," such as middleware, are becoming increasingly complex. The days where business application developers coded directly to the network (say, with sockets APIs) are gone. Moving complex items such as object (or component) transaction monitors into the platform and providing a "simple" API is the aim of the TOGAF application platform and the TRM.

In turn the architectural goals allow the organization to achieve strategic goals such as lower TCO, improve information integrity, reduce time-to-market.

The application platform, as depicted in Figure 6.5, should not be viewed as a physical entity. It is purely conceptual and does not suggest a particular application or deployment style. However, most all applications can be conceptually described using this model. Consider, for instance, the client/server model. Client/server topologies (whether they be two-, three-, or n-tier) are characterized by multiple machines distributed around a network performing various application functions. Each application function (for example, supported within the web, object/component, or database server) will require the use of platform services. The functions will be sufficiently distributed to require access to a communications mechanism of some type. Figure 6.6 demonstrates a method for describing a two-tier client/server model in TRM terms. As can be seen, platform services exist to support all of the client or server components of the business system. Additionally, the application platform provides (and isolates) the application with communications services.

We have presented the generic construction of the TOGAF technical reference model (TRM) and the concept of the application platform. We have also seen how the platform (and hence the application) is made up of distinct technology functions (or services). To complete the TRM, the categories (or types) of technology services provided by the platform must be overlaid.

There are many ways to describe platform services. The TOGAF foundation set is just one approach. Others are available from alternate standards bodies, such as IEEE. Individual organizations may also have their own taxonomies. There is no leader in this area but rather several parallel approaches. It is entirely up to the individual organization to adopt what it sees as sensible. We use the TOGAF taxonomy in this book for a number of reasons:

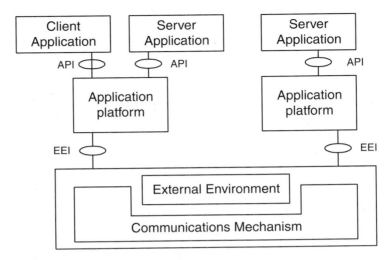

FIGURE 6.6. TRM for the client/server model.

- *Completeness.* The generic service categories are reasonably complete for most uses and provide an excellent basis to begin viewing the IT environment architecturally.
- *Extensibility.* Through the concept of the architectural continuum and the architectural development method, the generic TOGAF services can be modified, new services added to produce the organization's TRM.
- *The SIB.* A key advantage of the TOGAF services is that The Open Group has already defined an "organizational architecture" based directly on these services. The Open Group's standards information base provides an information source of all The Open Group's endorsed industry standards based on the its service taxonomy. This can be beneficial if the organization adheres to the standards provided by The Open Group.
- *Super services.* The TOGAF TRM easily supports our notion of "Super services"—architecturally significant services that use the foundation platform services.

The TRM was presented initially in Chapter 4 and is shown again in Figure 6.7. This figure focuses on the application platform showing the TOGAF foundation services. This taxonomy sits at the foundation architectures position on the architectural continuum (see Chapter 4 for an introduction to the architectural continuum).

The key conceptual components of The Open Group's TRM are:

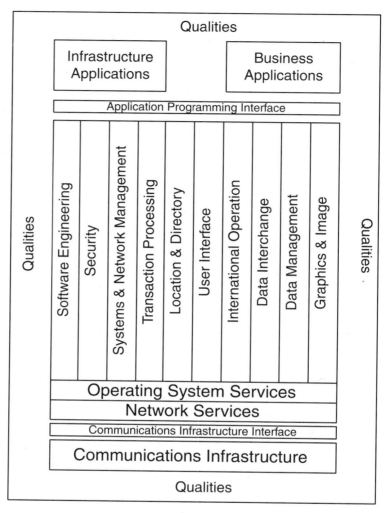

FIGURE 6.7.   Detailed TRM showing service categories.

- Application software
- Application platform
- Communications infrastructure
- Two service interface types: the application programming and the communications infrastructure interfaces

Using this model it is possible to describe almost any IT system. Furthermore, it encapsulates all possible technology services required by all systems in the IT environment (at least at the foundation-level). Any difference is unlikely to exist with the conceptual components but rather in the contents of the components. The TRM is critical to the enterprise technical architecture. Once complete the organizational TRM will represent the technology makeup of the organization and in essence define its technical direction. Let's consider in more detail the components of the TRM.

The Application Software

The application software component can be separated into two major categories:

- *Business applications.* These are the applications that directly support the business strategy and operational requirements. They are typically specific to a particular industry or vertical market. Examples include manufacturing, human resources, and business-to-business systems.
- *Infrastructure applications.* These are support applications, which provide the business with generic functions typically nonspecific to a particular industry. Examples include electronic mail, workflow, knowledge management, and so on. These applications are more likely to be common off-the-shelf products (COTS) and rely heavily on the underlying platform services.

The application programming interface (API) allows the application software to make use of the extant platform services. A single API may provide access to multiple services, or more than one API could be required to access a single service. This will depend on the technologies that will implement the services (selecting technologies to implement services is dealt with in later chapters).

The nature of the interfaces between applications and the platform has a huge bearing on the success of the technical architecture. Typically, the more rigorous the definition of this interface, the more likely the IT environment will support portability, interoperability, commonality, and isolation. The Open Group endorses and certifies a large number of robust API standards at this layer. It is the responsibility of each organization to determine how it will use industry standards. This point will be covered in greater detail in later chapters.

The Application Platform

We have already discussed the application platform at a high level. At this point we take a detailed look at its makeup. The application platform consists of a number of related services that provide support for the application software. TOGAF provides the architect with an initial baseline of services that will meet most general application software needs.

In TOGAF terms, the service baseline exists as part of the foundation architecture, at the foundation end of the architectural continuum. This is merely a starting point for architectural development. One of the underlying concepts of the architectural development method is to transition the application platform from the foundation architecture to an organization-specific architecture by augmenting, deleting, modifying, or adding services.

Coarseness of services is not specified, implying that the architect can adopt a granularity that is appropriate for the organization. For instance, a service may be as fine as an object (although this is unlikely to provide the requisite strategic intent), a component, a subsystem, or an entire system.

Physically, services can exist anywhere within an individual system; for instance they can be developed as part of a specific system, or they can be made more generic and used by more than one system (such as application frameworks). Conceptually, the TOGAF notion of platform services is those that have been moved out of the application and into "the platform" and hence standardized by the IT environment. This is the crux of the organization's technical strategy. Extract as many "common" services into the platform will ensure reuse and deliver to the organization's IT strategy. Platform services are then provided to the application or system through standard[22] interfaces (such as an application program interface—API).

Table 6.1 describes some of the key characteristics of platform services. This characterization is valid for all services identified during the architectural process, not just foundation services.

Key definition: **Services.**
Platform services are the crux of the organization's technical architecture. They define the functions the IT environment will provide all corporate applications.

Each service defined at the foundation level is not a specific technology (or product), rather it is a technology categorization. As the architectural is developed, the services will be realized by actual technologies. Again, at a foundation level, technologies are defined for these services in The Open Group's Standard Information Base (SIB). In the same way the services transition between the foundation and the organizational architecture, the technologies and the SIB will do likewise.

Throughout this text, we will refer to service categories as a descriptor for the high-level service areas pictorially described in the TRM and

---

22. The term "standard" used here does not imply an interface defined by an open standards body but merely an interface that is consistent for all corporate systems.

Table 6.1. Characteristics of platform services.

Service Characteristics
They primarily exist within "the platform"; that is, they tend to be generic, system-centered (as opposed to business-function-centered), and usable by cross-domain business applications.
They are encapsulated bundles of functionality.
They are accessed (by the application) through a published and stable interface (either based on standards, de facto, or proprietary specifications).
They typically interface with other services, providing a hierarchy (or embedding) of rich platform functionality. Some services interface directly with the external environment (i.e., network).
They can be replaced with other implementations (products, custom developments) without affecting the application as long as the interface is preserved.
They meet the service-quality requirements defined by the organization; for instance, performance or scalability.
The interfaces and internal machinery must adhere to the organization's architectural principles.
They typically do not implement organization-specific or domain-specific functionality (functions that are specific to an organization's business requirements).

service subcategories as the medium-level classification of individual services. Generically, when we use the term service we refer to both of these concepts. The following list shows the TOGAF foundation set of service categories and subcategories (the collection of which is called a service portfolio).

Key definition: **Service portfolio.**
The service portfolio is the collection of all services and their implementations that make up the organization's IT environment (or, in other words, the platform).

- Data Interchange Services
  - Document generic data typing and conversion services
  - Graphics data interchange services
  - Specialized data interchange services
  - Electronic data interchange services
  - Fax services
  - Raw graphics interface functions
  - Text processing functions
  - Document processing functions
  - Publishing functions

- Video processing functions
- Audio processing functions
- Multimedia processing functions
- Media synchronization functions
- Information presentation and distribution functions
- Hypertext functions

- Data Management Services
  - Data dictionary/repository services
  - Database management system (DBMS) services
  - Object-oriented database management system services
  - File management services
  - Query processing functions
  - Screen generation functions
  - Report generation functions
  - Networking/concurrent access functions
  - Warehousing functions

- Graphics and Imaging Services
  - Graphical object management services
  - Drawing services
  - Imaging functions

- International Operation Services
  - Character sets and data-representation services
  - Cultural convention services
  - Local-language support services

- Location and Directory Services
  - Directory services
  - Special-purpose naming services
  - Service location services
  - Registration services
  - Filtering services
  - Accounting services

- Network Services
  - Data communications services
  - Electronic mail services
  - Enhanced telephony functions
  - Shared screen functions
  - Video conferencing functions
  - Broadcast functions
  - Mailing list functions
  - Distributed time services

- Distributed data services
- Distributed file services
- Distributed name services
- Remote process (access) services
- Remote print spooling and output distribution services

- Operating System Services
  - Kernel operations services
  - Command interpreter and utility services
  - Batch processing services
  - File and directory synchronization services

- Software Engineering Services
  - Programming language services
  - Object code linking services
  - Computer-aided software engineering (CASE) environment and tools services
  - Graphical user interface (GUI) building services
  - Scripting language services
  - Language binding services
  - Run-time environment services
  - Application binary interface services

- Transaction Processing Services
  - Transaction manager services

- User Interface Services
  - Graphical client/server services
  - Display objects services
  - Window management services
  - Dialogue support services
  - Printing services
  - Computer-based training and on-line help services
  - Character-based services

- Security Services
  - Identification and authentication services
  - System entry control services
  - Audit services
  - Access control services
  - Nonrepudiation services
  - Security management services
  - Trusted recovery services
  - Encryption services
  - Trusted communication services

- ■ System and Network Management Services
  - ■ User management services
  - ■ Configuration management (CM) services
  - ■ Performance management services
  - ■ Availability and fault management services
  - ■ Accounting management services
  - ■ Security management services
  - ■ Print management services
  - ■ Network management services
  - ■ Backup and restore services
  - ■ On-line disk management services
  - ■ License management services
  - ■ Capacity management services
  - ■ Software installation services
  - ■ Trouble ticketing functions

In the same way that the application software uses the platform services via APIs, the services within the platform may make use of each other in a similar fashion. Some inter-service interfaces may be defined and published, whereas others may use private or unexposed interfaces. The valid interaction between services is a vital component of the integrity of the IT environment.

An interesting characteristic of services is the delineation from application software. In the past, we may have seen applications that implemented their own network services or e-mail services, or even developed their own programming environment. This usually occurred when such services were either not available on the platform or possibly not functional enough for the application. However, as services became more ubiquitous and more common to many applications, they slowly began to migrate into the platform, where the application merely has to issue an API call to use the service. An example of this migration is the network services. In the past programmers typically dealt directly within the TCP/IP stack (possibly at a socket level) to exchange information between distributed application components. Modern software platforms provide much higher layer interfaces to the network layers (such as Object Request Broker interfaces, WWW APIs, and others) isolating the programmer from the details of the network.

Analogous to biological evolution, this technology migration process is continually occurring. As new technologies appear, they are typically provided directly within applications. The style of the technology will then dictate how it will evolve. If they are seen as usable by a wide range of applications (i.e., if there is a large market into which they can be developed), they will become increasingly common (possibly even standards), and a greater vendor population will wish to get on the gravy train. At some point in this process, these technologies will be considered commodity and will be "formally" considered part of the platform. Other technologies that remain niche will continue to exist in high-cost, low-penetration applications and remain outside the platform. Workflow and decision support are examples of "niche" services that are still predominantly specialized and used by niche organizational applications. For both of these technologies, increased penetration is required to support their move to commodity status and hence to the platform. The advent of Web-technology based workflow may indicate the beginning of this process.

This brings us to a discussion on super services. We introduced this concept earlier in this chapter, mentioning that they are a collection and extension of the current platform services. A super service shares common themes with both infrastructure applications and services. We see them as a further refined (or even summarized) version of these two TOGAF concepts. For example, take the notion of object-oriented or component-oriented technologies. Most of the base technologies that provide object-oriented services already exist under the foundation services categories—they include transaction services, network services, data interchange services, and so on. However, clustering these services under an object-oriented super service can provide a convenient and useful categorization in its own right. In this way the platform can support a layer of services—the base (foundation) and the super services. The clustering of services can prove very useful when it comes to assessing products. For example, the current application-server market tends to sell an entire bundle of services as a single package. Assessing the technology against the relevant super service can aid the selection process. Super services are dealt with in detail in Chapter 9.

There is one further service category that is worthy of a mention at this point; namely, service qualities. These are the often-overlooked "nonfunctional" aspects of the architecture. Qualities consist of those operational and strategic characteristics of both individual systems and the entire technical environment that represent an organization's view of a quality IT environment. They include such components as (and are generally known as the –abilities):

- *Availability*—including manageability, serviceability, performance, reliability, recoverability, and locatability
- *Assurance*—including security, integrity, and credibility
- *Usability*—includes international operation
- *Adaptability*—including interoperability, scalability, portability, and extensibility

Qualities relate both to the application platform services and the application themselves, which is why they are represented in the TRM. In some respects, individual quality components are in conflict with each other. For example, manageability can affect security, or reliability can affect performance. However, it is important to be able to recognize these qualities in the current environment so that a complete analysis is achieved. We have used these quality aspects to lead the definition of an organization's strategic architectural principles. For example, an organization should have a definitive statement on portability. Is this a key factor? If it is, this will be a significant driver when selecting technologies and products. Another example is manageability. The quality of the environment would be severely affected if an organization had a limited understanding of how the environment should be managed. This is not just applying management technologies (which would be defined in the systems management service) but how these technologies are applied. Service qualities tend not to be technologies in their own right but rather they may be requirements, policies, guidelines, quality assurance checks, and so forth.

Communications Infrastructure

The communications infrastructure is now a ubiquitous part of all organizations' IT environment, whether it be a simple Internet connection or a worldwide corporate network. The communications environment provides the physical components to connect application platforms together. There is virtually no business system today that does not in some way rely on a networking medium. In fact, this reliance on the network will only increase as microdistribution of business system components continues to advance. This has had a significant impact on the network. In the past, the network was a strategic (and costly) corporate asset; today, it is becoming increasingly commoditized

Accepting this change in focus of the network, the TRM models the physical network as a service to the common platform services (not connected directly to the applications themselves). The infrastructure itself is the collection of network links, software, and hardware that make up the physical networks. Generally, the network service provides the technologies and interfaces that integrate with the physical network.

Commodity communications infrastructure interfaces exist between the platform and the network. Used by the platform services, these interfaces enable the higher-layer services to interact with the physical network medium.

It may be difficult to see where the network services stop and the physical network starts. For example, is ATM a network service or a physical network? There is no hard and fast rule on how the architect should pigeonhole the technologies within the TRM. Our call here is that ATM makes up the physical network as it is implemented within the hardware and software of the network, and the network service will include a technology that supports the formats and protocols for an application to use the "ATM network." However, this sort of classification is up to the individual. The only advice is to be consistent.

Views

Architectural views are an excellent approach for analyzing both a current environment and the target environment. We will be describing views in more detail in the target architecture chapters (and dedicate an entire chapter—Chapter 7—to a discussion on views), but a brief description of them here will demonstrate their usefulness in this phase.

Views are essentially slices through the architecture at different points. Typically, if we were to ask IT people to describe the makeup of a particular business system, their perception will be "tainted" by their particular expertise. For instance, the database developer will provide a different analysis of the system than the OO designer or security administrator. These perspectives are merely different views of the system, and each is important in building up a full picture of the system and environment. There are a number of views that can be taken of the current systems in this phase. The architect may consider only a subset important or that additional views should be added. The point here is, again, to ensure that a complete picture of the systems is gained before moving to the next phase. We have found the following views to be useful.

- Functional view. This could be obtained from the business systems architecture, if available.
- Builder's view. Takes a software development focus.
- Security view. Builds an understanding of the security requirements and implementation.
- Computing view. Includes how the hardware and software components are distributed within the organization. This view can also include a Communications view.
- Management view. Looks both at the quality aspects and how management is implemented.
- User view. Considers the user's interaction with the environment.

However, do not be constrained either by the views outlined here or those in TOGAF. Formulating alternate views that reflect the nature of the assignment or problem is encouraged. For instance, a commercial view may be important, so might an organizational view. In this area, there is no wrong answer; whatever is useful in providing input into the current environment analysis should be used.

6.5   *Current System Issues*

Balancing architectural decisions is a key facet of the development of the technical architecture. Understanding the constraints imposed on the architecture, determining necessary tradeoffs, and factoring sensitivities are tools we will use later when analyzing the target architecture. However, this analysis is also important in understanding the makeup of the current environment. Reviewing the various "architectural" or strategic processes available for describing the IT environment, it is noted that current state analysis plays an important role in understanding the problems to be solved. For instance:

- The information architecture considered how the current information needs were being met. Analysis of the current information uses and the organization's requirements identified information gaps. Gaps meant that additional business systems might be required to fulfill them.
- The business systems architecture determined business system information deficiencies. Additionally, review of the current business systems may have led to a decision to divest in favor of a new system.

The technical architecture analyzes the current environment determining both the technical gaps and technical deficiencies. As always it is important that this analysis be done in context with both the business and IT strategic directions (including the information and business systems architectures). For instance, there is no point in analyzing a system that the business systems architecture has already doomed to replacement or to recommend extending the internally managed network to more sites if the organization has decided to centralize its operations and attempt to compete on cost.

When describing and analyzing the current systems, the architect should therefore always be reflecting back on the business and technical strategies. This is the main purpose of the initiation and framework phase—establishing the strategic context.

There are a number of good analysis methods available, but the most important of these is the architect's experience and knowledge. Although a fairly limp phrase, applying the concept of "best practice" effectively is the secret of analysis in the context of the technical architecture, the context being the macro view. This experience manifests itself as knowledge of:

- Common IT industry practice and likely directions
- Trends in technology areas

- Access to vendor organizations, or trusted vendor analysts
- Knowledge of the specific vertical market and its associated technologies
- Knowledge of the business strategies

While collecting information on the current environment, the architect will be assessing this against his or her knowledge and experience. The objective is to uncover areas of the current environment that appear ineffective, misguided, or lacking focus. Typically, for an experienced architect these areas of concern will be fairly obvious. Most organizations tend to have similar problems, with only the scale and the technology being different. For instance, the following are common generic problems:

- Technology overlap—more than one technology filling a service role.
- Technology gaps—a defined service function that is not supported by technology.
- Policy gaps—colloquial guidance that needs to be institutionalized.
- Integration issues—applications and service that do not inherently interoperate.

The approach then is to further analyze these affected areas. Firstly, compare them with the business and technical strategies to understand the scope or likely effect of the problem. A technical deficiency that relates directly to a strategic objective will have a far higher impact than one associated with a purely operational area of the business.

Avoid digging deeply into the architecture of the individual systems, unearthing problems with application internals. This is the responsibility of the application architect and has little bearing on the overall environment unless an application service is being considered for migration into the platform. Although the application architect can describe the problems with the architecture of the system, the technical architect must view the individual system as part of an entire technical environment. The architect should be thinking in terms of the boundary of the application and how it interacts with the environment. This is one of the important concepts of the services portfolio and why the application itself is represented merely as a single block in the TRM.

We have found it useful to analyze the systems and the environment in alignment with the organization's specific (TOGAF) service portfolio. The first architectural project obviously will not have this artifact available, in which case using the TOGAF foundation service portfolio will suffice. This approach is constructive because it ensures that the architect does not miss key service areas when assessing systems. Tackling systems purely from the point of view of the information available has the effect of creating gaps in the analysis merely because the information is not there. Therefore, viewing each system in terms of the entire suite of platform services—viewing slices through the system if you will—ensures that no information is missed. For each system, and the enterprise environment, consider completing a table using criteria similar to those defined in Table 6.2.

There are a number of format methods available that the architect may find valuable in current system assessment. The TOGAF specification refers to two methods for analyzing architectural views:

- IEEE P1471—Recommended Practice for Architectural Description.
- The Architectural Tradeoff Analysis Method (ATAM) from the Software Engineering Institute and Carnegie Mellon University.

There are significant research papers on the ATAM, and its method provides a robust process driven approach to discover architectural problems based on the tradeoff of various different system attributes. The basic process is summarized in Figure 6.8.[23] ATAM provides a micro process to analyze system architectures in detail. It fits easily into TOGAF as an additional support tool for the overall architecture development method.

The key point of the current system analysis is to describe the issues that exist with the current environment. This provides the focus for the architectural work to follow. In essence, it provides the fuel for technical change. Once the issues have been discovered, the final step is to align them with the business and technical strategies so that they may be prioritized. This prioritization step ensures that the target architecture is concentrating on technical change that provides real business benefit rather than for technology's sake alone.

Table 6.2. System assessment criteria.

System: <system or environment name>				
Service Category	Summary of Technology that Provides Service	Issues Noted	Effect on Arch Principles, IT Strategy	Tech Assessment
<service cat name>				
<service cat name>				

23. For more information on ATAM, see www.sei.cmu.edu/ata.

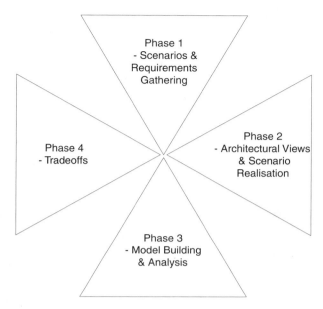

FIGURE 6.8.   Summary of ATAM.

6.6   Outputs

The final stage of the baseline phase is to ensure that all of the necessary documentation is up-to-date. The baseline will need to be documented in a form that allows for easy reference during later stages. Typically, such a document will describe each system and each infrastructure component in individual sections, stating necessary facts and analysis about each. All issues identified and described within these sections should be collected and summarized in the assessment section, including all rationales for highlighting issues. Each issue should be linked with either business or IT strategies that it affects. In TOGAF terms, this document is known as the technical architecture document. This document is a logical construct only; how it is physically described is a matter for the organization to decide. It is carried through the entire ADM, augmented at each phase, and is provided as the final key deliverable. This phase also adds to the business architecture. Again, this is a logical document only and consists primarily of information from the business systems architecture and the architectural TOR.

The final documentation tasks update the constraints, assumptions, or requirements documented during the first phase (initiation and framework). Typically, this will require updating the TOR or the architectural statement of work, if necessary. Remember that it is likely that the baseline activities will uncover further constraints that must be captured, and these are most likely to be technical rather than organizational. Be aware that should these new constraints have significant impact on the target architecture, they should be discussed with the architectural governance board with the aim of prioritizing their impact.

6.7 Example

Introduction

This section continues CFL's architecture program with the baseline phase. We do not provide a complete treatment of the CFL baseline but merely examples of some approaches in describing the current system baseline.

The CFL architectural program has progressed through the initiation phase as described in the previous chapter. The foundation documents describing both the project (the architectural statement of work) and the CFL business environment (the business architecture) have been produced. In this phase, the baseline, the next step is to delve into the current environment to provide the foundation information for the target architecture phase. During this phase, we will also update the "Phase A" deliverables if necessary.

Current System Background

Our first step, after reviewing the initiation documentation, is to map out a plan to capture the necessary current system information. We already knew from the ISSP that the CFL IT environment was separated into two streams, the legacy and the contemporary environments. The legacy environment appears to be characterized by stable management and mainframe-like disciplines. Gaining the necessary information should be reasonably straightforward here. The contemporary environment appears chaotic. Finding the key systems is going to be a challenge, as will be finding the correct people to talk in order to gain this information.

The ISSP also provided us with some key areas of focus, for instance:

■ Total cost of ownership (TCO). The CFL systems and environment have a high cost-to-value ratio. This ratio must be reversed either by lowering cost or increasing value (or both).

- The Internet. The ability of the organization to implement its e-business strategy is hampered by the lack of an Internet-ready environment.
- Systems management. User complaints and systems unreliability must be redressed through more proactive management.
- Technology duplication. A number of infrastructure applications are duplicated and do not cooperate. This also leads to TCO problems.
- Security. There is little control over the security of information within the environment.
- Reporting. Current reporting methods are not timely and are costly to produce.

The business systems architecture also provides some valuable insight into our areas of focus. The key points gleaned from this are:

- The need to support global operations
- The ability to reduce the cost of transactions
- The ability to provide CFL with the capability to develop faster solutions for future business problems
- The need to improve customer convenience
- Highlighting the major issues associated with duplication of core CFL information, including customer and product
- That retention of the core CFL systems was acceptable

The e-business strategy, a key foundation for the future of CFL, must also been considered.

Our information gathering plan looks like this:

- Make a detailed assessment of the "corporate" systems located at HQ, interviewing system support personnel (including help desk), system owners, and vendors where appropriate.
- Construct a questionnaire to be sent to remote office support personnel (or vendors) or office managers if no on-site support is provided.

We have decided to use native views to describe the entire environment. This is likely to facilitate timely gathering of information on the legacy (HQ-based) systems. Also this will not place any undue overhead on the remote offices when it comes to answering the questionnaire.

CFL's Current Systems

Network

We obtained the definitive network diagram from the Operations group, a summary of which is shown in Figure 6.9. Although it does not show

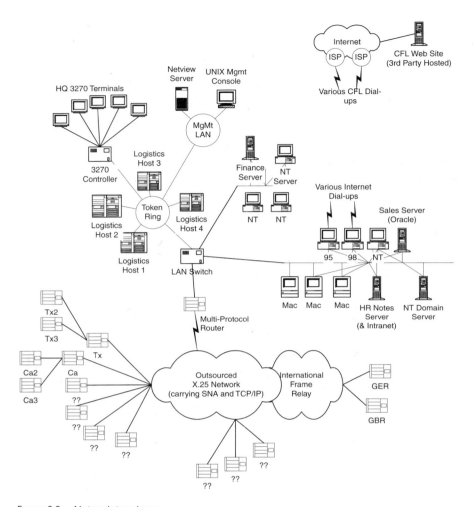

FIGURE 6.9.   Network topology.

a large amount of detail, it does allow us to understand the general environment. Additionally, it is interesting to note that the view of the environment is HQ-centric. From HQ's perspective, control appears to terminate at the regional routers, as in this diagram.

Coupled with this diagram, we were also able to obtain a detailed set of documents describing:

- The network hardware and software, including versions
- A list of all protocols supported

- Detailed service-level agreements, and vendor contracts
- Detailed configuration information
- A schematic of the Netview network management topology, including the properties of all managed objects (most of these consisted of the network equipment and the AS/400 systems)

Logistics System

The Logistics system is the key corporate business application, managing the manufacturing and materials requirements. Although it can be considered legacy, there appear to be no current plans to replace it (see the business systems architecture in initiation and framework). CFL continues to maintain considerable expertise in-house with both the application itself and the AS/400 technologies. We interviewed the systems analyst, the technical support leader, and a key business user to gain a better understanding of the system. Its key technical characteristics include:

- Mainframe-based architecture—"green screen" clients connected to several AS/400s. All business logic, data access logic, and data are maintained on the AS/400s.
- The system was developed in COBOL 74. The database has recently been ported to DB/2.
- Presentation is provided in 3270 data streams. Although there remain a number of terminals at HQ, all other regions use 3270 emulation software on PCs to gain access to the system.
- Logistics supports only SNA for client terminal access. However, recently a TCP/IP stack was installed on all hosts to allow for network management via Netview.
- The system has rigid response time and availability requirements. In summary, all on-line transactions must execute in 2 seconds or less, and the system (measured at the AS/400 end) must exhibit greater than 99.95% uptime.
- There are four AS/400s. One production on-line machine, one product batch and reporting machine, and two development/testing machines that double as hot-standby systems. Data are replicated between systems nightly.

Sales System

Information on the Sales system was gained by interviewing Development group developers, the Sales VP, and a key system user. Additionally, the data model provided for the information architecture was also analyzed with the corporate information architect.

The Sales system, developed in-house, is a recent addition to the enterprise applications portfolio. An analysis of CFL customers, which included a satisfaction survey, indicated that customer knowledge was ineffectively managed by regional sales teams. CFL regularly held misleading or outdated knowledge about customer activities (most of which had to come from the Logistics system via paper output). The CRM initiative was designed to increase the accuracy of customer information in the field, better manage promotions, and track customer interaction with CFL.

A "computing view" was obtained from the Development group. This is shown in Figure 6.10. Salient points are:

- The Sales system is a two-tier Oracle Forms application, modeled in and partially generated from Oracle Designer.
- There are at least two "static" PCs in each office that have access to the system. The limited network bandwidth (and SNA priorities) and the two-tier nature of the system limited the number of users that could be connected at any one time. This has been alleviated marginally through the use of Oracle's Multi-Threaded Server; however, the bottlenecks continue to be an issue.
- Many of the Sales users have a personal copy of the application running on their laptops. The laptop version consists of a sophisticated replication controller that allows salespeople to download core information about their customer to their CRM-lite database. They are able to work offline, including updating customer information. At regular intervals, they are encouraged to upload changed information to an offline replica database on the Sales server. This database contained significant rules that check for inconsistencies between the replica's information and that held on the online system.
- Laptop users can use a number of techniques to replicate information, including dial-up, Internet, and docked on the corporate network. The replication controller uses FTP to transport the information.
- The system does not make use of any management tools. All systems management is carried out by a local Development group resource. Any problems with a salesperson's laptop are either fixed over the phone or the laptop is sent back to HQ.

Interfaces

Gaining an understanding of the interfaces between systems proved to be difficult. We could not identify a single owner for the interfaces in general, and there were no intersystem contracts describing the interfaces. Most interfaces are run within the Operations group via standard batch jobs. Almost all required physical intervention to move generated files between systems. There were few error-recovery mechanisms in place. All systems (apart from HR) maintained a subset of customer information. Frequently, the view of a customer was different in each

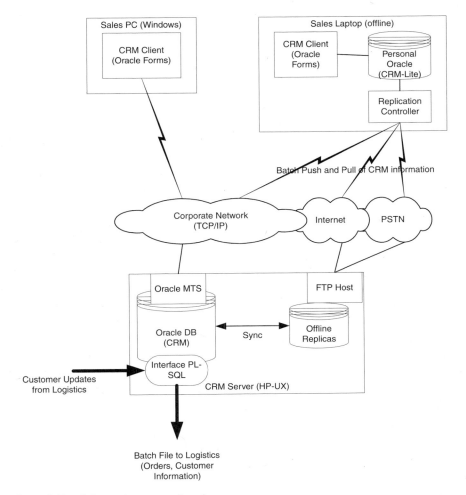

FIGURE 6.10. Sales system computing view.

system. During an interview with the Operations Manager, she indicated that the interfaces were "a mess"—each new interface requirement caused another point-to-point solution and exacerbated the problem. The help desk noted a number of irate customer calls relating to the inaccuracy of CFL's information due to interface difficulties.

We sketched a high-level diagram of the interface architecture, shown in Figure 6.11, from information provided by a number of support people in both the Operations and Development groups. We could not discover a detailed description of each interface (interchange formats, scheduling requirements, and so on).

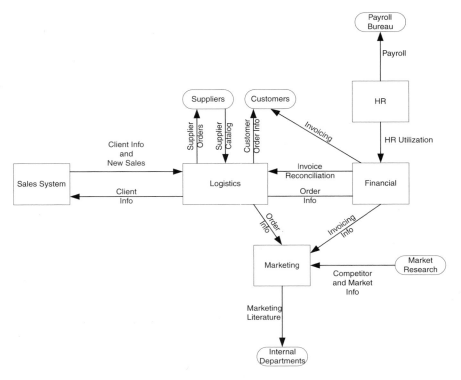

FIGURE 6.11.   Interface topology.

Regional Systems

We constructed a number of different questionnaires to support the discovery of the regional IT environments. Detailed and specialist technical questions were distributed to the known regional support personnel, the objective being to understand as much as possible about the technology environment. More general questions were sent to regional managers to gather an understanding of both the business systems regularly used at the site and the opinions of the users as to the effectiveness of the systems.

Figure 6.12 shows an example of infrastructure information received from the Texas regional HQ. This information highlighted that there was considerably more technology deployed within the regions than suspected, including a growing number of dialup Internet users. Additionally, although no new "corporate applications" were uncovered, the survey unearthed a large number of small regional applications supporting key regional functions. Many of these small applications were taking

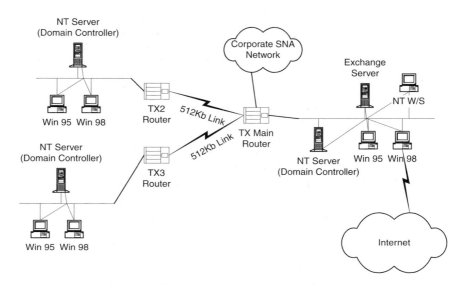

FIGURE 6.12. Texas system infrastructure.

information feeds from corporate systems and presenting them in a more usable form for the users.

Current System Assessment

In analyzing the current systems, we discovered and confirmed many of the problems described in the ISSP. Given our in-depth analysis, we were able to document them to a greater extent and understand some of the areas where changes would be necessary.

There were a few areas identified in the current system assessment that were not picked up in the ISSP. These were intersystem integration and security. This section looks at these two issues in more detail.

Additionally, through the interview process, we deduced further architectural constraints that were not already captured. The architectural TOR was updated to reflect this new information. The constraints identified were:

- IT management has just signed a hardware and operating system support contract with IBM for support of the Logistics system and the Logistics systems management environment (Netview). The contract runs for 4 years.
- The Marketing department is actively pursuing direct Internet-based customer ordering. This is in response to a competitor's efforts in

Service Category
Information Interchange
Summary of Technology that Provides Service
• Mostly batch integration between systems
• Some ad hoc file transfer used
• Sales system supports a custom developed replication systems
Issues Noted
• Unreliable
• No feedback mechanism
• n to n interface methods
• Requires significant manual intervention
• Costly to maintain integrity
Effect on Arch Principles, IT Strategy
• Management costs are high—negative effect on TCO
• Leads to information duplication across systems—corrupts corporate architecture
• Error prone—affects interface quality
• Reduces ability to change systems in a timely manner
• Limited the ability to integrate e-business applications into the corporate environment and therefore reduce supply chain costs
• Overall: major negative effect on achieving strategy
Tech Assessment (hype curve)
• N/A

this area. This service has been pitched to customers (mostly large supermarkets) for initial release in 6 months.

6.8 Summary

In this chapter, we concentrated on baselining the current environment. This is a key activity in understanding the systems and infrastructure components that make up the current environment and how they align with the business, IT, and architectural directions. We looked at mechanisms for describing the current environment, including in both native and TOGAF forms. From the TOGAF perspective, we introduced in more detail the concept of a service portfolio and its relationship with the standard technical reference model. Finally, using CFL, we provided some insight into what a baseline might look like.

In the next chapter, we take a more detailed look at architectural views.

Service Category
Security

Summary of Technology that Provides Service

- Security services specific to each application (e.g. Oracle DB security for Sales, RACF for Logistics)
- NT security provided in sites that have implemented NT domains
- Netware security provided in sites that have implemented Novell
- Lotus Notes public-key-based security
- Plus a number of others

Issues Noted

- User credentials duplicated in a large number of security repositories
- Users must remember a number of different passwords and user IDs to gain access to systems
- There is no overarching security policy governing security implementation, and therefore each system implements security to its own requirements
- There are little or no audit mechanisms to ensure that information security is maintained and that no attacks have occurred
- Ad hoc Internet connections have the ability to compromise internal security—there are no secure gateways preventing this
- The security environment is not robust enough, and does not have sufficient functionality to support e-business initiatives

Effect on Arch Principles, IT Strategy

- Unable to assure the integrity of CFL information or environment
- Limits the ability to implement Internet-based applications and supply chain integration
- Increases TCO due to maintaining numerous user repositories and handling help desk calls relating to forgotten passwords
- Reduces system and environment usability

- Overall: major negative effect on achieving strategy

Tech Assessment (hype curve)

- Most technologies providing security services are mature

CHAPTER 7

Architectural Views

7.1 Introduction

An individual system structure (say its application architecture) is a complex collection of components, building blocks, objects, hardware, networks, services, and nonfunctional requirements. Representing these aspects in a unified architecture can be difficult. This is complicated by the fact that an eclectic array of skills is required to specify, develop, and assure such an architecture.

This problem is multiplied for enterprise technical architecture development. All components of the IT environment are required to be modeled within the architecture to ensure that the end product (in this case, the organization's IT environment) is complete, logical, reasoned, and meets the organization's business requirements. The organization's technical architecture can be considered an n-dimensional space, each dimension presenting a single component of the architecture, with the points on the dimension being a specific element of each component. The complexity of such a representation limits its ability to be understood (a significant aspect of the architectural approach being the ability to support effective communication of the architecture) by those who created it and possibly not even then. It affects the architecture's ability to be assessed and assured by subject matter experts in the organization. Most of all, it affects the ability to deliver and maintain the architecture. We therefore need a mechanism to reduce the effects of these issues.

Architectural views provide us with such an approach. In general, views allow slices to be taken through the architecture at significant points to support increased understanding, assessment, and assurance and heighten the chances for successful implementation and maintenance. Views can be taken at any point through the architecture—there is no right way to slice up the architecture. The most typical approaches include:

- Platform service views
- Quality views
- Functional views
- Project views

This chapter presents a number of architectural views that can be used to describe the technical architecture. Because this is their purpose, the bias is toward platform service views.

7.2 The Role of Architectural Views

Depending on the area of responsibility of the architect, an architecture may be viewed from different perspectives. For example, the architect responsible for computing perceives the architecture with a different focus than the Architect responsible for data management. The architect responsible for the overall system has yet another focus.

These different areas of focus, or slices, are called "views."

A view therefore is a means of describing how an organization's specific needs are embodied in the architecture. Views are used as a method of cross-checking that a proposed technical architecture will meet all aspects of the computational needs that will be imposed on it or that a current architecture is fit for its intended purpose.

Pertinent views are taken of both the existing system and the target system to establish which elements of the current system must be carried forward and which must be removed or replaced. The use of views for describing the current systems environment was presented briefly in Chapter 6.

The views presented in the following sections describe architecture concepts from different perspectives. Each of these views addresses components, interfaces, and allocation of services critical to the view.

TOGAF presents some recommended views, some or all of which may be appropriate in a particular architecture development. This is not an exhaustive set of views, and those shown may be supplemented by additional views as required.

Recommended Views

We have separated the architectural views into three levels:

- The functional view focuses on the functional aspects of the system; that is, on what the new system is intended to do. This can be built up from an analysis of the existing environment and the requirements and constraints affecting the new system.
- Implementation views focus on how the system is implemented and how that affects its properties:
    - The management view examines the architecture from the point of view of the service provider. It covers issues such as initial deployment, upgrading, availability, security, performance, asset management, fault, and event management of system components from the management perspective.
    - The security view focuses on the security aspects of the systems for the protection of information within the organization. It examines the systems to establish what information is stored and processed, how valuable it is, what threats exist, and how they can be addressed.
    - The builder's view deals with aspects of interest to software developers. It considers what software development constraints and opportunities exist in the new architecture and looks at how development can be carried out in terms of both technology and resources.
    - The data management view deals with the storage, retrieval, processing, archiving, and security of data. It looks at the flow of data as it is stored and processed and at what components will be required to support and manage both storage and processing.
    - The user view considers the usability aspects of the IT environment.

- Physical views concentrate more on the location, type, and power of the equipment and software:
    - The computing view presents a number of different ways in which software and hardware components can be assembled into working systems. To a great extent, the choice of model determines the properties of the future organizational systems. It looks at technology that already exists in the organization, and what is available currently or will be in the near future. This reveals areas where new technology can contribute to the function or efficiency of the new architecture and how different types of processing platforms can support different parts of the overall system.

- The communications view examines various ways of structuring communications facilities to simplify the business of network planning and design. It examines the networking elements of the architecture in the light of geographic constraints, bandwidth requirements, and so on.

These views should not be considered an exhaustive set but simply a starting point. In developing an organization-specific architecture, it is very likely that some of these views will not be useful, whereas others not given here will be essential. For example, other views might be developed in response to specific business requirements such as performance, operating cost, uptime, or contract management.

The comparison of the views of the existing systems and the target architecture (as explained during the development of the target architecture) will often yield indications of where changes in environment and system requirements and objectives will lead to implementation constraints and to recognition of elements being retained or eliminated. This comparison should also yield a better understanding of relationships between the architectures of the existing and target systems.

7.3   *Business Process Domain View*

Introduction

A *business process domain* is a logical grouping of business systems dedicated to a common purpose. Such systems may be geographically colocated, thus emphasizing their purpose, or they may be grouped by some other constraint such as a common systems availability target.

To demonstrate the responsiveness of the technical architecture to the business needs of the organization, among the various architecture views that are developed a *business process domain view* should be considered. This describes the technical architecture from the perspective of the enterprise's key business process domains.

Role

A business process domain view is a set of functional views aligned with the business process structure of the enterprise. Business process domain views are used during architecture development as a means of verifying and demonstrating that the architecture being developed is addressing the business requirements. Specifically, they are an output of Phase C and are used in Phase D of the ADM.

Thorough and detailed application of the business scenario technique in the early stages of architecture development should provide an excellent foundation for a set of business process domain views. Business scenarios describe:

- A business process, application, or set of applications that can be enabled by the architecture
- The business and technology environment
- The people and computing components who execute the scenario
- The desired outcome of proper execution

Each business process domain view addresses components, interfaces, and allocation of services critical to the view. A typical structure is shown in Table 7.1.

Table 7.1. Business process domain views—description structure.

Introduction	A description of the domain, its key applications and attributes that characterize the applications within the domain
Business problem statement	A short description of the important business problems relating to the domain and how they are addressed in the target architecture
Applications deployed within the business process domain	A table listing currently deployed applications
Assumptions, constraints and guidelines	General guidelines for developers, implementers, and system suppliers
Domain structure	Target architecture/business process domain mapping: A table highlighting the services applicable to this domain Application topology: A figure showing the relationships between the major application elements within this domain
Domain service qualities	A description of the service qualities that are important for each business process domain and how they are achieved in the target architecture.
Deployment guidance strategy	Lessons learned with respect to deployment; the migration strategy for implementing the target architecture as it applies to this business domain; also any guidance for the implementation team responsible for deployment
Future directions	Any important directions identified for systems within the domain
References	Pointers to reference material

7.4 Functional View

The functional view considers the functional aspects of systems; that is, what the systems are intended to do. This can be built up from an analysis of the existing environment and of the requirements and constraints affecting the systems.

The architecture development method (ADM) outlines the process of analyzing and describing the existing environment in its own terms (Phase B) and then restating it in TOGAF terms to obtain information about what exists already (Phase C).

The new requirements and constraints will appear from a number of sources, possibly including:

- Existing internal specifications and lists of approved products
- Business goals and objectives
- Business process reengineering activities
- Changes in technology

Business scenarios are an important technique that may be used prior to, and as a key input to, the development of the architecture to help identify and understand business needs and thereby derive the business requirements and constraints that the architecture development must address.

What should emerge from the functional view is a clear understanding of the functional requirements for the systems that will exist in the new architecture, with statements such as "Improvements in handling customer inquiries are required through wider use of Computer/Telephony Integration."

7.5 Security View

The essence of security is the controlled use of information. This section provides a brief overview of how security protection is implemented in the components of information systems. Doctrinal or procedural mechanisms, such as physical and personnel security procedures and policy, are not discussed here in any depth.

Figure 7.1 depicts an abstract view of an information system architecture, which emphasizes the fact that information systems from the security perspective are either part of a local subscriber environment (LSE) or a communications network (CN). An LSE may either be fixed or mobile. The LSEs by definition are under the control of the using organization. In an open system distributed computing implementation, secure and nonsecure LSEs will almost certainly be required to interoperate.

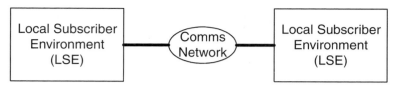

FIGURE 7.1.   Abstract security architecture view.

Basic Concepts

The concept of an information domain provides the basis for discussing security protection requirements. An information domain is defined as a set of users, their information objects, and a security policy. An information domain security policy is the statement of the criteria for membership in the information domain and the required protection of the information objects. Breaking down an organization's information into domains is the first step in reducing the task of security policy development to a manageable size.

The business of most organizations requires that their members operate in more than one information domain. The diversity of business activities and the variation in perception of threats to the security of information will result in the existence of different information domains within one organization security policy. A specific activity may use several information domains, each with its own distinct information domain security policy.

Information domains are not necessarily bounded by information systems or even networks of systems. The security mechanisms implemented in information system components may be evaluated for their ability to meet the information domain security policies.

Information domains can be viewed as being strictly isolated from one another. Information objects should be transferred between two information domains only in accordance with established rules, conditions, and procedures expressed in the security policy of each information domain.

The concept of "absolute protection" is used to achieve the same level of protection in all information systems supporting a particular information domain. It draws attention to the problems created by interconnecting LSEs that provide different strengths of security protection. This interconnection is likely because interoperable systems may consist of an unknown number of heterogeneous LSEs. Analysis of minimum security requirements will ensure that the concept of absolute protection will be achieved for each information domain across LSEs.

Generic Security Architecture View

Figure 7.2 shows a generic architectural view that can be used as an aid for describing the makeup of security services and the implementation of security mechanisms. This view identifies the architectural components within an LSE. The LSEs are connected by CNs. The LSEs include end systems, relay systems, and local communications systems (LCSs), described below.

- *Relay System (RS)*. The component of an LSE, the functionality of which is limited to information transfer and is only indirectly accessible by users (e.g., router, switch, message transfer agent). It may have functionality similar to an end system, but an end user does not use it directly. Note that relay system functions may be provided in an end system (ES).
- *Local communication system (LCS)*. A network that provides communications capabilities between LSEs or within an LSE with all of the components under control of a LSE.
- *Communication Network (CN)*. A network that provides inter-LSE communications capabilities but is not controlled by LSEs (e.g., commercial carriers).

The end system and the relay system are viewed as requiring the same types of security protection. For this reason, the view of security, the protection in an end system generally also applies to a relay system.

Implementing the necessary security protection in the end system occurs in three system service areas of TOGAF. They are operating system services, network services, and system management services.

Most of the implementation of security protection is expected to occur in software. The hardware is expected to protect the integrity of the end system software. Hardware security mechanisms include protection against tampering, undesired emanations, and cryptography.

A "security context" is defined as a controlled process space subject to an information domain security policy. The security context is therefore analogous to a common operating system notion of user process

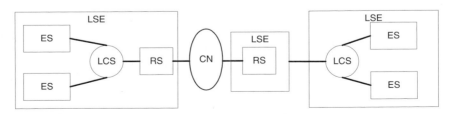

FIGURE 7.2.   Generic security architecture view.

space. Isolation of security contexts is required. Security contexts are required for all applications (e.g., end-user and security management applications). The focus is on strict isolation of information domains, management of end-system resources, and controlled sharing and transfer of information among information domains. Where possible, security-critical functions should be isolated into relatively small modules that are related in well-defined ways.

The operating system will isolate multiple security contexts from one another using hardware-protection features (e.g., processor state register, memory mapping registers) to create separate address spaces for each of them. Untrusted software will use end-system resources only by invoking security-critical functions through the separation kernel. Most of the security-critical functions are the low-level functions of traditional operating systems.

Two basic classes of communications are envisioned for which distributed security contexts may need to be established. These are interactive and staged (store and forward) communications.

The concept of a "security association" forms an interactive distributed security context. A security association is defined as all the communication and security mechanisms and functions that extend the protections required by an information domain security policy within an end-system to information in transfer between multiple end systems. Multiple security protocols may be included in a single security association to provide a combination of security services. IPSEC is an example of a technology that supports the forming of security associations.

For staged delivery communications (e.g., electronic mail), use will be made of an encapsulation technique (called a "wrapping process") to convey the necessary security attributes with the data being transferred as part of the network services. The wrapped security attributes are intended to permit the receiving end system to establish the necessary security context for processing the transferred data.

Security management is a particular instance of the general information system management functions described by the TOGAF Systems Management Service. Information system security management services are concerned with the installation, maintenance, and enforcement of information domain and information system security policy rules in the information system intended to provide these security services. In particular, the security management function controls information needed by operating system services within the end-system security architecture. In addition to these core services, security management requires event handling, auditing, and recovery. Standardization of security management functions, data structures, and protocols will enable interoperation of security management application processes (SMAPs) across many platforms in support of distributed security management.

7.6   Management View

The management view acts as a check and balance on the difficulties and day-to-day running costs of systems built within the new architecture. Often, system management is not considered until after all of the important purchasing and development decisions have been made, and taking a separate management view at an early stage in architecture development is one way to avoid this pitfall. It is good practice to take the management view after the security view because in general the system management personnel are also responsible for system security.

Key elements of the management view are:

- Which system and network management services are required
- The likely quantity, quality and location of management and support personnel
- The ability of users to take on system management tasks
- The manageability of existing and planned systems in each of the required system and network management service areas
- Whether management should be centralized or distributed
- Whether security is the responsibility of system managers or a separate group, bearing in mind any legal requirements

In general stakeholders are concerned with assuring that the availability of systems does not suffer when changes occur. Managing the systems includes managing components such as:

- security components
- data assets
- software assets
- hardware assets
- networking assets

Key technical components categories that are the subject of the management view deal with change, either planned upgrades or unplanned outages. Table 7.2 lists specific concerns in each component category.

7.7   Software Engineering View

Building software-intensive systems is both expensive and time consuming. Because of this it is necessary to establish guidelines to help minimize the effort required and the risks involved. Most organizations will

Table 7.2. Operational concerns.

Component category	Planned change considerations	Unplanned change considerations
Security Components	How does one propagate a security change throughout systems? Who is responsible for making changes, end users, or security stewards?	What should happen when security is breached? What should happen if a security component fails?
Data assets	How does one add new data elements? How does one import/export or load/unload data? How is backup managed while running continuously? How is data change propagated in distributed environment?	What are your backup procedures and are all the system capabilities there to backup in time?
Software assets	How does one introduce a new application into the systems? What procedures do you have to control software quality? How does one propagate application changes in a distributed environment? How does one restrict unwanted software introduction given the internet?	What do you want to happen when an application fails? What do you want to happen when a resource of applications fails?

Table 7.2. Operational concerns (*continued*).

Component category	Planned change considerations	Unplanned change considerations
Hardware assets	How do you assess the impact of new hardware on the system, especially network load?	What do you want to happen when hardware outages occur?
Networking assets	How do you assess the impact of new networking components? How do you optimize your networking components?	What do you want to happen when networking outages occur?

develop custom software therefore it is important to define the frameworks under which this will occur. This view helps the architect to analyze the current methods used by the organization to develop software and aids in positioning architectural styles for future development. This is one of the most obvious interactions between enterprise and application architecture. In the role of an enterprise standards-setter the technical architecture is required to develop an opinion as to how individual software development projects should operate. This view helps in determining the factors to consider. The view also relates to the less abstract system engineering view.

Major points for the technical architecture to consider in developing a software engineering strategy are:

- Development approach
- Software modularity and reuse
- Portability
- Migration and interoperability
- Architectural models

The development approach consists of the many lifecycle models defined for software development (waterfall, prototyping, etc.). A consideration for the architect is how best to feed architectural decisions into the lifecycle model that is going to be used for development of the system.

- Prototyping or rapid prototyping may be used to determine the overall feasibility of the system and also to demonstrate the user interface to be provided with the system.

- Iterative techniques may be combined with prototyping to incrementally develop the system in conjunction with potential system users.

As a piece of software grows in size, so the complexity and interdependencies between different parts of the code increase. Reliability will fall dramatically unless this complexity can be brought under control. Modularity is a concept by which a piece of software is grouped into a number of distinct and logically cohesive sub-units, presenting services to the outside world through a well-defined interface. Generally speaking, the components of a module will share access to common data, and the interface will provide controlled access to this data. Using modularity, it becomes possible to build a software application incrementally on a reliable base of pre-tested code. A further benefit of a well defined modular system is that the modules defined within it may be re-used in the same or on other projects, cutting development time dramatically by reducing both development and testing effort.

In recent years, the development of Object Oriented Programming Languages has greatly increased programming language support for modular development and code re-use. Such languages allow the developer to define "classes" (a unit of modularity) of objects that behave in a controlled and well-defined manner. Techniques such as inheritance, which enables parts of an existing interface to an object to be changed, enhance the potential for re-usability by allowing pre-defined classes to be tailored or extended when the services they offer do not quite meet the requirement of the developer. If modularity and software re-use are likely to be key objectives of new software developments, consideration must be given to whether the component parts of any proposed architecture may facilitate or prohibit the desired level of modularity in the appropriate areas.

Software portability, the ability to take a piece of software written in one environment and make it run in another, is important in many projects, especially product developments. It requires that all software and hardware aspects of a chosen technical architecture (not just the newly developed application) be available on the new platform. It will, therefore, be necessary to ensure that the component parts of any chosen architecture are available across all the appropriate target platforms.

Interoperability is always required between the component parts of a new architecture. It may also, however, be required between a new architecture and parts of an existing legacy system—for example during the staggered replacement of an old system. Interoperability between the new and old architectures may, therefore, be a factor in architectural choice.

Determining how software architectures are to be modeled represents a key decision point for the technical architecture. There are numerous modeling techniques, many of which are related to software development methods (Rational Unified Process and UML for instance)

Data Intensive versus Information Intensive Software Systems

The technical architecture must be cognizant of the fact that one software engineering approach does not fit all situations. Size, problem domain, and complexity are key differentiators. While the objective is to "unify" development methods in an integrated manner—interoperability with the platform being a key driver—it continues to be important to consider different techniques to tackle differing development types.

From an abstract point-of-view it is possible to view software systems in two general categories. First, there are those systems that require only a user interface to a database, requiring little or no business logic built into the software. These systems can be called "Data Intensive." Second, there are those systems that require users to manipulate information that might be distributed across multiple databases, and to do this manipulation according to predefined business logic. These systems can be called "Information Intensive."

Data intensive systems can be built with reasonable ease through the use of 4GL tools. In these systems, the business logic is in the mind of the user, i.e., the user understands the rules for manipulating the data and uses those rules while doing his work.

Information intensive systems are different. Information is defined as "meaningful data," i.e., data in a context that includes business logic. Information is different from data. Data is the tokens that are stored in databases or other data stores. Information is multiple tokens of data combined to convey a message. Typically, information reflects a model. Information intensive systems also tend to require information from other systems, and, if this path of information passing is automated, usually some mediation is required to convert the format of incoming information into a format that can be locally used. Because of this, information intensive systems tend to be more complex than others, and require the most effort to build, integrate, and maintain.

This view is concerned primarily with information intensive systems. In addition to building systems that can manage information, though, systems should also be as flexible as possible. This has a number of benefits. It allows the system to be used in different environments, for example, the same system should be usable with different sources of data, even if the new data store is a different configuration. Similarly, it might make sense to use the same functionality but with users who need a different user interface. So information systems should be built so that they can be reconfigured with different data stores or different user interfaces. If a system is built to allow this, it enables the enterprise to reuse parts (or "components") of one system in another.

Interoperability can only be achieved when information is passed, not when data is passed. Most information systems today get information both from their own data stores and other information systems. In some cases the web of connectivity between information systems is quite extensive. The United States Air Force technical architecture, for example, has a concept known as "A5 Interoperability." This means that the required data is available anytime, anywhere, by anyone, who is authorized, in any way. This requires that many information systems are architecturally linked and provide information to each other. The technical architecture must consider the way current systems interoperate and provide meaningful direction (technology, methods, guidelines) as to how integration will "improve" and how new systems will be designed for integration.

Software Tiers

Physically, software architectures are either 2-tier or 3-tier. Each tier typically presents at least one capability.

In a two-tier architecture the user interface and business logic are tightly coupled while the data is kept independent. This allows the data to be independently maintained. The tight coupling of the user interface and business logic assure that they will work well together—for this problem in this domain. However, the tight coupling of the user interface and business logic dramatically increases maintainability risks while reducing flexibility and opportunities for reuse.

A three-tier approach adds a tier that separates (an amount of) the business logic from the user interface. This in principle allows the business logic to be used with different user interfaces as well as with different data stores. With respect to the use of different user interfaces, users might want the same user interface but using different COTS presentation servers, for example, Java Virtual Machine (JVM) or Common Desktop Environment (CDE). Similarly, if the business logic is to be used with different data stores, then each data store must use the same data model ("data standardization"), or a mediation tier must be added above the data store ("data encapsulation").

An additional level of flexibility can be achieved through using a 5-tier scheme for software, extending the three-tier paradigm (see Figure 7.3). The scheme is intended to provide strong separation of the three major functional areas of the architecture. Since there are client and

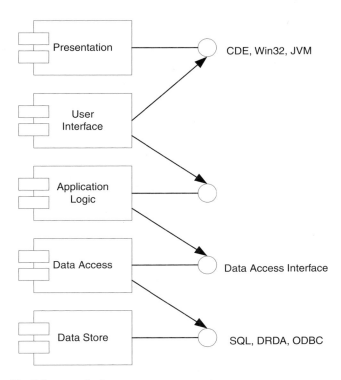

FIGURE 7.3.   The 5-tier organization.

server aspects of both, the user interface and the data store, the scheme then has 5 tiers.[24]

The presentation tier is typically COTS-based. The presentation interface might be an X-server, Win32, etc. There should be a separate tier for the user interface client. This client establishes the look and feel of the interface; the server (presentation tier) actually performs the tasks by manipulating the display. The user interface client hides the presentation server from the application business logic.

The application business logic should be a separate tier. This tier is called the "application logic" and functions as a server for the user interface client. It interfaces to the user interface typically through callbacks. The application logic tier also functions as a client to the data access tier.

If there is a need to use an application with multiple databases with different schema, then a separate tier is needed for data access. This

24. We use the technical architecture term "tier" as apposed to the application architecture term "layering" to highlight the detail differences inherent between the two concepts.

client would access the data stores using the appropriate COTS interface and then convert the raw data into an abstract data type representing parts of the information model. The interface into this object network would then provide a generalized data access interface (DAI) that would hide the storage details of the data from any application that uses that data.

Each tier in this scheme can have zero or more components. The organization of the components within a tier is flexible and can reflect a number of different architectures based on need. For example, there might be many different components in the application logic tier (scheduling, accounting, inventory control, and so on) and the relationship between them can reflect whatever architecture makes sense, but none of them should be a client to the presentation server.

This clean separation of user interface, business logic, and information will result in maximum flexibility and componentized software that lends itself to product line development practices. For example, it is conceivable that the same functionality should be built once and yet be usable by different presentation servers (e.g., on PCs or UNIX boxes), displayed with different looks and feels depending on user needs, and usable with multiple legacy databases. Moreover, this flexibility should not require massive rewrites to the software whenever a change is needed.

7.8   Data Management View

Data management services may be provided by a wide range of implementations. Some examples include:

- Mega-centers providing functionally oriented corporate databases supporting local and remote data requirements
- Distributed database management systems that support the interactive use of partitioned and partially replicated databases
- File systems provided by operating systems, which may be used by both interactive and batch-processing applications

Data management services include the storage, retrieval, manipulation, backup, restart/recovery, security, and associated functions for text, numeric data, and complex data such as documents, graphics, images, audio, and video. The operating system provides file management services, but they are considered here because many legacy databases exist as one or more files without the services provided by a database management system (DBMS). The DBMS is the most critical component of any data management capability, and a data dictionary/directory system is necessary in conjunction with the DBMS as a tool to aid the administration of the database. Data security is a necessary part of any overall policy for security in information processing.

A database management system (DBMS) provides for the systematic management of data. This data management component provides services and capabilities for defining, structuring, and accessing the data, as well as security and recovery of the data. A DBMS performs the following functions:

- Structures data in a consistent way
- Provides access to the data
- Minimizes duplication
- Allows reorganization, that is, changes in data content, structure, and size
- Supports programming interfaces
- Provides security and control

A DBMS must provide:

- Persistence—the data continue to exist after the application's execution has completed
- Secondary storage management
- Concurrency
- Recovery
- Data definition/data manipulation language (DDL/DML)

Database Models

The logical data model that underlies the database characterizes a DBMS. The common logical data models are listed below:

- *Relational DBMS*. A relational DBMS (RDBMS) structures data into tables that have particular properties. A collection of related tables in the relational model makes up a database. The mathematical theory of relations underlies the relational model—both the organization of data and the languages that manipulate the data. Edgar Codd, then at IBM, developed the relational model in 1973. It has been popular, in terms of commercial use, since the early 1980s.
- *Hierarchical DBMS*. The hierarchical data model organizes data in a tree structure. There is a hierarchy of parent and child data segments. This structure implies that a record can have repeating information, generally in the child data segments. Hierarchical DBMSs were popular from the late 1960s, with the introduction of IBM's Information Management System (IMS) DBMS, through the 1970s.
- *The Network DBMS*. The popularity of the network data model coincided with the popularity of the hierarchical data model. Some

data were more naturally modeled with more than one parent per child. So, the network model permitted the modeling of many-to-many relationships in data. In 1971, the Conference on Data Systems Languages (CODASYL) formally defined the network model.

- *Object-oriented DBMS*. An object-oriented DBMS (OODBMS) must be both a DBMS and an object-oriented system. As a DBMS it must provide particular data management capabilities. OODBMSs typically can model tabular data, complex data, hierarchical data, and networks of data. The following are important features of an object-oriented system:

  - *Complex objects*. For example objects may be composed of other objects.
  - *Object identity*. Each object has a unique identifier external to the data.
  - *Encapsulation*. An object consists of data and the programs (or methods) that manipulate it.
  - *Types or classes*. A class is a collection of similar objects. Inheritance subclasses inherit data attributes and methods from classes.
  - *Overriding with late binding*. The method particular to a subclass can override the method of a class at run time.
  - *Extensibility*. For example a user may define new objects.
  - *Computational completeness*. A general-purpose language, such as Ada, C, C++, or Java is computationally complete. The special-purpose language SQL is not. Most OODBMSs incorporate a general-purpose programming language.

- *Flat file Systems*. A flat file system is usually closely associated with a storage access method. An example is IBM's indexed sequential access method (ISAM). The models discussed earlier in this section are logical data models; flat files require the user to work with the physical layout of the data on a storage device.

- *Distributed DBMS*. A distributed DBMS manages a database that is spread over more than one platform. The database can be based on any of the data models just discussed above (except the flat file). The database can be replicated, partitioned, or a combination of both. A replicated database is one in which full or partial copies of the database exist on the different platforms. A partitioned database is one in which part of the database is on one platform and the other parts are on other platforms. The partitioning of a database can be vertical or horizontal.

  Whether the distributed database is replicated or partitioned, a single DBMS manages the database. There is a single schema (description of the data in a database in terms of a data model, such as relational) for a distributed database. The distribution of the database is generally transparent to the user. The term "distributed DBMS" implies homogeneity.

A distributed, heterogeneous database system is a set of independent databases, each with its own DBMS, presented to users as a single database and system. "Federated" is used synonymously with "distributed heterogeneous." The heterogeneity refers to differences in data models (e.g., network and relational), DBMSs from different suppliers, different hardware platforms or other differences. The simplest kinds of federated database systems are commonly called gateways. In a gateway, one vendor (e.g., Oracle) provides single-direction access through its DBMS to another database managed by a different vendor's DBMS (e.g., IBM's DB2). The two DBMSs need not share the same data model. For example, many RDBMS vendors provide gateways to hierarchical and network DBMSs.

There are federated database systems both on the market and in research that provide more general access to diverse DBMSs. These systems generally provide a schema integration component to integrate the schemas of the diverse databases and present them to the users as a single database, a query management component to distribute queries to the different DBMSs in the federation, and a transaction management component, to distribute and manage the changes to the various databases in the federation.

Data Dictionary/Directory Systems

The second component providing data management services, the data dictionary/directory system (DD/DS), consists of utilities and systems necessary to catalog, document, manage, and use metadata (data about data). The DD/DS is normally provided as part of a DBMS but is sometimes available from alternate sources. In the management of distributed data, distribution information may also be maintained in the network directory system. In this case, the interface between the DD/DS and the network directory system would be through the API of the network services component on the platform.

In current environments, data dictionaries are usually integrated with the DBMS, and directory systems are typically limited to a single platform. Network directories are used to expand the DD/DS realms. The relationship between the DD/DS and the network directory is an intricate combination of physical and logical sources of data.

A repository is a system that manages all of the data of an enterprise, which includes data and process models and other enterprise information. Hence, the data in a repository are much more extensive than those in a DD/DS, which generally defines only the data making up a database.

Data Security

The third component providing data management services is data security. This includes procedures and technology measures implemented to prevent unauthorized access, modification, use, and dissemination of data stored or processed by a computer system. Data security also includes data integrity (i.e., preserving the accuracy and validity of the data) and protecting the system from physical harm (including preventative measures and recovery procedures).

Authorization control allows only authorized users to have access to the database at the appropriate level. Guidelines and procedures can be established for accountability, levels of control, and type of control. Authorization control for database systems differs from that in traditional file systems because, in a database system, it is not uncommon for different users to have different rights to the same data. This requirement encompasses the ability to specify subsets of data and to distinguish between groups of users. In addition, decentralized control of authorizations is of particular importance for distributed systems.

Data protection is necessary to prevent unauthorized users from understanding the content of the database. Data encryption, as one of the primary methods for protecting data, is useful both for information stored on disk and for information exchanged on a network.

7.9   User View

The user view considers the usability aspects of systems and the environment in general. It should also consider impacts on the user such as skill levels required, the need for specialized training, and migration from current practice. The user view takes into account:

- The ease-of-use of the user interfaces and how intuitive they are
- Whether there is transparent access to data and applications, irrespective of location
- Ease of management of the user environment by the user
- Application interoperability through means such as drag and drop
- On-line help facilities
- Clarity of documentation
- Security and password aspects, such as avoiding the requirement for multiple sign-on and password dialogues
- Access to productivity (infrastructure) applications such as mail or a spreadsheet

7.10   System Engineering View

This view of the technical architecture focuses on computing models that are appropriate for a distributed computing environment and on hardware/software and networking. To support the migration of legacy systems, the section also presents models that are appropriate for a centralized environment. The definitions of many of the computing models (e.g., host-based, master/slave, and three-tiered) historically preceded the definition of the client/server model, which attempts to be a general-purpose model. In most cases, the models have not been redefined in the computing literature in terms of contrasts with the client/server model. Therefore, some of the distinctions of features are not always clean. In general, however, the models are distinguished by the allocation of functions for an information system application to various components (e.g., terminals, computer platforms). These functions that make up an information system application are presentation, application function, and data management.

Client/Server Model

Client/server processing is a special type of distributed computing called cooperative processing because the clients and servers cooperate in the processing of a total application (presentation, functional processing, data management). In the model, clients are processes that request services, and servers are processes that provide services. Clients and servers can be located on the same processor, different multiprocessor nodes, or on separate processors at remote locations. The client typically initiates communications with the server. The server typically does not initiate a request with a client. A server may support many clients and may act as a client to another server. Figure 7.4 shows how the client/server model can be drawn following The Open Group technical reference model, showing how the various entities and interfaces can be used to support a client/server model whether the server is local or remote to the client. In these representations, the request–reply relationships would be defined in the API.

Clients tend to be generalized and can run on one of many nodes. Servers tend to be specialized and run on a few nodes. Clients are typically implemented as a call to a routine. Servers are typically implemented as a continuous process waiting for service requests (from clients). Many client/server implementations involve remote communications across a network. However, nothing in the client/server model dictates remote communications, and the physical location of clients is transparent to the server.

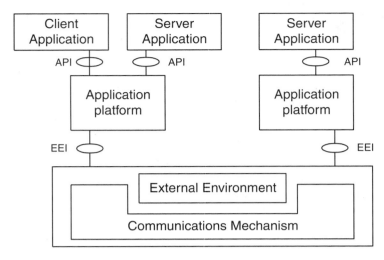

FIGURE 7.4.   Reference model representation of client/server model.

An application program can be considered to consist of three parts data management, business logic, and presentation. In general, each of these can be assigned to either a client or server application, making appropriate use of platform services. This assignment defines a specific client/server configuration (or deployment topology).

Master/Slave and Hierarchical Models

In this model, slave computers are attached to a master computer. In terms of distribution, the master/slave model is one step up from the host-based model. Distribution is provided in one direction, from the master to the slaves. The slave computers perform application processing only when directed to by the master computer. In addition, slave processors can perform limited local processing, such as editing, function key processing, and field validation. A typical configuration might be a mainframe as the master with personal computers (PCs) as the slaves acting as intelligent terminals, as illustrated in Figure 7.5.

The hierarchical model is an extension of the master/slave model with more distribution capabilities. In this approach, the top layer is usually a powerful mainframe, which acts as a server to the second tier. The second layer consists of LAN servers and clients to the first layer as well as servers to the third layer. The third layer consists of PCs and workstations. This model has been described as adding true distributed processing to the master/slave model. Figure 7.5 shows an example hierarchical model in the third configuration, and Figure 7.6 shows the hierarchical model represented in terms of the entities and interfaces of the technical reference model.

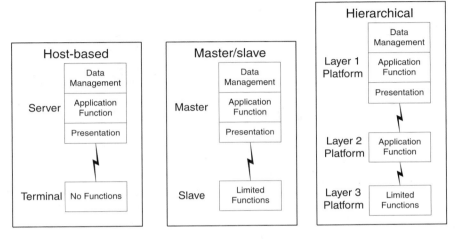

FIGURE 7.5.   Host-based, master/slave, and hierarchical models.

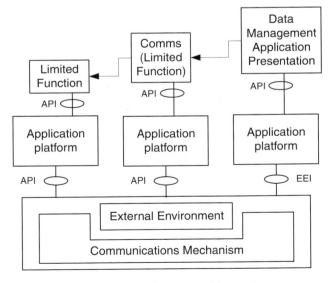

FIGURE 7.6.   Hierarchical model based on reference model.

Peer-to-Peer Model

In the peer-to-peer model there are coordinating processes. All of the computers are servers in that they can receive requests for services and respond to them, and all of the computers are clients in that they can send requests for services to other computers. In current implementations, there often are redundant functions on the participating platforms.

Attempts have been made to implement the model for distributed heterogeneous (or federated) database systems. This model could be considered a special case of the client/server model in which all platforms are both servers and clients. Figure 7.7 (A) shows an example peer-to-peer configuration in which all platforms have complete functions.

Distributed Object Management Model

In this model, the remote procedure calls typically used for communication in the client/server and other distributed processing models are replaced by messages sent to objects. The services provided by systems on a network are treated as objects. A requester need not know the details of how the object is configured. The approach requires:

- A mechanism to dispatch messages
- A mechanism to co-ordinate delivery of messages
- Applications and services that support a messaging interface

This approach does not contrast with client/server or peer-to-peer models but specifies a consistent interface for communicating between

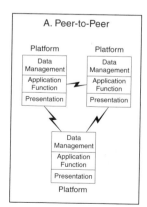
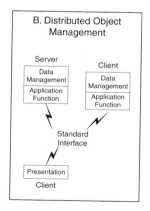
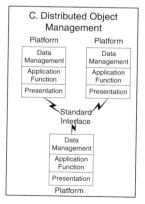

FIGURE 7.7.   Peer-to-Peer and distributed object models.

cooperating platforms. It is considered by some to be an implementation approach for client/server and peer-to-peer models. Figure 7.7 presents two distributed object model examples. Example B shows how a client/server configuration would be altered to accommodate the distributed object management model. Example C shows how a peer-to-peer model would be altered to accomplish distributed object management.

The Object Management Group (OMG), a consortium of industry participants working toward object standards, has developed an architecture—the Common Object Request Broker Architecture (CORBA)—that specifies the protocol a client application must use to communicate with an Object Request Broker (ORB), which in turn provides access to distributed object services (and the actual business objects). The ORB specifies how objects can transparently make requests and receive responses. In addition, Microsoft's COM and Java's J2EE provide similar distributed component services based on a similar model as CORBA but not the same technology (specifications).

7.11 Communications View

Introduction

Communications networks are constructed of end devices (e.g., printers), processing nodes, communication nodes (switching elements), and the linking media that connect them. The communications network provides the means by which information is exchanged. Forms of information include data, imagery, voice, and video. Because automated information systems accept and process information using digital data formats rather than analog formats, the TOGAF communications concepts and guidance will focus on digital networks and digital services. Integrated multimedia services are included.

The communications view describes the communications architecture with respect to geography, discusses the Open Systems Interconnection (OSI) reference model, and describes a general framework intended to permit effective system analysis and planning.

Communications Infrastructure

The communications infrastructure may contain up to three levels of transport—local, regional/metropolitan, and global—as shown in Figure 7.8. The names of the transport components are based on their respective geographic extent, but there is also a hierarchical relationship among them. The transport components correspond to a network management structure in which management and control of network resources are distributed across the different levels. Generally, available (cost-effective) bandwidth reduces by orders of magnitude as the geographic boundaries extend.

The local components relate to assets that are located relatively close together geographically. This component contains fixed communications equipment and small units of mobile communications equipment. Local area networks (LANs), to which the majority of end devices will be connected, are included in this component. Standard interfaces will facilitate portability, flexibility, and interoperability of LANs and end devices.

Regional and metropolitan area networks (MANs) are geographically dispersed over a large area. A regional or metropolitan network could connect local components at several fixed bases or connect separate remote outposts. In most cases, regional and metropolitan networks are used to connect local networks. However, shared databases, regional processing platforms, and network management centers may connect directly or through a LAN. Standard interfaces will be provided to connect local networks and end devices.

Global or wide area networks (WANs) are located throughout the world, providing connectivity for regional and metropolitan networks in the fixed and deployed environments. In addition, mobile units, shared databases, and central processing centers can connect directly to the global network as required. Standard interfaces will be provided to connect regional and metropolitan networks and end devices.

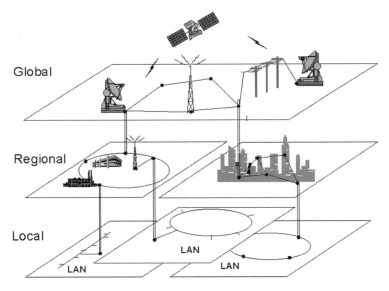

FIGURE 7.8.   Communications infrastructure.

Communications Models

The geographically divided infrastructure described earlier forms the foundation for an overall communications framework. These geographic divisions permit the separate application of different management responsibilities, planning efforts, operational functions, and enabling technologies to be applied within each area. Hardware and software components and services fitted to the framework form the complete model.

The open systems interconnection (OSI) reference model, portrayed in Figure 7.9, is the model used for data communications in TOGAF. Each of the seven layers in the model represents one or more services or protocols (a set of rules governing communications between systems) that define the functional operation of the communications between user and network elements. Each layer (with the exception of the top layer) provides services for the layer above it. The OSI model specifically aims at establishing open systems operation and implies standards-based implementation. It strives to permit different systems to accomplish complete interoperability and quality of operation throughout the network.

The seven layers of the OSI model are structured to facilitate independent development within each layer and to provide for changes independent of other layers. Stable international standard protocols in conformance with the OSI reference model layer definitions have been published by various standards organizations. This is not to say that the only protocols that fit into TOGAF are OSI protocols. Other protocol standards such as SNA or TCP/IP can be described using the OSI seven-layer model as a reference.

The OSI standards are essentially defunct from an industry perspective. Although a number still remain (X.500 and X.400, for instance), very few organizations are implementing the entire OSI stack; predominately, TCP/IP has filled this niche. However, the layered concept is still very much in vogue, and OSI is now probably better known as a euphemistic representation of the generic seven-layered model.

Infrastructure and business applications, as defined in TOGAF, are above the OSI reference model protocol stack and use its services via the applications layer.

A communications system based on the OSI reference model includes services in all of the relevant layers, the infrastructure and business application software that sits above the Application layer of the OSI model, and the physical equipment carrying the data. These elements may be grouped into architectural levels that represent major functional capabilities, such as switching and routing, data transfer, and the performance of applications.

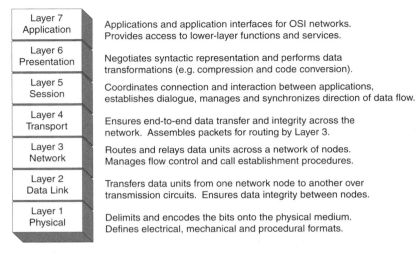

Layer 7 Application	Applications and application interfaces for OSI networks. Provides access to lower-layer functions and services.
Layer 6 Presentation	Negotiates syntactic representation and performs data transformations (e.g. compression and code conversion).
Layer 5 Session	Coordinates connection and interaction between applications, establishes dialogue, manages and synchronizes direction of data flow.
Layer 4 Transport	Ensures end-to-end data transfer and integrity across the network. Assembles packets for routing by Layer 3.
Layer 3 Network	Routes and relays data units across a network of nodes. Manages flow control and call establishment procedures.
Layer 2 Data Link	Transfers data units from one network node to another over transmission circuits. Ensures data integrity between nodes.
Layer 1 Physical	Delimits and encodes the bits onto the physical medium. Defines electrical, mechanical and procedural formats.

FIGURE 7.9.   Open systems interconnection (OSI) model seven-layer model.

These architectural levels are:

- The transmission level (below the physical layer of the OSI model) provides all of the physical and electronic capabilities that establish a transmission path between functional system elements (e.g., wires, leased circuits, interconnects).
- The network switching level (OSI layers 1 through 3) establishes connectivity through the network elements to support the routing and control of traffic (e.g., switches, controllers, network software).
- The data exchange level (OSI layers 4 through 7) accomplishes the transfer of information after the network has been established (end-to-end, user-to-user transfer) involving more capable processing elements (e.g., hosts, workstations, servers).
- In the TRM, OSI application layer services are considered to be part of the application platform entity because they offer standardized interfaces to the application programming entity.
- The applications program level (above the OSI) includes the infrastructure and business applications (non-management application programs).

The communications framework is defined to consist of the three geographical components of the communications infrastructure (local, regional, and global) and the four architectural levels (transmission, network switching, data exchange, and application program), and it is depicted in Figure 7.10. Communications services are performed at one or more of these architectural levels. Figure 7.10 also identifies the relationship of TOGAF to the communications architecture.

Allocation of Services to Components

The communications infrastructure consists of the local, regional, and global transport components. The services allocated to these components are identical to the services of the application program, data exchange, network switching, or transmission architecture levels that apply to a component. Data exchange and network-switching level services are identical to the services of the corresponding OSI reference model layers. Typically, only network-switching and transmission services are allocated to the regional and global components, which consist of communications nodes and transmission media. All services may be performed in the local component, which includes end devices, processing nodes, communications nodes, and linking media. Transmission, switching, transport, and applications are all performed in this component.

7.12 Summary

The ability to take various slices through an organization's architecture and present them in different ways is central to developing and understanding the overall architecture. The technique of using architectural views supports the slicing and dicing of the current and target architec-

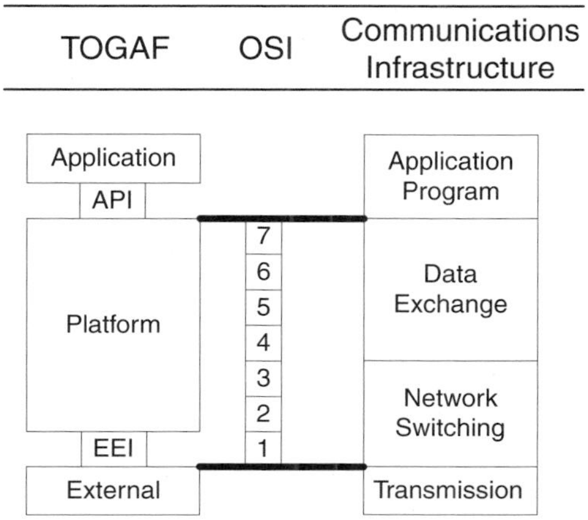

FIGURE 7.10. Communications framework.

tures. This chapter considered a number of TOGAF-specific architectural views, encompassing all aspects of the platform service continuum. We have already seen the use of a number of these views in the previous chapter describing the current environment.

In the next chapter, we continue the assessment of the current environment using further TOGAF-specific techniques to describe the environment in a way that allows us to develop further the understanding necessary to begin the specification of the target architecture.

CHAPTER 8

Target Architecture—Baseline Description in TOGAF Format

8.1   *Introduction*

This chapter begins the description of target architecture development. The first task in the target architecture phase (Phase C) of the architecture development method (ADM) is that of capturing a baseline description in TOGAF terms. The parent phase is depicted in Figure 8.1.

During this phase, we are primarily concerned with the alignment of the requirements, discovery, and analysis work to our chosen foundation architecture, which in this case, of course, is TOGAF. In essence, the concrete baseline is developed into a conceptual model from which the target architecture can be molded.

As we mentioned in Chapter 6, the technical reference model (TRM) is one of the fundamental pillars of the organization's technical architecture—it essentially describes the IT environment. Additionally, The Open Group has augmented TOGAF with a specific instance of the TRM to form part of its *foundation architecture*, at the leftmost end of the architectural continuum. The Open Group's TRM is based on their considerable experience both in open systems and distributed computing and brings together a view of the key service categories (and constituent subcategories) required to be supported by contemporary e-business architectures. It is an important tool at this stage, acting as the target lexicon onto which we translate our gathered information. To date, we have been content to document in organizational, native, or solutions

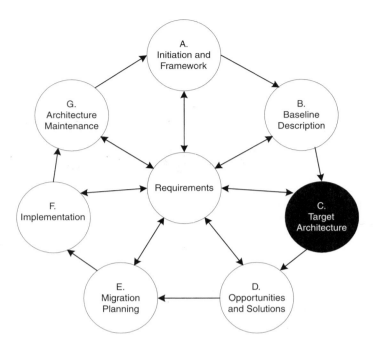

Figure 8.1.   ADM, with target architecture phase highlighted.

terms, but this acts as a barrier to communication, understanding, and progress once we enter the more abstract world of framework development. Figure 8.2 depicts the inception stage of the target architecture phase and shows the locations of the activities required to support the definition of the baseline in TOGAF terms.

Of course, TOGAF is not alone in this requirement for a standardized representation of parochial information. The general process of moving from organizational (i.e., domain) specificity to an abstract representation is a process that occurs in software development methods—the transition from requirements gathering to analysis (and then to design and implementation).

8.2   TOGAF Process

As we have noted before, TOGAF employs a standard and simple format of describing each phase (or activity) within the architecture development method (ADM). Each step is represented by an objective, ap-

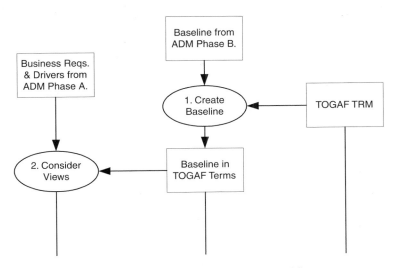

FIGURE 8.2.   Baseline activities of the target architecture phase workflow.

proach, inputs, steps, and outputs. Therefore, the following is the objective of the current tasks:

> The objective of this task is to convert the description of the existing systems into services terminology using terms of the organization's foundation architecture (e.g., the TOGAF Foundation Architecture's Technical Reference Model). The rationale behind this is to structure the existing system description in a way which makes it compatible with the breakdown of standards and the descriptions used within your foundation architecture.

Inputs

The primary inputs for the translation exercise have been gathered from our previous endeavors as we have employed the ADM in our quest for an idealized (or at least pragmatic) technical architecture (see Figure 8.3 for inputs and outputs). The TOGAF process lists the following artifacts as being key enablers:

- Reusable architecture building blocks (from the architecture continuum)—note that Chapter 6 discusses building blocks and why they have not been adopted for use in this text.
- Technical architecture document next version—this version augments the version generated by the baseline description phase described in Chapter 6.

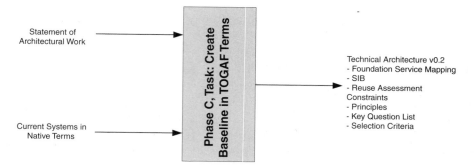

FIGURE 8.3.   Current systems in TOGAF terms wiring diagram.

- Request for architecture work. As we noted in Chapter 5, this may actually be manifest in a myriad of forms other than an actual request for an architecture style document.
- Statement of architecture work. The statement of architecture work was described extensively in Chapter 5 and includes the vision, scope, managerial support, and high-level project plan.
- Reusable solutions building blocks (from Solutions Continuum). Again, the comments relating to architecture building blocks apply here as well.

Steps

Again, TOGAF notes a rather simple partially ordered set of tasks that one can employ to satisfy the requirements of this task.

The activities noted for this task are:

- Collect data on current system description. In essence, this is the output of the preceding phases.
- Document all constraints. This is covered in greater detail in the *architectural constraints* section.
- Brainstorm architecture principles. Key architectural principles and mechanisms are covered in the *architecture principles* section.
- List distinct functionality.
- Produce affinity groupings of functionality using TOGAF TRM service groupings (or your business' foundation architecture).
- Analyze relationships among groupings—associations between groupings highlight interdependencies.
- Sanity check functionality to ensure that all of the current systems are considered. This is the equivalent of an informal gap analysis.

- Identify interfaces. All architectural components, whether as the result of serendipity or design, expose interfaces that other architecture elements depend on and use. Interfaces are covered in greater detail in the *architecture seams and interfaces* section.
- Produce an architecture model view.
- Verify an architecture model view.
- Document key questions to test merits of the architecture.
- Document criteria for selection of the service portfolio architecture.

Note that it is possible to defer or transfer some of these tasks to other phases, but, in keeping with the spirit of TOGAF, we leave their original set intact. However, some of the activities noted are worthy of greater consideration, and these are covered in some of the following sections before we consider the output artifacts that we should generate from our activities.

Architectural Constraints

To ensure that the target architecture is being developed under the correct assumptions, the architect is required to enumerate all constraints that must be reflected in the final product. A constraint is essentially a proposition or predicate that serves to restrain or impose a bound or condition of some sort. Architecturally, we encounter constraints of varying types that serve to help us better design an architecture—in other words, one that meets constraints!

Before we consider common architectural constraints, it is worth noting that we can only state that a constraint is satisfied if it is, in essence, quantitative and therefore provable (within the constraints of Godel's theorem) within some axiomatic framework. A common failing and criticism of constraints that are typically captured is that they are either qualitative or subjective to the extent that their fulfillment is either difficult or impossible to ascertain.

Key definition: **Architectural constraints.**
Constraints are essentially propositions that bound the architecture. Understanding the constraints allows the architecture to reflect the practical (and imperfect) world within which it exists.

Therefore, assuming that we are capable of capturing our technical constraints in a suitably measurable form, what constraints may exist within a domain? The following list suggests some common categories along with some fairly realistic examples:

- *Temporal.* This form of constraint offers key metrics that can guide (at least) the placement of architectural elements, their specifications and capacity. Apart from purely design-centric issues, temporal constraints will also normally form part of the basis of formal user acceptance. Some of the most prevalent temporal constraints include transaction execution times, total response time, ratio of network to client to server execution times, various forms of time out, and so on. Here are some representative constraints:

  > Transaction execution for query-only transactions will not exceed 3 seconds measured from initial transmission from the client through reception and full presentation of the response to the user.

  > The logon process will require no more than 5 seconds to execute, after which time a duly authenticated user will be able to use the system with all appropriate and assigned privileges without further delay.

  > The 95th percentile of transactions in the application server will execute within 2 seconds, with an interquartile range of no more than 1 second.

  > Any response generated from the middle tier to a client (be that an interactive or external "system" client) will be no greater than 20 Kbits in size.

  > The acceptance of an electronic business document from a customer portal should take no longer than 60 seconds to be processed and return a confirmation.

- *Quality attribute.* Such attributes (sometimes called nonfunctional requirements) measure other aspects of the architecture. Some familiar attributes include availability (7×24 and so on), concurrent user support, throughput (possibly in transactions per second or even the Transaction Processing Performance Council—see www.tpc. org—metric of tpm[25]), CPU usage, and disk storage requirements. Here are some relatively standard quality attributes:

  > The application server and database server will be deployed in redundant and load-balanced clusters (using the clustering technology as described in *some company reference*), with the initial cluster size being set at 2.

  > The application server software and associated application software (business components) will have an availability of 99.99%

---

25. Transactions per minute.

in each calendar month between the hours of 7 AM and 5 AM (22-hour day).

The server infrastructure must support a mixed update transaction throughput of 20 transactions per second with the application server configuration operating at less than 40% CPU time consumed and less than 50% of physical memory consumed.

- *Standards*. An important adjunct to the architectural effort is the employment of standards, preferably accepted or accredited ones as opposed to du jour. Standards are defined during the target architecture development, based on the service taxonomy, and described in the standards information base (SIB). The requirement for support or alignment with standards is assuming increasing importance as standards, platforms, and approaches merge or converge. The proprietary "standards" of old (as alluded to and described in Chapter 1) hold little sway in the modern technology landscape. Adherence to standards does not necessarily yield a binary result. For example, it is possible to state that a product supports SNMP. This is not entirely a true or false proposition. Support of SNMP may mean both SNMP v1 and SNMP v2 for example, or it may imply various, but not all, MIB views, in which case this is a conjunction of two or more possibilities (see Chapter 13 for various levels of architectural conformance). This hints at a key theme—that constraints must be as atomic as possible or at least allow deterministic choice among alternatives. Again, some regular examples are:

  The solution must employ the J2EE JMS 1.02 interface for asynchronous message exchange activities.

  Application-constructed and transmitted messages must conform to the defined enterprise message formats, referenced in *document*.

  Business components must be deployed either as CORBA 2.3 objects or as objects compliant with the J2EE Enterprise Java Bean 1.1 standard.

  The application server must support an SNMP v2 agent that supports integration with *Brand X* systems management software.

  The entire physical database model must be demonstrably in *at least* Boyce Codd normal form.

- *Existing TRM/SIB*. In a fashion similar to the standards "argument," organizations and architects can appeal to the extant technical reference model or standards information base of the business. Of course, this can on occasion be preemptive in that the current project is actually in the process of creating the TRM and SIB!

- *Organizational.* These constraints are derived from the function of the organization on the technical architecture. They are not typically technical but rather apply business-specific restrictions. These are the most difficult to discover because they may not have an immediate and obvious impact on the technical environment. Such constraints can include financial, personnel, operational, strategic, and competitive. Some typical examples include:

  The IT budget will be reduced by 10% over the next two years to reflect benefits ascribed to supply chain integration.

  New acquisitions in Europe mean that the IT organization is required to implement a support center in Germany.

  The organization will become a foundation member of the Automobile Standards Organization and adopt its interoperability standards.

- *Compliance and Conformance.* Issues of compliance and conformance can weigh heavily on the consciousness of the architect. An architecture will be deemed *compliant* if it acts generally in accordance with the rules of the technical architecture and *conformant* if it adheres to and acknowledges appropriate or notified standards (again, see Chapter 13). The distinction between the two states is easily blurred, and often one or the other term is used in isolation.

Constraint Satisfaction

The general problem of constraint satisfaction is of fundamental importance in all spheres of computer science. Generally, we are interested in *constraint satisfaction problems* or CSPs; that is, a problem whose solution must satisfy n constraints. Hence, a set of variables, each variable with its own state, can be measured against and shown to obey a set of constraints.

Constraints are relationships among variables and may appear in various cardinalities (unary, binary, and multiplicative, for example). Of course, as the cardinality of a constraint increases, so does the complexity of the problem at hand and therefore the time taken to reach a solution. Continuous domains and complex interrelationships can often lead to a large search space for solutions. A famous CSP, the 8 queens problem, has some 8^8 possible solutions. Yet to be encountered in the architecture space in which we typically operate in is the NP-hard or NP-complete style problem! Much research has occurred in the artificial intelligence community with respect to CSP's (and other generalized state and search-space problems), and many interesting techniques have been formulated that address the whole combinatorial expansion issue in naïve solution space investigation.

Simplistically, architectural constraints are often viewed as unary in nature. We note that this is a flawed view that can lead to significant downstream problems! However, the CSP for most architectural problems is simplified in that the variables have a discrete domain (as opposed, of course, to a continuous domain) and binary or ternary cardinality is the greatest we usually encounter.

For example, let us consider the two constraints introduced in a previous section, restated below:

> Execution time for transactions will not exceed 3 seconds measured from initial transmission from the client through reception and full presentation of the response to the user.

> The 95th percentile of transactions in the application server will execute within 2 seconds, with an interquartile range of no more than 1 second.

These constraints, stated separately, are nonetheless related. By this we mean that an architecture that satisfies constraint #1 at the expense of #2 will not be acceptable. It could also be argued that this problem is rather more difficult than we first perceived because the domain of each variable (in the case of #1, total execution; in the case of #2, a range) is continuous. However, as architects we will distill this problem to its essence and assume that the upper bound of each domain is that which will be acceptable (this can also be considered a vendor style stance!). Therefore, we have a ternary absolute constraint that is satisfied if[26] the total transaction time is never greater than 3 seconds, the application server execution time is never greater than 2 seconds, and 50% of the server execution times centered around the median occurs within 1 second. Although we can express this problem simply, it is still somewhat beyond our means to solve it within the confines of current knowledge. However, this apparently simple problem demonstrates the underlying complexity of architecture design decisions the type that we will be forced to make in the context of our example organization, CFL.

Architecture Principles

We hold that an architecture principle is essentially a canonical predicate. We use the term predicate here deliberately because the nature of a principle in this context very often precludes a truth functional out-

---

26. if and only if.

come. Hence we appeal to higher-order concepts and state that a principle is in fact a generalized (perhaps even idealized) notion. Simply, it is unlikely that one can ever state that a principle is fully upheld, only supported or not supported to varying degrees. Architectural principles are nonetheless guiding architectural mantras that summarize the overall intent of both the IT strategic direction and the ensuing technical architecture resulting from this process. Resulting principles provide necessary vision for all IT initiatives to follow.

Our engagements lead us to believe that principles often fall into the following categories:

- *Strategic.* Aspects that relate to a vision or direction. Such principles may be aligned with actual business strategies (e.g., alignment with industry standards bodies to support the strategy of integrating the supply chain). Conversely, they may be based in culture or "religion" and less substantiation (e.g., we will implement thin client technology).
- *Operational.* Aspects that are of greater concern in the realm of the operational; that is, that area of the (IT) business tasked with ensuring that operational characteristics of the technical architecture (among other things) meet business requirements.
- *Quality (Non functional, technical, pure architectural).* Principles that ensure the quality attributes of the technical architecture. In many instances, these principles intersect (logically) with operational concerns.
- *Functional.* Of less importance and focus in this text, functional concerns exist at a more domain-specific level. Functional principles presuppose the fulfillment of quality and operational principles.
- *Business.* An architecture principle always exists in the information technology domain but is traceable to business requirement, objective, or need. An architecture principle can be classed as more business-oriented in the sense that it exists primarily to fulfill a business requirement and the architecture itself easily with its information technology domain without the requirement per se. In other words, such a principle is primarily rooted in business need rather than the more usual business–IT equilibrium.

Why do we often assert that principles should be held inviolate? It would be convenient to appeal to a vaguely anthropomorphic ideation and note, perhaps even flippantly, that as humankind in its existence requires the presence and observance of principled behavior to ensure a level of civilization, IT architectures would likewise erode and crumble if such principles did not exist. In reality, this is the kernel of the argument and sacrosanct enshrinement of principles is at times slavishly followed. It is possible, with reasoned and accepted principles, to exercise control at a conceptual level with respect to the technical architecture and provide guidance that is inarguable. As we detail some standard principles, it will become apparent that the set of architecture constraints and architecture principles is not disjoint. Perceptually, it will be noted that principles exist on a higher (shall we say) plane than constraints, which are usually closer to propositions than principles. It is important to note that these principles act as an umbrella for the enterprise architecture, and thus affect at least the information architecture, business systems architecture, application architecture, and technical architecture. As the principles are introduced, the terms architecture, component, componentry, and so on should all be assumed as synonyms for enterprise architecture unless otherwise qualified.

Again, our experience leads us to suggest that the following principles are commonly identified by most organizations:

- *Flexibility*. The principle of flexibility notes that services and solutions exhibit the principle of flexibility. In this context, a flexible "solution" can anticipate, facilitate and implement changes in business operation. Changes in business operation vary from process, to legislative to functional.
- *Technology and/or vendor independence*. Many organizations (especially those in the government sphere) require that architectures, solutions, or services be vendor-independent, to facilitate contestability, replacement, or simpler interoperability or integration. Of course, vendor independence may also compromise one's ability to negotiate preferential rates or treatment, and it is not unusual for (larger) organizations to nominate a preferred list of suppliers for certain services, allowing a degree of negotiation to occur to support cost containment.
- *Secure*. Virtually all business operations require that confidentiality, authentication, auditability, and authorization be observed as key architectural requirements. Increasingly, the notion of nonrepudiation[27] is becoming accepted as another security aspect that cannot be overlooked.
- *Timely information*. Information should be delivered within certain timing constraints identified as necessary by the business. As a core principle, this has a rather more qualitative flavor than the other principles mentioned here. It in fact integrates more detailed quality attributions under a common banner that still captures a noble intent—see the discussion at the beginning of this chapter that explains why principles are often not propositional in nature or expression.

---

27. Nonrepudiation: the provision that an action issued by a party (organization, individual, and so on) cannot later be denied to have been issued by that party.

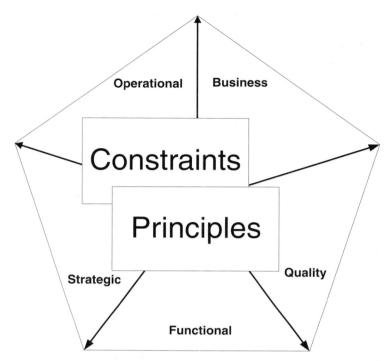

FIGURE 8.4.   Relationship among categories, principles and constraints.

- *Scalable*. This principle maintains the ability of the architecture to deterministically scale as the requirements of the business alter. This is of course usually a monotonic function of behavior (i.e., scalability encapsulates *increasing* demand).
- *Fault tolerant*. Many quality attributes concern themselves with the availability of the architecture and its hosted componentry. Although fault tolerance is a rather strong phrase, it states the apex to which services and the architecture should aspire.
- *Standards-based*. This principle has an identifiable tension with that of technology and vendor independence. Essentially, an organization endorses this principle to ensure contestability, replaceability, and longevity. This principle is often supported by the foundation architecture. In TOGAF, the standards information base underpins this idea.
- *Manageable*. This obviously relates to operational concerns, in that managing the architecture directly supports operations. Without the ability to manage the architecture (at a systems level) and its hosted applications, componentry and so on, chaos or at least uncertainty with respect to the delivery of business function will ensue.

- *Interoperable*. Another platform quality, concerned with enabling the effective integration of both intra- and inter-organizational information systems. Interoperability is an important issue in architecture design and deployment. The ability of solutions to be rapidly integrated with reasonable cost has never been more important than with the advent of Internet time. This principle is interdependent with standards and technology independence.

The preceding principle types represent a number of generic assertions. Organizations will often include principles that relate specifically to IT architectures. For instance, the declaration that all systems will follow a specific client/server model, or that centralized data storage is required, can reflect a reasonable, although rather detailed, architectural principle.

Each principle should also describe the rationale for its selection. This traces the principle to its intent. Also indicate the implications of executing under the principle. For instance a principle stating the use of open standards will require possible migration away from non-standard technology and the completion of a SIB.

We introduce Figure 8.4 to relate principle categories, principles, and constraints. Note the intersection of principles and constraints and the higher-level intersection with principle categories.

8.3   *The Nature of Service-Biased Mapping*

We return now to the underlying theme in the chapter and phase of the ADM—the mapping of the baseline captured in organizational-specific (or native) terms to one phrased in terms and concepts drawn from the foundation architecture.

To begin with we note again the fundamental tenets of TOGAF—the technical reference model (TRM) and the standards information base (SIB). The TRM presents, among other things, the taxonomy of logical services to be provided in support of business and infrastructure applications. The TOGAF TRM is the starting point for the definition of the organization's TRM. It prescribes a relatively simple taxonomy to facilitate effective partitioning of necessary services into the platform.

The SIB is effectively a standards reference library generated from the architectural development process, specifically in the latter stages of development, where the abstract notions of the service portfolio (embodied within the TRM) are described in concrete terms as technology standards. An organizational SIB represents those standards that have been specifically adopted within an organization's technical architecture.

We are mapping from native terms to TOGAF foundation architecture terms (i.e., from the concrete to the abstract) and concern ourselves in this phase with those aspects of the current systems that will come to make up the platform. The objective is to discover the platform services embedded within the current systems and position them within the TRM. In this case, we will use the TOGAF foundation architecture (the left most point of the architectural continuum) TRM. Figure 8.5 pictorially describes the process of service mapping.

"Current system" needs some definition. We adopt a more heuristic classification of current systems for the purposes of architecture development. Given that it is necessary to understand all of the services and technologies (embodied in the TRM and SIB, respectively) held within the IT environment, our segmentation of systems must ensure a full treatment of the environment. Therefore a "system," in relation to the architecture, can be any of the following:

■ *Business Applications.* These include Logistics, CRM, and reactor monitoring, for example.

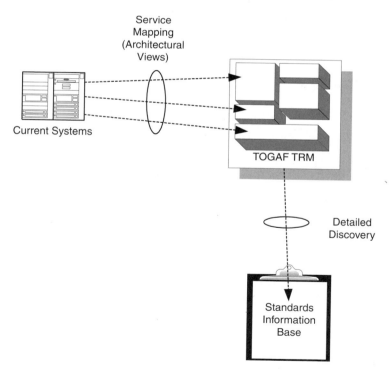

Figure 8.5.   Mapping systems to services.

- *Infrastructure Applications.* This provides general-purpose business support functions, such as e-mail, videoconferencing, file and document management, calendar/scheduling.
- *Infrastructure.* This provides underlying environments not tied directly to any particular business function but that support either business or infrastructure applications. It includes services and technologies not captured in the previous two classifications (e.g., the network, systems management).

Although we suggest that the use of the TOGAF foundation architecture is the de facto reference model for this mapping, the architect could if time permits consider developing a first-cut organizational architecture by moving along the continuum; that is, converging toward a tentative organization-specific view of the services through analyzing common services, industry, and specific organizational requirements of the current systems (for full details of this process, see Chapter 10's treatment of the target architecture service portfolio). However, this approach may not add the necessary value to the process, while consuming time. Focusing intensively on the structure of the current systems in TOGAF organizational architecture terms usually is not effective, especially because this work is likely to be invalidated, or superseded, by work done in determining the target architecture. This approach may also unduly affect the thinking surrounding the development of the target. It can be effective if the architectural project is driven by the need to document the existing environment in a consistent architectural format but major evolutionary changes are not solicited.

Given a TOGAF foundation service taxonomy for describing the current systems, the approach is that of service-to-service mapping; that is, assess the current system against each foundation service, determining whether it exists in the system. Furthermore, carry out this mapping not only by service categories but at a subcategory level as well. Test each system for service sub-categories by tracking linearly through the TOGAF foundation architecture, for instance:

Does the system use remote process access?

Is there any security auditing provided in the system?

One useful technique to use in carrying out the mapping is architectural views. Introduced in Chapter 7, views provide an excellent mechanism for drilling into particular service areas. Note from Chapter 7 that most TOGAF-focused views are aligned along service boundaries. Describing each system using the TOGAF views will support discovery of foundation services and SIB entries.

As we have postulated already, moving along the architectural continuum may not add the necessary value at this stage. However, changes to the foundation TRM may be necessitated by specific systems or requirements. It may be necessary to augment the foundation TRM by adding additional service categories or modifying individual service subcategories (TOGAF lists sub-categories for all services described in the TRM). This may be necessary if systems include specialized services not in the current TRM, such as robotic control services. This type of adjustment is encouraged, and should be carried forward into the baseline target TRM.

The final task is to build a SIB to describe the technologies that support each of the TRM's services. These two artifacts, the TRM and the SIB, provide an excellent snapshot of the enterprise technical architecture. They can be used effectively for communications purposes to describe the current technical structure (or environment) of the organization.

Building the SIB is based on cataloging the technologies that support the logical services. An issue to be cognizant of at this point is depth. There must be a conscious decision as to the amount of detail that will be collected on each service. The reader is encouraged to review The Open Group SIB[28] to understand the level of detail possible within the SIB. It is not mandatory that the architect analyze a system in this detail, however. For instance, it is possible to merely take a product view (e.g., transaction processing is provided by BEA WebLogic™). Further depth can be considered, for instance at a high-level specification level (e.g., transaction processing is provided by the J2EE suite of standards or by JTS / JTA). It is entirely possible to descend toward an application component level (e.g., the authentication service is a custom component that supports the following interfaces). This would be the lowest level we would recommend. The more detail considered, the easier it is to lose sight of the holistic view of technology within the organization. The idea is not to describe fully the engineering of the system but rather to capture a view of the important "platform" technologies present in the environment and used within the systems.

In formulating the SIB, each system and the interfaces between systems are treated individually. This leads to more effective recognition of service and technology gaps and overlaps. The objective is to extract all of the foundation services from a system, and align them with the foundation service categories. The most effective way of doing this is to walk through each foundation service category (and subcategory) and "test" against the system. For instance:

---

28. See http://www.opengroup.org/sib.htm.

What operating system services are used by the system?

What transaction processing service is it using?

How is the system managed?

What security services are supported and what interfaces do they expose?

When testing the system in this manner, it is important to consider the functional, technological, and quality aspects as a single package. The scope of most contemporary systems will include at least the following technology areas:

- Operating systems on which it runs
- Networks (and network protocols) supporting its distributed nature
- Security functions
- Systems management support
- Interfaces with other systems
- Databases
- Middleware to provide transaction management, messaging, distributed data, web serving, and other services
- Hardware
- Nonfunctional requirements (such as performance, availability, and security)
- Development tools used to support it (and possibly methodologies used in both development and support)
- Policies that guide the system's use

This list may look familiar. It is the basis of the TOGAF foundation architecture, the TOGAF TRM.

The next level of detail is that of the service subcategory. The subcategory provides an extra level of service specialization. Reviewing the specific TOGAF subcategories can provide a hint for the architect as to what characteristics a subcategory has and at what level the system should be viewed when considering technology, specifications, and products. In general, subcategories provide further refinement of the service (conceptual) taxonomy without implying exactly how individual services are demarcated. They could be considered categories in their own right, for instance.

The platform service categories, as defined by TOGAF, are reasonably self-evident; we know that applications require network services for communications and data management services for storing information. However, the TOGAF sub-categorization of the foundation services can appear less intuitive. For example, is a protocol that supports distribution of data categorized under network or data-management services? Which service categorizations represent the technologies embodied within an e-mail environment? TOGAF offers subcategories within the foundation architecture. For example, the network service is subdivided into:

- Data communications services
- Electronic mail services
- Enhanced telephony functions
- Shared screen functions
- Videoconferencing functions
- Broadcast functions
- Mailing list functions
- Distributed time services
- Distributed data services
- Distributed file services
- Distributed name services
- Remote process (access) services
- Remote print spooling and output distribution services

As can be seen, this is a reasonably eclectic collection, and there is bound to be healthy discussion regarding the validity of their placement here. Remember, however, that these are part of the foundation architecture (at the left edge of the architectural continuum). During the development of the target architecture, we will be augmenting and refining these categories as we move along the continuum toward the organizational architecture. For instance, we may move videoconferencing into a "multi media" service if this reflects the importance of such a service to the organization. Subcategories such as distributed time, data, name, and remote processes may move into a distributed computing or component computing service. Again, we are stressing the nonprescriptive nature of the framework approach and the general flexibility that pervades TOGAF.

The categories defined during this phase are not cast in stone; they will be refined throughout the process. At this stage, however, they can either be used as described or can be adopted as a guide and refined. Remember to be consistent. Furthermore, capture only those categories (and subcategories) that are reflected in the current systems. If there are no videoconferencing facilities used within the systems, do not adopt that categorization at this point. At the end of this stage, the architect should have a TRM encapsulating the service categories and subcategories present in the current systems only. Table 8.1 provides a summary template for capturing service and technology information for systems.

Table 8.1. Information collection template.

Information System <name> Application Type: <Business Application | Infrastructure Application | Infrastructure>			
	Subcategory	Present?	Technologies Supported
Operating system services			
Network services			
Software engineering services			
Security services			
Systems and network management			
Transaction processing			
Location & directory services			
User interface			
International operation			
Data interchange			
Data management			
Graphics & image services			
Platform qualities			

8.4 Reuse Assessment and Requirements Traceability

The ADM introduces but does not elaborate on the idea that requirements (from a number of different perspectives) can be captured in such a way to facilitate requirements traceability across the requirements, design, and implementation phases, a sort of tripartite gap-analysis tool if you will. Our treatment of constraints and principles provides information in this area. Key requirements for the architectural program will be based on these constraints and principles and include strategic input from the ISSP, business, and e-business strategies.

Key Definition: **Requirements traceability.**
Each stage of TOGAF's ADM stresses the need to review the stage's outputs with the established requirements. Gap analysis is a technique used to support traceability analysis.

The ADM does however, note that the architecture team should at least create a key question list. However, in spite of the fact that this artifact is a view over existing information, its value will be apparent when one conducts a gap analysis and attempts to understand the completeness of the key question responses to the architectural deliverables. The key question list is a living document that supports requirements traceability by establishing a set of questions to "ask" of the architecture. Its typical genesis is the initiation phase of the ADM (Phase A), where it is built from information gathered from processes like the ISSP or the business systems architecture. The key question list is extended in this phase until it supports the ability to test the defined target architecture. Chapter 10 provides a further treatment on this mechanism.

The nature of the ADM at this point indicates an understanding that, apart from concerns of completeness, the existence of an audit trail is often required to note, support, or illuminate architectural decisions. Certainly in governmental projects, architecture decisions are often subject to external (crown, state or federally appointed or nominated) quality-assurance processes.

The specific artifacts of the ADM requirements relevant to this phase are as shown in the following list:

- Acceptance criteria
- Criteria for choosing specifications
- Criteria for selection of portfolios of specifications
- Criteria to test merits of architecture (key question list)

As is reasonably obvious, the outputs shown are recasts of the basic constraints and principles we have already outlined. However, depending on one's organization or audience, such restatements can be valuable, providing insight or more easily digestible views of what is after all an important adjunct to target architecture design—the assurance that the design does in fact support key requirements.

The description of the current systems (in TOGAF form) represents little in the way of analysis. We have merely cataloged. Applying a traceability assessment is a key step in this phase to ensure that the development of the technical architecture is not carried out in isolation from the driving business factors (as is so often the case).

In each major phase of the ADM, the current technical architecture position is aligned with the requirements (see Figure 8.6). During the development of the target architecture it is typical to conduct a requirements traceability activity multiple times due to the long strides taken in each activity.

There are some key questions (hence the key question list artifact) we need to answer. Do the services provided by the current systems meet

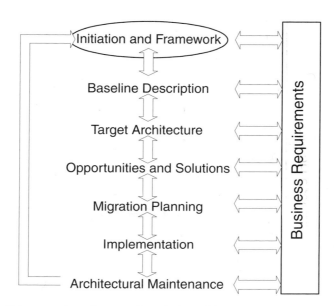

FIGURE 8.6.   Relevance of requirements through the architecture process.

the strategic requirements (both business and technical) of the organization? Is the technology implemented within these systems consistent with the organization's direction? What technology overlaps exist? What technology constraints are imposed, and how does this affect the target architecture? In short, what services and technologies are reusable and where are the issues?

Analyzing the current systems is enabled through the description of the environment in a formal way (that is TOGAF). We are able to investigate how the current environment will progress to the target architecture, taking into account external constraints, architectural principles, gaps and overlaps in the technology, and any inhibitors. This is shown in Figure 8.7. The objective is to understand how the current environment will transition into the target environment (i.e., understand what can be reused. At this stage, the key artifacts aiding the assessment include:

- Architectural vision and principles
- Business and e-business strategies and requirements (described in the business systems architecture)
- The ISSP
- Constraints
- Current system issues (from baseline)

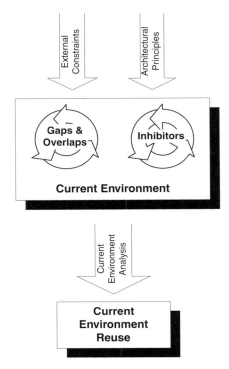

FIGURE 8.7.   Reuse assessment factors.

Usually a large amount of information has already been collected with respect to constraints, requirements, strategies, and so on. Effort is required to compile these into a form that supports their use in analyzing the current environment. A method we have used to do this is a form of gap table (an output of gap analysis). All relevant factors are gathered and classified together. Typically, the classification should bring together the following elements:

- *Strategic imperative.* These will come from the ISSP, the Business strategy, the architectural principles, and so on. Capture only those that have relevance to the technical environment.
- *Stated business requirements.* These are usually sourced from the business systems architecture, or equivalent document, and specific strategies such as the e-business strategy. Consider high-level business functions rather than detailed functional requirements.
- *Constraints.* Include all aspects of constraints, such as financial, temporal, organizational, technical, and so forth.

It is likely that the preceding elements have already been clustered during the strategic development process in some form of a strategy/ requirements hierarchy. Figure 8.8 shows a model that represents such a hierarchy. The technical architecture is driven by the ISSP and architectural principles. These, in turn, are influenced by the business strategy work completed (including an e-business strategy). The current environment should then be assessed regarding its ability to support these strategic elements.

When collecting the elements, attempt to restrict the assessment to those that have some bearing on the technical architecture. Avoid elements that are specifically tied to functional requirements—these are considered part of the business systems architecture, not the technical architecture. Be careful when making this separation, however; as we have already stated, there is always the possibility for collections of business functions to be identified as reusable platform services.

For each strategic element, we cluster the related elements, including

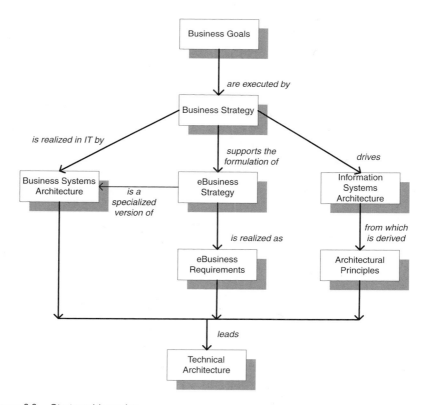

FIGURE 8.8.   Strategy hierarchy.

e-business strategy and requirements, information systems strategy, and architectural principles. Then, we determine how the current environment enables or inhibits the element. This need not be an in-depth assessment. We are merely looking for gaps or deficiencies in the IT environment so that they may be targeted during the development of the target architecture. For instance, given a strategy that states that cost of IT ownership be controlled, the architect need not conduct a full TCO analysis to form an opinion of the extent of a problem.[29] The TCO strategic imperatives can be realized through a reduction in the number of e-mail applications, an increase in the reach of systems management tools, and so on. Table 8.2 shows an example of a table that can be used for the reuse assessment.

Table 8.2. Current environment reuse assessment.

Strategic Element	Provided Through	Affecting Technology Service	Provision Assessment

It is possible that technology components of the current environment could hinder the meeting of the organization's strategic objectives. A technology component that inhibits the fulfillment of the strategic element is potentially a candidate for divestiture. At the very least, this indicates issues that will need to be tackled by the target architecture. On the other hand, a technology enabler indicates a candidate for reuse, moving unchanged or modified into the target environment.

During analysis, the architect should also consider technical gaps and overlaps. It is unlikely in this type of analysis that technical gaps will be found when comparing the logical services in the environment with the environment's systems, given that the services have been derived from the current systems in the first place. However, it is more likely that overlaps will be discovered. How many e-mail systems exist? How many different methods are there for exchanging interorganizational information?

To identify gaps, consider building a matrix like the one in Table 8.3. The cells in the matrix represent the technologies that provide the TOGAF services within each system. In the ideal (and unrealistic) world, each service will be supported by one technology across all systems (or at least a small, reasoned number of complementary technologies); for

---

29. In some circumstances, a full TCO analysis may be a requirement if this is a major area of concern for senior management.

Table 8.3. Service technology matrix.

		Systems		
		System 1	System 2	System n
Services	Service 1			
	Service 2			
	Service 3			
	Service 4			
	Service 5			
	Service n			

instance, one common security service, a single network protocol, one type of object request broker, and so on. This is an ideal because:

- System and environment integration is enhanced.
- Reuse (both platform and application service) is enhanced.
- Systems management is streamlined.
- Vendor relationships are clear.
- Organizational skills are maximized.
- The specification of new system technical requirements is clear.
- Development effort is reduced.
- There are many additional reasons leading to a reduction in the total cost of owning IT.

This is, of course, one of the objectives of the technical architecture. The ideal is somewhat utopian, but the objective for most organization types is to converge toward this utopia. Some Type A organizations may, however, be able to sustain this type of chaos to a limited degree.

We would not expect the current environment to show these characteristics immediately. Therefore, this matrix will aid the architect in understanding where some of the major areas of overlap are. These are documented in an updated current system assessment section of the technical architecture document. They can then feed into the target architecture development, allowing the architect to put in place strategies to mitigate the overlap.

During the assessment of the current systems in native terms (see Chapter 6) a similar, but less formal, analysis was carried out when assessing issues associated with the current systems. Consider the native analysis as a benchmark, and combine the gap analysis in TOGAF terms to support a full picture of the gaps. The gap assessment enables the architect to determine the problems to be solved during the development of the target architecture. Finally, the analysis should be summarized and cataloged against each of the current systems and each of the services. For each system/service combination collect:

- The relevant requirements that are either enabled or inhibited by the system
- The technology overlaps
- The match of the current services with the key TOGAF service characteristics

With this information we are able to make a first-cut judgment of the state of the current environment, the likelihood of a system being reused, and the problems that will need to be solved during the target architecture development.

Of course, there will always be conflict between requirements. IT constraints can affect business initiatives. Financial constraints will affect technical initiatives. IT and business strategies can be misaligned (although theoretically this should never happen, the odds are high). The architecture is often the first meeting ground for these issues as the architect attempts to realize the organization's business vision with technology. It is therefore important to implement a robust issues management process to ensure that these contentions are managed through to resolution. This would typically involve a well-positioned steering group who are able to make sure decisions on behalf of the business. Decisions in this area may then require changes of requirements, and these must be fed back to the relevant sources (e.g., the holder of the business strategy, the ISSP champion).

Selection Criteria

During the development of the target architecture, the architect will be required to assess and select technologies to fill gaps or meet new requirements. It is key, therefore, that there be clearly documented criteria available for selecting technology. At this stage in the process, the first draft of the selection criteria can be established. The criteria must be precise enough to be accurately measured against products and standards, for example, but general enough to relate to all service categories.

The organization's architectural principles should be carried forward and embodied within the criteria. The criteria will then be used for formal and/or informal technology "tenders." The architect can derive the criteria from a number of places:

- Architectural principles
- ISSP or IT guidelines/policies
- Business (or e-Business) strategy
- TOGAF

TOGAF provides a set of criteria used by The Open Group in the development of the foundation architecture. These are described in

Table 8.4, and can provide an excellent basis for development of the organization's own criteria. Before using (or adapting) the TOGAF criteria, the architect should ensure that there is alignment between the organization and The Open Group with respect to technology philosophy. The Open Group is primarily focused on standards-based technology, interoperability, and portability—this should also be the organization's focus.

More organization-specific criteria may include:

- Adherence to current technical architecture
- The ability to be supported by the skills currently available within the IT group
- The acceptability to the organization's outsourcer
- Supporting industry-sector strategies (interorganizational, and within the same domain)
- Adheres to regulatory constraints

Key Questions List

Key definition: **Key Questions List.**
The KQL is a TOGAF artifact, specifically in the requirements traceability area. The key question list is a set of qualitative and quantitative questions posed at the emerging architecture to test its adherence to requirements.

Another useful method for conducting requirements traceability is through the use of a *key question list* (introduced earlier). The key question list is a set of qualitative and quantitative questions posed to the emerging architecture to test its adherence to requirements. This is a list that will evolve through the architectural development process. Typically, the list is owned by the sponsor for the architectural development (this may be the Chief Information Officer), who will use the outcome to measure the success of the architectural program in general and the target architecture specifically. But the questions should also be managed and used by the architect throughout the project to ensure that output is continually being traced against the requirements (see Figure 8.6).

Although defining the key question list can occur during this stage, its contents are not usually answered at this point unless there is some benefit in retroactively assessing the current environment against the questions.

Defining the list can be a difficult exercise. It can be useful to imagine oneself as a "user" of the environment to be created by the architecture—

Table 8.4. TOGAF selection criteria.

Criteria	Explanation
Nondiscriminatory implementation	If the specification is taken from an existing product source licensable from a single vendor only, then implementations should be available to all companies on a nondiscriminatory basis. This includes pricing and licensing conditions.
Availability of dependencies	If an implementation requires other products or services to be usable (e.g., protocols), the complementary products or services must be publicly available, specified by The Open Group or obtainable from multiple sources.
Availability of implementations	Commercial availability of implementations.
Completeness of specification	The interfaces to be adopted must be specified sufficiently that a conformant product may be implemented (and usable) using only: • The specification itself • Products or services (e.g., protocols) that are publicly available or obtainable from multiple sources on a non-discriminatory basis • Formal standards from accredited standards development organizations • Other specifications originated or adopted by The Open Group • Other freely available information
Freedom to develop	Freedom for anyone to develop a practical product that either supports or uses the same specification, subject to the need to license any predisclosed patents.
Future access	The contributor to give The Open Group access to all future versions of the material with no obligation on The Open Group to adopt them.

Table 8.4. TOGAF selection criteria (*continued*).

Criteria	Explanation
Immunity from liability	An assurance that a person developing a product in accordance with the specification is immune from any liability to the contributor of the material in respect of the use by him or his customers of such material other than through failure to properly license predisclosed patents.
Market need	Evidence that there is a market need for the interface. For example: • Customer requirement • Requirement derived from The Open Group's product management activities • Vendor-submitted evidence
No proprietary lock in	The interfaces to be adopted are complete in that it is not necessary to use any additional interfaces retained as proprietary to create commercially usable products.
Nondiscriminatory patents	If the interfaces to be adopted are covered by patents, such patents must be licensed by their owners on a reasonable and nondiscriminatory basis.
Other activities	Understanding of activities in this area in other consortia and official standards bodies
Specification availability	The availability of a high-quality specification on which The Open Group activities can be based
Test suite availability	The availability of a test suite that could be used as the basis for conformance testing

"user" in this sense should be viewed somewhat abstractly; for instance, this may imply an application, a business objective, a senior executive, or even a competing organization. The objective then is to define a list of key questions to search the architecture for any deficiencies. The questions should fundamentally be based around the driving principles and strategies.

The list should contain quantifiable questions; that is, questions that can be ranked or measured objectively (bear in mind that few forms of question, except perhaps a mathematical proposition, can be totally objective). It is common to be able to provide answers to such questions based on a ranking or scoring mechanism. A ranking continuum would represent points such as:

- exceeds—meets—partially meets—does not meet—not applicable
- high—medium—low
- no change—better—worse

Scoring using such an approach is able to produce a single weighted measure describing the quantifiable level of adherence of the architecture.

The list could also contain quality-based questions. Typically, such questions will be more searching, more likely to contain subjectivity in the answers, and less likely to be fully measurable. These questions should focus on the critical success criteria that govern the architectural project. They should be phrased using openings such as "how" and "what." Reviewing the current technology environment issues is a good place to start.

In reality the key question list is derived from and becomes part of the overall requirements of the architectural program. Furthermore, it is able to provide important measures (some quantifiable) of the success of the program. Its contents will evolve through the development process as more of the architecture is discovered. The development of the service portfolio (see Chapter 10) is the first point at which answers will be provided to the questions in the list. The answers will also change during the process as further detail is discovered. This evolution is an important concept to ensure that the architectural development is successful.

Table 8.5. Example key question list.

Key Question List				
		Rating		
Quantitative Questions	**1**	**2**	**3**	**4**
To what extent …?				
Qualitative Questions	Assessment			
How will …?				
What will …?				

8.5 Outputs

The documented artifacts for this activity are encompassed within the technical architecture document, producing the next version, in this case version 0.2. This stage augments the document with the following:

- Technical reference model based on TOGAF TRM describing the current systems
- Standards information base for the current systems
- Constraints definition
- Architecture principles definition
- Requirements traceability for the current systems
- Current system re-use assessment
- Key questions list
- Selection criteria for selection of service portfolio

8.6 Example

In this section, we continue the development of the CFL technical architecture with the assessment of the current systems in TOGAF format.

Our first job is to collect CFL's strategic requirements (including constraints and principles) into a requirements hierarchy to support gap analysis and reuse assessment. The organization's strategic requirements have been collected during the initiation and early baseline phases. Table 8.6 brings together these requirements to allow us to assess CFL's systems. We have decided to use a numeric scale to determine the degree to which the current systems support the business strategies. In summarizing the technical environment, we note that:

- There is very little in the current environment that supports the e-business strategy. In fact, at this point, the environment inhibits the strategy.
- There are a number of constraints to supporting the control of internal process costs, and in particular, TCO. Issues such as the lack of interface quality and the inability to commoditize and generalize the IT environment significantly impact our ability to achieve TCO control.
- The internal environment has evolved without coordination and control—the Logistics system is the only system that supports any sort of robust IT discipline. The ability to support increased effective use of internal processes is inhibited by the environment.

Table 8.6. Requirements analysis.

Key:	Provision Assessment:
(IS) = ISSP Strategy	1 = Not provided for in Current Environment
(BS) = Business Strategy	3 = Some aspects exist in Environment
(ES) = e-business Strategy	5 = Fully provided for in Environment
(ER) = e-business Requirement	
(AP) = Architectural Principles	
(C) = Constraint	

Strategic Element	Provided Through	Affecting Current System	Provision Assessment
Support the development of high-value and differentiated products for continued growth. (BS)	Provide CFL with the capability to develop faster solutions for future business problems. (ES)	Internet infrastructure, Logistics, Sales, Network	1
	Provide a gateway into the internal business-to-business processes to our high-value customers. (ES)		1
	e-business initiatives are scheduled to be presented to the market in 6 months. (C)		n/a
	Offer a catalog browsing service to customers. (ER)		1
	Offer electronic ordering for key (yet to be identified) customers. (ER)		1
	Electronic supply chain integration with CFL's two leading raw material suppliers. (ER)		1
	Internet. Establish an Internet infrastructure to support e-business. (IS)		2
	Packages. Implement package solutions when requirements exhibit common functionality with industry solutions. Only build if the system is strategic and totally unique to CFL. (IS)		3
Be a best-cost producer. (BS)	Reduce the cost of business transactions—all (ES) will support reduction of cost. (ES)	Logistics, Internet infrastructure	1
Support pursuit of target growth opportunities, particularly in international markets. (BS)	All (ES) will aid in supporting growing target market growth through the provision of services not provided by our competitors.	n/a	1
	Reporting. (IS)		1

Table 8.6. Requirements analysis (*continued*).

Strategic Element	Provided Through	Affecting Current System	Provision Assessment
Manage the business globally. (BS)	International coverage. Extend the CFL IT environment to the International offices in a seamless way. (IS)	Network, Systems Management	3
	A UK support center is required. (C)		1
Deliver outstanding customer service and support. (BS)	Improve customer convenience. (ES)	Internet Infrastructure, Logistics	2
	Manufacturing is a 24×7 operation. (C)		5
CFL will be aligned with the Confectionary Manufacturers Association and is required to meet their standards. (BS)	Align technical architecture with CMA standards where possible and practical. (AP)	n/a	1
Streamline internal business processes for best cost. (BS)	Merge to a common architecture. (IS)	All IT Environment	1
	Control technology total cost of ownership. (IS)		2
	Interface Quality. Ensure the quality (both information and reliability) of interfaces between systems. (IS)		1
	Vendor partnerships. Reduce the number of vendors providing services and products for CFL. (IS)		2
	The IT group's budget will be reduced by 5% per annum. (C)		n/a
	No current plans to replace Logistics (renewed contract for 4 years). (C)		n/a
	Best of breed. Implement only best-of-breed (but not necessarily open), medium- to low-risk technology; do not play on the hype curve. (IS)		3
	Implement best-of-breed (not bleeding-edge) technology. (AP)		3
	Centralize processing and data at HQ where possible. (AP)		3
	All computers are networked together with a consistent architecture. (AP)		3

Table 8.6. Requirements analysis (*continued*).

Strategic Element	Provided Through	Affecting Current System	Provision Assessment
Improve ease of use of internal systems and processes. (BS)	Systems management. Centralize and streamline systems management tools and processes to increase user satisfaction. (IS)	Systems management, Interface infrastructure, Network, all business systems	3
	Usability. Reduce the effort users apply when interfacing with business systems. (IS)		3
	Computer technology must be widely employed. (AP)		3
	Computing and networking resources must be reliable, secure, and capable of delivering accurate information in a timely and consistent manner. (AP)		3
	Information must be within reach of all users, regardless of location. (AP)		2
	The mechanisms required to locate, access, and communicate data required by users must be transparent. (AP)		2
	Applications must be designed to allow users to work with data in ways most productive for them. (AP)		2
	Applications must work with each other. (AP)		1
	Software development must be consistent. (IS)		2
Ensure the integrity of our intellectual property. (BS)	Security. Ensure the integrity of CFL information and IT, especially in the opening up of business process to our partners. (IS)	All IT environment	2

The next activity is to create a catalog of services, based on the TOGAF TRM, and map them to the current environment. We take a minimalist approach, using the standard TOGAF platform service categories, and describe only those subcategories (again, directly from TOGAF) that exist in all of the current systems. The two leftmost columns of Table 8.7 highlight the services found in the current systems. We did not include all current systems (a number of regional systems could not be fully discovered) in this assessment. The in-scope systems included the following:

- Logistics (business application)
- Sales (Business application)
- Financial (Business application)
- Marketing (Business application)
- Logistics (Business application)
- Human Resources (Business application)
- Email / Collaboration (infrastructure application)
- Internet (Infrastructure application)
- Systems Management (infrastructure application)
- Network (infrastructure)
- Security (infrastructure)
- LAN Services (infrastructure)

For each "system", we researched the technology that supported each service category. Considering the problems discovered with the current environment, we restricted the depth of this analysis via the following rules:

- Specification (standard, protocol, etc.), if obvious
- Product, if it was too difficult to describe the technology
- Other stereotypes, such as *Manual* or *Custom*, if they aided the analysis
- A description, if no other rules would suffice

Table 8.7, Table 8.8, and Table 8.9 provide a summary of the details collected for the Logistics, Sales, and e-mail systems, respectively. The details of other systems are omitted for brevity.

Gap Analysis

Determining gaps and overlaps is a matter of reviewing the various system SIBs. Table 8.10 shows how we presented this information in the

Table 8.7. SIB analysis for the logistics system.

Information System Logistics			
Application Type: Business Application			
Service Category	**Sub-Category**	**Present**	**Technologies Supported**
Operating system services	Kernel services		OS/400
Network services	Data communications		SNA, TCP/IP, X.25, frame relay
	E-mail		Custom application (& Proprietary API based on APPC)
	Remote processes	X	
	Distributed data		DB/2 replication
Software engineering services	Language support		COBOL
	Specify, design, build services	X	
	UI building services	X	
Security services	Identification & authentication		RACF
	Audit		Custom
	Access control		RACF
	Security management		RACF
Systems and network management	Network mgmt		Netview
	Performance management	X	
	Configuration management		Manual
	Fault management		Netview
	Backup/restore		Manual
	Security management		Manual
Transaction processing	Transaction management		OS/400 Interactive
Location & directory services	Directory Services	X	
User interface	Character Based		3270 green screen
	Windows Mgmt	X	
Data interchange	Document	X	
	Graphical	X	

Table 8.7. SIB analysis for the logistics system (*continued*).

Information System Logistics			
Application Type: Business Application			
Service Category	**Sub-Category**	**Present**	**Technologies Supported**
	Electronic Data		CSV ASCII files (internal, external). All file interfaces in batch to physical media. Printed output (internal, external). All use proprietary (CFL-defined) formats.
Data management	DB Mgmt System		DB/2
	Repository	X	
Graphics & image services	Graphical Object Mgmt	X	
	Drawing	X	
Service qualities	Availability		Requirements of 2 seconds or less for all on-line transactions. 99.95% uptime.
	Adaptability		Scales by adding capacity within AS/400 (cannot scale beyond physical box).

technical architecture document. We were looking specifically along service lines; horizontally, if you will. In this assessment, the following are noted (again, Table 8.10 shows a subset of the full service analysis):

- We discovered international operation as a service omission—this service is already required within CFL branches in Europe.
- There are a large array of different products and specifications providing the same functions across the systems. For instance, technology overlap exists with internet working protocols, mail access protocols, and operating system platforms. Almost every service demonstrates this type of overlap. This is an indication of a nonarchitected environment.
- There are some service categories (e.g., security), where custom developments fulfill the service requirements. Remember that for a service to be in the platform it must be a commodity. Therefore, these

Table 8.8. SIB analysis for the sales sytem.

Information System Sales			
Application Type: Business Application			
Service Category	**Sub-Category**	**Present**	**Technologies Supported**
Operating system services	Kernel services		Windows NT HP-UNIX
Network services	Data communications		TCP/IP, PPP
	E-mail	X	
	Remote processes	X	
	Distributed data		FTP
Software engineering services	Language support		PL-SQL
	Specify, design, build services		Oracle Designer
	UI building services		Oracle Designer
Security services	Identification & authentication		Custom
	Audit		Custom
	Access control		Custom
	Security management		Custom
Systems and network management	Network mgmt	X	
	Performance management	X	
	Configuration management		Manual
	Fault management		Manual
	Backup/restore		Manual
	Security management		Manual
Transaction processing	Transaction management		Oracle
Location & directory services	Directory Services		DNS
User interface	Character Based	X	
	Windows Mgmt		Forms
Data interchange	Document	X	
	Graphical	X	

Table 8.8. SIB analysis for the sales sytem (*continued*).

Information System Sales			
Application Type: Business Application			
Service Category	**Sub-Category**	**Present**	**Technologies Supported**
	Electronic Data		CSV ASCII Files. All file interfaces in batch to physical media or FTP (depending on system). All use proprietary (CFL-defined) formats.
Data management	DB Mgmt System		Oracle, Oracle-Lite
	Repository		Oracle Designer
Graphics & image services	Graphical Object Mgmt	X	
	Drawing	X	
Service qualities	Availability	X	
	Adaptability	X	

custom developments should be viewed as candidates for replacement with products.

Using the information in Table 8.10, we were then able to analyze likely candidates for reuse within the environment. From a service perspective, consolidation of technologies will provide a degree of reuse in a number of service categories. For instance, we will consider rationalizing technologies in the corporate network, the systems management services, and the functionality provided by the Logistics security service (but not necessarily the security service itself), the e-mail and collaboration environment, operating systems, and others. The limited e-business services infrastructure currently provided by the environment (mostly ad hoc Internet connections and site) will require considerable rework to support the strategic objectives of CFL.

As for the current business systems themselves, there is no information to suggest that any would need to be replaced (in fact, a constraint was uncovered stating that the Logistics system must remain for at least 4 more years). This fact is borne out by the business systems architecture. However, from a technology perspective, none of the current systems fully enable the CFL business (and e-business) strategy. We must be cognizant during the development of the target architecture that any service deficiencies will need to be resolved.

Table 8.9. SIB analysis for the email infrastructure.

Information System: Email / Collaboration (corporate wide)			
Application Type: Infrastructure Application			
Service Category	Sub-Category	Present	Technologies Supported
Operating system services	Kernel services		Windows NT/98/95, Novell Netware, LINUX (Red Hat), Mac
Network services	Data communications		TCP/IP, IPX
	E-mail		Exchange, Groupwise, Notes, Messenger, ISP-based
	Remote processes		SMTP, MS-RPC, POP, IMAP, HTTP
	Distributed data		Proprietary to each vendor's product
Security services	Identification & Authentication		X.509 Certificate, HTTP Basic, Proprietary
	Audit		Proprietary
	Access control		LDAP, Proprietary
	Security management		Custom
Systems and network management		X	
Location & directory services	Directory services		DNS, NDS, NT Directory, Notes Directory, LDAP
User interface	Character-based	X	
	Windows management		Outlook, Internet Explorer, Netscape Navigator, Notes Client
Data interchange	Document	X	
	Graphical	X	
	Electronic data	X	
Data management	DB management system		Proprietary (to each vendor)
Service qualities		X	

Table 8.10. Service/technology matrix.

			Systems		
			Logistics	Sales	Email
Services	Operating system services	Kernel services	OS/400	HP-UX, NT/98/95	NT/98/95, Novell, LINUX, Mac
	Network services	Data Communications	SNA, TCP/IP, IPX, X.25, Frame Relay, PPP	TCP/IP	TCP/IP, IPX
		Email	Custom		Exchange, Groupwise, Notes, Messenger
		Remote processes			SMTP, MS-RPC, POP, IMAP, HTTP
		Distributed data	DB/2 Replication	Custom	
	Security services	Identification & authentication	RACF	Custom	X.509 certificate, HTTP Basic, Proprietary
		Audit	Custom	Custom	Proprietary
		Access control	RACF	Custom	LDAP, Proprietary
		Security management	RACF	Custom	Custom

Requirements Traceability

The final step of this stage was to produce the first draft of the key question list and the technology selection criteria (they will be refined during the development of the target architecture). Table 8.11 and Table 8.12 provide partial examples of these artifacts.

The architectural principles are also updated as follows:

- New principle: Execution of a common software engineering discipline (including tools, processes, and technologies) for all future development projects.

Table 8.11. Traceability—key question list.

Key Question List
Quantitative Questions
To what extent will total cost of ownership be changed?
To what extent will international operations be improved?
To what extent will supply chain integration be supported?
To what extent are the Confectionary Manufacturers Association standards supported?
To what extent will the efficiency of intersystem integration be improved?
Qualitative Questions
How will security be managed with the integration of a partner's systems into our environment?
What implementation costs are likely for this architecture?
How will this architecture aid interdepartmental communications?
How will the new services fit within the "legacy" environment?
How will the architecture deal with the organizational constraints?

Table 8.12. Technology selection criteria.

Technology Selection Criteria
Completeness of specification
Leading position in the market
Adherence with CMA specifications
Coordinated integration between systems
Alignment with strategic vendor relationships
Support for e-business and business strategy requirements
Support architectural principles
Can be supported effectively with skills that are widely available
Can be provided to CFL based on a contestable process
Produces applications that can scale to meet user demands, are able to effectively interoperate with other systems, and are portable enough not to be tied to a single vendor's technology

8.7   Summary

In this chapter, we have looked at the activities involved in understanding and assessing the baseline environment in TOGAF terms. This baseline assessment is fully grounded in the business strategy, requirements, and constraints that drive technology within the organization. We introduced, for the first time in detail, the TOGAF concepts of the technical reference model and the standards information base. We combined these artifacts with a number of other techniques to analyze the current environment, revealing problems that will need to be tackled during the development of the target architecture.

In the next chapter, we take a brief sojourn from the architectural development process. Instead, we look at the makeup of super services.

CHAPTER 9

Super Services

9.1   *Introduction*

We have already introduced the base concepts of the TOGAF platform and its associated service portfolio—the foundation architecture. Chapter 6 detailed the service categories (and subcategories) that exist within TOGAF's foundation architecture. Chapter 8 described how the current environment might be portrayed using the TOGAF concept of services and represented as a technical reference model (TRM).

To this point, then, we have dealt only with the basic services described within TOGAF's foundation architecture. Later, in Chapter 10, we take a detailed look at how services are refined as they progress along the architectural continuum. However, a number of issues may have become apparent with respect to the way services are defined in TOGAF:

- There is no overt layering concept, given that layering seems apparent within the foundation service categories and subcategories.
- There is no obvious concept that describes the transition of services from systems into the platform.
- Services are not cognizant of how vendors collect technologies into products.

It is important to remember that our summary of service problems uses a more concrete form than is the intent of TOGAF. Services should be viewed more generically and will support massaging to fit particular organizational requirements for the definition of the architecture. This is the purpose (and strength) of TOGAF as a framework rather than a specific method. We therefore suggest that there are different service types, the classification of which will aid in the development and understanding of the technical architecture.

In this chapter, we introduce the concept of *super services*, a type of service that will help the architect remedy some of the issues just described and provide an additional tool for the definition and understanding of the architecture.

9.2   Services and Super Services

Background

Super services provide an increased specialization of a generic service; that is, they inherit all of the characteristics that would be expected of a general service (Table 6.1 is reproduced from Chapter 6). Using the same approach, services described along the architectural continuum—from the foundation services already cataloged in TOGAF to the organization-specific services from which the IT environment is established—are also specializations of the generic service concept.

In essence, then, all services are equal. However, we think that some services are more equal than others; that is, a super service represents a

Table 9.1. Characteristics of Platform Services.

Service Characteristics
They primarily exist within "the platform"; that is they tend to be generic, system-centered (as opposed to business-function-centered), and usable by cross-domain business applications.
They are encapsulated bundles of functionality.
They are accessed (by the application) through a published and stable interface (either based on standards, de facto, or proprietary specifications).
They typically interface with other services, providing a hierarchy (or embedding) of rich platform functionality. Some services interface directly with the external environment (i.e., network).
They can be replaced with other implementations (products, custom developments) without affecting the application as long as the interface is preserved.
They meet the service-quality requirements defined by the organization; for instance, performance or scalability.
The interfaces and internal machinery must adhere to the organization's architectural principles.
They typically do not implement organization-specific or domain-specific functionality (functions that are specific to an organization's business requirements).

collection (and augmentation) of foundation services into a collective (i.e., a unit that closely depicts a specific service requirement and can be easily mapped to procurable technology) that are naturally closer to the application. A super service can be distinguished from a foundation service in that it collects foundation services while adding other services. Of course, there is already an implied hierarchy in the foundation architecture—services are made up of subservices (service subcategories). Super services add an additional layer to the hierarchy. Not all new services are super services, however. For instance, a newly identified service may be granular enough to be presented as a new subcategory to an existing service category.

Key definition: **Super services.**
Super Services are a specialization of the TOGAF notion of a service that provides a mechanism of collecting together individual services (or whole service categories) into a "service-of-services". In a service hierarchy, super services are close to the application and tend to encapsulate more basic (or the foundation) services.

The position of a service in the service portfolio of an organization's TRM is never cut-and-dried. Consider a number of TRMs available in the public domain (government bodies that undertake architectural work will sometimes publish that information on the Internet). Many show the platform services as a loosely coupled, nonhierarchical collection. This is by no means a flawed approach—especially considering the level at which the technical architecture is defining—but in many cases, services can appear in a more layered fashion to the applications that use them. This layering is driven by:

- The platform concept; that is, as services descend from applications into the platform, they become super services initially, then continue to descend deeper into the infrastructure as they become ubiquitous.
- New technologies tend to collect services together and provide applications with simpler access to those services.

Service categories evolve as the platform evolves. Consider the example shown in Figure 9.1. In the early 1980s, most applications had to make almost direct use of the network protocols to support client/server style applications. Although we could easily call this cluster of functionality a service (the network service, in fact), the platform provided only very basic interfaces to this service. As network functionality became more sophisticated, the applications were able to use more generalized interfaces to the network (typically socket-based APIs). Remote procedure call interfaces generalized the network service even further; at this point, the application (and the infrastructure) did not have to rely on a single-protocol model. Today's applications use highly featured object brokers to obtain the services of application components almost anywhere while also isolating the network service completely.

The salient point described with this example is that the network service was continually pushing "dated" interface functionality further into the platform. This functionality was hidden, but not removed; for instance, ORBs use remote procedure call interfaces, which use socket APIs to put information onto TCP/IP networks such as the Internet.

As we ascend up the stack shown in Figure 9.1, the services provided become far more specialized from the applications point of view. Only

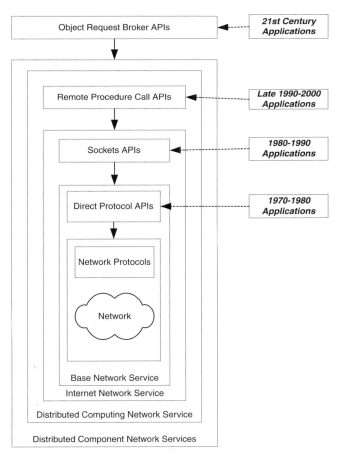

FIGURE 9.1. Example of service evolution.

distributed components will use ORB-type services, whereas many general network-centric applications can use socket interfaces (directories, security services, transaction management systems) perhaps with other interfaces layered on top.

So, using the TOGAF taxonomy, should all of these interface types be classified within the network service? On the other hand, should we consider a number of more specific services that use the basic functions of the network service? This is the basic idea behind super services.

Application–Service Relationships

Logical View

The concept of discrete services grouped into logical service categories underpins the TOGAF service model. The categorization of services is loosely based on their type, not how products may implement them.[30] For instance, mail, distributed time, and remote procedure call services are classified, under the TOGAF foundational architecture, within the service category *Network Service*, as may seem logical. On the other hand, this may not be exactly how the architect wishes to model service functions. Of course, the framework nature of TOGAF allows the architect to consider any other grouping of classifications that is seen fit. We therefore present super services as a useful specialization of foundation services.

From a logical point of view, the service groups are simply arranged. Figure 9.2 shows an example of a subset of services used by an application. Applications make use of an eclectic array of foundation services across many of the service categories. This is a simplistic view of service usage.

However, digging a little deeper, this view can become somewhat more complex. For example (see Figure 9.3):

- The database management system has its own security and transaction management functionality. This may be the same technology described by the security service or it may be additional (remember our aversion to a single service represented by multiple implementations).
- The application uses the mail service as an interface to a workflow engine, which in turn uses distributed processing services (such as RPC and Time), security services, and DBMS services to support workflow. On the other hand, an e-mail client application uses the

---

30. From The Open Group's point of view service classification is also related to areas of standardization.

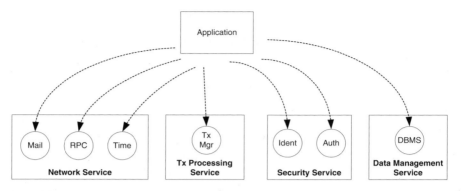

FIGURE 9.2.   Application use of services.

mail service directly for no purpose other than to send and receive mail.

■ The application may not even use transaction management services directly if it is deployed into an environment that understands and manages transactions on behalf of the application (such as J2EE containers or COM+ transaction servers).

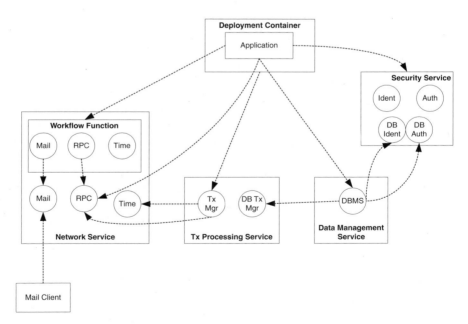

FIGURE 9.3.   Complex service interactions.

Given these examples, the problem is that a flat view of services does not necessarily aid in the understanding of how services are used by applications and how the individual services are clustered and possibly duplicated. This is not a criticism of the TOGAF service model. The TOGAF model described in the foundation architecture will accommodate almost all circumstances. The issue, however, is whether this is the best way to describe the services.

Physical View

The logical view of services is usually unencumbered by how they will be implemented. This is the typical practice for the development of reference models. However, it is important to consider how the service portfolio (the collection of platform services that complete the IT environment) may be implemented within the environment. The objectives of the service portfolio are to:

- Describe fully the breadth and depth of the services used
- Depict how services interact
- Illustrate how services are clustered in the physical environment

We believe that the foundation architecture services are a useful starting point but that a specialization of these services is required to support fully the objectives of the portfolio. Furthermore, the logical services are required to support the definition and selection of actual technologies, specifications, and products with which to build the IT environment. The flat view shown in Figure 9.2 does not depict the intricacies of the final implementation environment which in reality looks more like Figure 9.3.

In the physical world, products implement services. Some products are based on standards and specifications, others implement proprietary interfaces, and all are required to support the functionality defined in each service (Chapter 11 provides tools for describing the functionality of individual services). However, products are driven by the market, not by the TOGAF (or organization) service portfolio. There is a tendency in the IT industry for vendors to cluster a suite of functions within a single product. We have seen this with desktop productivity tools, the application server market, enterprise application integration (EAI), and even database management systems. Vendors typically support this type of bundling for a number of reasons:

- From the marketing perspective, it demonstrates increased functionality (value?) in an individual product.

- From the vendor perspective, it involves a certain amount of "follow the leader".
- From the organization's perspective, it can support a "one-stop shop" approach for platform functionality.

Vendors who provide bundled functionality may support "open" standard interfaces for some of the bundled services but will rarely encourage the use of alternate product components to provide a single service. For example, vendors in the EAI space tend to deliver a bundled product that provides all necessary EAI services. They may support an industry-standard API for messaging or workflow but are less likely to encourage the use of an alternative product to their own. In some cases, the organization is hampered in even considering such a substitution because the vendor incorporates "added value" functionality to the standard interface. However, organizations are not rioting over this situation; in fact, the procurement of a single, integrated package can be seen as more beneficial than pulling together different products to provide the EAI solution for example. Of course, this can lead to significant duplication in the IT environment. The EAI product implements a messaging product, as does the application server, the B2B portal product, and so on.

Product bundling can also hide service implementations. This is not necessarily undesirable from the perspective of the service portfolio. After all, the hiding of services in a product demonstrates the transition of

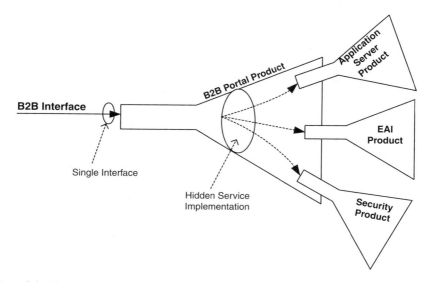

FIGURE 9.4. Functional bundling through a single funnel.

such services to a commodity platform status. This hiding can be taken to the extreme by the product. Consider the example of B2B portals. It is entirely possible that interaction with such a product is via a single published interface (say, an XML interface). Behind the scenes, however, the portal provides a huge array of services such as distributed component execution, core systems integration, and security. In turn, these services hide a number of other services. Underneath all of this are the foundation services.

As can be seen from these examples, the fundamental approach for service modeling (i.e., single-layered services) does not aid in the clear understanding of how services will be realized into products and how products are likely to affect the service structure.

Architectural View—Super Services

We use the notion of super services to help in the logical illustration of service bundling. The super service inherits its characteristics from a generic platform service. It also has additional characteristics that help in our understanding of the physical implementation.

Super services are likely to exist in a hierarchical relationship with the application and the foundation services. In most circumstances, we see that super services will sit at a higher level than foundation services, and applications will access the foundation services through the super service.

Super services will use, replicate, consume, replace, or add individual foundation services. Super services also support the hiding of foundation services (and possibly other super services) within their functionality. For instance, super services may[31] consist of:

- Direct copies of the foundation service in that they can be implemented by exactly the same foundation service as is used directly by a "simpler" application (replicated). Potentially, the super service may support the use of the foundation service in this instance.
- The foundation service may become bundled inside the super service, without being exposed, but in all other respects is identical to the foundation service (consumed).[32] Consumed services cannot be reused by other applications or services.
- Replacements of the foundation services, in that they provide addi-

---

31. The word *may* is used here deliberately. At this point in the modeling of services, it is usually too early to tell how the services will be implemented in technology and how that technology will be used. Certainty occurs during the realization of technologies against services.

32. Consumed services can be seen as a corruption in the service model and the final IT environment because there may be the requirement to support multiple individual products that perform the same function.

tional functionality to enable the super service. Such services therefore will be supplied by different technology and possibly treated as
a service separate from its more primitive cousin. However, each instance of the service has the same classification with respect to the
TRM taxonomy.

- Additions that do not currently exist within the foundation services
  but are a distinct service subcategory within the super service.

Super services may or may not support increased functionality (in
relation to the foundation services), but they will provide access, for the
application, to their encapsulated functionality via a simpler interface.
It is the fundamental concept in the evolution of services. The industry
is continually attempting to make the development task easier, thus supporting greater productivity, by providing increased functionality with
higher-level interfaces. Consider the example shown in Figure 9.1. In the
1970s and 1980s, developing an application that communicated across
machine boundaries required specialist knowledge of network-layer protocols, how to put data onto a network, how to get it off, what error
checking to apply, and so on. In the 21st century, applications use verbs
such as SERIALIZE on their objects, and the infrastructure takes care
of the rest. The developers who write the infrastructure applications
must still understand the intricacies of networks, but these developers
are producing platform services, not business applications.

Super services will have a tight bond with actual products and technologies—possibly one-to-one. Although the mapping between foundation services and products can be somewhat abstract, super services are
structured with implementation in mind. This supports a simpler transition from the logical service portfolio (Chapter 10) to the physical service realization (Chapter 11), thus making the reference model accessible to a wider audience.

Figure 9.5 summarizes the logical structure of the super service. It is
a collection of services from either the foundation architecture, other
super services, or unique to itself. Although super services provide an
application with a potentially simple, more powerful interface, certain
applications will require the use of services directly (this is particularly
true of infrastructure applications such as e-mail). This modeling of the
super service allows the architect to mitigate the issues described in the
early part of this chapter without corrupting the overall notion of a
service.

We discuss the treatment of the service portfolio in more detail in
Chapter 10. However, it is worthwhile to touch briefly on a complexity
introduced into the TRM with super services. Given a flat (nonhierarchical) service portfolio, individual services (subcategories) are easily classified based purely on their service category. Super services introduce

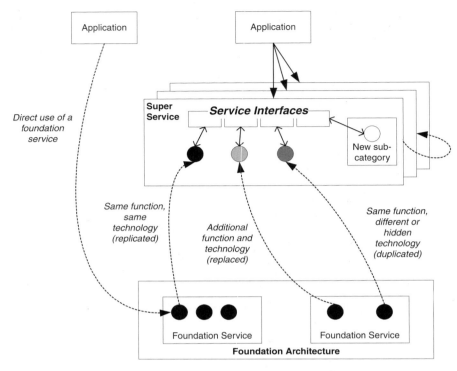

FIGURE 9.5.   Super services and foundation services relationship diagram.

the concept of replicating, duplicating, and replacing foundation services. The complexity is associated with representing super services and foundation services in a way that promotes understanding and does not corrupt the model. There are a number of strategies for service definition:

- Describe super service subcategories both in the foundation and super service. Although this duplicates service sub-categories, it does allow straightforward viewing of how foundation and super service functionality and technologies relate. This is especially important when attempting to avoid overlapping technologies. This strategy is valid when applications use both the foundation and super service directly.
- Maintain the hierarchical nature of the services, isolating foundation and super service subcategories. This reduces the ability to assess for service overlap. However, it is effective when applications predominantly interface with super services, not foundation services.

9.3 Example

In this section we consider an example of the identification of a super service for CFL. CFL's e-business strategy zeroed in on the following high-value initiatives:

- Integrate electronic supply chain with CFL's two leading raw material suppliers.
- Offer a catalog browsing service to customers.
- Offer electronic ordering for key (yet to be identified) customers.

In this example, we concentrate on the modeling of the business-to-business requirement; namely, electronic supply chain integration with CFL's two leading raw material suppliers. We conducted research into the typical facets of B2B functionality. This included an assessment of significant standards initiatives in this arena, such as RossettaNet, eCo, ebXML, and BizTalk. Additionally, an investigation of notable products was also carried out. The result was the definition of a number of key services required to support commodity B2B trading. These included:

- Business document definition and interchange formats
- Process flow definition and execution environment
- Ensuring the privacy of information transferred between parties
- Identification (authentication) of both parties
- Authorization of the actions a party can perform
- Proof of origin and receipt (nonrepudiation)
- The Internet as a network transport
- Synchronous and asynchronous session protocols
- Remote process routing application protocols (to support trading hubs)
- Permanent message (and message metadata) storage
- Development tools and environment to support customization

It can be seen from this collection of services that they are derived from a number of foundation services, including network, software engineering, data management, data interchange, and security services. It is our preference to cluster these services into a single super service called *B2B Commerce Service*. We do this for a number of reasons:

- A single service aids in the logical definition, and communication, of a major functional area for CFL (i.e., business-to-business integration).

- Product selection criteria will be derived from the functionality (and interfaces) embodied within this super service.

Figure 9.7 outlines the relationships between the super service and the foundation services. Points to note about the B2B commerce super service are:

- We anticipate that the majority of the basic network-oriented services will be directly replicated from the foundation services.
- It is considered that the information interchange service (of the super service) may not be fully exposed as a standard service. Rather, its specialized nature may cause it to be bundled within the selected product.
- Both the process routing and the development environment are likely to implement additional functionality specific to e-business and therefore may not be fully reusable (unless other CFL systems were built in this manner).
- A new service has been identified that is not currently present in the foundation services. This service includes the definition and execution of partner interface processes supporting business-to-business interchange.

In Figure 9.7, we have used the notation shown in Figure 9.6 to describe the relationship between the super service (and its categories and

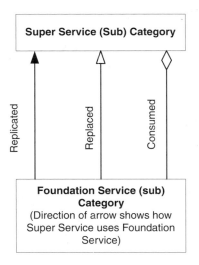

FIGURE 9.6.   Super service notation.

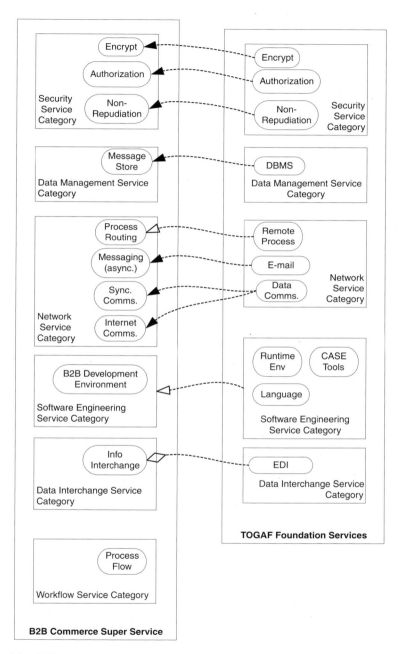

FIGURE 9.7.   B2B commerce service relationship diagram.

subcategories) and the foundation services. The relationship is derived from three stereotypes:

- Replicated.
- Replaced.
- Consumed.

9.4 Summary

In this chapter, we have introduced the concept of super services. A super service is a specialization of the generic TOGAF service (both of which are derived from the services defined in the foundation architecture step of the architectural continuum). Super services provide the architect with a specific mechanism to describe higher-order services, thus allowing the hierarchical structuring of the final service portfolio (in the TRM).

Super services collect together a bundle of services from the base service taxonomy. In this structure, they provide an effective tool for communicating key organization functional requirements of the platform. Additionally, they can be more closely related to the products that will implement them. The concept of super services will be used when we discuss the definition of the organization's service portfolio in the next chapter.

Target Architecture— Selecting Service Portfolios

10.1 Introduction

The preceding chapters have dealt with describing, in various forms, the organization's current technology environment. This chapter takes a first look at defining the technical direction by the definition of the target service portfolio.

The selection of the service portfolio is one of the key steps in the development of the technical architecture. The selection is the taxonomy of services that represent the IT environment and the technology to be supported within that environment. The development of a service portfolio is supported by the architectural continuum. As the architecture is further refined, the architect moves from the foundation toward the organization-specific end of the continuum. With this, the services become increasingly more relevant to the organization.

Once the architect has defined and agreed on the technical services to be supported by the technology environment, the next step is to assign actual technologies to each service. This increasing layer of detail is dealt with in the next chapter.

The TOGAF architectural development method (ADM) positions the development of the service portfolio within the target architecture phase (Phase C). Figure 10.1 presents the now familiar input–output wiring notion for this activity. Figure 10.2 shows the ADM's view of where the portfolio definition is incorporated within Phase C. This chapter also deals with activities 5 and 6 in Figure 10.2. The development of the target service portfolio necessitates activities surrounding requirements traceability and the definition of the individual services.

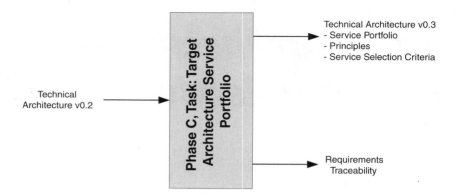

FIGURE 10.1.   Target architecture service portfolio wiring diagram.

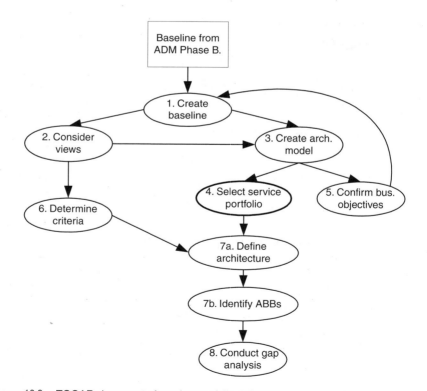

FIGURE 10.2.   TOGAF placement of service portfolio definition.

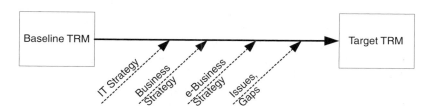

FIGURE 10.3.   Transition to target architecture.

10.2   Transition

The logical architecture (encapsulated within the service portfolio) is developed to transition the current environment to the target environment. Along this journey, the following aspects influence the transition (see Figure 10.3):

- *Business strategy*. The business strategy positions the organization for its likely future. Taking into account the current strategy, and the issues with its current implementation, it describes the business roadmap for the organization. Additionally, it presents the aspects of technology enablement required to support the strategy.
- *IT strategy*. The IT strategy provides significant input into the problems identified with the current IT environment. It offers valuable analysis of the evolution of the IT environment and how it must change to support new business initiatives (provided in detail by the business systems architecture).
- *E-business strategy*. The e-business strategy specifically concentrates on competitive (and cost-controlling) initiatives enabled by a specific technology set. This therefore has a bearing on specific service areas within the architecture.
- *Issues and gaps*. A key aspect of architectural planning is the resolution of the issues and gaps in the current environment.

10.3   The Baseline Description

In the last chapter, we discussed the definition of the organization's current technical environment in TOGAF format. In general, the baseline analysis would have been primarily conducted at the organizational end of the architectural continuum, producing a technical reference model and service portfolio in line with a TOGAF view of the architecture; that is the foundation end of the continuum. The baseline is pure gold for target architecture development—in virtually every case, the architect will not be required to start with a clear sheet of paper.

The baseline provides the starting point of the definition of the target architecture. It has established the architectural "givens"—the necessary services and subservices—that the organization will expect from the target architecture. It has defined the constraints that must be considered (e.g., functional, financial, organizational, technical). From the e-business perspective, the baseline also provides the necessary analysis of the current environment's ability to support e-business initiatives.

The baseline does, however, represent a static point in time, usually before the IT strategic planning process has been undertaken. The task of this stage is then to factor in the intended strategic direction, evolving the baseline into the target architecture, delivering to the requirements established by the strategic process.

Before proceeding through the continuum, it is important to form an initial view of the state of the baseline with respect to the strategic requirements. At this stage, we are considering the services to be provided by the IT environment rather than the technology that will implement the services. As such, the architect should pass quickly over the baseline, noting the state of the services (and service subcategories) in relation to the strategy. This may include the need to assess each service in terms of its effectiveness (this should have been completed during baseline definition). This is a partial gap analysis. The likely state of services found in the baseline:

- Basic platform service effective and to be provided in the target architecture.
- Service does not effectively support the strategic requirements and should be replaced (define as legacy, to be transitioned).
- Service partially supports the strategic requirements and should be considered for extension.
- A combination of the above.

A future stage of the process, the migration phase, will define the projects required for the organization to transition from the current environment to the target architecture. Therefore, the architect must be cognizant of how this transition will occur and the effect it will have on the current environment when defining the target architecture. For instance, the ability to support both business-as-usual and transition activities for each service will be an important aspect of an effective transition.

10.4   *Gap Analysis*

Key definition: **Gap analysis.**
Gap analysis is a general technique for the discovery and management
of gaps that result during the planning of a transition between an initial
state and a target state.

Throughout this text, we have talked about gap analysis. Gap analysis is
a tool (or technique) often used in a strategic-planning context. As we
have shown in a number of the examples, it relates to the assessment of
a desired (or target) state against a current state, with the objective of
understanding the gaps between the two (see Figure 10.4).

FIGURE 10.4.   Generic gap analysis model.

Gap analysis is an important tool within TOGAF, especially in the role
of requirements traceability. Gap analysis supports both a model and
approach for understanding the viability of the target architecture by
determining:

- That the full requirements have been catered to
- The requirements that have been forgotten
- The aspects of the architecture that have been intentionally removed
- The aspects of the architecture that will need to be enhanced or
  added

Before progressing into target architecture development phases, the
architect should define a gap model and method that will be used for
gap analysis during traceability assessment.

The model and method will depend on the types of gaps that are to
be assessed. For instance, strategic, technical, quality, and organizational gap models have the same basic structure (model) but may have

significantly different measurement requirements and points (method). In general, the model will provide the perspective for the identification of gaps and the factors that will be considered during the analysis.

The gap model will have an effect on how requirements traceability is carried out. Figure 10.5 presents an example of a gap-analysis model for the assessment of the service portfolio against strategic requirements. Note from the example model that gaps are measured at three points:

- *Strategic gap.* This measures the gap between the target environment and the strategic expectations of the environment.
- *Customer gap.* This is a quality gap. It measures the gap between the customer's (internal and external groups) expectation of the target environment and perceptions of the environment.
- *Organizational gap.* This measures the gap between the organization's strategic expectations and the customer's expectations of the target environment. Although this may not have a direct bearing on

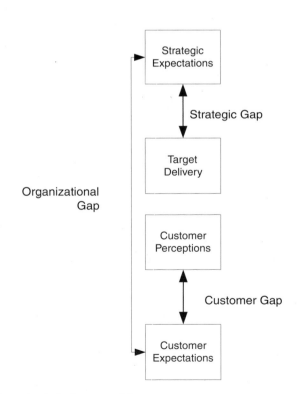

Figure 10.5.   Example strategic gap model.

the target architecture development, it does indicate a gap in either the strategic or customer expectations.

This example model shows where gaps will be measured and generally describes which gaps are important. The reason for establishing this model up front is obvious; it defines what measurement points are important and communicates ultimately how the architecture will be measured.

Coupled with the gap model is the gap method. The model presents the key gap relationships; the method defines how the model will be applied. The method should determine how the gaps defined by the model are identified, measured, and documented (especially gaps based on expectations or perceptions). There are a number of techniques for measuring gaps. Typically, they fall under two classifications:

- *Quantitative analysis.* Quantitative analysis relies on assessment and delivery of concrete, usually mathematically based, factors that are immutable and support absolute decision-making. Such a technique will produce weighted scores or similar numeric outputs that can be generated from analytic or simulation techniques.
- *Qualitative analysis.* Qualitative analysis is derived from the need to measure perception-based aspects that cannot be described by absolute metrics. Techniques such as focus groups, surveys, and so forth are used to determine nonconcrete gaps. The key question list provides a form of qualitative analysis. Chapter 3 provided an example of such an analysis adapted for plotting a system's business contribution against its technical quality.

The objective of gap analysis from TOGAF's perspective is:

. . . to identify areas of the current and target system for which provision has not been made in the technical architecture. This is required in order to identify projects to be undertaken as part of the implementation of the target system.

The TOGAF method adopts gap analysis as a major activity within Phase C; in fact, it is the last step. This does not mean that the architect should only carry out gap analysis at the end of target architecture development. If significant change is anticipated between the current and target environments, conducting multiple gap-analysis activities (one each at the service portfolio and architectural definition phases) is encouraged. This is the reason for emphasizing the development of a gap-analysis model and method before continuing with architectural development.

10.5 Services

The technical services are the cornerstone of the target architecture and hence the organization's strategic technical direction. Services were introduced in Chapter 6, we demonstrated how they might be used in describing the current systems in TOGAF form in Chapter 8, and we introduced a specialization of the service (i.e., super services) in Chapter 9.

In essence, the organization's technical architecture is built from a number of interrelated services. Services are typically discrete bundles of functionality that support an application in providing business or infrastructure functionality. The coarseness of services is not specified, which implies that the architect can adopt a granularity that is appropriate for the organization. For instance, a service may be as fine as an object (although this is unlikely to provide the requisite strategic intent), a component, a subsystem, or even an entire system.

Physically, services can exist anywhere within an individual system; for instance, they can be developed as part of a specific system, or they can be made more generic and used by more than one system. Conceptually, however, TOGAF's notion of platform services is those that have been moved out of individual applications and into "the platform." Platform services are then provided to applications or systems through standard[33] interfaces (such as an application program interface or API). The key characteristics of platform services were described in Chapter 6.

The TOGAF notion of services is encapsulated within the TOGAF technical reference model (TRM). The TOGAF TRM provides two main components:

- A taxonomy, which defines terminology and provides a coherent description of the components and conceptual structure of an information system
- An associated technical reference model graphic, which provides a visual representation of the taxonomy as an aid to understanding

A reference model allows groups interested in a particular domain to agree on a common vocabulary, definitions, and standards. The IT industry is generally enamored with reference models. They exist within most domains; some are useful, whereas others represent a more marketing view. Even the industry's standards bodies (organizations such as The Open Group, IEEE, ISO, OMG, and others) tend to compete in this area, providing similar but not fully compatible models. We intend to

---

33. The term "standard" as used here does not imply specifications from open standards bodies but rather specifications that have been defined by the organization through the architectural process.

continue with and build on the TOGAF TRM in this text; however, the architectural development method does not similarly mandate that the architect do the same. We assert that architects should start with whichever high-level TRM they feel comfortable with and understand.

Other TRMs to consider include the IEEE Open System Environment (otherwise known as POSIX.0) reference model, shown in Figure 10.6. The reader will note that the IEEE TRM has some similarities with the TOGAF TRM without breaking down the application platform into the same detail (although the detailed standard is more specific in this area). As a TRM, POSIX.0 has goals slightly different from TOGAF. POSIX.0 aims to promote, among other things, application source code portability, data portability, application software interoperability, and application platform interoperability. TOGAF, in contrast, is an architectural framework designed to support generic architecture development, resulting in actual architectures that may or may not have the same goals as POSIX.0. The result is that TOGAF includes a considerable amount of material on architecture development that is lacking from POSIX.0, whereas POSIX.0 includes a considerable amount of detail in service category definition and in the recommended lists of standards and specifications that is lacking in TOGAF.

As technologies become commoditized—that is, as vendors see the volume of (certain) product use increasing—it is more likely that such a technology will be "pushed" into the platform. For instance, not too many years ago, most organizations had to purchase TCP/IP networking

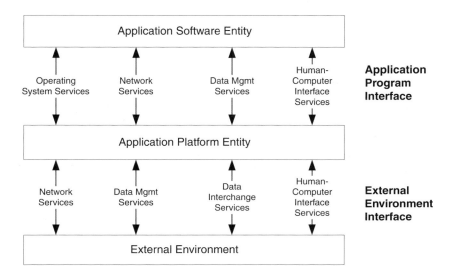

FIGURE 10.6.   Open software environment TRM.

services if they wanted their applications to run in such an environment. As the Internet exploded, some vendors realized that delivering TCP/IP networking within their operating systems (at "no cost") was immensely beneficial in driving operating system sales. Nowadays, no vendor would even consider delivering an operating system without this service. This is a classic example of a service that has moved from "the application" into the platform. The technical architecture is concerned with these types of services.

A service may adopt a different characteristic. Some technologies are sufficiently specialized or niched to reduce the chances that they will transition into the "generic" platform.[34] These technologies tend not to have the necessary market penetration, or interest, to drive the volumes necessary to move them to the platform. Such products are seldom commodity, and organizations usually pay a premium for their use. Technologies in this class tend also not to suit "platform-ization" because they are not generic enough to be used by a large percentage of systems within the organization. Examples of technologies in this area include data warehousing and business intelligence, workflow, geographic information systems, medical imaging, and many others.

Table 10.1 shows some of the drivers that push technologies into the platform.

These platform drivers are based on a generic industry view of technology—the foundation end of the architectural continuum. On the other hand, individual organizations represent a specialized and micro view of the technology industry. The technologies that the industry considers niched and not fit for the platform may be seen as commodity and

Table 10.1. What drives services into the platform.

Platform Service Drivers	Application Service Drivers
• High demand • Well-defined or standard interfaces • Major vendor(s) uptake • Implemented to support access by any application "user"	• Niche • Proprietary interfaces • Typically only a small number of vendors implementing the technology • Integrated within a single application • Not normally implemented in a way that supports multi-application access

34. The definition of commodity and niche may differ between the overall industry and individual organizations. Organizations may consider industry niche technology commodity if it is used extensively internally. It is all a matter of perspective.

therefore be platform candidates within the organization. For example, data warehousing technology could be implemented throughout the organization, making it a candidate as a platform service. These two different notions of platform services are embodied within the concept of the architectural continuum. Architectural development moves along the continuum, applying an increasingly organization-specific view.

TOGAF describes individual technology services as components (subcategories) of a foundation service category. For instance, TCP/IP is a particular technology service that can be subcategorized within the network service category. TOGAF does not prescriptively define how and what services should exist in particular categories. It merely provides this layering of services and categories for use by the architect. As described in the last chapter, super services not only extend this hierarchy but also define additional rules for the classification of technology services into a category.

The identification of services and their categories is one of the key aspects of the development of the technical architecture. Service categories provide the basis for positioning and selecting the actual technology that will form the organization's technical environment. The organizational service categories will be an amalgamation of the current technical environment (described in the baseline) and the strategic direction of the organization. The service categories become the high-level table of contents for the detailed technology standards. In the next chapter we investigate converting (realizing) the platform services in actual technologies. In this chapter, we concentrate on building the organization's service portfolio (we use the term *service* as shorthand for both service categories and subcategories).

10.6   *The Enterprise Continuum*

As described in Chapter 4, the enterprise continuum is segregated into two interrelated streams; the architectural continuum and the solutions continuum. In this chapter we use the architectural continuum to aid in the development of the service portfolio. In the next chapter, the solutions continuum is our tool for realizing service categories as technologies.

The architectural continuum was shown in Figure 4.1. The architectural continuum demonstrates how architectures are developed from the foundational architecture (such as that provided by TOGAF), through common systems architectures and industry-specific architectures, to an organization's own individual architecture.

The arrows in Figure 4.1 show a bidirectional flow. The flow from the left to the right represents the increasing need to describe the organization's specific needs and business requirements. This is plain enough and is generally the path the architect will follow in describing the organization's architectural direction. The leftward flow, from organizational to foundation, is more esoteric but important. It shows the ability to leverage from a set of "packaged" architectures in building the architecture. No architecture sits in isolation. There are very few (perhaps no) organizations whose requirements are so specific that their technical architecture is totally unique, containing components not seen in any other organization's architecture. Most industries have domain-wide bodies that provide at least some technical guidance. Many organizations use common technology components when building their technical environments. The majority (should) use standard styles for the implementation of technology.

These concepts are personified in the architectural continuum, and the characteristics of each point on the continuum are summarized in Table 10.2.

The continuum is also a valuable communications tool. It provides a simple and reasonably heuristic and common vocabulary to describe technology and technology strategy. Once an organization becomes familiar with the continuum points and their contents, the continuum can be used to effectively communicate the concepts of both technology and the architectural process. For instance, we have been involved in discussions where the key architects and business owners were determining whether they should be looking for common service or industry-specific solutions to a particular procurement problem. This level of understanding enhances the success of the corporate technical architecture. The makeup of the continuum is easily understandable by both technical and nontechnical people and provides a pragmatic view of the technical strategy.

The organization's technical architecture is made up of a number of technical services gathered into the service portfolio. The definition of these services is aided by moving from the left end of the continuum (the foundation architecture) to the right end (the organization architecture). The reason why the architect should not tackle the organizational architecture immediately is due to the intellectual property encapsulated in the continuum's other architectural components. Each point on the continuum relates directly to collectable services and can provide a wide base for the architecture without undue effort. During the architectural process, the architect will build on, augment, replace, redistribute, and delete services as the development moves through the continuum. There is no one correct embodiment of services. It is the responsibility of the architect to use the services discovered along the continuum in a way that best fits the organization's requirements.

Table 10.2. Architectural continuum-point characteristics.

Continuum Point	Characteristics
Foundation architecture	• Reflects general computing requirements • Reflects general capabilities • Contains strategic "open" protocols components • Provides direction for products and services • Reflects the function of a complete, robust computing environment that can be used as a foundation • Provides "open" system standards, directions, and recommendations • Reflects directions and strategies
Common systems architectures	• Reflects common system-specific requirements and capabilities • Contains selection of one or more "open" protocols • Provides super services for easy reuse and lower costs
Industry architectures	• Reflects industry-specific requirements, standards, and capabilities • Contains industry-specific logical data and process models • Contains industry-specific applications and process models as well as industry-specific business rules • Contains industry-specific protocols • Provides guidelines for testing collections of systems • Encourages levels of interoperability throughout the industry.
Organizational architectures	• Provides a means to communicate and manage the information technology environment • Reflects organization-specific requirements and capabilities • Contains organization-specific physical data, applications, and process models, as well as business rules • Contains organization-specific protocols

Table 10.2. Architectural continuum-point characteristics (*continued*).

Continuum Point	Characteristics
	• Provides a means to encourage implementation of appropriate information technology to meet business needs • Provides the criteria to measure and select appropriate products, solutions, and services • Provides an evolutionary path to support growth and new business needs.

In this chapter, we follow service development along the continuum, noting the key aspects of each point and how they can add value. This is typically not the method used during architectural development; it is more likely that the architect will consider all points simultaneously.

The basis for the organization's service portfolio rests in the foundation architecture.

The Foundation Service Portfolio

The Open Group is a standards consortium acting as custodian over a number of the important standards in the IT industry. It was born out of an amalgamation of the Open Software Foundation and X/Open. Its mission is to:

. . . deliver assurance of conformance to Open Systems Standards through the testing and certification of suppliers' products, with the objective:

■ To deliver greater business efficiency
■ To lower the cost and risks associated with integrating new technology across the enterprise by bringing together buyers and suppliers of information systems

The Open Group is the owner of the UNIX trademark and as such they continue to strive for greater value from its use. They work toward:

■ Being neutral toward vendor, product, and technology
■ Ensuring multivendor information technology matches the demands and needs of customers
■ Developing and deploying frameworks, policies, best practices, standards, and conformance programs
■ Pursuing the vision—the concept of making all technology as open and accessible as using a telephone

As the keepers of TOGAF, they have also enumerated the contents of the foundation architecture. The foundation architecture provides a taxonomy of services that are generic enough to suit almost all organizations. In fact, some organizations will find that The Open Group categorization will be sufficient for their entire architecture; such is the complete nature of the foundation service categories.

It is tempting for polarized views to appear with respect to foundation architecture provided by The Open Group. The Open Group is primarily the UNIX custodian, and in viewing the foundation standards information base[35] (SIB) provided by The Open Group it is common to recognize many UNIX-related technologies. Furthermore, the concept of industry standards (or in fact industry standards bodies) may be abhorrent to some organizations. Although The Open Group will have an opinion on the benefits of standards (and in particular, their branded standards), TOGAF has no such bias. The foundation architecture, as provided by The Open Group, is merely a first step in defining the organizational architecture. The service categories, as we will see, are sufficiently generic to fit any organization. The technologies defined in The Open Group's SIB serve two purposes in our opinion: firstly they offer an indication or what types of technologies the TOGAF designers intended to exist within each category (the subcategories, if you wish); and secondly, if the organization is Open Group technology aligned, it can provide an almost "instant" architecture.

Chapter 4 provides a table that outlines TOGAF's foundation architecture service categories. Described also were the subcategories, or the types of technologies positioned by TOGAF in each category. It may be useful to review that table before continuing.

The reader will notice a number of interesting aspects of the foundation services. There is considerable alignment with the Single UNIX Specification (and IEEE POSIX) style of presenting the categories. Each of the subcategories tends to represent the APIs that should be provided by the UNIX platform to support the Single UNIX Specification and/or The Open Group's technical standards (formally known as the Common Application Environment, or CAE) adherence. The foundation service categories are generally aligned with The Open Group's own standards.

Another interesting point is that a number of the service categories are not actually technology-related. A case in point is the *service quality* category. Service Quality describes the behavior of systems with respect to their nonfunctional requirements. Examples include system availability or the ability to change given new requirements. The security category can also include policy and guideline information, or even man-

---

35. The standards information base is the set of standards, technologies, and guidelines that implement (or realize) the service categories.

ual procedures. These services are important as they apply to all technologies that provide services to applications.

In general the foundation architecture can be used, without modification, as the starting point for the target architecture development. It provides a reasonable description of the services of the basic platform, and at this stage the generic nature of the foundation services is usually sufficient. The architect has ample opportunity to modify the service definition as the analysis moves toward the right hand side of the continuum.

An important point to reemphasize is the distinction between the platform and the application with respect to the services. The foundation architecture positions its services within the platform. This is a logical notion only—physically, they may of course be implemented in a product such as an operating system or an application server, or alternatively within a custom application. The point is that a platform service is generally available to any application or system that may need it through a well-defined interface (such as an API). Individual applications or systems are likely also to contain "services" of varying types. They will provide and/or enhance the functionality of the individual system but are unlikely to be implemented and exposed in a way that allows them to be used by any application. On the other hand, the organization may also have implemented services within its applications that meet many of the requirements of a platform service. This could have been intentional or otherwise.

To reiterate, from the TOGAF perspective, the more services the platform offers, that relate directly to the business and technical goals the more effective the technical architecture. This is one of the central concepts of the TOGAF architectural approach.

The foundation services provide excellent examples of what TOGAF considers to be a service and what it deems to exist within the platform, at least at a foundation level. As an exercise, the architect could select one of the organization's applications and analyze it with respect to the TOGAF foundation services (this will have been done to some extent if the architectural method included describing the current systems in TOGAF terms; see Chapter 8). It should be easy to identify that most of the services exist and are used, how they are used by the application, what technologies provide the service, and what interfaces provide access to the service. Looking deeper into each service, the architect should also be able to identify the functions supported and relate these to the subcategories summarized in Chapter 6.

The TOGAF foundation architecture does not consider that there may be other candidate services that exist within the organization's applications. However, TOGAF provides a framework for modifying current services and defining additional services and for representing these services in an enterprise TRM.

The in-depth analysis of the local applications for service harvesting occurs at later points on the continuum (typically, the industry and organization points). For now the architect should validate the foundation services. This does not mean that they must to be accepted regardless, although this is typically what can occur without affecting the target architecture.

It is recommended that the architect review the platform services with a view toward accepting them as valid for this stage of the architectural development. For example, the organization may be constrained to a single geographic location and therefore does not need international operation services. Also, the service subcategories should be reviewed both for completeness and validity within the organization's own technical environment. For example, although the organization is likely to require the services of data interchange, it may not have any requirement to support multimedia functionality.

Although the foundation analysis should not be overly concerned with organizational specifics, it is always valid to consider the organization's systems and the strategic business requirements (such as the business systems architecture). If the architect already knows of additional enterprise platform services that may be required to support new information system initiatives, these can be captured now and revalidated later.

The categorization of the foundation services may also require some work. For some organizations, the architect may believe the categories are not totally representative of the style of technical environment. Additionally, the architect may have some philosophical difference with the categorization as laid out in the foundation architecture. TOGAF is not prescriptive in this sense. The architect is freely able to modify the services as he or she sees fit; only the characteristics of a service must be preserved. For instance, we have found it beneficial to add a distributed computing service in a number of our client's TRMs. Such a service could merely borrow from a subset of subcategories in the foundation services. Using our vocabulary, distributed computing also has the characteristics of a super service and so may be seen, for emphasis, as above the base (foundation) platform in a more prominent position. Its categorization as a super service is enhanced, considering that it can be realized in current application server products as a "single unit." A newly identified service may also need subservice categories that do not currently exist within the foundation architecture.

TOGAF has similarly adopted this "super service" approach with the inclusion of object-oriented provision of services. This service is not actually included within the TOGAF technical reference model but merely uses this service as an example of how a higher-layer service may be described and what it may borrow from other services.

The outputs of the foundation architecture analysis should be as follows:

- A list of foundation service categories that is relevant to the organization
- A list of foundation service subcategories that is relevant to the organization
- Notional list of organizational services to be considered at a later date
- Notional categorization of new services (whether they be reclassifications of existing services or new super services).

The Common Systems Service Portfolio

Common systems services provide the ability to augment and extend the foundation services through the adoption of well-known and favorably positioned technology services. The foundation architecture merely provides the architect with the basis for a detailed technical architecture. It does not provide the detail necessary to describe each of the individual services in a way that will be meaningful as a technical strategy. The strengths of the foundation architecture are in the provision of a taxonomy of services that can be built on or at successive points along the continuum.

The objective at this point in the continuum is to concentrate on identifying and applying services adopted as standard or best-of-breed within the IT industry. Adopting such services allows the architect to apply "IT industry" best practice in extending the foundation architecture.

Many services, including each of the foundation services, are sufficiently fundamental that the IT industry is likely to provide a great deal of resources that can aid the architect. Such intellectual property tends to be related to a technology domain rather than an individual service. In some cases a domain and a service match one-to-one; however, it is also possible that a domain will relate to multiple services. This value derived from this point may include:

- Technology reference models describing the details of the service or domain using a taxonomy similar to the concepts behind the TOGAF TRM. It is highly likely that a specific domain may have both competing and complementary models.
- A set of standards and specifications representing the domain's TRM. "Standards" are likely to take a number of forms—international stan-

dards, standards from industry consortia, and de facto standards controlled by a single vendor. Again, the competition for standards mind share is likely to be rugged.

- Vendors producing technologies and products. This is generally the acid test of the models and standards defined within a particular domain. The number of vendors delivering products is a sure indicator of the current and likely success of technology services and therefore an indicator of the likely placement of the service (i.e., in the platform or in the application).

In essence, at this point in the continuum, the requirement is to consider building a library of reference models that drill into the identified service or super service. The TOGAF model exists at the root, while each service category can be exploded into a reference model of its own. This is not a mandatory step, but identifying service category models is beneficial in understanding further detail about the service and the concept of a TRM is an excellent way of capturing their composition. It should also be noted that finding reference models that provide this further detail can be difficult and confusing. Many common industry services, such as B2B commerce, can be represented by a number of different and competing models that describe different parts of the service. For example, a single service could be described by a communications protocol model, a metadata model, and a process flow model, as is the case with many of the e-business models. However, all of these can be important in understanding and describing the makeup of the service.

Selecting common systems services models also must follow the architectural principles defined in the early phases of architectural development. For instance, the stance on open systems tend to push the architect in a particular direction. Should a principle dictate open systems, then the most useful domain models will come from open standards bodies. Conversely, a best-of-breed approach may lead the architect to select vendor-specific reference models.

As an example of the application of common services models, consider the current trend of the consolidated application server, which we will call the distributed component super service. Generally, the application server is an entire deployment environment for component-based applications, typically based on a Web delivery model. There are a number of vendors working in this space, and the products of this effort can provide an indication of what technical services the organization may need to support if it required such a service. Assessing the products in this area, and the major specifications, gives the architect valuable insight into how the foundation platform services may be molded and augmented to provide for component-based deployment. The organization should review how the current major players in this area structure their products if this is a style of application development they intend to adopt.

For this example we will consider three specifications which drive actual application server products; namely, CORBA, Java 2 Enterprise Edition, and COM+ (or .Net). Our primary requirement for analyzing these common industry specifications is to convert them into a reference model of some type that highlights the services that make up the platform and can be used to augment the organization's TRM. Additionally, the architect may then decide to compare the reference models with actual products to gain further insight into the service-technology mapping.

The Common Object Request Broker Architecture (CORBA) specification produced by The Object Management Group defines a set of interface standards and service specifications that allow distributed objects (or components) to interoperate in a distributed environment. Initially defined in 1993, it preceded other specifications (such as J2EE and COM) by a number of years and was the first serious attempt at defining services for distributed object computing. Readers will note that the service models for these other specifications have borrowed heavily from the CORBA work. Although it is generally felt that CORBA will be superseded by these other distributed component standards, the service portfolio is still worthy of consideration. The CORBA service portfolio is shown in Figure 10.7.

The Java 2 Enterprise Edition (J2EE) specification is another example of a model that could further extend our component execution super service. It is shown in Figure 10.8.[36] This simple model is not provided directly in the J2EE specification; however, we were able to distill its construction from the major service components described in the standard. It is typical that such models can provide a greater amount of detail with respect to the individual subservice categories and their associated technologies. The J2EE specification provides absolute reference to application program interfaces; for instance, it states explicitly what transaction APIs to implement (JTA) or what messaging APIs to use (JMS), for example. It is therefore reasonable to compare its structure with that of TOGAF's TRM. The services provided in the J2EE specification can be considered definitively platform-based, providing standard APIs for Java applications to use these services. This is an excellent example of the power derived by moving technology into the platform. Because this is a super service the application is provided with a set of powerful APIs that isolates it from some of the basic services.

The J2EE model/specification is controlled by a single vendor (i.e.,

36. From the Java 2 Enterprise Edition Specification, v1.3, proposed final draft, 20 October 2000.

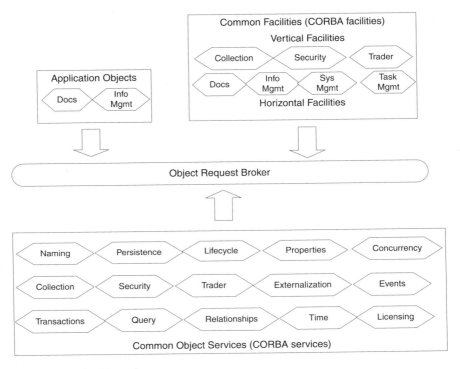

FIGURE 10.7.   CORBA services.

Sun) but is available for implementation by any vendor. Depending on the philosophy of the organization, J2EE could be considered a proprietary specification or an open standard, or in fact anywhere along this continuum. Unlike some of the other reference models we discuss here, the J2EE model is generally considered to be specific to a single language; that is Java. The organization would need to ensure that this aspect is aligned with their direction before integrating the model as part of a common service.

Microsoft is not a member of the Object Management Group and is unlikely to consider Java as strategic. Therefore, Microsoft has yet another specification, known currently as COM+,[37] which also provides the services of the component execution super service. The major difference with the Microsoft offering is that it is also an actual product. Both CORBA and J2EE are specifications and rely on vendors to implement products. COM+ is based on a number of Microsoft distributed component technologies that are integrated into the Windows operating

37. Microsoft's distributed component architecture is being transitioned to their *.Net* initiative.

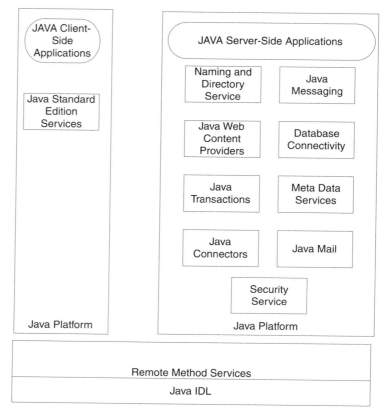

FIGURE 10.8.   J2EE reference model.

system—that is, directly into the platform. Figure 10.9 shows a view of the basic services provided by COM+.

The interesting aspect of each of these reference models is the similarity between each specification's service categories. That is not to say that the categories are interoperable (because they are not without significant translation) but rather that the types of services necessary to support distributed component-based computing are consistent between the different models. Each collects together a number of key services within the platform. Table 10.3 summarizes the subset of services that are common to all of the models. Notice that some of the subservice categories exist as TOGAF services already, such as security, network, and data interchange. Others are new, such as legacy integration.

The information gathered in assessing these common service offerings can now be used to determine how it might be worked into the organization's TRM. The architect may decide to summarize the services

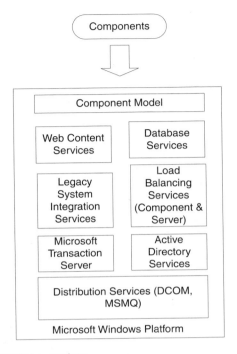

FIGURE 10.9.   Microsoft COM+ services.

Table 10.3. CORBA, J2EE, and CO+ service summary.

Service category	Service Sub-Category
Distributed component communications bus	• Synchronous and asynchronous network services • Location services
Component platform services	• Transaction management services • Data interchange services • Directory and naming services • Legacy integration Services • Web content Services • Data management Services • Deployment services (such as clustering and load sharing) • Security services • Systems management services

described by these specifications and highlight where they would appear in the TRM. In essence, putting placeholders in the TOGAF TRM to indicate each service has some relationship with distributed component computing. This may be relevant even when distributed component computing is not the only strategic direction for the organization. If other models of application development and deployment are being considered, it is likely that they too will have a similar service portfolio, except that the services will be provided through different technologies.

An alternative approach to consuming the services into the TOGAF foundation TRM is to represent them as a super service. A super service collects together services from the base platform and augments them with any additional services required to form a subject-area-specific service. The super service can then be represented directly within the organization's TRM, affirming a degree of importance to the service.

Furthermore, it is then possible in some cases to break down the subcategories into further reference models. This provides even more detail with respect to the style of the service and possibly its implementation. Considering implementation at this point is not a sin either. For example, take the transaction service embodied within the distributed component models. This can be broken down further by using The Open Group's XA reference model (see Figure 10.10). This provides a tertiary model, giving increased detail (implementation specifics) about the transaction service.

Other TOGAF foundation service categories can be treated in a similar way. What is important is to leverage off the work already available in the IT industry in defining how technologies are put together. For instance, the classic International Standards Organization (ISO) Open

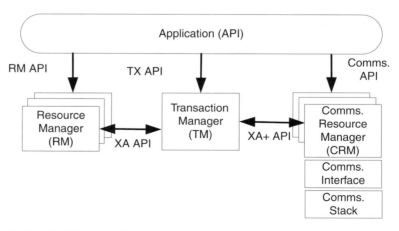

FIGURE 10.10.   The XA transaction reference model.

Systems Interconnection (OSI) reference model, a summary of which is shown in Chapter 9 in the communications view, represents an excellent method of describing the general layering of communications services. Although originally specific to the OSI protocol suite, its general service layering is applicable to Internet communications technologies.

It is impossible for the architect to have significant depth of understanding with all technologies. The service categories within the TOGAF TRM have been extensively researched worldwide. The fact that these services exist within the platform indicates their maturity and the number of associated standards and products. What is important is to understand the services that are relevant to the organization and the technologies and standards that should be reviewed as likely candidates to fulfill these services. Then, the architect need only leverage off the work undertaken on a particular subject area by the experts.

The security service is an interesting example of this leveraging concept. TOGAF indicates that this service should contain the following subcategories:

- Identification and authentication services
- System entry control services
- Audit services
- Access control services
- Nonrepudiation services
- Security management services
- Trusted recovery services
- Encryption services
- Trusted communication services

Each of these individual subcategories obviously is critical to supporting a secure information system, especially in an Internet-facing environment. However, the problem of understanding how these services are made up can be a lifelong pursuit. There is a huge amount of research into security available from a wide variety of organizations—vendors, government, standards bodies, and others. In fact, each of the subservice categories mentioned earlier can be supported by a large number of differing products, standards, and approaches. For instance, The Open Group has published a document entitled "An Architecture for Public Key Infrastructure"[38] that provides a set of reference models describing how an organization may go about implementing a public key infrastructure (one of which is shown in Figure 10.11). If the organization deems that this type of security service is required in its environment, leveraging from such an architecture can both save time and

38. Open Group Guide, Document Number G801, ISBN: 1–85912–221–3.

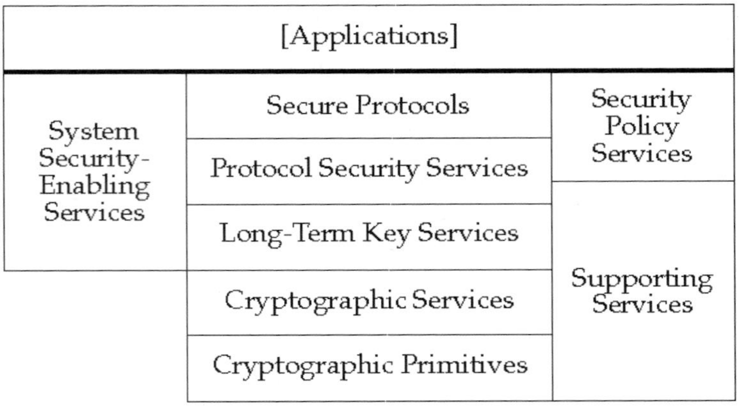

[Applications]		
System Security-Enabling Services	Secure Protocols	Security Policy Services
	Protocol Security Services	
	Long-Term Key Services	Supporting Services
	Cryptographic Services	
	Cryptographic Primitives	

Figure 10.11.   Public key infrastructure architecture.

ensure that best practice prevails. Such a model can then represent the second level of hierarchy of TRM for the security service.

The common services point of the continuum aids the development of the target architecture by leveraging off services already researched and described within the IT industry itself, the objective being to build a better understanding of the services that already form part of the foundation architecture and to convert common industry products and specifications into the TOGAF service framework (possibly through the specification of super services). The output of the common services architecture analysis typically includes:

- A more complete service and subservice categorization
- A reordering of the standard foundation services based on current products and specifications
- The identification of possible super services
- A second layer of reference models to aid both service definition and the alignment of technology

The Industry Service Portfolio

Much as the common services point on the continuum leverages off the IT industry's products and specifications, the industry architecture point leverages off the IT initiatives of the organization's own industry. Many large industries sponsor the formation of industry bodies to maintain the IT "well being" of the overall industry. Commonly, these sector groups will provide some (or all) of the following services to their members:

- Political (both domestic and international) advocacy
- Industry watch
- Global marketing
- Professional development and customer education
- Technical standards development
- Promotion of innovation
- Facilitation of member interaction (either commercially or professionally)

Key success criteria for industry bodies include the development of industry technology standards. These tend to be categorized as technical (non-IT) specifications associated with the particular domain and IT specifications that aid and enhance individual member internal (and external) IT environments. Many of the IT specifications defined by the industry bodies aid the standardization and interchange of electronic information among their members.

The architect must be aware of the industry bodies to which it belongs, the specific industry-driven specifications that may need to be supported by the organization, and the impact of these specifications on the organization's technical architecture. This can tend to be a reasonably binary decision. The organization is aligned with one or more industry consortia, and therefore their standards should either be considered for inclusion within the architecture or not. The organization may be a contributing member or associated by virtue of being involved in the same industry. Alternatively, the organization has no compulsion to be involved with industry consortia, and therefore any standards may be safely ignored.

There is a situation whereby the architect can add value to both the organization and the architectural process. An organization may not even be aware of the IT artifacts generated from associated industry bodies. Most organizations will know of the existence of any related industry consortia; however, the focus is most likely on the industry-specific services they might provide. What may not be known are the IT standards services provided. The architect should work with the business to understand which industry bodies should be considered for IT standards.

Industry specifications and standards should not be adopted without assurance, except in situations where adoption is mandatory for the organization. The following factors should be considered:

- The architect should assess the specifications resulting from the consortia's work, determining how they relate both to the currently defined target architecture and to the architectural principles. For instance, the organization may wish to interchange all information via

XML message formats, whereas the aligned industry consortia are generating specifications calling for SGML.

- The stated technical direction of the consortia is also important. Their technical strategy will be, after all, augmenting the organization's strategy. There must be "vision" alignment for this relationship to be effective.
- The status of the consortia needs to be understood (their level of penetration within the industry). Some industries have competing groups, usually due to political division.
- The acceptance of the specifications by the organization's peers is key. Although lack of acceptance may not be a reason to ignore the consortia's recommendations, a low level of acceptance may make their use invalid.

At the industry architecture point in the continuum, the architect is looking to further enhance the current service taxonomy with services provided by relevant industry bodies. The majority of industry bodies are particularly interested in interoperability of information among their members typically in support of efficiency gains. In a few cases they will provide reference models describing their offerings. Generally, the consortia will also provide a catalog of standards and specifications. These standards will become useful in the next stage of architectural development—defining the technology to match the services. This process occurs within the solutions continuum.

The aim at this stage is to ensure that the standards provided by the industry consortia are accommodated within the TRM. This allows the architect to cross-check that the services required to support the industry standards are present in the TRM. Usually, the standards can be easily categorized within the foundation services without further refinement. Using this categorization, the architect is then able to consider whether the services provided by the industry specifications can be re-categorized across existing services or described more completely as a super service. Depending on the richness and breadth of the standards, they can normally be left in the foundation service categorization.

There are many industry consortia providing a wide range of services to their members. A very small subset include:

- *Health Level 7.* Provides standards for the exchange, management, and integration of data that support clinical patient care and the management and delivery of health services.
- *Petrotechnical Open Software Corporation.* Provides standards for the definition of petrotechnical information and supports its exchange and its integration within applications.
- *Electronic Industry Association.* Acts as political advocate for its

members, guiding trading organization for the community, and provides business strategy and industry strategy assistance.

- *Society of Automotive Engineers*. Provides technical information and expertise in designing vehicles.
- *Telecommunications Industry Association*. Provides standards relating to telecommunications in wireless, fiber, user premises, network, and satellite. Additionally, the TIA provides a business-to-business portal for its members' products and services.

The TOGAF documentation makes reference to the Petrotechnical Open Software Corporation (POSC). POSC is a typical example of an effective industry consortium. POSC is an international not-for-profit corporation formed to advance information sharing and business process integration within the petrochemical exploration and production industry. A strength of POSC, and in fact most industry consortia, is its status as a neutral forum for collaborative learning and sharing. This allows the industry to focus on business solutions rather than on information technology problems.

POSC provides specifications in the following areas:

- Logical data models describing the information within the domain
- Application interface definitions for accessing the domain data models
- Information interchange between POSC-compliant systems
- Interapplication communications interfaces
- Graphical interchange formats (for domain-specific images) between POSC-compliant systems
- Test data and operational information for building POSC-compliant systems

The POCS specifications are structured into an entity known as the POCS software integration platform, within the specification. It is interesting to discover the common theme with respect to positioning functionality within "the platform." There is no single reference model that describes the POSC platform; however, there are a number of implementation models describing the interaction among various components provided within the POSC specifications. Figure 10.12 shows an example of one of these models—in this case, a definition for component interoperability.

The figure reasonably clearly delineates the various POSC specifications. Translating this into TOGAF service format is fairly trivial. An organization that intends to build a majority of its computing infrastructure to a particular consortium's specifications may wish to modify its reference model to align directly with the specifications. However it is

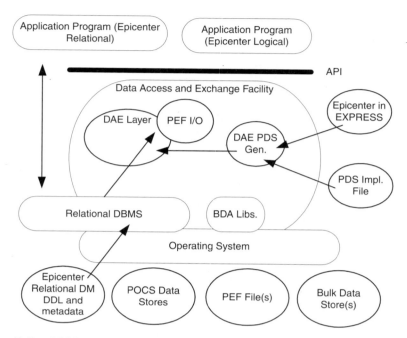

FIGURE 10.12.   POSC implementation model.

possible to adopt a more convenient (and most useful) method. Simply identify the particular service areas provided by the specification and incorporate them within the **TOGAF TRM** directly into the service portfolio already identified during the previous stages. For example, the **POSC** specifications provide standards in the following foundation service categories:

- Data interchange
- Data management
- Graphics and imaging
- Networking

In summary the industry architecture position on the architectural continuum aids the definition of the target architecture service portfolio by ensuring that industry-specific services are discovered and described within the reference model. The output of this analysis typically includes:

- List of aligned industry consortia
- Collection of relevant industry reference models, standards, and specifications

- Analysis of each industry-accepted service and specification with respect to its inclusion within the architecture
- Possible update of the evolving technical reference model

The Organizational Service Portfolio

The organizational architecture is at the rightmost end of the architectural continuum. The objective at this final point on the continuum is twofold:

- Organization-specific services must be considered and factored into the overall reference model (service portfolio).
- The building of the first full draft of the target architecture TRM.

Organizational services are derived directly from the organization's business functions. The business systems architecture will provide this detail. The functional requirements of the organization can be separated into two categories:

- functions that are specific to a particular business subject area and a particular business need.
- functions that may be specific to a particular need but may also be provided in a more generic way.

The second type can be readily considered for inclusion within the service portfolio. However they can be difficult to identify for two reasons. Firstly, they can be wrapped up in application function requirements. The architect should always be looking for functions that can be moved from the application into an application supporting role and hence into the platform. These are services that have not already been discovered in the previous continuum steps. Secondly, they may not exhibit all TOGAF-defined service characteristics. For instance, they may not be generic, commodity, or exposed through a standard interface. However, the important characteristic to look for is the ability to provide cross-domain functionality.

Organizational functions that are identified as platform services generally come in a couple of forms: custom-developed services and procured services.

Custom Services

It is not uncommon for an organization to have built custom sets of services to augment the enterprise platform. However, as vendor products become increasingly sophisticated, encapsulating more advanced services within the platform, the need for custom-developed services will move to higher domain—specific functions; that is, the "platformization" of procured services changes the scope of custom enterprise services. For instance, a number of years ago, when sophisticated middleware was not commonly available (particularly outside the mainframe), applications had to rely either on lowest-common-denominator remote procedure support, or in-house developed middleware-like services.[39] Organizations would not typically do the same today, when some advanced middleware products are available for only a few thousand dollars.

Even though, these new platform services, such as application servers and e-business platforms, at times encourage the implementation of custom services to be plugged into the products. There are a number of reasons for this:

- The standard that describes the product implementation may not have mandated a specification for a service.
- The vendor may be providing a value-added service outside the standard specification.
- A unique enterprise service is expected.
- The complexity (or simplicity) of a common approach to the problem may not be sufficient for all implementations.

Whatever the situation, most, if not all, organizations will have a number of custom-developed services. These need to be discovered and assessed for their suitability for inclusion in the TRM as an enterprise service. This is not an easy task. Services can be buried deep within applications, with little or no indication of their potential usefulness. Organizations that maintain a project, but not architectural, culture (systems delivered within project silos) are more likely to develop (or redevelop) embedded services without appreciation of the significance of doing so. This is because project pressures (cost and delivery) outweigh any corporate architectural imperatives. Others that have exerted some control over component reuse, and engender a corporation-wide architectural approach, are more likely to develop and to identify enterprise services.

At this point in the ADM new custom services or gaps in the current service offerings (through traceability efforts) should be considered. The two options available to meet these gaps are custom development or

---

39. A number of large organizations attempted to build the "super-API" to support all in-house platform services.

product procurement. The organization must determine which path is best aligned with its strategy for service delivery. Many have a "develop-first" culture. This can be valid if it has sufficient expertise over the long term to maintain and enhance custom services. As a personal prejudice, we have maintained a strategy of buying in the first place and only building if there is no other tenable option. Even the decision to move an organization-specific service into the platform may mean that wider vendor support is increased for the service. Most organizations will not be able to justify the same development investment in such services as a vendor would, so why compete with them? After all, the organization is typically in business for reasons other than building IT products. We would strongly suggest that organizations consider a similar strategy for services, even to the point of remolding user requirements to fit a product rather than undertaking custom development. However, this is very much going to depend on the organization's business and IT strategies. For example, in a highly competitive industry, an organization may need to innovate above lowest-common-denominator vendor products.

The suitability for the platform of custom-developed services must be determined. The service must exhibit many of the characteristics required of an enterprise service (see Chapter 6). Typically this will mean that it has been designed in this way from the beginning. It can be difficult to retrofit a custom component with the necessary service characteristics after development.

Custom services may not merely be pieces of technology. Guidelines, policies, processes, and standards are instances of nontechnological organization-specific services that may be available. For example, an organizational security policy can (and should) be viewed as a key architectural attribute of the organization's technical architecture. Enterprise data models are another example.

Armed with a list of custom services the next step is to assess which will be considered for inclusion within the target TRM. Remember that at this point we are only concerned with the service not the technologies that will implement it. Given that the identified custom services can be considered candidates for the service portfolio, it is usually enough to include them without prejudice. However, it is also important to understand what competing vendor services (and technologies) may exist to implement (and replace) the service. Adopting a product in place of a custom service may have positive impact on the overall total cost of ownership of the IT environment.

Procured Enterprise-Specific Services

There is one category of service that we have not considered fully up until this point and that is the enterprise-specific service delivered typically as a procured product. At the foundation point on the continuum, we have been concerned mostly with the classic type of service—those that are driven into the platform by the industry acceptance, as defined in Table 10.1. Niche functionality, which is not considered at the other points on the continuum must now be taken into account and reviewed for its inclusion within the TRM. Procured business functionality can either be specific to a particular set of business requirements or alternatively, it is possible that such functionality can be viewed as generalized across a number of different systems and hence be a candidate for a service. This classification is dependent on a number of factors:

- Whether the functionality is likely to be reused either by current or new systems described in the business systems architecture
- Whether the functionality exhibits the characteristics that represent a service
- Whether the product meets the architectural principles of the organization

One example of procured business functionality that can be considered for the platform is workflow. The basic constituents of a workflow system will use the underlying platform services already defined (e.g., network, security, systems management). In this way, the workflow system behaves just like any other organization application. However, the higher-level functions of workflow (e.g., process definition, process enactment) can also be considered as a platform service (probably a super service) and as such may be moved into the platform if required. These higher layer services are not in the foundation model, and so must be described (modeled) if workflow is a candidate for the platform.

Procuring a workflow product gives the organization the opportunity to consider the product as a service or collection of services. Of course, the organization may be intending to use workflow for a single business requirement, in which case the package may continue to live outside the platform. This type of decision, platform service or application function is constantly being made during this stage of the target architecture development. There is no right or wrong answer here; it is dependent on the requirements of the organization and, interestingly, on the style of the architect. However, making a procured application a platform member gives it a different status. Essentially it will become more strategic.

Functionality, such as workflow is, however, typically moved to the platform because it meets all of the characteristics of a service. Most leading workflow products are structured around a service paradigm (as would be expected), which therefore adds weight to its consideration as a service. As a platform service, any application that wishes to utilize workflow is required to use this service. This begins to introduce commonality and interoperability while also removing the temptation of the development teams to build another workflow system (or even individual service subcategories of workflow). Furthermore, one of the roles of the architecture project is to recommend what changes should be made to existing applications. This may include recommending that existing systems that implement workflow directly in the application be migrated to the standard workflow service.

The next logical step is to determine how to describe workflow as a service for the purpose of the TRM. The architect must be able to describe the services of workflow. This can aid in the procurement of a product, if necessary. There are a few methods of approaching workflow service definition, any of which has merit:

■ Determine whether a workflow standards body exists that publishes workflow specifications and adopt these as the service definition. Understanding the "success" of the specification is also important in making the decision to use this method.
■ Review a number of industry-leading products, understand their architectures and build a service definition that amalgamates the key functions.
■ Build a service definition based on the organization's business requirements for workflow.

The Workflow Management Coalition (WFMC) is an industry provider of specifications for workflow systems. It publishes a set of reference models and specifications that describe a workflow system. Figure 10.13[40] presents the WFMC high-level reference model, and the specification describes a further breakdown of this model into more specific services. Using a model such as the one provided by the WFMC allows the architect to leverage from the detailed work carried out by experts in the particular field.

It should also be understood that the technical architecture is not required to delve deeply into the architecture of a particular service (the service's application architecture, if you will). The objective is to describe the service in enough detail to be able to assign technologies and understand how the services and the organization's applications will interrelate and best suit the organization's strategic objectives. The service is in effect treated as a black box defined by an interface (or collection of interfaces) and described by its encapsulated functions. The services will need to adhere to the technologies selected to fulfill the service portfolio (we look at this in the next chapter). There is no point in a procured product running on an operating system or a DBMS that cannot be supported as part of the IT environment.

40. Workflow Management Coalition, Workflow Reference Model – Document Number TC00-I003, 1995.

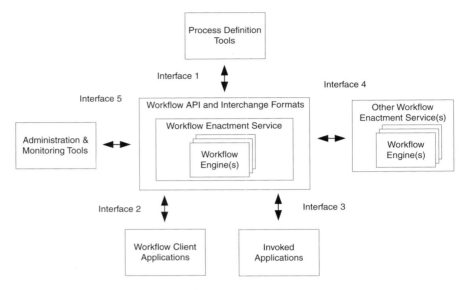

Figure 10.13.   Workflow reference model.

At a later date the organization is likely to initiate a project to procure technology to provide the service. At this time, a more detailed systems (or solutions) architecture will be defined for this purpose. This will obviously be driven by the technical architecture (it is envisaged that all technology development and procurement is in some way driven by the technical architecture) but is not in the scope of the Technical Architecture.

Iterations

The journey from the foundation to the organizational point of the continuum is not linear. At all points there is a feedback process that allows the architect to revisit any instant along the continuum to add, remove, or modify the defined service portfolio. This process is not restricted to the service definition either; during technology definition the architect may also decide that a particular service area needs further investigation due to problems with technology alignment. The objective is to provide a stable service taxonomy for describing the organization's technical strategy.

Our experience indicates that the definition of the organizational services is typically likely to lead to rework in the industry and common services points of the continuum. Analysis of custom organizational services may lead to the decision to refactor how custom services are delivered. For instance, it may be decided that a particular custom service should in fact be procured. Therefore, it will be necessary to revisit the industry or common service point of the continuum to find solutions to the problem.

The continuum points can be more conceptual than physical. When working with TOGAF for the first time, it can be valuable to think specifically about the points along the continuum. However, as the organization's technical strategists become familiar with TOGAF, they will find that they can think intuitively in continuum terms without cognitively considering each point individually.

10.7 The Technical Reference Model

The TRM Graphic

The aim of the TRM is twofold: firstly, it provides a high-level (conceptual) diagrammatic representation of the organization's strategic view of its IT environment; secondly, it provides a detailed list and description of the organization's services to drive the selection of technology to align with the services. In essence, the TRM provides a taxonomy and visual representation of the organization's platform functions.

The TRM brings together all of the modeling work completed during the journey along the continuum. It will describe all super services and foundation services, including service categories and subcategories discovered.

The method of visually representing the TRM is a personal (or organizational) preference. The architect may decide to adopt the TOGAF block representation method; certainly, most reference models are presented in this fashion. However, there are many other techniques, including rich pictures, animated models, hyperlinked models, "wiring" diagrams, and others.

The architect may also consider describing the TRM in terms of the architectural continuum. If the continuum is deemed to be a useful communications tool and is becoming part of the organizational vocabulary, then this method of presentation can be incredibly valuable. Using this method, all services are plotted against the continuum at the points where they were added assuming a linear progression through the continuum.

From the purely visual perspective, it is important to provide a single-page summary view of the TRM. This does not mean that the TRM should be restricted to such a size but rather that the overview should fit on a single page. This supports the communication of the model and is easily able to be accommodated within all sorts of organizational literature, such as tender documents, requirements definitions, IT strategies, management reports, standards documents, and so on. Condensing such information into a single page can be a challenge; however, the hierarchical structure of the service taxonomy can aid this tremendously. Figure 10.14 presents a simple model for describing the service taxonomy. The primary TRM presents and summarizes the key service groupings, particularly the enterprise-specific and super services.

The detailed breakdown of the primary services is achieved through a set of secondary and tertiary models that can be linked back to the primary TRM. Bear in mind that each service (from the primary TRM) may have one or more reference models that describe it. These must be referenced as part of the encompassing TRM. It is these more detailed models that provide the necessary information to create service subcategories. This information can be critical in the next phase when technology is assigned to the services. The detailed TRM should contain all services discovered and defined as necessary for the corporate technical

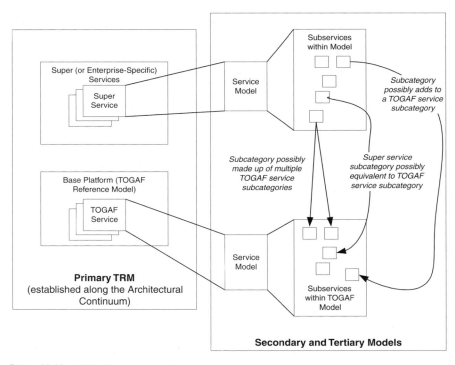

FIGURE 10.14.   TRM hierarchy model.

architecture. This will include any baseline services that remain. This information is likely to be less viable for the organizational groups not directly connected to the architecture. Therefore, this can be provided in simple textual format (possibly table-formatted) in a way similar to that provided in TOGAF. Both the primary TRM and the secondary and tertiary models and taxonomy are then captured in the Technical Architecture Document.

The individual models used to describe the super (or organization-specific) services would contain within their structure a set of their own service categories (or subcategories). These categories may already exist within the foundation services. As the TOGAF foundation architecture continues to mature, this will increasingly be the case. At any point, the subcategories within the super services may specialize, overlap, or replace those within the foundation services (we introduced the notion "new", "duplicate", "consume", and "replace" in Chapter 9 to describe how super service subcategories relate to the TOGAF foundation subcategories). This should be catered for in the architecture, for although the service category may be the same, the technology used to implement it may not be.

For example, a super service such as application integration services will include a security subcategory that is likely to provide principle authentication as will a distributed computing super service. The TOGAF security foundation service also contains identification and authentication subcategories. From a service category point of view these are identical services. From the perspective of the TRM, showing these subcategories in more than one place represents its number of different uses (and potential technical duplication). When the time comes to look at the technology to implement the subcategory, the architecture must be able to meet all of these security requirements and, of course, there may be a number of ways that these services can be fulfilled with technology.

We, of course, suggest that the organization adopt the TOGAF TRM as the de facto model for the foundation platform. All other, more specific, services should sit on top of the TOGAF TRM.

Selection Criteria

At this stage, the architect will have developed a good understanding of the "functional" makeup of each service area. This is a natural by-product of the detailed discovery process. As has already been stated, the next stage deals with aligning technology with the selected services. Therefore, at this point it is important to define the criteria that may be used for technology selection and the functional aspects of each service.

The selection criteria for technology will have been touched on during the development of the architectural principles (during the initiation and framework stage; see Chapter 5) and during the development of the baseline definition in TOGAF format (Chapters 6 and 8). These will have provided high-level guidance with respect to technology but should be re-tested in light of the service portfolio.

The architectural principles (which represent strategic selection criteria) state those aspects of IT that the organization holds dear. They tend to be aligned to the IT cultural briefs and are not so much quantifiable as they are religious. To effectively select technology during the next stage, it is imperative to redefine these sometimes "religious" statements in pragmatic terms. In essence, the architect is required to ensure that the principles are definitive, measurable, and achievable.

The other point to consider when developing selection criteria is the problems raised during the initiation and baseline description. A strategic analysis of the IT environment, usually conducted during the ISSP exercise, will have unearthed some key problems that must be solved to ensure that the strategy implementation is effective. We warrant that a technical architecture development is key in resolving strategic issues. Furthermore, the baseline phase will discover and describe more in-depth technology-related problems with the current environment. These problems must be addressed by the target architecture (see the overview of the process in Figure 10.3). Therefore, the architect should review the problems identified and attempt to distill criteria that, if met, will lead to the resolution of the issue. For instance, consider the following problem identified during an ISSP, and elaborated during the Baseline phase:

The application of IT security is ad hoc and unmanaged.

An architectural principle that may have been derived from this problem would be:

Where possible, all security services should be provided via an integrated service based on a corporate security policy.

The architect would be able to distill (at least) one selection criterion from this information, which may state:

Security services (especially authentication and authorization) must be provided through a published, and commonly accepted, interface, and delivered generically to all applications.

The other component of the selection criteria to consider at this point is an early "functional" draft of the service requirements. Each service will be required to provide functionality to both the platform and the applications that use it. These requirements will need to be captured to allow functional assessment of the technology selected to provide the service. During the service portfolio development, the architect will begin to develop an excellent understanding of the functional structure of the services. This can come about for a number of reasons:

- Assessment of specific industry or common service architectures and reference models will lead to an understanding of the generic requirements for that service.
- The review of the organization's applications for the purpose of service discovery will provide further understanding of the way the application (and hence service) is implemented.

An initial draft of the functional requirements for the services should be captured as part of the detailed view of the technical reference model. Consider the generic characteristics (see Chapter 6) of services, and describe how a particular service might support the characteristics. Service requirements definition will be covered in greater detail in the next chapter.

The Technical Architecture Document

The technical architecture document is the key descriptive deliverable from the entire architectural process. This document collects information from the entire architectural development into a single repository. It should contain information that describes the technical architecture, the basis for the architecture, and tracks any important decisions made during the process. At this point in the process, the document should contain at least the following artifacts:

- Architectural principles
- Constraints (both organizational, project, and technical)
- Key organizational requirements and strategic references.
- Baseline description
- Draft primary TRM.
- Draft detailed service (and subservice) taxonomy
- First draft of service technology selection criteria
- First draft of service functions (requirements)
- Key service selection decisions
- Service taxonomy alignment with the continuum (optional)
- A mapping describing the transition between the baseline and the target service portfolio

10.8   Requirements Traceability

The last stage of the service portfolio definition is requirements traceability. It is not unusual for the architect (and other contributors to the service portfolio) to stray somewhat from the functional and strategic drivers of the architecture. This phase of architecture development is reasonably technical (although less so than the next), and the strategy and business drivers can sometimes be lost in the effort required to discover, model, and document technical services.

There are various techniques that can be used to ensure requirements alignment. Typically, the most effective approach is to undertake a gap analysis (based on the associated model) defined at the beginning of the chapter and shown in the Chapter 7 baseline assessment. After the creation of the first draft of the service portfolio and TRM, this can be achieved through the production of a number of matrices, relating significant requirements with specific services, and applying standard gap techniques.

An important comparison to undertake is to ensure that each of the major services meets the architectural principles. Consider a matrix that plots these two dimensions. At each intersection consider how the principle may be met by the service. Analyze the functions of the service and the subcategories and understand how each exists to aid the principles. At this stage we are matching service function with architectural demands. Table 10.4 shows a skeletal table for this purpose. There are no hard and fast measures to use in this comparison (i.e., the intersections in the matrix). The architect must adapt the measures to make sense when read against the principles. As a suggestion, we have used the following successfully:

- Primarily provider
- Contributes
- Is not related to
- Modified or enhanced to meet
- Does not provide (or inhibits)

Focus on those gaps that represent nonprovision or principle inhibitors. The architect must then consider why principles are not being met. Is this purely due to a misunderstanding of the principle? Is there a missing service? Does the principle need to be reconsidered or dropped? Furthermore, it can be important to consider the spread of measures for a principle across all of the services. For instance, a particular principle may require that it be provided by all services to be delivered successfully (e.g., reduce total cost of ownership).

Table 10.4. Principles and service comparison.

Architectural Principles	Major Services								

Another useful matrix is the comparison of services against key strategic factors (i.e., strategic drivers, business requirements, or constraints; see Table 10.5). This is a rehash of the analysis carried out during the baseline assessment. As with that assessment, this takes the target service portfolio and ensures that there are no inhibitors to meeting the factors defined. The combination of this assessment with that done in Chapter 7 begins to establish a transition map.

A typical gap-analysis view of the target architecture is a one-for-one service comparison with the current services. For each service, map how the current service subcategories are provided by the target subcategories. To complete this effectively, the current environment should be described in TOGAF terms. Using a table such as the one in Table 10.6, the architect will be able to describe subcategories:

- Where no change is anticipated
- That will be amended
- That will be greatly enhanced
- That will be fully replaced
- That are new in the target architecture
- That will be eliminated
- Where the intersection represents a gap in the target architecture (i.e., has not been considered)

When the exercise is complete, anything in the "Eliminated Services" or "New Services" category's are a gap, which should either be explained

Table 10.5. Business drivers and service comparison.

Strategies, Requirements, Constraints	Major Services								

as correctly eliminated or marked as needing to be addressed by reinstating or developing/procuring the function.

Another area to consider is how various problems identified during the current systems assessment are mediated by the target architecture. This information may already be captured in the key question list but it can provide the architect with piece-of-mind that the intending direction is actually solving the organization's problems.

It is also pertinent to update the key question list. Questions will be refined, added, and deleted based on the service portfolio discovery process. The key question list was first devised during the baseline development. This, however, is the first point at which the questions can be answered. The architect need not provide formal answers to the questions at this stage but must be able to explain (preferably to both the sponsor and him or herself) how the architecture might help answer these questions.

Another point to consider is the acceptance process. The development of the service portfolio and the TRM is a key deliverable of the process and should represent an important milestone in the architectural development process. It is therefore important to ensure that the requirements analysis be accepted and signed off by the sponsor and/or the program's steering group. This is a significant checkpoint and ensures that the project is on track, is actually targeting the organization's requirements, and is meeting expectations.

It is also important that the IT group have a detailed understanding of the current state of the target architecture. The IT group will be the people who must implement it, so their buy-in is key. The group will usually have been significantly involved in the process anyway. However, it is also important to obtain feedback and signoff on the validity of the TRM and the portfolio before embarking on the next stage. This may seem like stating the obvious, but we have been involved with organizations whose IT groups have "rejected" the new architecture due to

Table 10.6. Service transition gap analysis.

Service: <service name>

	Target Service Subcategories									Eliminated Services
Current Service Subcategories										
New Services										

their lack of involvement. The architect (who may or may not be a member of the IT group) should always attempt to negate the "ivory tower" concept—the shop floor disregarding the architecture because it was viewed as an academic exercise produced by people who have no real understanding of the real world outside HQ. This is one of the barriers to architectural success—even more so than an invalid architecture.

This is also a good time within the project to consider updating the acceptance criteria. These have been defined at a high level during the initiation and framework phase. Further discovery and the completion of the key question list will provide additional input into updating the acceptance criteria.

In summary, the output of the requirements analysis will include one or more of the following:

- First draft of key question list
- First answers to key questions
- Updated acceptance criteria
- Gap analysis
- Overall report on how the architecture meets the requirements

10.9 Outputs

The documented artifacts for this activity are encompassed within the technical architecture document, producing the next version, in this case version 0.3. This stage augments the document with the following:

- The target technical architecture model—the organization-specific TRM
- Further constraints definition, if required
- Further architecture principle definition, if required
- Requirements traceability
- Additions to the key questions list, if required
- Selection criteria for selection of the target services

10.10 Example

Introduction

We continue the development of the CFL technical architecture with the development of the target service portfolio. To develop the portfolio, we have serialized the steps along the architectural continuum, beginning at the foundation services, moving to the common system services, incorporating the industry services, and finally arriving at the organization-specific service portfolio. Again, it is worthwhile to emphasize that this is not a complete treatment of CFL's IT environment—such a treatment would run to a volume in its own right. Instead we pick on specific requirements for this section of the example.

Foundation Service Portfolio

We begin with the foundation service portfolio discovered during the description of CFL's systems in TOGAF format. We could equally have adopted all of the foundation service categories and subcategories, but we felt that this would not give an accurate view of the requirements of the IT environment as a whole and be likely to cause wasted effort because nonrelevant subcategories would require the assignment of technologies.

At the granularity of a service category, the international operation service is a key area that is missing from the current systems and needs to be added into the foundation service portfolio.

Some of the key problem areas to be solved by the target architecture include:

- Significant integration issues
- Lack of an e-business infrastructure
- Ineffective reporting infrastructure
- Ineffective e-mail and collaboration environment

Common System Service Portfolio

The common systems services allow us to refine the already adopted foundation services and begin the discovery of super services. We highlight some of the key service areas that need a secondary model of their own. Their significance leads to the conclusion that they exhibit super service characteristics. At this point, we can only postulate that they are in fact super services. Later, it is possible that they will need to be extended with additional functionality or chopped up into smaller units. These service areas represent key components of the CFL IT environment that will enable business strategy and requirements to be met.

For each of these services, we have conducted significant research within the IT industry to determine the industry-leading service models that reflect CFL's requirements.[41] Adopting a specific model does not mandate that we will also adopt any technology or products that underpin the particular model. The model merely provides us with a better understanding of the service category. Table 10.7 presents a partial view of the candidate super services and the proposed secondary reference models to describe them.

Business-to-business (or B2B) commerce is an important part of CFL's future direction. To ensure that the IT environment supported the B2B requirements, we needed a model (or set of models) that described the types of service subcategories present in B2B implementations. We discovered a number of (competing) specifications and products in the industry that would help us map the technology required to deliver to CFL's B2B requirements. After analysis, we selected the RosettaNet specifications for a number of reasons. They appeared to target the particular e-business areas we were concerned about and, secondly the Confectionary Manufacturers Association have also built their model on the RosettaNet specifications.

Other similar decisions were made in selecting models to provide both secondary and tertiary service categories. For instance:

Table 10.7. Common service models.

(Super) Service	Proposed Model
Business-to-business commerce	RosettaNet framework
Distributed component computing	CORBA model
Security	TOGAF foundation security, and common data security architecture Open Group PKI architecture
Systems management	Tivoli (product) TOGAF foundation systems management
Enterprise reporting	Metadata consortium (partial)
Software engineering	Rational (partial) Software engineering institute capability maturity model
Enterprise application integration	CFL service model Confectionary Manufacturers Association

41. Of course, by requirements, we refer to the full gamut: business (and e-business) strategy, ISSP (and the other architectural components—information and business systems architecture), and issues and gaps.

- It is essential that CFL move into the world of multitier application development in a reasoned and consistent way. Currently, CFL does not have a standard approach to the architecture of applications; nor does it have an understanding of the optimum method by which applications should be deployed. We conducted a detailed assessment of the market and see the gradual (some may say, fanatical) move toward distributed object computing based on object transaction middleware. There are a number of competing models in this area; however, at this point it is important for CFL to at least understand the services to be provided within the IT environment to allow distributed, multitier computing to be successful. We selected the Object Management Group's CORBA as an indicative model with which to plot the services required for distributed computing. It is generic (and mature) enough to provide the necessary information for the CFL reference model and does not imply any particular direction.

- The standard TOGAF security service model appears adequate to describe all security requirements for CFL. However, we believe that security based on public key based is important to emphasize in light of its likely use in e-business applications (for authentication and nonrepudiation, for instance). Additionally, PKI is an approach for solving a number of CFL's disparate security implementation problems. Therefore, we have selected The Open Group's PKI architecture to represent the services required in this specialist area.

- Systems management is an area of concern in all but the Logistics environment. For this reason, we have adopted the Logistics systems management models to present "best practice" for the implementation of systems management throughout the organization. In this case, systems management is based entirely on the IBM Tivoli products, and therefore we have adopted the Tivoli service architecture. Additionally, CFL's move into new international markets, plus the drive to centralize (or coordinate) support for IT, will necessitate the delivery of increased remote management services within the IT environment, particularly software distribution, remote console takeover, and remote fault logging. These subcategory services already exist within the TOGAF systems management service.

- Enterprise application integration is an area of significant pain for CFL. We looked around in the EAI market for likely products or standards that could adequately represent this area. However, we found a significant amount of fragmentation in the market and no clear "winner" on which to base our model. In light of this, we decided to distill the essential services for the EAI (super) service from a number of the leading products. The model (see Figure 10.16) was then developed internally. This fact may mean that it is an organization-specific service. However, we believe that the model is generic enough to represent best practice in the industry and therefore can easily be considered in this section.

Industry Service Portfolio

A key component of the CFL business (and e-business) strategy is alignment with the Confectionary Manufacturers Association (CMA).[42] An architectural principle derived from this strategy is that:

> CMA standards and specifications should be adopted where possible and practical.

The CMA Information Exchange Model (IXM) (see Figure 10.16) has a number of objectives:

- Provide specifications for information exchange for domain-based information
- Define loosely coupled service layers to facilitate machine-to-machine integration, over the Internet
- The IXM is targeted at aiding improved material procurement and order fulfillment.

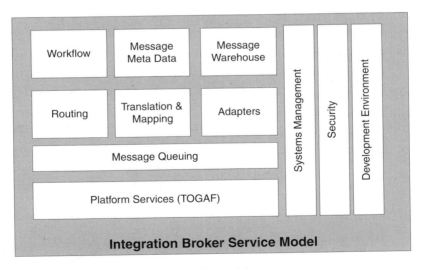

FIGURE 10.15. Enterprise application integration model.

Due to its alignment with many of CFL's own e-business needs, the CMA's IXM will be adopted as a key secondary model. Its generic nature is such that it may also be considered as a model for more generalized uses in the overall reference model. There is noticeable overlap with many of the foundation services; particularly information interchange and network. In fact, it does not add any new service categories. However, it does show some of the elements of a super service in that it collects together these foundation services into a more functional grouping. Including this service does not corrupt the TRM. It merely provides a greater recognition of the importance of the CMA standards in the model.

Organization-Specific Service Portfolio

We looked into the key organizational systems (at an application architecture level) to determine three things. Firstly, we wish to understand the "service nature" of the CFL application architectures. Secondly, we wanted to locate any services within the current applications that we had not accounted for in the TRM to date. Finally, we wanted to understand whether any of these services might be candidates for harvesting. There are a number of points to note here:

■   A custom-developed collaboration application that supported remote scheduling using calendars was discovered within the Sales CRM

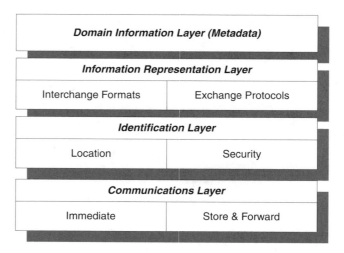

FIGURE 10.16.   CMA information exchange model.

system. This system can be driven by the CRM application but can also be accessed by a browser interface. It is essential to the management of the distributed sales force. We consider this application to have enterprise appeal (and related directly to a CFL technology issue) and that it should be considered for an organizational service. This is an area that is also well-served within the IT industry (i.e., the common systems point on the continuum), and we have chosen to model this service's subcategories using the Internet calendar standard models.

- A custom security service was discovered within the Logistics system on the AS/400s. It provides a proprietary API that supports authentication and authorization. This service was not considered for harvesting due to its proprietary nature.
- A GUI framework that has been reused within a number of small regional systems has the potential for incorporation within the TRM as an organizational service. Additionally, a quality GUI standards document was discovered that could be reused as a policy component of the user interface service.

CFL Technical Reference Model

We use the TOGAF "block" reference model graphical style to represent the top-level CFL TRM (Figure 10.17). Note that, in a fashion similar to TOGAF, we have used the concept of key business components interfacing with the model. For instance:

- The CFL corporate applications interface with the platform. These applications are typed and include infrastructure, tools/utilities, and domain-specific business applications from the business systems architecture.
- An element of the model is the point at which CFL users integrate with the platform. From our perspective, we describe this interface as through the various application types. Another way of showing this is via a specific human/computer interface type, as shown in the Open Software Environment TRM (see Figure 10.6).
- We show physical entities that interface with CFL over communications connections at the bottom of the model. These include both the physical communications infrastructure (not part of the model itself) and the infrastructures of customers and suppliers that are integrated through communications connections. Note that partners and customer are also represented as CFL users in that they make use of the high-level platform services.

Underneath the top-level services are a number of service models that help describe the details of each of the services. Some we have already discussed. Others (not shown) include:

- A custom-developed Web services model (that supports the consumer-to-business initiatives) represented in two layers, a set of secondary-level Web service categories, and the specialization of those services within the TOGAF platform services.
- The e-business service category model, developed in this text, describes the service requirements of CFL's B2B initiatives.
- We adopted the ISO seven-layer model to represent the communications service.

Requirements Traceability

Table 10.8 provides a subcategory gap analysis for the security service. The acronyms adopted for the comparison are NC for no change, EN for enhanced, RE for replaced, and NE for new, and Gap denotes an unintentional omission. Additionally, various points of intersection are annotated, and additional detail is provided after the table. Services that have entries in either New or Eliminated services indicate a gap, which should either be correctly eliminated or marked to be addressed and included within the target architecture.

{1}: Although current authentication mechanisms will remain embedded within a number of the legacy systems (notably Logistics) the entire method for users representing themselves to individual systems will be rethought. The target architecture service realization is to consider single sign-on technologies. This will also be tied to the need for e-business technologies to support external party authentication. In supporting this enhancement, the target environment is required to consider a single-user information repository.

{2}: System-entry control services were unintentionally omitted from our original assessment of the security service. Their importance is recognized, and it has been reinstated as a key security service.

{3}: There are no nonrepudiation services provided within the environment at this point. e-business initiatives, especially the commitment of funds and orders, will require the ability for both sender and receiver to be nonrepudiated. This will also require additional audit functionality to support the retention of signed messages.

{4}: CFL does not currently conduct any significant business over open networks. However, the e-business strategy mandates a number of ini-

tiatives, including the transaction of supply chain information with
CFL's partners. New facilities will be required, within the trusted communications subcategory, to ensure the privacy of this information as it
is passed over public networks.

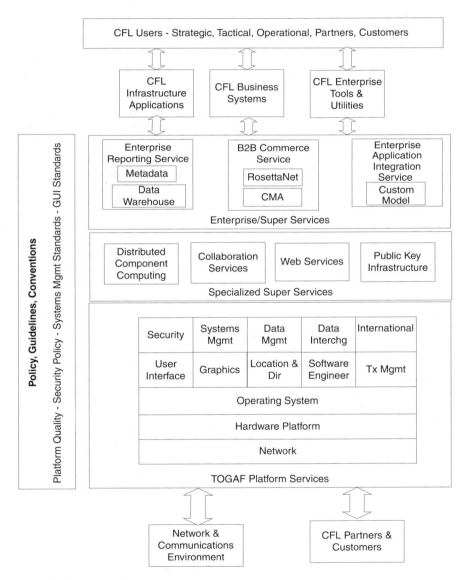

FIGURE 10.17.   Partial CFL target technical reference model.

Table 10.8. Security service subcategory gap analysis.

Service: Security — Current Service Subcategories	Identification and Authentication	System Entry Control Services	Audit	Access Control	Non-repudiation	Security Management	Trusted Recovery	Encryption	Trusted Communications	Eliminated Services
Identification and authentication	EN {1}									
System entry control services										
Audit			EN							
Access control				EN						
Nonrepudiation										
Security management						EN				
Trusted recovery							NC			
Encryption								EN		
Trusted communications										
New services		Gap {2}			NE {3}				NE {4}	

10.11 Summary

In this chapter, we took a detailed look at the development of the target architecture with the objective of developing the organization's service portfolio. We introduced the development of the portfolio as a linear progression through the architectural continuum. Finally, we considered methods of presenting the technical reference model, the need to develop the service requirements more fully, and a continuation of requirements traceability.

In our example, we developed a reasonably complete model for CFL's TRM by following the method outlined in this chapter.

We are how ready to consider how the service portfolio becomes represented by technologies. This is the topic of the next chapter.

CHAPTER 11

Target Architecture— Architectural Definition

11.1 Introduction

This point of the architectural development method (ADM) is where the rubber meets the road. It is at this stage that the target architecture is defined in a way that can be implemented and the logical service model (the technical reference model, or TRM) is realized as actual products and technologies.

This chapter describes a process to facilitate the realization of the abstract TRM, a product of the architectural continuum, into an enterprise solution. As with the service portfolio (discussed in Chapter 10), the enterprise continuum aids the development of the final solution-specific architecture; in this case, we use the solutions continuum to support service realization.

We also define the target standards information base (SIB). The SIB was introduced in Chapter 7 as a method of presenting current technology. In this chapter we use the SIB more extensively and as such it becomes an important artifact in the final definition of the enterprise architecture.

We continue to track through Phase C of the ADM (target architecture). The tasks of Phase C are shown in Figure 11.2 with the current task highlighted. From the TOGAF perspective this task covers both the definition of the architecture and the identification of architectural building blocks. As we have already stated, we have dropped the concept of building blocks from our treatment of the enterprise architecture. We instead dictate a service-based view to all architectural components.-

Thus, this chapter specifically shows a process to convert the architectural services identified in the last chapter to solution services.

Because this activity is still very much within Phase C, the inputs and outputs continue to revolve around the technical architecture document. During this task, it transitions from version 0.3 to 0.4. As usual, Figure 11.1 shows the wiring diagram for the activity.

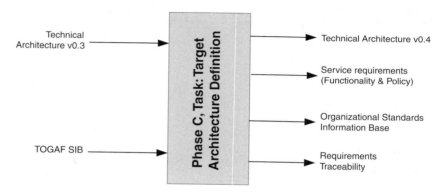

FIGURE 11.1.   Architectural Definition Activity wiring diagram.

11.2   *The Solutions Continuum*

As described in Chapter 4, the enterprise continuum is segregated into two interrelated streams: the architectural and the solutions continua. In this chapter we make use of the *solutions continuum* to aid in the final development of the technical architecture (the realization of services with technology). In the previous chapter, the *architectural continuum* was our tool for defining the logical service portfolio.

The solutions continuum represents the actual implementation of the architecture at the corresponding points of the architecture continuum. At each point, the solutions continuum is the realization of the service portfolio with either purchased products or custom-built components (or systems). The realization of the logical services represents solutions to the organization's business needs (strategic, operational, tactical).

As the solutions continuum is populated (that is, the architecture becomes defined), it develops into an inventory or reuse library of technical and nontechnical components. The inventory—embodied in the SIB— forms the basis of the platform that is the organization's IT environment.

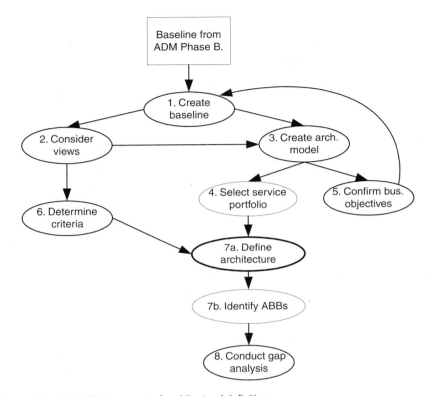

FIGURE 11.2. TOGAF placement of architectural definition.

This platform will be seen as the ideal encapsulation of all of the organization's business and technical requirements and the baseline for future development of the architecture.

Much as the architectural continuum is structured, the solutions continuum, shown in Figure 4.3, represents a bidirectional flow. The flow from the left to the right represents increasing delivery to the organization's specific needs and business requirements. This is the path that we will use to describe the organization's technology direction.

The leftward flow, from organization solutions to products and services, represents the provision of solutions value. It is highly unlikely that an organization will build every component of its IT environment. Also, it is unlikely (although less so) that an organization will use only standard purchased products. The leftward flow represents this. Products and services provide value in creating systems solutions, systems solutions provide value to create industry solutions, and industry solutions are used to create customer solutions.

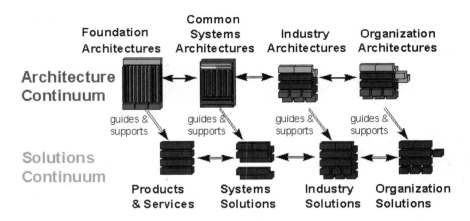

FIGURE 11.3.   Relationship between the architectural and solutions continuum.

The combination of the architectural and solutions continua constitutes the *enterprise continuum*, as illustrated in Figure 11.3. The relationship between the architectural continuum and the solutions continuum is one of guidance, direction, and support. For example, the foundation architecture supports the creation or selection of common industry products and services. It also guides development by providing descriptions of required functions, and the rationale for those functions, to build open computing systems. A similar relationship exists among the other elements of the enterprise continuum.

The enterprise continuum conceptualizes mechanisms to help improve productivity through leverage. The architectural continuum offers a consistent way to understand the different architectures and their components. Whereas the solutions continuum offers a consistent way to understand the different products, systems, services, and solutions required.

The enterprise continuum should not be interpreted as a strict chained relationship. The organizational service portfolio will have components from the common systems architecture, and products or services are provided by organizational solutions. The relationships depicted in Figure 11.3 are a best case for the ideal leveraging of architecture and solution components.

Finally, it is worth emphasizing that the beginning and end of the enterprise continuum lie at the foundation architecture, which serves as a tool box or repository of reusable guidelines and standards. For The Open Group, this foundation is The Open Group's own TOGAF technical reference model and standards information base.

11.3   The Standards Information Base

The standards information base is a significant artifact output from the realization of the service portfolio. The SIB is essentially a database of dynamic entities structured according to the taxonomy of the service portfolio in the TRM. The Open Group maintains such a SIB, indexed under the taxonomy of its foundation architecture. Neither the structure nor the contents of The Open Group's SIB need to be directly adopted by the organization, merely the concept. Note, however, that The Open Group SIB is an excellent reference for open, adopted standards under the now familiar TOGAF foundation taxonomy and can be a mine of information for architectural development in any organization.

We recommend that the organization use the SIB to describe the alignment of its chosen technology with the organizational TRM. The SIB does not provide all details for each service category (detailed design and architectural documents are required for this purpose). However, it does present, in a single place, the summary of all technical standards, specifications, policies, and products that make up the organization's IT environment. The SIB forms part of an excellent communications tool-set describing the enterprise architecture. We have also used the SIB, in its entirety, as part of the contractual schedules for IT projects.

The SIB is not specifically formatted for standards (or specifications) only. The SIB can be used to hold aspects such as preferred products, vendor relationships, policy and guidelines, organizational responsibilities, and others. In its basic form, the SIB will be formatted to hold the realization of the organization's TRM taxonomy (i.e., the identified service categories and subcategories).

Table 11.1 shows an extract from The Open Group SIB. The extract shows a microcosm of the Software Engineering Service standards. From this small subset, the eclectic use of the term "standard" can be seen. This extract contains references to textbooks, to an entire framework (TOGAF in this case), and a specific standard describing a conceptual overview.

11.4   Service Realization

Services and Service Instances

Service is a central concept of a TOGAF-based architectural development. Up to this point the definition of service has remained reasonably

Table 11.1. Extract from The Open Group SIB.

Reference	Year	Title	Description	SIB Status
ISBN 0-201-63459-7		Java Application Programming Interface, Volume 2	The Java Application Programming Interface described in one of two volumes by J Gosling, F Yellin, and The Java Team, published by Addison Wesley, Reading MA 1996 (ISBN 0-201-63459-7)	Adopted
TOGAF6	2000	The Open Group Architectural Framework (TOGAF) Version 6	Describes a framework for developing enterprise architectures based on open standards, comprising an architectural development method (ADM), a generic foundation architecture, and a resource base. Provides guidance to architects, and management responsible for IT governance, in customer, integrator, service and vendor organizations in developing enterprise architectures that will meet their business requirements.	Adopted
ISO /IEC/14252	1995	Guide to the POSIX Open System Environment	ISO/IEC Std 14252 is identical to IEEE Std 1003.0. This guide presents an overview of open system concepts and their applications. Information is provided to persons evaluating systems based on the existence of, and interrelationships among, application software standards, with the objective of enabling application portability and system interoperability. A framework is presented that identifies key information system interfaces involved in application portability and system interoperability and describes the services offered across these interfaces. Standards or standards activities associated with the services are identified where they exist or are in progress. Gaps are identified where POSIX® open system environment services are not currently being addressed by formal standards. Finally, the concept of a profile is discussed with examples from several application domains.	Adopted

abstract. During the development of the service portfolio (Chapter 10), the emphasis was on capturing the required service categories and subcategories without too much consideration of how they would be assembled to build the IT environment. To realize the organizational services, it is required that a more detailed view of services is taken, including exactly how they will be integrated into the architecture. The time has come to consider the technologies that will provide the services. In doing this, we introduce a new concept, that of the *service instance*.

Before considering the definition of a service instance, we must first state our meaning of the term *technology*. We have used the term *technology* liberally throughout this text to describe a number of related but different notions. It is an adequately generic term that begins to lose cohesion at this point in the process. In the context of this chapter, we use *technologies* to refer to the specifications and products used to detail services and implement service instances.

- Specifications describe the functional (and nonfunctional) aspects of service interfaces and implementations, can be proprietary or open, and can be produced by vendors, industry consortia, standards bodies, or the organization itself.
- Products are actual procurable or buildable implementations of specifications.

Specifications and products provide the realization of the service portfolio. The relationship between specifications and products is not clearcut. Ultimately, every product will have been derived from (or will implement) specifications. However, the specification's level of importance to the service realization process is murkier. Much depends on the organization's view of standardization and openness (see later in this section for a commentary on this issue). For instance, products that are derived from "open"[43] specifications are likely to hold the specification in high regard while the product is merely an implementation of the specification. From the organization's perspective, a focus on open standards is likely to lead to the service being realized primarily as a specification (with a possible addendum stating a preferred product). For example, operating system services are provided by the Single UNIX Specification APIs (the product that implements these will be less "important" to the realization process).

On the other hand, an organization may be less concerned with openness and may have more of a focus on limiting vendor relationships, for instance. In this case, a service will be realized as a product, which may (or may not) have a specification important enough to also be refer-

43. See the discussion on the continuum of openness later.

enced. For example, operating system services are provided by Microsoft Windows 2000 (the specification being less "important" to the realization). Of course, the product may in fact be derived from an open specification; however, this may not be as important, and the specification will be hidden from the SIB. An organization with this focus is more likely to implement a proprietary product.

Of course, we have opinions as to the focus an organization should place on specifications and products, but seldom is there a single approach. For most it will be a matter of pragmatism. Technologies must meet the organization's requirements (both functional and architectural), so inevitably a mixture of the two methods will be adopted. However, organizations will tend to bias one way or another.

Getting back to services, we introduced the characteristics of a platform service in Chapter 6. We also refined the generic term *service*[44] by noting that each service is more specifically described as a *service category*, each category consisting of a number of *service subcategories*. Regardless, both categories and subcategories exhibit the characteristics described.[45] Figure 11.4 shows a pictorial representation of the salient points of a service (that are also a truism for a service instance):

- A service must always have an interface of some type. In fact, from the architectural perspective, this is arguably its most important characteristic. Through the interface, the implementation is accessed by applications and other services. Of course, a single service instance may have multiple interface types supporting access to different parts of the implementation. The interface should be defined via a describable, published, and stable (but not necessarily open) specification. The service will also provide something across the interface, such as a set of bits written to a network link or a signed public key certificate.
- A service will have an implementation that provides the functionality accessible by the interface. The functionality implements some form of platform requirement; that is, in the context of TOGAF, an architectural service does not implement domain-specific or business functions. The combination of an interface and an implementation is generally delivered by a product (either custom or procured).
- A service implementation is highly likely to use other platform services in performing its functions. It would access such services

44. When we refer to service during this chapter, we do so generally. This term may be used to refer to an entire service category (such as distributed computing) or a single subcategory (such as remote method invocation). However, we will use the term *service* interchangeably for both meanings unless further clarification is required.

45. The nontechnical services, such as policy, quality aspects, standards, and so on, do not entirely conform to this model.

through an interface in the same way it itself is accessed. The recursive arc on the box labeled "Other Platform Service" shows that a chain of service integrations can occur.

- Applications are the key users of platform services. A constant requirement in application code is the need to access platform services. Whether it be a call to perform an operating system function (such as I/O to a file) or a request to start a transaction, the application is required to use the service's interface to perform the function. The interface called by the application (and the implementation of the service) is a first-class citizen from the architecture perspective. The entire reason for the IT environment is to support applications that provide a business benefit. Although some services occur deep in the bowels of the infrastructure (i.e., one not accessed by an application, only other services), those that are accessed directly by applications have significant bearing to the overall quality of the IT environment. Interestingly, the architecture can be viewed as responsible for influencing the interfaces that will be used by applications, as opposed to the applications determining what technologies should fulfill services (this is a bottom up approach to architecture—more on this later).

- Some services integrate with the external environment. This includes those that interface directly with a communications network or possibly to a system user.

TRM services are implemented (realized) in technology by *service instances*. A service instance is a physical incarnation of a logical service and is described by a specification(s) and/or product(s). Table 11.2 shows an example of service categories and service instances. In general, although each TRM service has the potential to be implemented by one or more products, each service instance should be implemented by a single product, allowing the occurrence of functional overlap to be eliminated. The organization may, however, choose to implement more than one product to provide a single service instance (allowing some cases of overlap). A product, on the other hand, could potentially implement one or more service instances.

During this stage, every service within the portfolio must be realized as a service instance. However, it is not vitally important that each service instance be defined by a product. It is entirely valid to identify instances with a specification, with no relationship to a product. This may occur for a number of reasons:

- The architect is not in the position to select a product, possibly due to a number of viable alternatives that must be assessed. During the next phases (opportunity and solutions, and migration planning), a

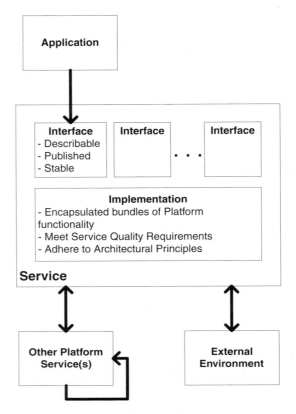

FIGURE 11.4.   Service (and service instance) characteristics.

task will be required to identify and procure a product that matches the specification.

■ A service instance may merely consist of an interface specification and cannot be associated directly with a product or the organization does not wish to mandate a product. This may occur where the interface is implemented as part of standard libraries in multiple products.

The relationship between service instances and service categories and subcategories is the crux of this stage of architectural development. Up to this point, the main protagonist has been logical services within the service portfolio (the TRM). Its treatment in Chapter 10 presented a purely logical view of services. This process has a tendency to throw up subcategory duplications; that is, a single subcategory could exist within more than one service. The mandate, however, for the portfolio was logical, not physical, and such problems could reasonably be ignored.

Table 11.2. Service instance examples.

Service (Category)	Service Instance	Product and/or Specification?
Location and directory service	LDAP	Specification
	Novell NDS	Product (with specification)
Operating system service	Microsoft Windows	Product (with specification)
	Single UNIX Specification 98	Specification

Now, however, we are required to convert the logical into the physical and in doing so, ensure that the realization is robust. Seldom, if ever, will there be a one-to-one mapping between the logical services and their physical realization (i.e., service instances). Although it would be convenient, it is unlikely that a specific instance of a service subcategory could be described neatly by a single technology no matter how hard the architect attempts to massage the services. Likely scenarios are shown in Figure 11.5:

- A single service instance (specification/product combinations) could span multiple service categories and subcategories.
- A single service instance could, in fact, implement a single subcategory.
- A single service instance could span and encapsulate an entire service category.
- A single service instance could include only a sub-set of a category's subcategories.
- A single service instance could encapsulate subcategories already provided by another technology.

A logical service therefore can be implemented by one or more physical service instances, each service instance being a product/specification couplet. The decision to create a service instance is driven by a number of (overlapping) factors:

- The desire for reuse of the functionality
- The desire to control cost attributable to execution of the functionality
- The desire to avoid duplicating the functionality
- The recognition of the functionality as a strategic enabler
- The desire to control procurement through standardization

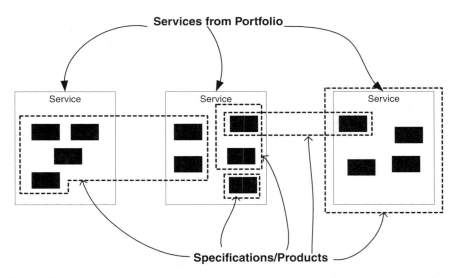

FIGURE 11.5.   Logical and physical services.

Should a service category exhibit these factors the functionality and interface should be bundled into a discrete service instance. On the other hand if the service category does not exhibit these factors then its functionality (and interface) should be consumed into a larger service instance.

For example, the service portfolio is likely to contain a database management system service subcategory (in the data management category). This service functionality can exist in (or be used by) a number of other super services. Additionally it can be implemented in many different products and technologies. If the organization decides to control costs by limiting vendor relationships and product types this service category may be considered to have both strategic and cost-saving influencers. As such it will be described by a discrete service instance.

Service Instance Relationships

The collection of all service instances provides the basis for the actual IT environment. We will take a look at some of the ways service instances interwork with each other.

Figure 11.6 shows a hierarchical relationship; that is, where one instance uses the services of another instance to complete a task for an application (or another service). The service hierarchy can be many layers deep. Each service instance in the hierarchy may be interservice or intraservice. For example, a web service instance calls a XML parsing service instance.

Figure 11.7 presents a web of service instances. This relationship is typical in a modern computing environment. The service instances are essentially peers with an application possibly invoking many of them directly as well. For example, transaction managers, database management systems, security servers, and name servers all are inexorably linked.

An embedded service instance, shown in Figure 11.8, is a discrete

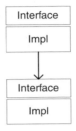

FIGURE 11.6. Hierarchical relationship of services.

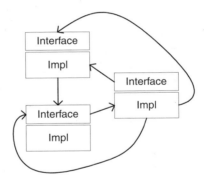

FIGURE 11.7. Web of service relationships.

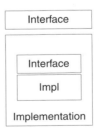

FIGURE 11.8. Embedded service instances.

service within another service. Embedded services may be used by another service instance independently. The embedded service is significant because its limited exposure to the outside world may mean it does not exhibit the characteristics of an instance at all. For example, the LDAP service is embedded within a federated name service and is not called directly.

A hidden service instance, shown in Figure 11.9, is specialized embedded service. The definition is the same except that the recognition of the hidden service in the architecture is not important. This may be due to the service being encased in a commodity service, the service having no other external service interfaces. The service may not be important for the organization to standardize. For example, subnetwork services (such as Ethernet, frame relay, and others) are hidden within an overall TCP/IP network stack.

Figure 11.10 shows the concept of a common service. Common service instances are ubiquitous. They are used by many other service instances. Their fundamental nature can influence the entire IT environment, including how business applications are developed. A common

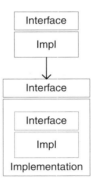

FIGURE 11.9.   Hidden service instances.

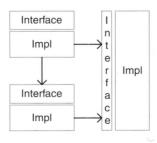

FIGURE 11.10.   Common services.

service instance is an extreme example of the platformization of a service. Operating systems and their individual service instances (such as kernel operations) are the ultimate common service.

Some service instances may have multiple interfaces, as shown in Figure 11.11. This implies a number of different interface types leading to a common implementation. The implementation would be responsible for transforming the individual interfaces into a common internal vocabulary. The architecture may stipulate such a service instance to support different application types gaining access to the same service, such as an interface defined in either HTTP/XML, HTTP, or SMTP/MIME used by a collaboration implementation. This service instance type is common when a single implementation encapsulates multiple service subcategories.

Figure 11.12 shows an example of the relationships among a selected set of service instances and provides some insight into how logical service categories are realized as physical service instances. The example considers two applications' (business and infrastructure) use of the location and directory service category (for a description of its subcategories, see Chapter 6). An application may use DNS to look up network resource objects (such as hosts) or LDAP to find security principles and credentials, distributed business objects, or individual company personnel. Both DNS- and LDAP-based directories provide all subcategories of the location and directory service category, with the possible exception of accounting. DNS and LDAP both provide subtly different functions, although one could assert that an LDAP-style directory service will replace DNS. Therefore, both will normally be in the technical architecture. The architect may also decide on a federated naming service, such as that provided by The Open Group Federated Naming API (XFN), to isolate the application from the various types of name service instances. XFN again provides all subcategory services (excluding accounting). All of these service instances, DNS, LDAP, and XFN, are specifications and

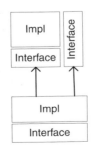

FIGURE 11.11.   Services with multiple interfaces.

not products. Defining a complete naming service instance will require the selection of products to provide the implementation(s).

In discovering the instances in this example a number of conclusions were reached:

- The federated naming service instance is able to embed (or hide) the other naming service instances.
- However, applications do make use of DNS and LDAP directly (i.e., not via the federated interface). This implies that the DNS and LDAP instances should not be hidden.
- The duplication of technology implementation in this service category represents a significant cost and usability for the organization.
- Therefore, most significant aspects of the service will be modeled as discrete service instances.

The ubiquitous network operating system (NOS) also implements a directory service to provide a naming structure around its file-sharing facilities. Contemporary products are increasingly providing standard interfaces (such as Microsoft's Active Directory or Novell's Netware Directory Service) and so are important to consider. Depending on the NOS product, there may be considerable implementation (and interface) overlap between a "standard" LDAP directory and the NOS directory, although the interface in the NOS world is likely to differ somewhat (and be hidden). The NOS directory may even support integration with an LDAP directory, although it is unlikely to allow its replacement with a "standard" LDAP implementation.

The implementation of an LDAP directory service can be an example of a hidden (or embedded) service relationship. Unlike its big uncle the X.500 Directory, which described many of the internal distribution mechanisms (including security), LDAP merely specifies the interface to a directory service but does not define the implementation and how the directory will be managed or distributed. LDAP products may even hide a relational DBMS within the service instance. It is the architect's choice whether to consider the LDAP directory as a black box implementation provided by a single product or as an open service described by its external and internal protocols.

DNS is essentially an example of a full directory standard (including distribution and other protocols). The DNS standards provide a specification that allows a full distributed directory to be built using a number of different products (this after all is how it operates in the Internet).

All the directories use a data communications service (a subcategory of the network service) to provide the distribution. With an organization that wishes to adopt a single internet working protocol, the data communications service instance may consist of a TCP/IP socket interface

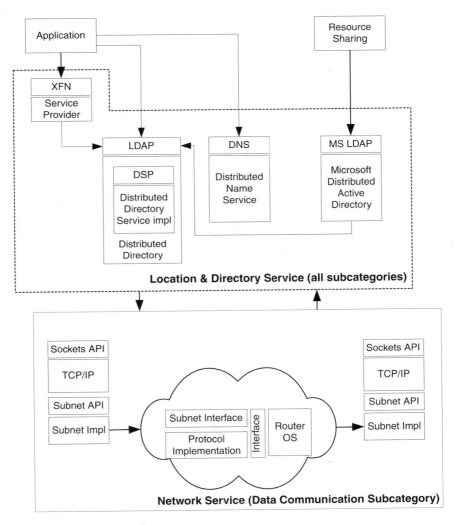

FIGURE 11.12.   Directory Service Instance Examples.

followed by a TCP/IP network implementation. This would seldom be the case because many networks will continue to be multiprotocol in the foreseeable future. The subnetwork protocols may also be considered a service instance (i.e., possibly a hidden, rather than embedded).[46] Most sophisticated network equipment includes an advanced operating

46. Subnetwork protocols can be considered embedded also, particularly if the architect wishes to use the technical architecture to specify network protocol, topology, policy, and technology, obviously not at a detailed level but at a level that is sufficient to provide the vision for detailed network planning work.

system. There is no subcategory within the Network Service to hold such a service instance, so one could be added or it could be considered an instance of the operating system service. The same approach can be applied to the hardware and specific hardware products providing the physical network implementation.

Whereas Figure 11.12 considered a number of specific foundation services, Figure 11.13 provides a partial view of an organizational super service, the distributing component service. In defining this service, we have already declared the need for remote method invocation, transactions, naming and lookup, persistence, and many others. Figure 11.13 provides a view of the service instances that may implement these four service subcategories using a Java engineering strategy. Note that from the applications point of view, it is provided with a set of high-level interfaces. Within the service, however, there are a greater number of "hidden" (at least to the application) service instances that provide the underlying machinery.

For instance, the transaction service instance uses a number of native (database-specific) service instances as well as an Open Group standard

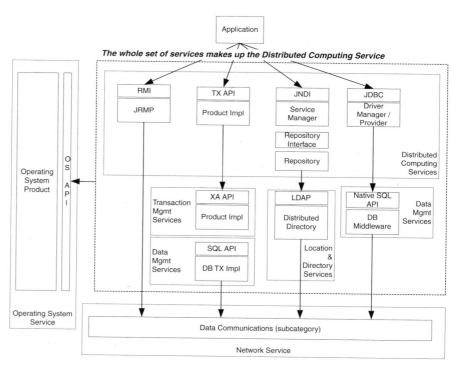

FIGURE 11.13. Distributed computing service instances.

(the XA specification) in the provision of the service. Therefore, in exposing this one instance to the application, the platform is making use of transaction management, data management, data communications, and, of course, operating system service instances. This is, of course, the power of the current "application server" technologies (and the platform concept). Isolating the developer from the vastness of the infrastructure through a "simple" API is immensely powerful, but the architect must take a view as to how these underlying service instances will be treated—either hidden or embedded. If they are considered hidden, the technical architecture need only define the distributed component service instances (including the application server products that implement them). If embedded, the architecture is required to state the specifications and products of these underlying service instances as well.

If the application server product "does everything," and the organization will not implement (or does not currently have) other applications in different technologies, then adopting the hidden strategy is workable. On the other hand, if the application server does not provide all aspects of the service (e.g., it is required to be integrated with a third party DBMS product) or the organization will not adopt a single approach to application development (which is the reality in most organizations), then the architecture should explicitly treat these instances as embedded and define them as they may be reusable elsewhere.

Another interesting point is the placement of service subcategories such as remote method invocation, transactions, naming and lookup, and persistence. In one sense these services may be placed within a distributed component super service. Additionally, they may (indeed are likely to) also exist in the foundation services: remote method invocation (network), transactions (transaction management), naming and lookup (location and directory), and persistence (data management). From a logical perspective, this overlap is not a significant problem. However, how does this affect the physical definition of service instances? Table 11.3 suggests a process.

Standards and Their Incarnations

The term *standard* has a wide variety of interpretations in the IT industry. It is important to ensure that there is an agreed-upon understanding of the concept, and how it will affect the selection of technologies for the IT environment. The term will become well-used on completion of this phase of the architecture.

There is often confusion between standards and openness. The two do not necessarily mean the same thing. It depends on the context. From the perspective of an organization's IT environment, a standard can easily relate to (what would be termed by the industry as) proprietary tech-

Table 11.3. Effect of service overlap.

No.	Situation	Strategy
1	If the service instances are likely to be implementing both within and outside the super service.	Reference the subcategory in both places, and duplicate the service instances from the super service into the foundation service. Multiple implementations may be tolerated.
2	If the service instances are likely to be pertinent only to the super service.	Reference the subcategory service instances only in the super service. Optionally, the service instance can be duplicated into the foundation service if it is likely that situation 1 will exist in the future. Multiple implementations are not encouraged.
3	If the service instances are likely to be pertinent only to the foundation service.	Remove the subcategory from the super service in the service portfolio. Multiple implementations are not encouraged.

nology. In general, an organizational technical standard is one that is documented in the enterprise technical architecture (in the SIB, in fact), and its use is enshrined in policy—generally it will be mandated. On completion of the ADM, all selected technologies will represent technical standards.

Open is more difficult to define. The open systems movement has evolved over the last 20–30 years. There appear to be a couple of major reasons why it became popular. Firstly, there was a reaction (both from customers and competitors) to a small number of large vendors "owning" the industry. Secondly, the birth of UNIX (in part due to the first reason) and its metamorphosis into numerous variants within the research organizations necessitated the concept of application (and therefore system) interworking. The general style of openness early on was a set of lowest-common-denominator specifications, agreed upon among a number of interested parties, which allowed applications to be:

- Moved around between different UNIX variants without significant hardship (i.e., portability)
- Integrated with other applications on different platforms transparently (i.e., interoperability)
- Transferred from graduated series of platforms to a more powerful series (i.e., scalability)

Key definition: **Open standards.**

While a standard can refer to any type of technology that an organization mandates usage of in policy, an *Open Standard* refers to specifications that have been developed in an environment of consensus that are "freely" available for vendors to implement. The degree of openness can be judged by the level of consensus and the availability to the specification.

The euphoria attached to these monumental objectives gave birth to the open standards movements. Organizations such as X/Open, the Open Software Foundation, and others championed the definition of portable and interoperable specifications (mostly interface-based—API), sometimes in active competition with each other. These consortia usually rallied their standards around the UNIX (operating system-specific) flag. The main protagonist in the networking arena is the International Standards Organization (ISO) with their Open System Interconnection (OSI) standards. The seven-layer model proposed a set of networking interoperability standards, most of which are not widely implemented, although the model itself is now ubiquitously associated with networking.

Using the models and experience of these "open" standards bodies, it is possible to describe a generic graduated openness litmus test. Table 11.4 provides this continuum.

The implementation of open standards is not an architectural driver, goal, or objective (although it can be a principle). Open standards are a means of fulfilling drivers goals or objectives. Interoperability and portability are architectural objectives that *can* be delivered through a technology environment that embraces open standards (of course, this is not the only method of delivering to these objectives). The architect, when assessing technologies for service instances, should form two views:

- Generally, where does the organization sit in its attitude toward technologies with respect to the openness scale?
- Where is it pragmatic to place a particular service category (or subcategory) on the openness scale?

Obviously, the higher a technology on the scale, the more likely that the organization will achieve interoperability, portability, scalability, and vendor independence. At the proprietary end of the openness continuum it is more likely that these objectives will not be met unless the organization pursues a limited number of vendor relationships but then only partially met. The perceived benefit of openness does not come free, of course. There are a number of problems with open standards, and the propensity for issues increases the farther up the scale the technology is. Some of these are:

Table 11.4. Openness scale.

Degree of Openness	Consensus Scale	Description
High	Formal standards	Standards that are specified by formal standard-making bodies (membership of which is available from any quarter) and are available in the public domain without restriction
	Industry consensus	Standards developed and maintained by industry consortia. Control is not with one vendor; however non-vendor representation is limited
	Published specifications	Standards that are controlled by one vendor but are widely available for implementation by any organization
Low	Proprietary	Specifications that are controlled by one vendor and whose technology is not available to any other group

- Open specifications are usually committee-based. The side effects of the consensus process can be a reduced speed to market and possible compromises. International standards can be 6 to 18 months behind proprietary products. Not only must the standard be agreed upon, but the products must then be built from the standards.
- Open standards can suffer from the lowest-common-denominator scourge. The standard, when implemented, is required to operate on a variety of different platforms, lessening the chance that a fully functional specification can be supported.
- Many standards suffer from "the intellectual process." Debates of academic subtlety increase time to market. Specifications can be notoriously difficult to read and understand (and therefore implement) due in part to the authors' requirements for "formal English definition".
- Many standards suffer from a lack of reference implementations. This means that actual implementation experiences are not factored into the specification. Many standards bodies lack a robust certification process (or their process is too robust). Thus, different vendors' products may not necessarily interoperate.
- There are a plethora of "standards bodies," many of who overlap in their scope. Some are even used by vendors to give the illusion that their technologies are indeed open. The work of many of them will be quickly consigned to the "standards library in the sky."

- Open standards have a limited life span. Technology changes around them necessitating changes to their structures, and the whole process starts again.

We have seen that there are pluses and minuses for the implementation of both open and proprietary specifications, so what should the organization and the architect do? If the benefits associated with open standards are desired, then the higher up the "openness scale" a technology is, the better. But choose carefully. In order to avoid the problems mentioned previously selected standards should be from consortia that:

- Represent a large number and cross section of vendors
- Have a robust (but not abhorrent) certification process
- Are being readily implemented within many organizations
- Allow active participation from member organizations and customers of the final products
- Can demonstrate a number (i.e., more than two) of actual specification implementations, that they interoperate, and that the vendors of these products are seen to be successful (i.e., sound financial basis, and so forth)
- The total cost of ownership (not just procurement) is positive.

Organizations that align with open standards should consider building a generic selection list of desirable standards consortia to be used when assessing each technology area. For example:

1. The Internet Engineering Taskforce
2. The Open Group
3. The Institute of Electrical and Electronics Engineers (IEEE), International Standards Organization (ISO), and National Standards Body
4. De facto industry standards bodies to include the Object Management Group (OMG), the Distributed Management Task Force (DMTF), BIZTalk Consortium, and others

An assessment (and review) process should be defined with which to add and subtract consortia from the "preferred" list.

However, organizations should not choose the openness path by default. The issues associated with open standards must be weighed against the stated benefits derived from them. Also, the benefit statements should be tested for validity. For instance, portability is an oft-stated ideal. But what does this actually mean in practical terms? Sure, an open SQL API (and exchange format) would allow an organization to switch database products. But is this a likely occurrence? Most organizations invest large amounts of time and resources into implementing database products. Many of the skills are proprietary to the product (e.g., administration, systems management, development). Furthermore relationships between the organization and the vendor will have been forged over a considerable period. Would the organization consider dropping the product just because implementing a standard means it can? Most probably not. Consider, also, the cost of using this standard. To meet portability requirements, application developers are required to code to the standard API—typically, providing lowest-common-denominator functions. The developers, and hence the application, miss out on the high-value, but proprietary, features. Does this approach provide a valid return to the business? It could potentially increase total cost of ownership not control it.

What about interoperability? The Internet is possibly the ultimate argument for the benefits of interoperability. Hundreds, possibly thousands, of different products are integrated to provide a single service (consider the Internet DNS, for example). But does this hold up within the organization? The DNS servers in each department can be from different vendors (or freeware), running on different operating systems and hardware, and they will almost certainly interoperate to provide the organization with an effective directory service. But such an approach would be untenable from the point of view of maintainability—think of the skills that would be needed to maintain such an environment. Higher support costs are a direct contributor to increased cost of ownership (it all comes down to cost in the end). In fact, the overall cost of implementing a proprietary directory service (but with a standard interface for applications) could be much lower.

From an e-business perspective, the issues of standards and openness become more crystallized. The e-business services that provide outward-facing functionality must be implemented through standards that exhibit a high degree of openness (and success). Specifications for interchange formats and protocols, business process protocols (such as procurement), security (especially authentication and nonrepudiation), and service discovery must be open enough to allow interoperability with e-business partners (after all, the organization has no control over its partner's technical environment). Actually selecting the correct specifications is more of a minefield. As with most high-profit technology subject areas, the competition among "standards consortia" can be fierce. Selecting the right standards is a factor of experience and understanding the industry. Use the criteria defined in this section to help select the right consortia. Selection is also a factor of understanding relevant business partners and the specifications they have chosen (consider establishing a partner group to agree on specifications). In the consumer-to-business market, there is seldom the luxury available to "ask your customers." In such a case, safe bets are lowest-common-denominator specifications or widely deployed (read de facto) technologies.

Architectural Definition

The final definition of the architecture—the realization of the service portfolio with technologies—can be described in a number of steps:

- Determine the approach, validate criteria, and document services
- Finalize service functionality
- Iterations of defining and assigning technologies
- Requirements traceability

Determine Approach

This step is preparatory. It establishes the general approach to be used in selecting technologies that will implement the IT environment. Defining the approach requires that the architect factor in the organization's overall IT philosophy. This may seem overly process-driven; however, our experience is that it is difficult to know from what point to begin. It is like beginning a large jigsaw puzzle: a decision must be made as to the point at which it will be started (normally where two or more pieces are immediately obvious).

During this step, the selection criteria are finalized, including the architectural principles. Knowledge of the current systems environment is reviewed, and the architect should be cognizant of any notable vendor relationships.

Finally, it is important that the services be documented to a level that allows the assessment of specifications and products for them.

A single, universal architecture will never fulfill every organization's requirements for an IT environment. Certainly, the philosophy of TOGAF is the generalization of the platform. However, the final makeup of the platform will be very dependent on the organization's market sector, their position in that sector, the effects of competition, the approach to delivering products and/or services, and the degree of focus on technology to provide competitive advantage. A government and a telecommunications organization will have vastly different market approaches and require different technical strategies (and hence architectures). Two important dimensions in determining how technology will be selected are the degree to which control of the cost of IT ownership is important and the requirement to be innovative in the face of market competition. Figure 11.14 shows how these two dimensions may be related and what effect the relationships may have in terms of technology-selection strategies. Industries in which innovation (at least from an IT perspective) is not as important as cost control can build a successful IT environment through a program of standardization, commoditization, and the limitation of product sets. Organizations at the opposite ends of these dimensions are more likely to rely on agreeing interoperability specifications to ensure that the environment will interoperate regardless of the products being used. Limiting actual product implementations is unlikely to be successful.

The TOGAF approach to realizing services is to walk along the solutions continuum (the continuum also communicates relationships of logical and physical architectural artifacts). Rather than using the solutions continuum in the same fashion as we used the architectural continuum—that is progressively moving along it toward an end state—there are a number of complementary approaches that can be applied. Figure 11.15 represents a bottom-up approach to service instance development. This approach has the greatest alignment with the solutions continuum. From the products and services point on the continuum, through the systems solutions, the industry solutions, and finally the organizational solutions, the journey is from the general to the specific, from the foundation to the organization. In general, this graduation will also be reflected within the layered TRM. The foundation (general) services will gravitate toward the base of the TRM, whereas the organizational (specific) services are likely to be at the top.

Should the bottom-up view be well suited to the organizational TRM, the solutions continuum prescribes the selection of foundation technologies in the first instance. Such technologies would include operating

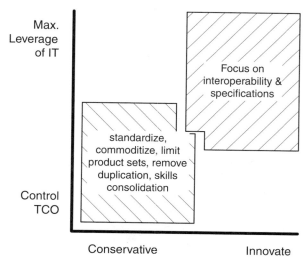

Figure 11.14.   Organizational influences.

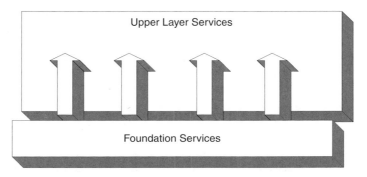

FIGURE 11.15.   Driven from the platform (solutions continuum).

systems, networks, databases, and so on. At the products and services point of the continuum, a number of technologies easily stand out as being highly generic, such as those just outlined. Others, however, are more complicated to define in this way. With security, for instance, no obvious candidates may spring to mind. In such a case, delay these decisions until farther up the continuum.

The technologies selected at the system solutions point continue to exhibit generic, cross-sector appeal. Distributed computing application servers fit into this point on the continuum.

The industry and organizational solutions points continue to drill into the organization specifically, encompassing their position in the sector. With reference to the TRM, such solutions tend to provide direct benefit to the organization's actual applications.

It is recognized that the TOGAF solutions continuum provides a method for selecting technology that relates directly to the method used to create the service portfolio in the first place. This is one option. On the other hand, the architect need not adopt a full continuum approach, although the continuum is generic enough to establish a viable mapping with the continuum points regardless of the method used. There are a number of other approaches that can be employed.

Another approach is to consider the applications that are currently running, and are planned to run, on the platform. This is a top-down approach (see Figure 11.16). For each application, abstract the technologies intrinsic to providing platform functional value or high-level infrastructure support (i.e., those technologies used directly by the application). For example, an application may require a workflow service directly or need the services of an application server. Once these application-facing services are defined in technology, examine each of these services with the intention of extracting the lower-layer services used. Continue until there are no undefined technology relationships.

Typically, technologies representing the operating system and network services would be defined last, considering their generic nature. Ensure that all service categories are covered. Some services have a tendency to be neglected in this approach such as systems management services.

This approach allows the applications to select the technologies of the platform. It works well in a stable application environment where an organization is not expecting much change in its application portfolio in the short to medium term. If the application environment is reasonably dynamic (as it can be with an organization with e-business drivers), or a large-scale change in application "style" (reinvention of the whole software engineering approach) is expected, then this approach may not be effective. It is far more difficult to begin at the application if the current application set is about to be replaced.

An approach that deals with some of these issues is to select a sweet-spot service and fully define it (see Figure 11.17). Selecting the technologies to describe a key service will logically progress to the services clustered around it, and so on. In our jigsaw analogy, this is akin to beginning in the middle of the jigsaw and moving out in concentric circles. The sweet-spot service will depend on the type of organization. However, with most, beginning with the software engineering service can be useful. This service is responsible for describing the programming languages, engineering tools, user-interface tools, and run-time environments. These subcategories directly affect the styles of applications to be built and therefore can be related to other key services. For example, a language can (but will not necessarily) dictate a run-time environment, a type of distribution style, and ultimately the technologies and overall platform into which the application is deployed. A "dot.com" organization may decide to base its technology selection around its business-to-business (or consumer-to-business) service. An organization that spe-

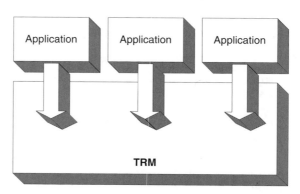

FIGURE 11.16. Service realization driven from applications.

cializes in providing service centers could focus selection around a workflow service.

An "anomaly" to be aware of when selecting an approach is the services that are intrinsically related to all other services (see Figure 11.18). This is the case with security, platform quality, and possibly systems management (the organization may also define others in this category). Security has a relationship with many of the foundation services, such as network security, systems management security, directory security, operating system security, and database security. Furthermore, it can also be highly prominent within individual applications (i.e., custom access control). This infers that when reviewing the approaches described earlier, consideration should be given to how security service instances are defined.

The approaches presented here are reasonably generic. The architect may have other approaches that have been used successfully. However, the idea is to decide (and agree) on a general method for realizing the service portfolio in technology. Using a single approach will ensure that the resulting technology definition will be consistent and likely to lead to fewer iterations as the technologies are integrated (integration is on paper at this stage). Of course, validate the model using one of the other approaches, if required.

An additional aspect to consider is the question of whether the specification or the product should come first. This is more of an organizational philosophy than a practical assertion. To paraphrase, it is important for the architect to understand how the technology decisions will be driven. There are basically two options:

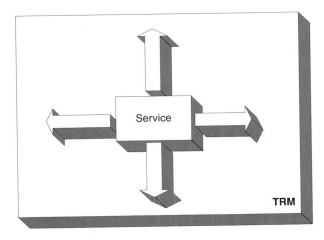

FIGURE 11.17.   Driven from a Sweet-Spot Service.

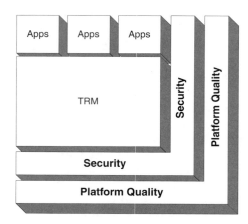

FIGURE 11.18.   Universal services.

- *Consider the specification foremost.* Using this approach the organization recognizes the specification, not the product, as the strategic entity. Such organizations tend toward the openness. They may not have centralized control of IT, implying that product selections are distributed to business units, and thus interoperability is a key issue. Open tender processes are normally followed, which cannot always be circumvented with preferred supplier arrangements. Using specifications can be more difficult in defining a workable collection of service instances, however. Multiple products can implement a single specification, implying that a robust selection process is required. Additionally, specifications do not necessarily imply interoperability or portability—much depends on the scope of the specification as already discussed earlier.
- *Consider the product foremost.* Using this approach the organization places the product as the strategic entity, with the specification merely being derived from the product selected. With many services, a contemporary approach is to select preferred products as organizational standards, mandated from a central IT policy body. Areas typically targeted are operating systems, databases, networking, and application servers. With this approach, the integration of service instances becomes less complicated, with the additional side effect that the architect is working in the physical world with actual products where interoperability can be easily tested. Deriving the specifications is still important because other service instances may need to be defined by specification, and the applications will use the interface specifications to gain access to the product.

Ultimately, the approach will include a combination of these two options. Some technologies will be selected by specification whereas others will be driven from products. However, a preferred approach should be selected that matches the characteristics of the organization. This is important because the preferred approach requires a set of processes to be solidified, such as tendering, policy-driven specifications, or preferred supplier agreements.

Platform service categories are another interesting aspect of service realization. Service quality describes behaviors such as adaptability or manageability and has a pervasive effect on the operation of most or all of the functional service categories (and therefore on the applications that use the platform).

In general, a requirement for a given level of a particular service quality requires one or more of the other service categories to cooperate (for instance, performance is universal throughout the platform services). Usually, this means that the software that implements the platform services contributes to the implementation of overall platform quality. Service qualities may also require support from the application software and the external environment as well as the platform. However, the more effective the platform is in providing quality, the more likely it is that applications will have the job done for them.

In some cases, service qualities affect each of the service categories in a similar fashion whereas in other cases service qualities have a unique influence on one particular service category. For instance, international operation depends on most of the service categories in the same way, both providing facilities and needing their cooperation for localization of messages, fonts, and other features of a locale. It may, however, have a more profound effect on the software engineering services, where facilities for producing internationalized software are required.

During the process of architecture development, the architect must have fully defined the qualities required of the platform. A method to ensure that qualities are not forgotten is to create a quality profile documenting the quality requirements and describing the relationships between each functional service and the qualities that influence it.

In conclusion, be aware that in only a small number of cases will the technology to be applied to a service be self-evident. There is a high likelihood that each service area will throw out a number of competing and overlapping, technologies when modeled as service instances. At this point, this is not an issue. Document each of the options available. This information will be used during later steps to make the final assessments and decisions. Do not bother making any more than a cursory assessment of the technology; essentially, determine that it has the potential to fulfill the service.

Finalize Service Functionality

Before beginning the task of selecting technologies to create service instances ensure that the service requirements are fully documented. This process has been ongoing since the definition of the current environment and continued during the development of the service portfolio. In fact, the definition of the logical view of services would have been a key milestone in the finalization of service functionality.

However, there may still be areas of vagueness about the service requirements. Now is the time to bring them to a level necessary for realization. The definition of requirements is not analogous to, say, the description of an application software component. At the application level, full, formal, and precise descriptions of functionality (and architecture) must be provided. Defining the functional requirements of service instances only requires the detail necessary to a) select a product or b) determine the scope of a custom-development.

TOGAF provides a number of templates to support service description at a logical level. The service instances will be defined from these requirements. While all services can be defined using these templates it is more typical to concentrate on upper-layer services (such as super services)—a number of foundation services are "basic" enough not to require description in this way (e.g., elements of the network service). There are two useful templates worth considering when describing a service:

- *Functionality table* (Table 11.5). This table lists each of the subcategories within the service and describes the specific functionality required. While analyzing the functionality, always be cognizant of specific interfaces that will provide access to the functionality. The definition of interfaces, even at a generic level (at this stage), begins to focus on the actual service instances, considering many service instances are accessed through a single interface.
- *Policy table* (Table 11.6). This table notes any corporate policy that currently exists and has some bearing on the service (for example, existing security policies, systems management policies, e-business directives). Furthermore, it is used as a placeholder to capture areas where policy may be required, bearing in mind that the establish-

Table 11.5. Service functionality table.

Service: <Service Category>		
Functionality category	**Functionality**	**Interfaces – APIs, Formats and Protocols**

Table 11.6. Service policy table.

Policy	Entity	Remarks

ment and maintenance of technical policy is a responsibility of the technical architecture. Note the agency (either internal or external) that owns the policy (or is the potential owner).

Key definition: **Policy**
Policies are the nontechnical artifacts that support the governance of the architecture. Policy defines the mandatory rules of the architecture.

Technology Selection Iterations

The third step of the process is iterative. The architect will now have all of the information necessary to facilitate the selection of technologies within each service category. Many organizations will require formal tender processes in some categories to make final technology decisions. Formal tendering will not occur during this step, as such the SIB will be completed after the tenders have been run. It is recommended that this be an activity during phases D (opportunities and solutions) and E (migration) of the ADM.

The selection of specifications and, finally, products can be a major undertaking. Not only is there the struggle with the selection of the right product, there are also many internal political and legislative pressures applied to the decision; however, at least these pressures should be known as they were captured during the earlier ADM phases. We have worked in organizations where the selection of any product for the technical architecture had to follow a full tender process. With others, we have had the opposite experience—the "whatever you say is OK by us" syndrome. It is important therefore to fully understand the organizational process for product selection (and procurement). The process may be enshrined as part of policy. If not, it is the responsibility of the architect to ensure a clear understanding of the process to be used has been accepted (formally signed off) by the architecture steering group before selection begins.

Should a service category require a formal tender, there is limited ability to actually select a specific technology to implement a service at this stage. Therefore, instead of defining a technology explicitly, the architect should document likely technology options (products) that would fulfill the service requirements. These options would allow a possible short list set of vendors and provide the architect with enough information to ensure that service instances are valid.

It is interesting to note that organization's that require formal tendering for products do not have the same requirement for specifications. The architect can freely select specifications to fulfill services without being pressured into tendering. The more "open" the specifications the more unreservedly they will be accepted. This is then a good approach when tendering is required. Describe the service at least in specification form. The tendered products can then be measured against these specifications.

All of the platform's services can be subject to tender. Although it is likely that many of the foundation services (e.g., databases, networks) will require tenders to select a product, anything is possible. Software development tools, application servers, workflow products, and geographical information systems all could be the subject of tender.

At this point final definition of the criteria for accessing and selecting technologies is required. The selection criteria have evolved throughout the architectural process. This is now the point at which they must finally be accepted. Although the focus of the criteria at this stage is both architectural and requirements-driven, it is important to consider other, more holistic elements. Here are a number of generic criteria we usually apply to product selection:

- The product should meet the functional and nonfunctional (the "qualities") requirements of the service.
- The product should adhere to the architectural principles.
- Feedback from independent consultants and industry analysts should be considered.
- Determine the relative position of the vendor in the market and/or sector.
- Consider the stated future direction of the vendor in general and the product (or specification) specifically.
- Determine the degree of cohesion of the technology area in the market—if it is fractured, a tactical approach may be required.
- Do not forget the advice on picking standards and standards bodies.
- Look for vendor financial stability.
- Follow the Joneses. The power of the market tends to throw out natural leaders. Follow the vendors and products in this position.
- Diverge from the Joneses. Increases risk but is sometimes a critical strategy in highly competitive markets.
- Assess the stability of the product—ever-changing interfaces can provide considerable ongoing problems.
- Consider the key vendor relationships already in place. Vendor partnerships, with the requisite amount of control with the customer, can have considerable benefits with respect to ongoing maintenance

costs. In technical areas dominated by aggressive competition, the organization has considerable power in negotiations.

- Always consider how the product will be supported once it becomes part of the IT environment. What skills does the organization currently have, and what will it need in the future? How does the product affect any outsourcing arrangements (consider whether the organization is able to mandate technologies to the outsourcing vendor)?
- How will the products be interconnected to make up the IT environment. For instance, is the product compatible with other selected products (use the solution map—introduced later—as a tool to discover interoperability problems)?

Technology development does not stand still; there is a continuous ebb and flow of technologies. As a technology is introduced, it is difficult to predict the extent to which it will be adopted and how long it is likely to remain viable. In general terms, a broadly accepted industry standard leads to a low adoption risk but may not satisfy those that must innovate to compete due to its commodity status.

The generic life cycle of advancing technologies, the 'S' curve (see Chapter 2), shows an initial decline in benefits as expenditures accrue until such a time that usefulness and acceptance emerge and benefits begin to rise. The benefits increases until saturation or maximum capability is reached and remains until another technology renders this technology less beneficial.

The point along the "S" curve at which technology is adopted by an organization depends on its nature. Gartner Group classifies organizations into three types (A, B, and C; see Chapter 2) in terms of technology adoption. In the identification and selection of technology, the architect must be cognizant of the organization's "technology usage rating" and map that rating onto technology at the correct point along the "S" curve. As a rule, technologies in the early part of the life cycle seldom exhibit significant platform service characteristics, whereas stable technologies will, although it is possible that organization-specific services will be included in the platform that break this rule.

In deference to the technology life cycle, and the fact that architectural development represents a point in time, there is a danger that the architecture will quickly become out-of-date as technologies travel between adoption and declination. Primarily, we suggest that architectural development should not represent a point in time and should be continuous (this point is discussed in more detail under the heading of governance in Chapters 13 and 14). But in many respects the architecture is required to make a "now" choice to support the succeeding migration efforts. To neutralize this dilemma and to emphasize the continual progression aspect of the architecture, we suggest adopting a timeline approach to selecting technologies. As shown by Table 11.1, for each service, define a SIB entry that represents the following dimensions:

- A *"now" dimension.* This represents the technologies that are currently fulfilling the service instance (from the current system analysis) and any technologies that can realistically be implemented before the medium term.
- A *"medium-term" dimension.* This focuses on a period within the medium-term business and technology planning cycle; for instance, 6–18 months.[47] This dimension positions the technologies to be implemented within the term that states the immediate migration requirements of the IT environment.
- A *"long-term" dimension.* This focuses on a vision for both individual technologies and the IT environment in general. This is likely to represent a period beyond 2 years, which would coincide with a next planned business and architectural development term. Incorporated in this timeline would be stated vendor directions for the current technology sets. The only difference between a medium- and long-term technology for the service instance may be merely a change in version.
- Include any rationale, policy statements, or guidelines that would aid the reading of the SIB entry.

This technique provides a sliding timeline, providing a communicated technology direction. Technologies move from the right to the left. Long-term technologies become medium-term migration objectives. Medium-term technologies are implemented and become current. Also, it recognizes that there is no such thing as a "big bang" implementation of the technical architecture—it highlights a transitional approach.

Table 11.7. Technology selection timeline.

Service: <logical service category / subcategory or service instance>		
Now	**Medium Term**	**Long Term**
Technology a	*Technology a* *Technology b*	*Technology c* *Technology b*
• *Guidelines* • *Rationale* • *Policy Statements*		

47. The actual scale of time representing a dimension will differ for each organization. Much will depend on the type of organization and its stated business strategies. The scale may even change across service categories.

Instance Mapping

The first step in the definition process defined a preferred approach for transforming services into service instances[48] and thus products and specifications. Using the approach, the architect constructs (or realizes) the service portfolio in technology. This process must include recognition of dependencies and boundaries of functions (i.e., services) and must take into account what products are available in the marketplace.

The architect will need to progress through a number of iterations with respect to the service instances. In essence, the early iterations start with relatively abstract realizations of services, defined by standards and including services that map most easily to the architectural framework. These service instances can be referred to as architectural instances in deference to their relationship with the architectural continuum. Typically, the first iterations will provide a one-to-one mapping between services and their implementations.

However, the architect may notice a number of deficiencies with the solutions model built in the early stages (as discussed in Services and Service Instances, previously):

- Technologies do not relate one-to-one with service categories.
- Products and specifications have inherent gaps or overlaps across service.
- The relationship between technologies does not fully provide the environment.

One particular area to be aware of is the duplication of service instances within a single logical service, meaning that modeling the interface between an application (or another service instance) and a service instance would be problematic because more than one instance can provide the necessary services.

For example, consider Table 11.8. The medium term provides for multiple LDAP implementations (Netware and both Microsoft implementations), which provide functionality identical to the application. The long term states that a single LDAP implementation is planned, a single "NOS," and a single network resource directory. However, there is confusion in the medium term as to what LDAP service instance is strategic (this also indicates the pragmatic view the same service will be realized by different specification to support different usage). To clarify, consider showing that one instance will be superseded (see the following SIB classifications) by another over a defined migration period. Present ap-

---

48. TOGAF uses the term solution building blocks to show the transition between the logical view of services and their physical realization in implementable building blocks as well as reflecting their positioning on the solutions continuum. The same terminology can apply to service instances (i.e., solution instances).

Table 11.8. Service confusion.

Service: Location & Directory Services		
Now	**Medium Term**	**Long Term**
DNS	DNS	DNS
NDS (Netware)	NDS (Netware)	LDAP
	LDAP (Microsoft)	Active Directory (Microsoft)
	Active Directory (Microsoft)	
• Unify directory products to a single corporate directory (based on Microsoft's AD) and migrate from other directory implementations in the medium to long term. • Unify directory specifications to the IETF directory standards (DNS & LDAP)		

plications may continue using the instance; however, no new implementations are warranted.

Integration between service instances (in their provision of the service categories) is paramount to the integrity of the architecture and the final IT environment on which it is built. Using a technique to diagrammatically trace service instance interrelationships can aid in ensuring integrity. The architect should consider representing the service instances in a solution map. Each entry in the SIB could be shown in this manner. An indicative notation is shown in Figure 11.19. The notation provides a basic way to test the service relationships rather that providing a full specification of the target environment. The notation extends the earlier discussions on the characteristics of service instances and the types of relationships between them.

The map provides a visual tool to aid in testing the final architecture. It will aid in proving that instances will interoperate, that the interoperation is sensible, that duplicates are identified, and that application requirements for platform services can be met. Broken links, overlapping instances (i.e., where the use of a service is confused among multiple instances), and gaps will become evident during the mapping.

As development proceeds through the iterations, the service instances become more implementation-specific. The solution service instances provide increased detail of the service's functionality (documented in the Functionality table—see Table 11.5). The final service instances will pay careful attention to the current system analysis performed previously because it provides a detailed view of the currently implemented service instances. The architect will have already formed a view of the relative merits of reusing various current service instances. It is never practical to totally rebuild the IT environment from the ground up, so the target architecture must be sympathetic to both the current environment and to the issues (and gaps) within this environment. Furthermore,

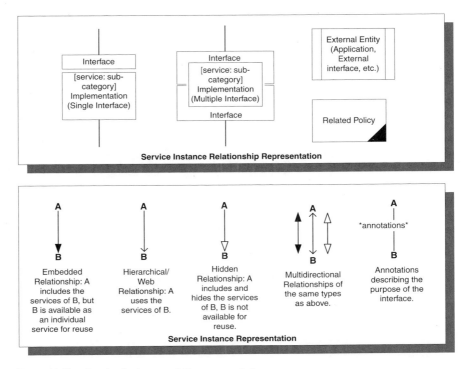

FIGURE 11.19.   Service instance solution map notation.

the migration from the current to the medium-term environment must be realistic. The steering group or the management team will not accept significant or wide-ranging change, and the architecture will fail. Consider small, progressive transition to the target architecture.

As mentioned in Chapter 10 there is a possibility that changes to the logical service portfolio will be required as the service instances are defined. As instances are realized, gaps within the current portfolio may be uncovered, particularly in subcategories. Do not be reticent to make such changes if they are required; it is all part of the iterative approach. It will require changes in (already completed) documentation such as the current version of the technical architecture and may require a review of other (related) service instances. However, resist applying the physical service instance structure on the logical service model.

The final set of technologies forms the SIB. The SIB is a key component from the process. Furthermore, the SIB should become a key architectural artifact for the organization. Typically, the SIB will be ordered by the logical service categories. Each service instance will also be associated with a service category. The SIB then contains the interface and implementation details of all technologies (and policies) selected to fulfill the logical services. Current, medium-term and long-term technologies can be entered directly within the SIB. As may have been noticed from The Open Group SIB template, the SIB can contain a status attribute, and its use is encouraged. This implies both a classification for each technology and a "workflow" process to support its management. The classification of SIB entries is left up to the organization. We have used the following classifications:

- *Adopted*—the current organizational standard
- *Proposed*—technology that has actively entered into the standard process
- *Suggested*—a long term replacement for the current standard
- *Withdrawn*—an adopted, proposed, or suggested standard that no longer represents organizational policy
- *Superseded*—a current, proposed, or suggested standard that has been replaced by a later release

Requirements Traceability

The final step in this ADM task is that of requirements traceability. As was introduced in Chapter 7, traceability is important in ensuring that the development of the technical architecture is not carried out in isolation from business-driven factors. There is considerable collateral built up during the process to support this activity. From the requirements perspective, the ADM has provided:

- The key question list
- Architectural principles
- External constraints
- Various business and strategic requirements
- Selection criteria
- Service instance definitions

Of these, the principles and selection criteria have been used in the selection of technologies and therefore are likely to have been respected. The business requirements and constraints are embodied with the principles and criteria while also being captured in the service functionality tables.

Gap analysis provides another method of undertaking requirements traceability. During Chapter 10, we asserted the necessity of understanding how gap analysis would be undertaken for the target architecture development, identifying the need for a preemptive model and method.

Gap analysis conducted at this point would represent a specific and quantifiable analysis of the technology difference between the current and target architectures. Generally, the current environment, plus strategic requirements, minus current issues and gap should equal the target environment.

The target architecture is required to take into consideration the outputs of the various gap analysis activities conducted during service portfolio development. To ensure that this has been effective, consider an analysis of the current and target technologies using a matrix similar to that shown in Table 11.9. In some ways, such an assessment is provided by the SIB entries. The SIB describes, through the use of timelines, the transition between the current and target architectures. The SIB is not, however, designed to represent gaps but rather technology standards and transitions. Using Table 11.9, it is possible to understand those technologies that will be new to the environment (i.e., require development or procurement) and those that are to be eliminated.

The key question list is the final part of the traceability jigsaw puzzle. By this point, the steering group will have confirmed the questions and an initial assessment completed during the development of the service portfolio (see Chapter 10). Now that the services have been realized, this is an opportune time to re-answer the key questions and complete any rating required. This information, along with the proposed state of the target technical environment should be reported back to the steering group as a final assessment of the target architecture's effectiveness.

One other activity that may be considered is a final validation of the service portfolio in the face of the target architecture implementation. If the process has been followed, there should be no change. However, anything is possible.

Table 11.9. Technology transition analysis.

Service: <service name>											
	Target Service Subcategory Technologies										
Current Service Subcategory Technologies											Eliminated Technologies
New Technologies											

11.5 Output

As with the other tasks in the target architecture phase, the output of
the architectural definition task is embodied within the technical architecture document. The next version of this document is produced, in
this case version 0.4. A summary of the outputs is:

- Latest version of the TRM
- Final selection criteria for technologies
- Detailed service functionality definitions
- Draft of selected technologies
- Draft standards information base
- Optional solution map
- Requirements traceability, particularly full sets of answers to the key
  question list

11.6 Example

Disclaimer

An issue to which we have been sensitive about throughout the book,
and that is particularly important in this chapter, is that of technology
bias. To this point we have attempted to deliver examples that are reasonably independent of specific technologies. This obviously is not entirely possible at this stage because we must use actual technologies
(including products) to illustrate the examples effectively. Actually, we
would have preferred to use fictitious technologies because this would
not affect the concepts we have been trying to purvey. But developing
understanding through example is important. Therefore, we have decided to use actual technologies in the examples, but this does not imply
the monotechnology approach of TOGAF. TOGAF is successful in describing contemporary, legacy, and niche technologies. Our only bias is
to concentrate on Internet-based technologies. This suits our purpose of
framing B2B requirements against a typical organizational technology
backdrop. Furthermore, they are reasonably familiar to those who might
read this book.

Introduction

The development of CFL's technical architecture continues in this chapter with the realization of the service portfolio from Chapter 10. As in
the last chapter, we intend to limit the definition of the realization to a

small subset of CFL's TRM. We will concentrate on the B2B commerce and enterprise application integration super services. Some other notable realization decisions will also be summarized. Again, we do this for reasons of brevity.

Approach

It is important to assess CFL's relative position on the conservative–innovative continuum. This will aid in our selection of technologies. The inference from analyzing initiation and baseline information is that CFL is reasonably conservative in its approach to technology, the cost of IT ownership being more important than the "risky" technology enabling of the business. This assessment was validated with the architectural program's steering group and the CIO, accompanied by a presentation on the implications of each point on this continuum.

Based on the assessment of organizational influences, we have decided to adopt the following strategies for realizing the services (note that many relate directly to architectural principles and strategic objectives):

- Adopt mature commodity technologies where possible.
- Focus on specification and product equally.
- Reduce technology duplication where possible—unify under single technologies.
- Limit (or control) the number of major products.
- Work from the B2B commerce and enterprise application integration super services outward.

Service Functionality

The second step is to finalize the service functional requirements for the CFL TRM. Primarily, we have concentrated on the super services defined in the TRM. The functionality descriptions are provided at a high level because it is anticipated that these services will be acquired through product procurement (not built). The interface information is provided through a cursory cataloging of desirable technology specifications. They represent likely candidates and have been selected based on the technology defined in other service areas (although not shown here). For example, it has been decided that CFL will pursue a software engineering path based on component and object-based technology. Further elaboration includes the selection of a Java path due to a stable relationship with IBM (logistics and systems management) and a number of skills available within the IT group in these technologies. Although this plots the medium- to long-term future for CFL software development, existing software engineering disciplines will remain due to legacy system support. The success (or otherwise) will be measured over a number of development projects to come out of the architecture, and the decision will be revisited. The software engineering strategy and policy are to be developed as part of the technical architecture policy requirements.

To ensure brevity, we have summarized the B2B commerce and enterprise application integration super services (see Table 11.10 and Table 11.11). The actual functional description for CFL extends to all services, including foundation. B2B service functionality is based on the super service definition from the example in Chapter 9. EAI service functionality is based on the EAI reference model developed internally in Chapter 10. The italicized rows show nonfunctional, or quality, aspects of the service.

The technical architecture must be supported by policy. A number of new policy initiatives have been identified for development—see Table 11.12.

At this point in the realization, we have made little attempt to select actual products for both super services just described. We realize that the markets in both B2B and EAI spaces are reasonably unpredictable, so finding a "known" commodity product is unlikely. Although the B2B service must adhere to the RosettaNet framework (which is also in line with CFL's strategy to support CMA specifications), RosettaNet is a specification, not a product. It is our recommendation that CFL tender (either formally or informally) for products in both areas. Alignment will be sought for the functional requirements sketched out earlier, including the likely adherence to the technical specifications defined. Main selection criteria include:

- Meet the functional and nonfunctional requirements of the service.
- Adhere to the architectural principles.
- Implement market leaders (with best-of-breed status)—CFL to select an external technical analyst/consulting organization to support this research.
- One product, one super service.
- Product integration—the various products must integrate so that common service overlap is avoided.
- Focus on current vendor relationships before considering new vendors.
- Product capital and ongoing operational costs must not exceed tangible benefits.
- Adhere to all relevant technical policies and standards (to be developed), including software engineering strategy and the corporate SIB.

Table 11.10. B2B commerce super service functional description.

Service: B2B commerce super service		
Functionality Category	**Functionality**	**Interfaces—APIs, Formats and Protocols**
Data interchange	Business document definition, document manipulation, document parsing	XML, XML-schema, CMA standards, RosettaNet, DOM, XML parser
Security	Privacy of transported information, nonrepudiation of origin and receipt, authorization of business partners	S/MIME, X.509, DES, MD5, SHA-1, RSA
Data management	Message storage (for persistence, audit, and nonrepudiation), message meta data storage	Relational, see SIB
Network	Synchronous and asynchronous interchange, remote process delivery mechanism (B2B hub intermediary)	TCP/IP, HTTP, SMTP, RosettaNet delivery
Software engineering	Customization of B2B environment	Java, HTML editor, Java IDE, JRE (see SIB)
Process flow	Definition of business activities and signals, the flow of activities, the roles involved in the interaction. Execution of business activity instances based on partner or internal stimulus	Proprietary, RosettaNet
EAI	Integration with EAI, via messaging, to support internal system integration	See EAI service
Location & directory	Maintain partner attributes, including security components	LDAP, See SIB
Transaction management	Concurrent message processing, integrity of business transaction, load-sharing	XA, J2EE
Operating system	Scalable.	UNIX, NT
Performance	*20,000 business interchange activities per day.*	
Availability	*24 by 7.*	
Manageability	*All planned management disciplines, integration into enterprise management system.*	*See Systems Management Service, and SIB*

Table 11.11. EAI super service functional description.

Service: Enterprise application integration super service		
Functionality Category	**Functionality**	**Interfaces—APIs, Formats and Protocols**
Data interchange	Corporate EAI header definition and message payload guidelines, document manipulation, document parsing	XML, XML-schema, DOM, XML parser
Security	Authentication of system using integration service	
Data management	Persistent message storage, message metadata repository, message warehouse	Relational, see SIB
Network	Synchronous and asynchronous interchange, predominantly based on message queuing	TCP/IP, JMS, Message Q product
Software engineering	Generation of adapters. Generation of translation and mapping. Graphical. Includes prebuilt adapters for JDE. Note: Adapters are considered infrastructure applications with respect to the TRM	Adapter IDE, Java implementation
Workflow	Definition of message flows, including exceptions, routing, and translation and mapping. Execution of instances of message flows	Proprietary
Transaction management	Concurrent message processing, integrity of business transaction, load-sharing	XA
Operating system	Scalable	UNIX, NT
Performance	*100,000 message integrations per day, to 5 major CFL systems.*	
Availability	*20 by 6.*	
Manageability	*All planned management disciplines, integration into enterprise management system.*	*See Systems Management Service, and SIB*

Table 11.12. CFL new policy initiatives.

Policy	Entity	Remarks
Security and audit	CFL HQ	Information Manager
Business interchange standards and guidelines	CFL IT group	Based on RosettaNet implementation framework
Software engineering processes, policy, and guidelines	CFL IT group	
Technology standards	CFL IT group	See SIB
Systems management design guidelines	CFL IT group	

Realization

We decided to create a number of service instance maps depicting key services, particularly the super services, to understand how the technologies might be integrated. Figure 11.19 shows a partial example of the B2B commerce super service (the final map is more "complex"). All super services were built into the same instance map to establish relationships and valid technology selections. This process allowed us to determine whether the super services were to be realized as separate products or whether it was possible to reuse some instances across multiple super services. We found that both cases were evident. A few points to note from the mapping are:

■ Many of the hierarchical relationships indicate the ability to establish separate reusable architectural components, such as the message database, directory service, and XML document manipulation. A number of services can use these services, and as such they should be physically separated for implementation if possible. Criteria was then added to the super service definitions to indicate that CFL wished products to interface, rather than hide, these service instances.

■ Some technologies, although inexorably entwined within the bowels of the service, are nonetheless globally reusable. Consider the public key libraries, for instance. Although they exist as internal application components, their library structure and the use of a standard API allows them to be reused across many services. In this case though reuse would be achieved through copying. For more information, see the security service definition (not shown in this example).

- The map also considers where policy is required. For the B2B service, policies relating to security, systems management, and messaging standards are identified.
- A number of proprietary components were identified (e.g., the process flow "service"). The fact that we were unable to map these effectively as services may mean that they are not actually services, rather internal application components that do not belong in the platform. Although the B2B super service must provide this functionality, there is no re-usable candidate technology identified.
- A number of the service instance implementations were difficult to describe in anything apart from a generalized manner. This suggests that a technology standard for the implementation (but not necessarily the interface) need not be defined in the SIB.
- Some instances have specific interface and implementation definitions, such as Microsoft Exchange for e-mail transport and DB/2 for relational DBMS. Others are undefined; such as the LDAP implementation. Undefined technologies will need to be defined before the completion of the program. Generally, there are two strategies for this: define them now or suggest that they should be defined through a tender-like process.

There will be no SIB entries defined for each of the super services, with the exception of those service categories that have been created by, and are unique to, the super service. The technology definitions for each of the super service's subcategories are referenced back into the foundation services, where possible. The super service therefore exists as a logical representation within the TRM, a functional description, a service map, a collection of related SIB entries, and, finally, a product that adheres to all of these aspects. New super service subcategories (such as the workflow and messaging of the EAI super service) have been given their own categories and SIB entries.

This section provides only a sample of the SIB entries making up the CFL corporate SIB. A number of points regarding the standard selections are raised:

- Table 11.13 demonstrates the fact that CFL has no current architectural implementation for intersystem integration. Basically, flat files (and other ad hoc mechanisms) made up the interchange formats of the ineffective integration environment. The medium and long term show greater reliance on formatted messages based on enterprise and industry standards.
- Table 11.14 demonstrates the issue of overlap. Currently, there are

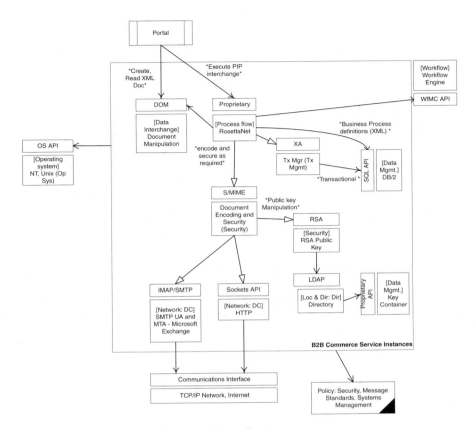

FIGURE 11.20. Partial Realization of B2B Super Service.

six technologies that fulfill the electronic mail service subcategory. This overlap is characterized by high ownership costs and poor interoperability. The SIB entry shows a concerted effort in the medium term to unify CFL onto a single internal e-mail product. Also note that guidance is given with respect to a long-term review of the situation.

■ Table 11.15 shows a reasoned approach to the server operating system situation in CFL. The current spread of OS products needs little rationalization. Each product fills a necessary niche as a server platform. This entry also recognizes the ongoing existence of the Logistics system. Also shown is an example of how policy statements are a fundamental part of the SIB entry.

Table 11.13. Data interchange SIB entry.

Service: Data Interchange/Electronic Data Interchange		
Now	**Medium Term**	**Long Term**
Proprietary flat files	XML, XML-DTD, XML-schema Enterprise message formats RosettaNet PIPs CMA IXM interchange formats IBM XML parser	XML, XML-Schema Enterprise message formats. RosettaNet PIPs CMA IXM interchange formats IBM XML parser
• Enterprise message formats will be defined in-house and based on XML standards. They will be used to support a common intersystem vocabulary for internal system interchange.		

Table 11.14. Electronic mail SIB entry.

Service: Network/Electronic Mail		
Now	**Medium Term**	**Long Term**
CFL custom Exchange Groupwise Notes Messenger Generic SMTP / POP	Generic SMTP / POP / MIME Exchange/Outlook	Generic SMTP / IMAP / MIME Exchange/Outlook
• The current plethora of e-mail technology (both user agent and message transfer agent—refer to logical e-mail reference model) greatly impacts the usability and maintainability of the infrastructure. E-mail use will be migrated to a single product in the medium term as a priority. • Internet messaging (e.g., SMTP, POP, IMAP, MIME) will be supported for all external (interorganizational) requirements. This need not be the case within CFL, where proprietary messaging specifications are sanctioned because there will be a single product providing mail. Standards-based internal messaging is to be reviewed in the long term.		

11.7 Summary

In this chapter, we have discussed the realization of the logical service reference model in actual technologies. This is a last major step in defining the target technical environment for the organization. The tech-

Table 11.15. Operating system SIB Entry.

Service: Operating System (Generic Application / DB Server)		
Now	**Medium Term**	**Long Term**
OS/400 Netware Windows NT HP-UX	OS/400 Windows NT / 2000 HP-UX	OS/400 Windows 2000 HP-UX
• OS/400 to remain for the Logistics system only; no further investment is to be made in this product. • Windows NT / 2000 for all small to medium system requirements (see hardware SIB entry for clustering information). • HP-UX for major corporate systems; server rationalization required.		

nical environment embodies a number of service instances (specifications and products) that interrelate to provide an actual implementation of the logical service portfolio. We investigated a number of approaches to transitioning between the logical and the physical, including the TOGAF solutions continuum. We also introduced a simple notation for mapping technologies together in a unified environment. Finally, we continued the theme of requirements traceability, ensuring that the physical realization meets the overall business requirements.

In the next chapter, we discuss ways in which opportunities may be identified in the implementation of the IT environment to the defined architecture.

CHAPTER 12

Opportunities, Solutions, and Migration Planning

12.1   Introduction

In the preceding chapters, we have transitioned through a number of key stages in the development of the organizational technical architecture. However, it must be emphasized that while the technical architecture defines the means; the end is meeting the strategic objectives of the organization through IT initiatives. Using TOGAF, we have understood how to depict and understand the current environment and its problems; that is, where we are today. We have formulated the ideal target environment (to meet strategic objectives and solve the problems); namely, what the future may look like. The glue is the *How*. How do we get to this ideal picture?

In this chapter we take our first view of implementation. We look at techniques to uncover the various activities necessary to make the transition between the current and target environments. These activities become work packages and are finally clustered into architectural projects managed as a program. Furthermore, we must consider the impact of change and contemplate strategies for ensuring that the change is managed.

We also consider aspects surrounding planning for the migration. We introduce the concept of project initiation. Under this umbrella, we discuss the execution of cost-benefit analysis and the process of project prioritization.

12.2 *Opportunities and Solutions*

Background

This section considers the next major phase in the architectural development method (ADM): the opportunities and solutions phase. Its position in the ADM is shown in Figure 12.1. The objective of this phase, as defined in TOGAF, is:

> . . . identify the parameters of change, the major phases along the way and the top-level projects to be undertaken in moving from the current environment to the target. It will form the basis of the implementation plan that will provide the target architecture.

This is the first phase where implementation is the primary focus. Now that the organization has a tenable technical architecture, effort must be put into determining how the transition will be carried out from the current environment to the proposed architecture.

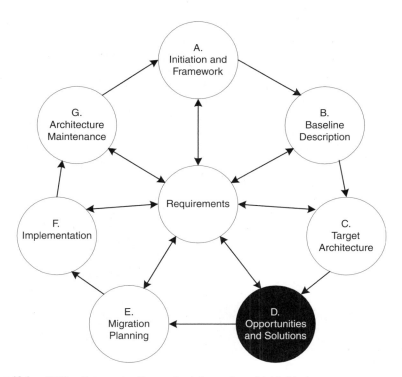

FIGURE 12.1.   ADM, with opportunities and solutions phase highlighted.

In doing this, the phase identifies the necessary parameters of change, the major activities needed to complete the transition, and the top-level projects to be undertaken in moving from the current environment to the target. It will form the basis of the implementation plan that will provide the target architecture.

This phase accepts the (signed off) technical architecture from Phase C. The business architecture, completed outside the technical architecture project and augmented with strategic technical discoveries (such as architectural principles, the key question list, and organizational constraints), provides the necessary business context for this planning activity. It must be emphasized that this phase does not implement the projects or plan the implementation in detail. This phase is high-level, strategy-based, planning required to determine the likely options and structure for implementation. The output is a selected set of work packages for input into the next phase, that of detailed migration planning. The inputs and outputs are shown in Figure 12.2.

Transition Assessment

One of the interesting by-products of any architectural process is the experience gained by those involved. Many IT groups, and organizations in general, are not typically required to think in a strategic way about IT. Characteristically, IT groups focus on the tactical aspects of running IT day-to-day. This is a fact of life. The stability of the current systems, ongoing integrity of data, robustness of the enterprise networks, and maintaining control over faults are all real concerns for the entire organization, and deserve a fair degree of focus.

It is interesting to contrast this with the disciplines associated with strategic planning. The strategist views things beyond the immediate

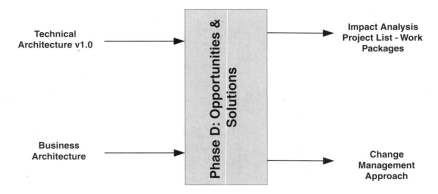

Figure 12.2.   Opportunities and solutions wiring diagram.

and into the distance. The concern is not how the current systems are maintained (although this does have a significant input into the planning process) but what the systems will look like in the future. The strategic view must meet the strategic requirements of the organization, whereas the tactical view is governed by service level agreements.

However, the development of the technical architecture is where worlds collide. Seldom will an architecture program such as this be carried out purely by the architects. As an exercise, count the number of personnel in either the IT group or wider organization that are solely responsible for technical strategy. If the organization is fortunate, there may be more than a couple. Senior technical and business subject matter experts, therefore, are critical in aiding the definition of the target environment. During development roles can change; the architect is required to understand the current environmental issues, whereas the practitioners are encouraged to look beyond the current environment. This provides an interesting adjunct to the process. Those from a tactical background will be exposed to the architectural or strategic process and have the ability to think somewhat outside the square they normal are required to inhabit.

Once version 1 of the technical architecture document has been defined, this phase allows for brainstorming around the opportunities that surround the implementation of the architecture. Applying the knowledge of subject matter experts is critical in achieving this. There is no generic way to classify opportunities that may be uncovered; however, the following generally could be exposed (this list is by no means exhaustive):

- A new service—likely to be a super service—category that was not considered
- New service subcategories or the reclustering of the current subcategories.
- Innovative approaches to eliminate duplicate service instances in the target architecture
- Approaches to speed the transition between the current and target environments
- Intelligence (either positive or negative) on the state of the products selected in the target architecture
- Intelligence on the state of standards bodies and their impact on the product market
- New business initiatives that may not have been considered.
- Ways around difficult transition problems.

As opportunities are identified, changes to the target architecture (both logical and physical) may be required. This infers that phases C and D may iterate around each other until opportunity identification is complete. There are a number of dangers with this approach:

- Iteration costs time and money, especially at this stage of the architecture development. With software development projects, changes in design are far easier to invoke at design time than during user-acceptance testing. This premise also holds true for architectural development. Although nothing has been physically implemented, the addition of major architectural components to the architecture at this stage may require significant rework. It is suggested that the opportunities phase be bound in some way; time and/or cost are practical metrics. After all, the perfect architecture is an illusion, and can never be reached.
- Opportunity brainstorming can have the effect of circumventing the process (embodied within the ADM). Those in the organization who are not intimately involved in the entire project may only have a limited understanding of the ADM, various approaches, and the TOGAF artifacts. The danger, therefore, is relitigation of the process, circumvention of the process, and production of outputs that cannot be fed back into the process. Ensure that everyone involved in opportunity brainstorming is fluent enough with TOGAF (and whatever local character has been added by the architect), and able to discuss opportunities using TOGAF terminology.

Change Management

A critical aspect of the architectural program is that of change management. Our experience is that most organizations will either be resistant to or cynical of the changes implied by the architectural program, and maybe of the architectural development itself. The reasons why organizations embark on the strategy path may be many and varied. It would be naïve to assume total commitment to the program. We have seen the development of corporate technical strategies merely because an external consultant has advised the organization that they should have one. Such an attitude is not amenable to success. Alternatively, we have experienced IT groups that understand the true value of architectures, and are passionate about their execution, but do not have the political muscle necessary to engender the same enthusiasm at a senior management level.

The architectural program is destined to impart significant change on the organization. IT systems implement business processes. Changes in those systems—as will be expected of a migration to a new target technical environment—could have far-reaching effects on the entire orga-

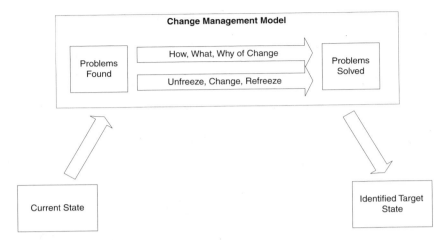

FIGURE 12.3.   Generic change management framework.

nization. Consideration should also be given to external partners. Initiatives associated with e-business bring change not only to the internal organization but to business partners, suppliers, customers, and consumers. Each will require a degree of change management.

The management of change is a complex but essential discipline to understand. It is backed by an entire academic and research base. A large number of consulting companies specialize in this arena, and much theoretical capital is available. Basically, from a sociological perspective, change is difficult. Why is this so?

- There is resistance to the unknown.
- People can be cynical about change.
- There is doubt that there is an effective means for conducting change.
- Organizational change can clash with the values of it's the organization's members.
- Change may conflict with other organizational goals.

In making changes, the agents of change need to be aware of these difficulties. Usually, the selection of a change model that best handles the anticipated difficulties is a key introduction to the process. Figure 12.3 presents a general framework that underpins change management. Essentially, change is the process of moving from a current state to a proposed state. This is also the essence of the TOGAF ADM—the migration from current to target technology environments. Although there are many change models, in general they all reference the need to identify problems and provide a means of solving them. This transition from a problem identification state to a problem solved state can be determined by the how, what, and why of change:

- *How* questions analyze the change problem in terms of the means to an end. The goal state (the problem being solved) is more often than not implied by putting how questions.
- *What* questions focus on the ends, not the means.
- The ends and the means are relative to the questions being posed. *Why* questions allow us to drill into the specifics of the ends–means relationships.

Once the current position and the end state are understood (or at least known), a general change process is required for the transition. A planned change model supports three generic operators: unfreeze, change, and refreeze. In other words it is a staged approach to undergoing change—one that implies a degree of relative stability between periods of change.

In general, there is no single strategy that will support change in all circumstances. There are a large number of factors that affect the application of change, from organizational type to an individual's values and beliefs. In the late 1960s, Bennis, Benne, and Chin undertook significant study into change strategies. Table 12.1 highlights the results of their research.[51]

In general, however, technical change—as with any other form of change—can be facilitated based on a number of straightforward guidelines:

- Do not underestimate the need for wide communication. Communicate the need for change and the change process during the change and post-change.
- Ensure that the change process is facilitated by a properly positioned change agent. A position in senior management is important.
- Change is managed by teams of people, not by individuals. Build an effective change team.
- Plan for change. Set goals and measures to determine when goals are achieved.
- Enlist feedback at multiple points within the change, and modify the strategy if required.
- Ensure that organizational structures will be valid in the changed environment. If not, plan for the need to restructure to support the change.

---

51. Warren G. Bennis, Kenneth D. Benne, and Robert Chin (Eds). *The Planning of Change* (2nd Edition). Holt, Rinehart and Winston, New York, 1969.

Table 12.1. Four basic strategies of change management.

Strategy	Description
Rational–Empirical	People are rational and will follow their self-interest once it is revealed to them. Change is based on the communication of information and the proffering of incentives.
Normative–Reeducative	People are social beings and will adhere to cultural norms and values. Change is based on redefining and reinterpreting existing norms and values and developing commitments to new ones.
Power–Coercive	People are basically compliant and will generally do what they are told or can be made to do. Change is based on the exercise of authority and the imposition of sanctions.
Environmental–Adaptive	People oppose loss and disruption but they adapt readily to new circumstances. Change is based on building a new organization and gradually transferring people from the old one to the new one.

Project Identification and Classification

The identification and classification of a set of projects that represents the transition to the target architecture is process-oriented. The objective is to describe at a high level the various units of work required to support the transition. Although the term project is used here, the practicality of actual project planning does not occur until the next phase. The work packages identified may not have a direct one-to-one relationship with actual funded and executed projects.

The process-oriented nature of this step is derived from the architectural method. As can be seen in Figure 12.4, the enactment of the ADM inherently provides a focus on the transitional activities required. The ADM stipulates an understanding of the current environment, and identification of architectural problems within the environment. The target architecture embodies the solution to the problems given a starting point of the current environment. The set of projects, therefore, is the "difference" between the current and the target environments.

Furthermore, the TOGAF artifacts provide additional support in performing project identification:

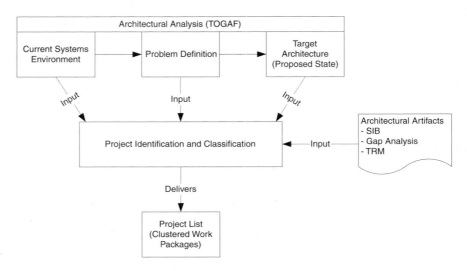

FIGURE 12.4.   Project identification process.

- The standards information base (SIB) views service instance implementation on a temporal basis—using the approach defined in Chapter 11, the timelines described are *now*, *medium*, and *long term*. This provides technical input as to the changes required to support transition.
- The gap analysis provides a different view of the transition. Gap analysis has been performed throughout the process, typically to measure a target state with the organization's strategic direction. The gap analysis will have identified new items (i.e., gaps) that will need to be implemented. The identified gaps, hopefully now filled by the target architecture, represent a business focus on the transition.
- The technical reference model (TRM) provides a blueprint of the end-state of the changed environment. The TRM is a very useful tool for supporting the vision of the change strategy.
- Service functionality has been documented over the period of the architectural development. Beginning during the assessment of the current systems in TOGAF format (see Chapter 7), the service functionality provides a detailed view of the contents of each service, but without the temporal aspects of the SIB. The functional description is useful in one particular area: identifying changes to existing functionality. This is one of the more difficult areas to identify with respect to migration.

In summary, the architect will use the artifacts from the process to identify the work packages (documented as a project list) required to bring the IT environment in line with the strategy. Changes that will be identified fall under the following broad classifications (note that these change categories are relevant to both technical and policy-based changes):

- *New functionality*. As suggested before, this is a relatively trivial process, using artifacts such as the SIB and the gap analysis. This will include new services (i.e., implementing the newly identified service instances). However, the target architecture may not have identified a specific product for implementation but rather a selection of likely products. In such a case, the first step in the change process will be to select the actual product.
- *Amendments to existing functionality*. Changes to existing functionality are not only more difficult to identify but it is more difficult to determine a likely action. Combing of the service functionality documents will aid in identification. An action strategy will need to be based on a pragmatic approach and based on how the service is provisioned in the current environment (i.e., a product, custom-developed, bureau). Significant changes to an existing service can necessitate a total rewrite (for a custom service), the replacement of the product (for a procured service), or a change in partner (for a bureau-provided service). Minor changes may not require the same approach. The scale of change is an important factor in determining the likely outcome.
- *Removal of functionality*. The removal of functionality is necessary when, among other things, service functionality changes, a service is no longer required, or an overlapping service is being replaced by another. Decommissioning a service may be a trivial exercise if the service provides only limited functionality. However, it may necessitate significant changes in the entire IT environment if it is currently a major offering. For instance, what will the organization do with the support personnel whose responsibility is exclusively to manage this service or the support contracts currently in place?

The change associated with the target architecture must be considered holistically, not purely from a technical point of view. This is one of the key messages of an effective change-management approach. If the IT organization considers the transition to the target architecture merely as a technology project, then it is likely to be unsuccessful. As shown in Figure 12.5, there are a multitude of other, nontechnical factors that must be considered when planning the transition. These range from the obvious, such as supporting business as usual during the transition, to the obscure, such as reworking measures associated with IT performance (after all, if a target objective is the control of cost of ownership,

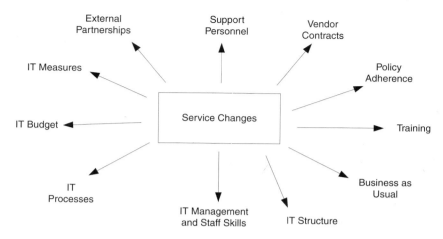

Figure 12.5.   Factors affecting transition.

the success of this needs to be quantified and measured). Of course, many of the nontechnical changes may be handled under a wider context, such as the IT strategy program, of which the technical architecture is a single aspect. This should not be taken for granted, however.

The potential for a wide variety of work packages to be identified is high. It is important, therefore, to assign them some sort of classification to aid their later clustering into projects. A suggested categorization is as follows:

- *Technical.* Cluster all technical change around the logical services described in the TRM. This implies that changes (add, change, delete) to service instances will be associated with their respective service. For example, "implement an **LDAP** directory service organization-wide" is less effective (and far too granular) than the same change enacted under the "implement changes to organizational directory services" work package. Granularity can be reduced even further using the layering inherent within the TRM, such as foundation services (e.g., "implement infrastructure changes"), super services, or organization-specific services.
- *Policy.* One of the aspects inherent within the target TRM is that of policy and guidelines. The implementation of the target technical environment relies heavily on policy surrounding the implementation. Typical policy areas will include security, systems management, software development, and business-to-business contracts. Furthermore, there should exist an overarching *architectural policy* that describes how the architecture is maintained (governed), how new

initiatives are to factor into the architecture, and other polices. Policy need not be technically focused. Other areas in this category include project management, training, and personnel retention. This category is grouped separately from the technology in awareness that different skills are required to develop and implement policy.

■ *Change management.* As discussed previously, it is impossible to be bound up in the implementation of a new technology environment and ignore the change aspects of the implementation. This category should contain the change management approach and the change management initiatives to be implemented during the change period.

The organization has funded the development of the target architecture. However, it is unlikely that there will be funding for migration work. This effort will need to be justified on its own merits. Each work package will be viewed in terms of its costs and benefits. The likelihood that all work packages will be implemented is low, so we will tackle project prioritization in the next section.

For each work package, consider establishing metadata that captures and summarizes its major attributes. A format such as Table 12.2 is suggested. This can be valuable during the later phases when detail is required, such as during project prioritization. Such a description can be used for all categories of work—technical, policy, and change management.

Output

The outputs of this phase are those of project (work package) identification, structure, and classification. A list of unprioritized projects are produced and described that capture the full gamut of change necessary to transition from the current environment to the target environment.

Table 12.2. Work package metadata table.

Work Package Description	
Work package name	
Description	
Objectives	
Categorization (technical, policy, change management)	
Related service category	
Classification (new development, procurement, selection, redevelopment)	

12.3 *Migration Planning*

Background

This section considers the next major phase in the ADM, the migration planning phase. Its position in the ADM is shown in Figure 12.6. The objective of this phase, as defined in TOGAF, is:

> . . . to sort the various implementation projects into priority order. Activities include assessing the dependencies, costs, and benefits of the various migration projects. The prioritized list of projects will go on to form the basis of the implementation plan.

The activities in this phase involve the disciplines of project management. The fundamental activity is the initiation of the architectural work packages identified during the solutions and opportunities phase. This phase is cognizant of the inevitable limited resources (e.g., time, people, dollars, equipment) that hamper any organization. The organization is

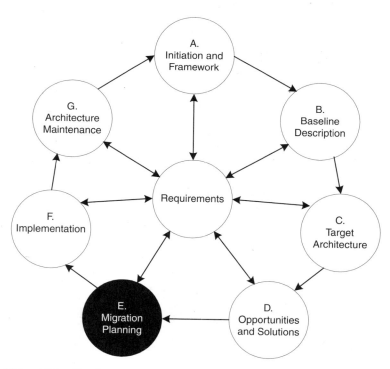

FIGURE 12.6.   ADM, with migration planning phase highlighted.

required to make decisions between various competing initiatives (not limited to the architectural program) to maximize the strategic value, for a given level of investment, based on a defined risk profile.

Project initiation is awash with analyzing the tradeoffs between a number of seemingly beneficial projects. Basically, the organization is required to make strategic decisions that lead to the investment of capital in the desire that some sort of gain will be realized. Making these key decisions is complex, and there are a number of factors that add to this complexity:

- Decisions have inherent risk and uncertainty.
- Decisions will require more than one decision-maker from more than one area of the business.
- Decisions require that the decision-makers be well-versed in a number of disciplines.
- All decisions requiring (significant) capital outlay have long-term impacts that cannot be readily predicted at the outset.
- Decisions are loaded with multiple alternatives and (conflicting) objectives.
- Decisions affect various departments within the organization (not just the IT department).

No decision-making process, given these factors, can be wholly accurate. The stochastic and dynamic nature of organizations and markets can affect a seemingly prudent decision in a matter of months. The individuals that back the decision, the stakeholders, have a further dramatic effect on success or failure. As yet there is no statistical model that takes into account the behavior of these societal factors (at best, it is merely science fiction, as anyone who has read Issac Asimov's *Foundation* novels will attest).

The important aspect of this phase of work is to allow decision-makers access to sufficient quantifiable information to support the making of pragmatic decisions. As may be appreciated from this introduction, the processes and capabilities required to achieve this goal are not solely restricted to the TOGAF ADM or the architect. These disciplines can be summarized under the project management body of knowledge. As such, they are generic to any IT project and, in fact, to strategic asset management in general. Therefore, although we will touch on some of the processes used within this phase, we do not consider this a complete treatment by any means. The reader is encouraged to initiate his or her own research on the matter. Furthermore, although the architect will be required to provide considerable input into the definition of the architectural projects, it is more likely that individuals with project management expertise will provide most of the necessary structure and process.

This phase accepts the list of work packages provided from the solutions and opportunities phase. The outputs required will differ among organizations, and much will depend on the incumbent project management processes; however, the minimum output from this phase will include a migration plan, cost–benefit analysis, and a list of prioritized projects. Figure 12.7 provides the usual wiring diagram.

Project Initiation

We have positioned the migration phase of the ADM under the general process known as project initiation. Project initiation involves the steps required to take the set of planned work packages (representing the transition to the target architecture) and turn them into a set of projects that will be prioritized and implemented. Figure 12.8 represents a summary view of a generalized project initiation framework.

The initiation process has the following key activities:

- *Cost/Risk assessment.* During this stage, the work products are (optionally) clustered into projects based on preselected criteria; for instance, a desirable maximum duration, a particular skill area, functional delivery, a strategic subject area (e.g., e-business initiatives), the logical services or other self-supporting parts of the TRM. An initial view of the project schedule is devised, and an initial cost–benefit analysis is completed for each project.
- *Asset management decision-making.* The information provided during the assessment stage supports the prioritization of all of the architectural projects against each other (and probably other IT projects vying for funds at the same time). Projects that are "above the line" are likely to require further elaboration of their costs and sched-

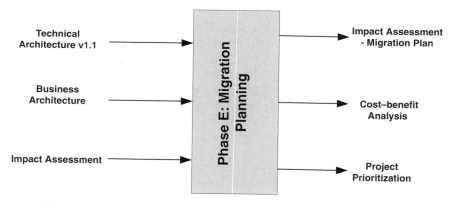

FIGURE 12.7.   Migration planning wiring diagram.

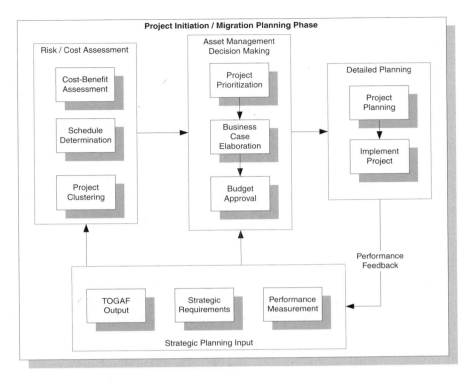

FIGURE 12.8.   Project initiation framework.

ules (usually in the form of a business case). Final budgetary ap-
proval is given.

- *Detailed planning*. Detailed planning sits within the ADM's implementation phase and is shown here for completeness.
- *Strategic input*. Initiation requires significant strategic input encompassing both the information gathered for the architectural program
  and additional "business" content required for decision-making. The
  framework incorporates feedback mechanisms showing that the initiation process (especially cost, risk, and prioritization models) requires vital input from past projects to support further improvement
  of the process.

There are many initiation models available within the public domain.
We based the framework described here on the total cost management
(TCM) framework developed at the Association for the Advancement of
Cost Engineering (AACE).[51]

51. See www.aacei.org.

Cost–Benefit Analysis

Cost–benefit analysis (CBA) is a primary step in providing quantifiable measures to support the prioritization of projects. Analysis components reflect not only "real" costs or benefits (e.g., costs of developers, products, or hardware), but intangible costs and benefits. Intangible costs and benefits reflect those aspects of the project that have a negative or positive impact on the project but cannot easily be quantified in pure dollar terms. Also inherent in CBA is the ability to determine the economic value of a project over a finite period, a process that requires the "discounting" of future costs and benefits in present terms.

The development of a robust CBA is critical, but often neglected, in e-business initiatives. The organization must be realistic with respect to both the costs and benefits of e-business systems, and constructing a CBA can be immensely helpful. E-business systems can be made to pay, but particular focus must be applied to those functional areas that will generate real value, while cost control is also an important strategy to ensure e-business success. The rash of "dot.com" failures can be related to riding the waves of e-commence hyperconfidence without a sound understanding of how initiatives would be structured to succeed. Many of the problems in this space have not been directly associated with technology. Cavalier decision-making has also had a noticeable effect.

CBA is ostensibly a discipline that can be executed through any number of alternate methods. It is likely that the organization will already have a CBA process in place to manage the organization's capital assets (either in IT or organization-wide). The assessment of the architectural projects should "borrow" whatever is available as opposed to reinventing an architecture-specific process.

We present here, however, a general CBA process for reference purposes. It is not, and in fact need not be, related to the assessment of strategic technical projects. Figure 12.9 outlines a CBA process derived from U.S. government guidelines.[52] It is likely that most other CBA processes will contain the same or similar components.

The early components of the CBA process have already been completed as outputs of the ADM. There is already a well-documented set of objectives (both strategic and architectural). The current and future environments have been defined. What remains is to document the assumptions used in building the CBA. The CBA cannot be purely quantitative, so there will be a number of assumptions associated with the cost and benefit assessment. Furthermore, assumptions provide a vehicle for defining the components that are inside and outside the scope of the project.

---

52. For full CBA guidelines, see the National Institutes of Health (NIH) guide for CBA in IT projects (see irm.cit.nih.gov/itmra/cbaguide.html).

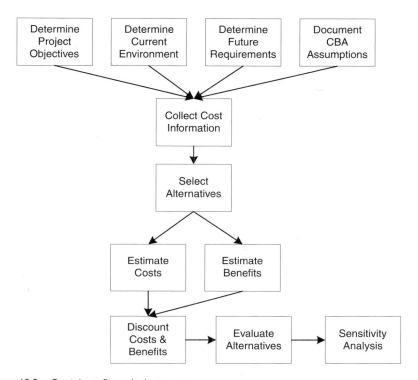

FIGURE 12.9.   Cost–benefit analysis process.

An area that has not been fully defined by TOGAF is the assessment of the current cost of IT. In the context of the CBA, the current cost assessment is restricted to the specific area within which the project is dealing (e.g., migrating the distributed directory service or building a public key infrastructure). However, costs associated with the entire environment covered by the architectural program should be understood. This is especially the case when the overarching strategy is the control (or reduction) of total ownership cost—most of the defined architectural projects will quote a positive benefit (either tangible or intangible) of reducing TCO. The IT group may already have done the necessary benchmarking to provide this information (in a perfect world this is the likely outcome because there is little point in setting a goal of reducing TCO without understanding whether the current TCO is too high for the particular industry sector). If not, it befalls the architecture program to conduct this at least at a high level. There are plenty of models and consulting organizations available to carry out this work, or it may be done in-house using a commercial (or home-grown) benchmarking approach.

An aspect to consider when the work packages have been clustered into projects is the evaluation of technical alternatives. Typical CBA is executed against freestanding projects that has little or no relationship with other IT projects. Therefore, the CBA usually dictates that multiple alternatives be considered. This allows decision-makers to compare the relative returns of different options in a single project. Some of the architectural projects will be considering alternatives. An organization may have a tendering policy that dictates going to the market for the solution. In such cases, architectural projects that require the replacement of a current part of the IT environment will have presented a number of options during target architecture development. In other areas where the new technology is not disputed the project's CBA need not consider any alternatives. The only objective of the CBA for such projects is to determine benefits in relation to costs. Remember that the CBA is a necessary step in the project initiation process that will eventually prioritize each project against all others.

The completeness and accuracy of cost information are critical to the quality of the project initiation process. There are a number of sources for this information, including:

- Historical/current organization data
- Current environment costs
- Market research
- Publications
- Industry analysts
- Specially funded studies
- Vendors
- Commercial cost models (e.g., software development costing tools)

The next step is to estimate the costs associated with the project using the cost information gathered. The reliable estimation of costs in IT projects has historically been difficult because the estimation of size or duration is problematic. There is a huge amount of cost-estimation collateral available. However, regardless of the countless number of IT projects that have gone before, new estimations never appear to be completely reliable. There are numerous models that the estimator can use. The method depends on the type of project. For instance, in the software development space, models such as function point counting, COCOMO, and COSMIC-FFP, are applicable. The estimation of package implementation relies on the methodology, the experience of the selected vendor (remembering that at the time of the CBA, there may be no selected vendor), or organizational experience of a previous implementation. Infrastructure implementation is estimated in a manner similar to that of packaged applications. Never take costs and estimates at face value. For instance, it is our experience that the costs provided in vendor responses to a tender are unlikely to provide an accurate estimation method.

Figure 12.10 shows a fundamental aspect of the estimation of IT projects. We have seen this chart quoted in so many sources that it is difficult to determine where it may have first originated. It presents an absolute truism about IT project estimation. While it is a cliché it is seldom used effectively. What it shows is that the accuracy associated with estimating a project (cost, duration, resources, etc) increases as the project moves through its life cycle. It is not until near the end (testing) that the true and final cost of the project is "estimated" accurately. During project initiation, the accuracy of the estimates can differ by an order of magnitude. Although Figure 12.10 shows ±100%, the actual magnitude of the difference is governed by many factors, including the quality of personnel, the type of technology, the tools used by the project team, the location of the teams, and the maturity (from an IT perspective) of the organization. The reason for this is obvious. At the initiation stage, there is normally a conceptual understanding of the structure of the end product, but no detail is available. Estimation models rely on detail for the accuracy—the number of function points, the number of objects, the number of HTML pages, and the number of elements in interchange documents. Without this detail, estimates can develop a significant divergence from the actual outcome. As this detail is gathered, the estimates converge. Notice how quickly this occurs in succeeding phases.

The important lesson to be taken from this is that expectations within the organization must recognize that estimation is not an exact science. In the early stages of the project life cycle, never consider a "point" estimate (an estimate stating an absolute answer such as 95 days or $500,000) no matter what the pressure. Always provide a range estimate (e.g., 75–100 days, $350k–$600k, 70% certainty) and refactor as the project proceeds through its life cycle. This is particularly important with the CBA because it fits squarely in the initiation phase, where the lack of detail exacerbates the estimation dilemma.

Accurate costing relies on a full sweep of cost categories and is likely to include both capital and operational cost considerations. Furthermore, costs must be estimated for all phases of the life cycle, including annual maintenance costs. Costs for both internal and external personnel must be factored in. Many organizations do not attempt to cost internal resources. This can hide the true cost of IT projects and hence reduce the effectiveness of future estimation based on the project. Indirect costs (such as depreciation, rent, utilities, insurance, and overhead associated with direct labor) may also need to be considered.

The estimation of benefits is the most difficult aspect of the CBA. It is inconceivable that an IT project be accepted without significant benefits to justify the expenditure. However, there are two primary challenges

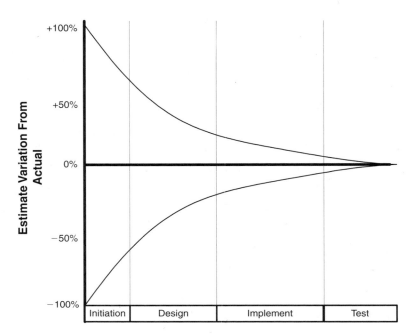

FIGURE 12.10.   Estimate variation convergence.

in understanding the benefits; ensuring benefit coverage is complete, and actually measuring benefits. Generally, benefits can be classified as either cost savings, productivity gains, strategic enablers, or competitive influences. Some general benefit categories include:

- Integrity (information, system, process)
- Maintainability
- Security
- Reliability
- Efficiency
- Changeability
- Speed to market
- Increased market share

Each of the categories identified can either be described in terms of an absolute cost saving (i.e., a tangible benefit) or a business-based gain leading to a perceived cost saving or increased revenue (i.e., an intangible benefit). Both are valid; however, whereas the first can be measured in dollars the latter requires a more subjective assessment.

Tangible benefits, such as a reduction in hardware and software costs associated with coordinating disparate systems management services, reflect an actual and estimatable monetary value. It is important to consider the period(s) in which the benefit will be realized. In other words over the lifetime of the system, how will the benefits accrue?

Intangible benefits are not usually reflected in dollar amounts. A (subjective) rating system of some predefined type is required. Such a system requires that benefit criteria be defined. Criteria should be based on performance measures that reflect the organization's strategic direction. Performance measures should include both business (e.g., improves customer satisfaction, reduces product cycle times) and IT (e.g., reduces project schedules, increased information quality). Avoid assigning actual costs to intangible benefits. Also be aware of double counting of benefits, either between tangible and intangible or between projects.

The discounting of costs and benefits is derived from the need to represent the dollar values of multiyear initiatives to a common baseline. In essence, discounting converts future costs and benefits into present dollars. The present value, or discounted value, can be calculated using the formula shown in Figure 12.11, and represents the fact that to achieve the equivalent value, future dollars must be greater than present dollars.

Sensitivity analysis tests the sensitivity of the input parameters to the final result. This is especially relevant when alternatives are being considered. Given the importance of the CBA in the overall prioritization, decision-makers must be sure that the costs and benefits reflect the likely outcome. Sensitivity analysis varies key input parameters to test how the final result is affected. For instance, it may be applicable to view all estimated costs in three dimensions: worst, best, and most likely. During the prioritization process, the decision-makers may look at how each project fairs when individually assessed against these dimensions. For

$$P = F \left(\frac{1}{1 + I^n} \right)$$

P = Present Value
F = Future Value
I = Interest Rate
n = number of years

FIGURE 12.11.   Present value formula.

example, will the same projects come out on top if worst case costs are used?

The output of the CBA process is a full cost assessment for each of the architectural projects. Some of the projects will include a number of alternatives, which will also be assessed on their costs and benefits. The next step in the initiation process is to prioritize the projects.

Project Prioritization

The completion of a detailed CBA for each project can provide all of the necessary input into the prioritization process. The implication is that the CBA has considered all of the important factors, not just those with a dollar value. However, whereas CBA is an approach for providing quantitative cost and benefit data for a project, project prioritization is a never-ending cyclic process that underpins project initiation decision-making. This concept is shown in Figure 12.12.

Prioritization is very much process-driven. There is a constant flow of new project initiatives as well as projects in the execution phase, hence the cyclic process. All projects are competing for scarce resources, particularly money and personnel. This is why the prioritization process, as part of the overall project cycle, is important. As new initiatives are defined (for the technical architecture project this is the activity of the migration phase of the ADM), they will be assessed against peer new initiatives and projects currently executing and, based on the resources available, will provide a portfolio of projects to execute over the next period.

We suggest that a single organization-wide prioritization process for IT projects is vital. The objective is to take a collection of new initiatives

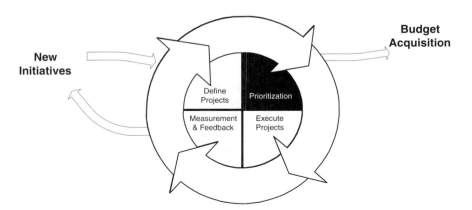

FIGURE 12.12.   Project cycle.

and weigh them against a standard set of factors (usually strategic) to determine which are the most likely to provide maximum benefit for the capital investment. Circumventing this approach, possibly with a number of independent business units performing their own prioritizations independently, or initiating projects in an ad hoc manner is counterproductive. Such an ad hoc approach is also counter to the architectural approach to IT, which emphasizes a coordinated approach to the IT environment, and is likely to cause a rapid degradation of the architecture once implemented.

One of the main reasons for unifying IT prioritization is that the organization must settle on both a common set of drivers for prioritization and a common approach. As we have mentioned, the output of a CBA could be directly fed into the prioritization approach. Those projects that generate maximum return on the capital investment, given the capital outlay, would decide the relative positioning. There are, however, many factors not directly related to cost that must be considered as part of the prioritization. A way of measuring these factors is required much as there was a need to assess intangible benefits and costs in the CBA. In fact, the same techniques can generally be used.

Usually all factors, including absolute cost, are converted into a weighted score so that all can be leveled. Each project is then scored against the factors, and the application of the weighting provides a final total. Thus, the project is positioned with respect to all others.

There are many techniques. For instance, the identification and isolation of the two most important determinants and a set of factors describing the determinants are assigned. The project is scored on all factors, and an average is produced for each determinant. The results are then presented as a quadrant, where each of the four segments represents a priority. For example, key determinants may be value and resource. Value can be measured by factors such as political pressures, customer benefit, customer demand, or time urgency. Resource can be measured by the levels of personnel requirements required, capital outlay, or scope of the project, for example. In this case, the organization will be looking for projects that maximize value and minimize resource usage. From Figure 12.13 it can be seen that a high positive determinant (in this example, value), and a low negative determinant (i.e., resource) provide the highest-priority project.

The differentiation of strategic initiatives, particularly those that are driven from the architectural program, can be difficult in terms of prioritization because the architectural method is responsible for highlighting projects with high strategic value. General advice is to view the projects in terms of their ability to maximize the short- to medium-term wins, that is, the projects that have low to medium resource require-

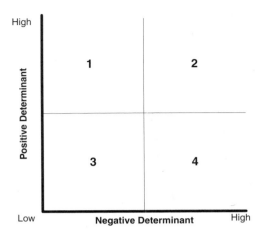

FIGURE 12.13.   Prioritization quadrant.

ments and have the ability to quickly provide the greatest gains in terms of key business strategy (e.g., TCO reduction).

The list of prioritized projects must then go through a final step. Resource limitations are likely in almost every organization—we have not come across an organization that has unlimited resources to undertake IT projects (hence the prioritization process). The final cut is typically the capital budget available to the IT group for new initiatives. Running down the list of projects, in priority order, there will be a point at which the money runs out. This represents "the line." Projects above the line are likely to be executed whereas those below will have to wait (see Figure 12.14). At the same time, new initiatives are being added to the prioritization process all the time. Some even displace current above-the-line projects.

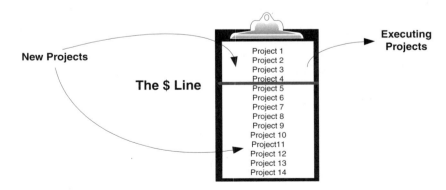

FIGURE 12.14.   The cut.

There are two significant feedback mechanisms required in the process:

- Many of the factors associated with prioritization are qualitative (that is, based on some sort of subjective reasoning). There are methods to remove much of the subjectivity, but the fact remains that it can never be as quantitative as absolute costs. Therefore, a key aspect of the project cycle is to feed back experience from the executed projects to recalibrate the model. For example, did the way market share was assessed during prioritization stand up to the actual experience of market share, and if not, how should the assessment be changed?
- IT budgets are not static and are generally reassessed each year based on the anticipated capital and operational requirements of the IT group. The CBA and prioritization activities provide an excellent feedback mechanism into the new round of IT budget reviews. Depending on the organizational budget framework, projects that are awaiting execution represent a "best possible" budget scenario. This will be tempered by organizational budgets, however. It is possible that "the cut" line will move during the budget rounds.

This entire process is conducted in direct consultation with senior management and the senior executive team (either IT or organizational) will generally take custodianship of the process. IT prioritization is likely to be conducted and maintained by a team headed by the CIO and containing senior IT managers. Of course, the process should exist higher up the organization so that all projects (not just IT) are managed through a single process.

Project Roadmap

The generic project initiation processes will treat the architectural projects individually. However, the entire portfolio of architectural work packages affecting the transition should be tracked independently of the generic processes. To this end, an architectural roadmap should be constructed (based on the output of the prioritization process) to act as a tracking tool for the overall transition. The roadmap should contain:

- Estimated timelines for each architectural project, including the major activities. Do not descend to task level; this will be handled within the individual projects.
- The priority assigned by the prioritization process.
- The architectural dependencies among the individual projects. Project dependencies will have already been factored in during the apportioning of the work packages into projects. These architectural

dependencies track how the various components of the service port-folio come to realization.

Most architectural programs will generate a large number of potential delivery projects, which will be delivered over a number of years. The architectural roadmap provides a valuable communications tool to all parts of the organization as to the progress of the architectural initiatives. Furthermore, it provides positive reenforcement that the organization is continuing the architectural program. This supports the change-management processes already in place.

Output

The outputs of the migration planning phase include:

- Cost–benefit analysis of each of the architectural projects
- An assigned priority for each project, produced via the prioritization process
- An architectural roadmap, providing a holistic view of all architectural projects

12.4   Example

Introduction

This chapter presented approaches for opportunity, solution, and migration planning, phases D and E of the ADM. In this example, we look briefly at some of these aspects for CFL. As is the style for the examples in this text, the treatment is not designed to be complete but rather to illustrate several of the key points.

Change Management

There are some significant changes to be made in the CFL IT environment to support the architectural direction. Although the impact will be felt in all areas, the regional IT centers will be affected the most. The unification of the environment (E-mail, operating system, Internet access, and systems management) will reduce their ability to act autonomously. Although regional subject matter experts have been involved in architectural development, the reality of the actual changes will need to be carefully managed. The same can be said about CFL's raw material suppliers. Achieving cost-effectiveness of the B2B solution will require motivated and open-minded suppliers as partners. Generally, we support a normative–reeducative change model. The culture of CFL reflects the social–cognitive approach, which best supports change through the development and commitment to new behavioral norms and values. Change management strategies include:

- Promote the architecture to the organization (especially the regional IT groups). The selling proposition is based on the problems faced by the existing environment, the new initiatives required, and the selected direction. Regional subject matter experts will be enlisted to act in project-steering activities.
- Establish a clear architectural governance structure to support on-going maintenance of the architecture. Ensure that governance is driven by senior business representatives.
- Consider restructuring the IT group to support a greater centralization of operational aspects.
- Enact a process for partner (supplier) advocacy.

Work Packages

We have identified a number of work packages that represent the architectural change necessary for CFL. Table 12.3 shows a partial list. Each work package is aligned with its most likely service and is assigned a generic type: technical, policy, governance, and change management.

Project Initiation

The first step in the project initiation phase is to cluster the work packages into sensible project divisions. The clustering of work packages into projects is always a difficult process. From an architectural perspective, we would have preferred to cluster along service boundaries. However after discussion with the architectural steering group and the CIO, we are using the following criteria for clustering:

- Constrain the likely length (and cost) of project to under 6 months and under $1 million.
- Policy is to be clustered together.
- Change management will form part of the change–management program instigated by the architecture project (but not driven by it).

The next aspect is to undertake cost–benefit analysis for each of the architectural projects. This information will be fed into the prioritization process owned by the Chief Financial Officer. Table 12.4 shows the sum-

Table 12.3. Architecture work packages.

Work Package	Service	Type
Select and implement B2B commerce platform based on super service and SIB architectural requirements.	B2B	Technical
Pilot and implement supply chain project with selected partners on B2B and EAI infrastructure.	B2B	Technical
Deliver customer-facing B2B applications as required by e-business strategy	Web	Technical
Select integration (EAI) product to conform to EAI super service.	EAI	Technical
Implement EAI product and integrate core systems via EAI solution.	EAI	Technical
Development of security policy and change-management requirements.	Security	Policy
Implement security enhancements as defined by SIB.	Security	Technical
Implement a PKI infrastructure commensurate with internal PKI applications. Engage external PKI certification authority.	Security	Technical
B2B partner identification and business interchange document standardization (including recognition for RosettaNet and CMA's IXM) with partners.	Information interchange	Policy
Establish unified Internet connection model and infrastructure (including firewall). Bring outsourced Internet (including e-mail) in-house.	Network, Security	Technical
Unify e-mail product implementations based on SIB.	Network	Technical
Implement organization-wide calendar and scheduling functionality based on SIB.	Collaboration	Technical
Integrate core systems (including regional infrastructure system) into enterprise systems management environment according to Logistics ESM policy.	Systems management	Technical
Develop software engineering strategy to support a contemporary approach to development and based on technologies defined in the SIB.	Software engineering	Policy, Governance

Table 12.3. Architecture work packages (*continued*).

Work Package	Service	Type
Unify the network infrastructure (and applications) to support a single internet working model.	Network	Technical
Extend WAN into international market offices, and increase WAN bandwidth of overall network according to SIB.	Network	Technical
Establish relationship with external IT analyst.		Policy
Establish architectural maintenance and governance processes.		Policy, Governance, Change management
Internal (and outsourced) skills review, including training strategy.		Change management
Training for users facing functionality changes.		Change management
Partner advocacy.		Change management

mary of the CBA for the B2B commerce project. This project consisted of the following work packages:

- Select and implement B2B commerce platform based on super service and SIB architectural requirements
- Pilot and implement supply chain project with selected partners on B2B and EAI infrastructure
- B2B partner identification and business interchange document standardization (including recognition for RosettaNet and CMA's IXM) with partners

Only tangible costs and benefits were considered. The basic breakdown of the CBA for this project included:

- *Costs*. Development (products, vendors, internal development); operational and maintenance (support resources, licenses, maintenance contracts, hardware, software, communications).
- *Benefits*. Avoidance of costs (manual supply chain handling, reduced stock on hand).

The CBA is an input into the prioritization process used by CFL. Strategic projects must have either a neutral or positive ROI. Limited return is supported for strategic projects if intangible analysis provides a positive outcome. Prioritization consists of a number of techniques to determine "above the line" projects including SWOT, force field, choose by advantage, and criteria analysis. Intangible determinant ranking is also adopted as a tool. Projects are rated on the following determinants:

- *Value* includes political, support of business strategy, support of e-business strategy, and time urgency.
- *Resource* includes, level of resource required to complete project, variation from existing projects, and the scope of the project.

Prioritization analysis assigned projects along a continuum of high, high–medium, medium, low–medium, and low. Based on the current budget position, low–medium and low–priority projects are delayed until further funds are allocated. Table 12.5 notes the priority position for each of the architectural projects, and Figure 12.15 shows a summary of the overall program on a timeline.

Table 12.4. B2B commerce project summary.

Description / FY	2002	2003	2004	2005	2006	Total
Annual Costs	1,240,000	1,240,000	1,240,000	1,240,000	1,240,000	6,200,000
Annual Benefits	1,312,620	1,432,400	1,432,400	1,640,000	1,760,000	7,577,420
Discount Factor	0.9825	0.9483	0.9154	0.8836	0.8529	
Discounted Costs (DC)	1,218,300	1,175,892	1,135,096	1,095,664	1,057,596	5,682,548
Disc. Benefits (DB)	1,289,649	1,358,345	1,311,219	1,449,104	1,501,104	6,909,421
Disc. Net (DB-DC)	71,349	182,453	176,123	353,440	443,508	1,226,873
Benefit/Cost Ratio	1.0586	1.1552	1.1552	1.3226	1.4194	1.2159

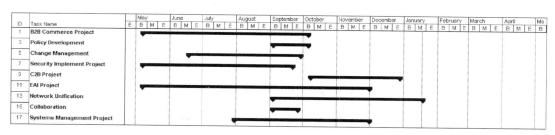

FIGURE 12.15.   Architectural program timeline.

Table 12.5. Project priority.

Priority	Project
High	B2B commerce project
	EAI integration project
High–medium	C2B project
	Security project
	Policy development project
	Change management project
Medium	Network unification project
	Collaboration project
	Systems management project

12.5   Summary

This chapter has considered the activities associated with the implementation of the target architecture. This is the first phase to truly attempt to quantify the delivery aspect of the architecture. The definition of opportunities and solutions is principally dedicated to the aspects of change management and work package identification. These are significant components of TOGAF. The chapter stressed the clustering of the target architecture initiatives into individual packages of work as well as initiatives to support change management.

The migration planning phase (Phase E of the ADM) takes a project management slant on the development of the architecture. The work packages are clustered into projects. These projects must then be justified though techniques such as cost–benefit analysis and prioritization. The result is a list of projects that will enter the next stage of the ADM, the implementation phase. This is the subject of the next chapter.

CHAPTER 13

Implementation and Maintenance

13.1 Introduction

In the last chapter, we looked at the identification of architectural projects. Further, we discussed the inclusion of the architectural projects into the organization-wide project initiation process. The outcome of this process was a prioritization of the projects (along with other IT project initiatives) and a final order in which they would be undertaken.

In the first part of this chapter, we take a more detailed view of the implementation of the individual architectural project. Although we consider implementation a generic activity—the subject of uncountable industry collateral—there are individual components of the implementation that have specific bearing on the architectural program. We review the types of projects required to build the architecture and consider the role of the architectural contract in ensuring delivery to the architecture.

The "last" phase of the architectural development method (ADM) is the maintenance of the architecture. Maintenance does not have the same project-like characteristics of the other phases. It does not have a defined endpoint but rather it consists of the ongoing disciplines required to maintain the architecture delivered during the process. The architecture delivered is prone to erosion—that is, it diverges from the ideal path established during the program. This erosion, or architectural drift, is influenced by many factors, including changes in business strategy, changes in technology, changes in constraints, or even changes planned as part of the ongoing development of the architecture. We look at a number of approaches to control drift. Primarily, to be successful, the maintenance of the architecture must exist as part of

IT-governance that takes into account the control mechanisms, including feedback, required to maintain the charted course.

13.2   *Implementation*

This section considers the next major phase in the ADM, the implementation phase. Its position in the ADM is shown in Figure 13.1. The objective of this phase, as defined in TOGAF, is:

> . . . to formulate recommendations for each implementation project and construct an architecture contract to govern the system implementation and deployment. The projects are then implemented and deployed during this phase.

Whereas the first four phases of the ADM (from initiation to opportunities and solutions) can be considered specific to the domain of ar-

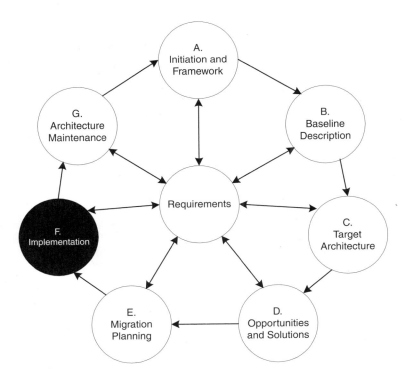

FIGURE 13.1.   ADM, with implementation phase highlighted.

chitecture, this is not the case with phases E and F. Both migration planning (discussed in the previous chapter) and implementation rely significantly on in-place organizational processes for:

- Cost–benefit analysis
- Project prioritization
- Project planning
- Project implementation

We do not suggest that the organization adopt specific TOGAF-related processes in these areas. Even if the processes do not exist (which is highly unlikely in a mature IT organization), adopting an architecture view in these areas will not be beneficial. Instead we suggest that the architect defer to the organizational processes. In fact, our feeling is that migration planning and implementation phases exist within the ADM merely for completeness. Therefore, the implementation of the architectural projects will be handed over to the standard organizational "development" (or implementation) process.

Although we use a generic term (i.e., the architectural project) to refer to each initiative, in reality individual projects may look very different. Each of the architectural projects identified is required to be implemented to enable the organization to transition to an "architecturally stable" situation. The types of those projects can include:

- Policy development (e.g., security policies, architectural conformance policies, software development guidelines)
- Product customization and deployment
- Software development
- Interorganizational negotiations (this is particularly likely with e-business initiatives)
- Vendor relationship transition or amendment
- Systems integration
- Organization structure changes, and recruitment
- Marketing initiatives
- Market research
- Internal technology reviews
- Governance changes
- Performance benchmarking

As can be seen, the preceding list presents an eclectic range of project types. Although many IT groups are familiar with a number of them (for instance, software development or product implementation), they may be unfamiliar with others (e.g., marketing, governance, interorganizational negotiations). Although general project management disciplines will cover such a wide range of project types, determining the right approach for undertaking a project of a specific type cannot be generalized.

There is a wide range of literature, research, and commercial and noncommercial organizations available to aid in the management of all of the project types listed. In the IT industry, volumes of research are available with respect to software development because supporting a software engineering discipline is paramount in most organizations. Consortia, such as the Software Engineering Institute (SEI), provide a wealth of information on this topic. Additionally, each specific project subtype, such as data warehousing, will generally also have supporting consortia and research (in this case, the Data Warehousing Institute would be an example). In the previous chapter, we briefly introduced the subject of change management. It is likely that at least one of the architectural projects will include change management. As highlighted in the last chapter, the information available on this discipline is also large and wide-ranging.

Providing specific advice on individual project types in this text would be futile. However, there is a TOGAF architectural artifact that should accompany every architectural project to aid in its successful implementation and bring together the necessary information for delivery; that is, the architectural contract.

The architectural contract is a formal agreement between the enterprise technical architecture (or rather the custodians of the architecture) and the project. The architectural contract also forms a significant part of the overall architectural governance process. Each project (not just those identified as part of the architectural process) represents an addition or amendment to the IT environment and therefore has an effect on the architecture. The contract provides a type of contextual reference for each project—that is, guidelines and policy as to how the architecture will be maintained by the project. The fact that we are currently concerned with the projects necessary to reach the target architecture does not alleviate the need to be bound by the architectural requirements. This is especially important considering that the projects are generally run individually and independently of each other. Obviously, some integration may be required, where many of the projects are tested and delivered together; however, some projects are totally self-contained.

The contract also acts as a communications mechanism for the project team. Although they may be working on a small and seemingly unrelated component, the contract provides the necessary background to give team members an understanding of the full strategic direction. Consider also that internal resources may not carry out the projects. The contract is able to provide the necessary input into contract management of the external organization.

Table 13.1 shows the basic contents of an architectural contract. The organization may alter this as necessary to support any internal policy requirements.

As already mentioned, the architectural contract is not an artifact exclusive to the development of the architecture. As part of the architectural governance process the contract should become a standard project input for all IT projects. This approach is embodied in the process to maintain the architecture (which we discuss in the next section and the last chapter) beyond the point where it is actually delivered—that is, when all of the architectural projects have been completed. The architectural requirements for any IT project are as critical as the functional requirements and should be given at least equal importance during project initiation. In other words, an IT project of any type cannot be deemed successful unless it has delivered to the architectural requirements, these requirements having been stated in the contract.

At this point, the project passes through the organization's standard project management processes. This falls outside the TOGAF development method. In fact, other architectural disciplines may take over. The solutions architecture is a solution- or project-specific medium-level architectural view of the solution. Solutions architectures are typically required when a project must implement a number of interconnected parts (or major functional groupings), that have a reliance on, and may modify, certain infrastructural components (such as network, directory services, or network operating systems). The solutions architecture can easily adopt the TOGAF taxonomy and representations to describe its aim. In fact, we have used exactly this technique in a number of projects. This has the advantage of leveraging off the formal TOGAF method with which the organization should now be familiar and supporting an effective relationship with the enterprise technical architecture.

Key definition: **Solutions architecture.**
Solutions architecture is a particular instance of an architecture that deals with the design of multisystem solutions.

Projects that are tasked with the delivery of custom software will require the adoption of formal application architecture disciplines. We do not believe that TOGAF has applicability in this area due to its current weakness with respect to building blocks and the lack of detail available for expressing interservice and intraservice functionality. There are a huge number of methods, techniques, and supporting tools available in this space—some would say too many. Methods and models include Rational Unified Process, Waterfall, Spiral, Incremental, eXtreme Programming, and vendor-specific techniques. Modeling techniques in-

Table 13.1. Contents of architectural contract.

Category	Contents
Background	The background positions the project in the context of the entire program. It describes the overall business strategy and objectives. Included are the general assumptions and constraints.
The nature of the agreement	The contract will state a certain degree of adherence for the project team. It may be considered to provide (non-enforcing) guidelines for an internal team, or its contents may reflect contractual requirements, related to performance milestones, for an external team.
Scope	Much in the way the project's terms of reference (and other functional documents) would describe overall scope, this section provides the scope from an architectural perspective. Typically, this provides a high-level view of included service and super service functionality. It is important to indicate items that are not in scope, thus ensuring that the project remains focused on the planned outcomes.
Strategic requirements	This section describes the key strategic drivers that the project must support through its outcomes. These are taken directly from the business and technical architecture and generally will consist of all business and technical objectives, not just those that are specific to the project.
Criteria measuring effectiveness of projects	The architectural program, as a whole, embodies a number of criteria to measure its effectiveness which were discussed during the initiation phase. This section provides individual criteria that relate to this project, communicating clearly the goals and objectives of the project with respect to the entire program.
Roles and responsibilities	The roles and responsibilities referenced here do not relate to the project itself but rather to the key stakeholders and custodians of the architecture and the strategies. This provides the project team with a list of those who will provide guidance on architectural issues, who can make project governance decisions, who manages IT budgets, and other decision-makers.
Roadmap	The program roadmap was discussed in the previous chapter. Presenting it in this context allows the project team to understand the relationship between their project and the overall program. Furthermore, by providing dependencies, it allows the project team to understand any interproject interactions required.

Table 13.1. Contents of architectural contract (*continued*).

Category	Contents
Conformance requirements	The project is responsible for putting in place a part of the transition to the target architecture. Thus, the scope of the project should directly map to architectural conformance. However, there will be aspects of the target architecture (embodied within the TRM and SIB) that provide mandatory requirements on the project. For example, a specific interface specification, the product to implement, an integration standard between systems, or a number of specific products to evaluate in a tender process. Furthermore, a number of services (called universal services in Chapter 11) have a relationship with all other services (and applications). The requirements for services such as service qualities and security are mentioned here as well. Additionally, policy requirements should also be provided (distilled from the service policy table discussed in Chapter 11).
Target architecture mapping	This section provides a detailed view of how the project scope relates to the target architecture. The solution maps and the SIB produced during the target architecture definition provide the project with a detailed architectural context. Furthermore, the service functionality table (discussed in Chapter 11) affords a view of the functional requirements of the project. In some areas, this level of detail may not be available (e.g., policy development), but the TRM (including subcategories) should still be provided.
QA milestones	Quality assurance (QA) is a key discipline for the successful delivery of any project. QA implies a planned set of points at which the project and parties external to the project will assess progress and deliverables. This section states the project milestones at which architectural quality assurance will be undertaken. A detailed list of deliverables and criteria for success is supplied for each milestone.
References	The references section provides links to relevant architectural documents. Such references would include the business and technical architectures and cost–benefit analysis as well as pointers to relevant industry research and background relating to any of the secondary and tertiary reference models that form the TRM.

clude; Unified Modeling Language, Patterns, CASE, structural varieties, and C2 Modeling.

Although it may seem that TOGAF and the methods and techniques just noted have no defined relationship, this is not entirely a correct representation. In one respect, TOGAF acts as a metaframework for all other software development methods. The TOGAF software engineering service category is a critical enterprise technical architecture component that defines how the organization develops software and generally operates software development (or customization) projects. The development of software (and purchase of software packages) has a huge impact on the entire technical environment. The development languages, the modeling techniques, and the development processes have an impact on every other aspect of the technical architecture. This is because the platform is required for one reason alone—to support the applications (business and infrastructure). Development languages can have a far-reaching effect on application server choices, service interface specifications, service qualities, and policy. The maintenance of the IT environment in an architectural manner relies on control of software engineering disciplines. Therefore, we can see that even before the target environment is delivered, the proposed technical architecture may actually already be setting conformance requirements (or architectural constraints, depending on your view) for the architectural projects in the area of software engineering services. These constraints will then drive the types of application architecture methods and modeling techniques used.

13.3   Maintenance

Background

This section considers the last major phase of the ADM, the architectural maintenance phase. Its position in the ADM is shown in Figure 13.2. The objective of this phase, as defined in TOGAF, is:

> . . . to establish a maintenance process for the new baseline that is achieved with the completion of the implementation phase. This process will typically provide for the continual monitoring of such things as new developments in technology and changes in the business environment, and for determining whether to formally initiate a new architecture evolution cycle.

The first six phases of the ADM have put in place the organization-specific target architecture environment. These phases are, in essence, a program of work that has progressed in a linear fashion from the spec-

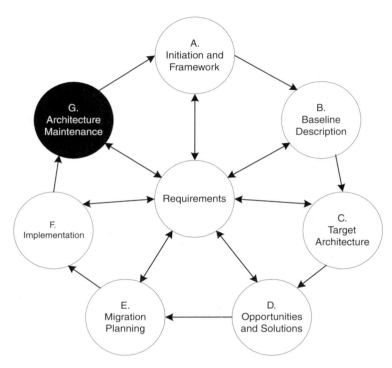

FIGURE 13.2.   ADM, with maintenance phase highlighted.

ification of the conceptual architecture (the ideal architecture) to the implementation of projects (and individual work packages) to realize the ideal. Certainly, there would have been a number of compromises made along the way. There may have been conflicts within the architecture team over the right product or specification for the job, or individual projects may not have been executed due to time and/or money constraints.

All of the projects in the architectural program have been responsible for moving the organization closer to the target. Now that this is complete, two areas of focus remain:

■ How does the organization remain true to the architecture?
■ How does the organization allow for continuous architectural improvement?

In TOGAF terms, this is the phase known as architectural maintenance. However, unlike the other TOGAF ADM phases, architectural maintenance should be seen as a continuous cyclic process in its own right. This process must exist at the very heart of the organization's IT discipline and is part of the overall IT governance processes.

The Cyclic Architecture Process

No organization is a static entity. Constant change is necessary for an organization to grow and remain profitable in today's market. Every change event, whether it is the opening of a new market, the acquisition of another company, or a change in leadership, has an impact on the operation of the organization. The same is true for technology. In a manner that is agnostic to individual organizations, technology is dynamic. The technology life cycle (presented in Chapter 2) shows that individual technologies never remain static. In fact, in the era of the Internet (and e-time), the pace of technology change is increasing. Both of these factors have considerable effects on the target architecture.

The execution of the TOGAF ADM has progressed the organization from its current environment (its baseline technology environment) to the target architecture, with the objective of meeting all strategic requirements. In essence, the target environment becomes the new baseline. From day one, outside influences are acting on it, causing it to slowly erode. There are a number of key reasons why erosion occurs:

- The current state of the business changes, fundamentally driven by a change in the organization's strategic objectives. The target architecture has been specifically based on meeting the organizational strategies and is therefore sensitive to change in this area.
- The ideal technology position changes; that is, the technology from which the architecture is built transitions through the general life cycle. Products become obsolete and new trends occur. Bear in mind that the target architecture incorporates educated "guesses" as to where technology will be in the short, medium, and long term. The architecture has essentially "bet" on potential winning technologies, with the chances of complete accuracy being less than 1:1.
- After the new baseline has been achieved, an initial static state will occur, driven by a focus on operational stability that necessitates limited change. Furthermore, the architectural program is basically complete, its focus diminished within the organization.
- Industry and organizational chaos. The unexpected should never be discounted. Changes in political climates, movement of personnel, and external factors, all can aid in architectural erosion.
- Planned erosion. The standards information base maintains an evolutionary path for technology. Depending on the approach used in describing the SIB, it will contain a short-, medium-, and long-term view. This therefore predicts how erosion might happen and how technologies should transition to reduce drift.

Key definition: **Architectural drift.**
Architectural drift describes the movement away from a chosen architectural direction based on external influences.

Figure 13.3 attempts to present the concept of drift based on these factors. The implication is that the current baseline and the ideal architectural positions are seldom aligned. Once alignment does occur—say through the initiation and completion of an architectural program—the ideal position erodes under the influence of both technology and business changes. During that period the new baseline does not react to the change and begins to lag and complete control is lost. This gap between the optimum and the current positions is called architectural drift. As shown in Figure 13.3, one method to effect realignment is the execution of another architectural project. This is the concept embodied within the ADM, whereby the maintenance phase precedes the next initiation phase.

The execution of regular architectural realignment is a sound strategy for fighting drift. This infers that the IT environment will need to be realigned after a defined period has elapsed, and a new architectural program will be initiated to facilitate the realignment.

If an organization has never undertaken an architectural review (and possible realignment) of its IT environment, the first architectural program will be painful. It is typical in such cases that major change is required and that almost nothing in the IT environment appears to be

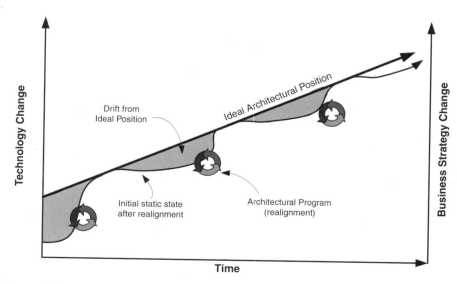

FIGURE 13.3. Architectural drift.

valid. This may be true because the environment may have built up many years of accumulated grime as the change factors continue their glacial movement. However, once the target architecture is reached, the next initiation of the program will be less painful. This is facilitated by the fact that the IT group should now have a better understanding of the architectural process. The degree of drift may not be as significant. Furthermore, the process has generated a number of key artifacts that will be useful for ongoing maintenance; that is, the technical reference model (TRM) and the standards information base (SIB).

The degree of required change will depend on the period between the end of one program and the start of the next. There is no best-practice information to determine the best duration between programs. Much will depend on the organizational type and the business and technology climate of the organization. As a general rule, the period between programs appears to be shrinking in line with the pace of technology improvement. A decade or two ago, once every 5 years would have been enough. Today, that number is more likely to be a maximum of 2–3 years. As a pointer, the organization should use the time defined as the medium-term duration, referenced in the technology selection timeline of the SIB (see Chapter 11).

Instead of using a fixed period, of course, a "when needed" approach can be taken. Such an approach highlights the critical aspects of architectural capability (dealt with in the next chapter) and measurement feedback. To determine the point at which drift is deemed unacceptable, there must first be a quantifiable understanding of what constitutes drift. Secondly, the measures must be in place to provide the metrics for measuring drift. Using TOGAF, the architectural program has provided a vast array of metrics that not only determine the structure of the target environment but also can be used to measure drift. Metrics are embodied within the following:

- Business strategy, objective, and so on (e.g., are we increasing online customers)
- Information system strategic plan output (e.g., is all information available)
- Architectural principles (e.g., have we reduced the number of security breaches)
- Short-, medium-, and long-term service instance standards (e.g., have we standardized on a single mail system).

A change in any of the measures may indicate drift. At the macro level, a change in key business strategies could invalidate parts of the architecture or could require additions not considered (or discounted) during the process. Consider the paradigm shift caused by the Internet and the viability of e-business. Given this external influence, most organizations are considering ways to use this new channel for increased market share. The Internet as a delivery channel would not even have been considered more than a few years ago. Another example is a noticeable change in service quality requirements—caused by, for example, a merger with another organization requiring a two-fold increase in scalability requirements of much of the platform, and an increased need for interoperability—may necessitate technology changes or upgrades.

Changes in technology can have a significant impact on the organizational architecture. From the outside, it appears that the IT industry is in a constant state of change. A vendor's products are continually being upgraded with new features and modified functionality. Industry standards ebb and flow in such a manner that it is possible for an organization to back one standard only to find it superseded in short order. Products grow to fill the ever-increasing capacity of the hardware and operating system platforms. In IT industry segments, vendors blossom, only to face consolidation as the strong acquire the innovative and the weak. Apart from a few notable exceptions, the rising stars of yesterday can be rapidly overtaken and consumed by the rising stars of today.

We, along with many IT executives, lament this pattern and the effect it has on the IT environment. But in reality, the IT industry functions like any highly competitive industry—the maxim being "Innovate or Die." Outside the IT industry, the users of technology feel the same pain (and/or exhilaration), say, as those who religiously follow the fashion industry. But we are perpetuators of this IT fashion. Even as the analysts begin discussing the new technologies, we want them in our IT environments; we want to be ahead of our competition. A couple of years ago no one had even heard of XML, but now we demand that it be the very hub of all B2B and integration products. We will not consider products without it. Consider the engineering disciplines required to tool up to be able to provide XML products. Compare this with the ability of your own organization to respond in months to new customer demand. We drive the IT industry; make no mistake about it. Therefore, we must understand how the internal IT environment should react.

Of course, some organizations can blissfully remain static for a number of years, reducing the impact of continual IT change. The important aspects of their environments are functionality and stability. Such organizations typically exist in markets with little or no competition, such as government. On the other hand, others must continue to innovate to survive (much like the IT companies). In industries with aggressive and relentless competition, organizations are required to ride the technology wave, implementing new technologies and paradigms before their competitors in the hope of grabbing key market share.

The IT organization must maintain a watching brief on the IT industry. The target architecture provides a technology roadmap using the short-, medium-, and long-term stakes in the ground. The state of these predictions must be continually monitored and periodic improvement noted that necessitate altering course. In particular, volatile technology areas should be monitored. At present these include such areas as the distributed component tool market, the integration tool market, and the application server market. Other areas are less vulnerable to change and can be monitored less aggressively, such as operating systems, databases, or network equipment. Interestingly, the volatile markets tend to be characterized by:

- Significant vendor competition
- New areas with limited or no standardization
- Areas with analyst-driven elevated market revenue predictions

It requires an eclectic person, or a team of people, to truly understand how the technology industry (and specific product) is evolving. To obtain an accurate assessment requires significant research. The industry functions primarily on rumor and competitive positioning. Therefore, do not rely on hearsay and innuendo. Do not rely exclusively on the vendor either. Gather information from multiple sources. It may seem extreme, but making IT research a specialist role in the organization is not outrageous. We have experience with an organization that invested $10 million in the implementation of an operating system that detailed research (i.e., not asking the vendor) could have refuted, so there is value in this role. The areas of research should include:

- *Vendor product information* provides the current state of products plus any (marketing embellished) planned upgrades. Mostly this can be found from vendor Web sites.
- *Internal vendor relationships.* Forming honesty-based relationships with people in the key areas (such as engineering, product strategy, and customer service) can provide valuable insight on the state of current and future products, new acquisitions, and product retirements. View any market position information with a grain of salt, however.
- *Product (or specification) special interest bodies* can be independent of the vendor or vendors and can provide honest—if somewhat biased—feedback on the technology. Typically, these bodies also provide discussion forums where salient views can be aired.
- *Industry periodicals* provide a more general appraisal of industry segments and can have useful information on the state of a particular nation.
- *Independent consultants* provide valuable services with respect to analyzing market segments and presenting crystal ball prognostications. Never underestimate the information provided by consultants because they usually have well-developed relationships in vendor organizations and are able to gain access to information not usually

released. Furthermore, they specialize in this area and have a considerable knowledgebase on past trends. Of course, a bit of cynicism is also recommended.

- *Reference organizations* can provide real-world experience and opinions regarding the use of a particular technology.
- A *wider view of organizational usage* can help plot a product (or specification) on the technology life cycle. Look at all of the organizations in a particular industry or geographic region and determine what is being implemented and what is being replaced. Obtaining industry research through an independent organization can provide these types of metrics (many consulting organizations conduct this type of research).
- *Textbooks* can provide some information with which to understand industry trends; however, their lack of immediacy tends to limit such information gathering. On the other hand, the fact that texts are being published on one technology area but not another can also provide valuable insight (at least in where the hype is).
- *Monitor the Web sites of consortia* (including the organization's industry consortia) producing specifications and standards. We have noticed that a lack of activity on the site (whether that be page views or periods between information updates) can indicate flagging enthusiasm. Furthermore, a standard that has only periodic version changes or no indication of working drafts can mean doom.

The researcher must absorb all of this information and put it into an organizational context. It has no direct relevance unless related to the organizational condition. This context includes the organization type, the industry, and the strategies employed. This last aspect is particularly important because there is a balance between the organization's strategic intent and the state of the IT industry. Remember that organizations employ technology as an enabler. Although it is likely that a change in strategy will drive an alteration in the IT environment, it is equally likely that a change in technology could drive a change in strategy.

Architectural Governance Model

At this point in the architectural process (i.e., the end of implementation), the IT environment should represent the (tenuous) balance between the organization's strategy and the state of technology. Continuous improvement relies on the reduction of drift and the application of course changes at defined intervals. Figure 13.4 represents a general governance model for management control. This model reiterates the TOGAF-specific cyclic ADM; architectural maintenance is heavily reliant on the "check" process, feeding back into the initiation and framework phase. The point to take from the governance model is that the key activity between checking and replanning is to correct the position. In the architectural context, this implies eliminating drift. The architectural governance control objective is to manage technology change and implemenation.

Using the generic model for management control, it is possible to overlay the concepts embodied within TOGAF's architectural maintenance phase. The generic "check" stage evolves to include a specific control component. The organization is not likely to let architectural drift occur through inactivity, waiting for change factors to effect erosion. The control component of the maintenance phase relates to IT governance and architectural conformance. Conformance will be discussed in the next section.

There is no specific correction phase in TOGAF (see Figure 13.5). Correction implies taking remedial action to affect small changes in direction. Large directional changes are made by initiating another TOGAF cycle. Obviously, the full cycle comes at a considerable cost and effort investment. However, in some cases it is necessary:

- Should the organization adopt a periodic realignment strategy, the TOGAF process may occur every 3–5 years.
- A significant change in the organization, such as a merger or acquisition, can necessitate a full TOGAF approach.

Minor corrections can be an optimum method for avoiding (or at least reducing) architectural drift. Minor corrections can take many forms. However, the aim is to provide for the two key requirements that reflect architectural alignment: the impact of (unanticipated) change and the planned evolution of the architecture (embodied within the SIB). The types of corrections depend on the final makeup of the architecture and the plans (and budgets) the organization has in place for ongoing architectural development, and they can include:

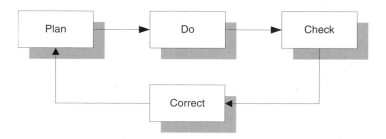

FIGURE 13.4.   General governance control model.[53]

53. IT Governance Institute, COBIT Management Guidelines, July 2000.

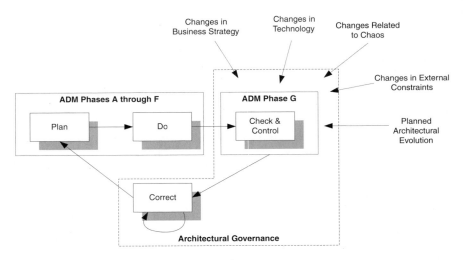

FIGURE 13.5.   TOGAF and management control.

- Continuous migration to new product versions.
- Planned replacement of products as the SIB timeline dictates.
- Focus on, and isolation of, service areas that require significant change or addition. Often major business change can be isolated to individual parts of the TRM. In essence, consider conducting a miniarchitectural project. Ensure that the amendments are worked into the reference model (and other artifacts).
- Plan for progressive migration of large-ticket items.
- Exert architectural control on every IT project—using tools such as the architectural contract—the aim being to eliminate some aspects of drift. This topic is considered in more detail in the next section.

To support continual improvement, the artifacts of the architectural process must be maintained and updated, such as:

- The SIB is modified to reflect changing product versions and new (or modified) medium- and long-term views. Remember that the SIB is on a constantly ticking timeline. The medium-term predictions become the short term, and the long term becomes the medium term. New long-term projections are made.
- The service functionality is updated as new versions add functions or functions are changed.
- The TRM is modified with the addition of new categories and subcategories. The addition of categories is an unusual event, reflecting

a major technology change. Subcategories, on the other hand, are added more frequently due to product changes.

- The service instance map, representing the interconnection of all realized services, will change as all other components change.

Architectural Compliance

In the previous section, we discussed approaches for the maintenance of the architecture in the face of major change factors. However, one of the most significant factors influencing architectural drift is business-as-usual initiatives. Simplistically, the activities of an IT group can be pigeonholed in the following manner:

- *Strategic activities*—many of the activities covered in this text
- *Operational activities*—the ongoing tasks of ensuring that the current IT environment is operating effectively
- *Project activities*—capital-funded initiatives to introduce new capability

Both operational and project activities have a continued effect on the architecture established by the architectural program. There are a large number of decisions made in the operational environment that can potentially alter the technical environment. In many organizations these decisions are typically ad hoc and tactical. They are made to fix operational problems or fight fires associated with functionality not currently available. They slowly but inevitably impact drift. Operational groups tend to have the budgets to implement what is necessary to maintain operational integrity. However, in some instances, the scope of the budget allows for significant changes to the environment. We have seen major client/server systems implemented within operational budgets and outside the normal project initiation processes. Ad hoc bespoke systems spring up to provide for functionality that is not fully available in existing systems, such as the replacement of one product with another based on the need to replace a component due to failure.

Even formally defined and capitalized projects can also affect the architectural position. Large organizations may have a number of projects running at any one time. Although architectural control may have existed during initiation, project pressures and problems can cause drift from the architectural position. Furthermore, in some cases lip service is paid to any architectural quality-assurance process throughout the project. Although the QA process is identified as part of the project, the budget required to alter aspects of the solution is not available. On the other hand projects that are destined to deliver package solutions may not be able to guarantee the architecture of the package application. Formal tender processes are underpinned by criteria in a wide variety of sometimes conflicting areas. The best architectural solution may not provide the best functional solution.

Management-inspired drift should not be underestimated. Management is generally charged with acting in a strategic manner. However, execution style is very dependent on the individual and his or her own philosophies. No organization can plan for every eventuality, so in some circumstances management is required to act tactically and immediately. Due care is applied to ensure that such an action does not impact the organization; however, in some circumstances this is just not possible and something must give. Sometimes, this is the architecture. The effect of this factor is heightened due to the availability of discretionary budget.

Management—in fact, everyone—can be swayed by salespeople. On the other hand, incumbent vendors can lose favor over a period of time.

The structure of the IT group and the entire organization can have an impact especially where that structure aligns with budget responsibility. A distributed IT group, containing individual IT centers responsible for their own budgets and fulfillment of their own customer's requirements, has a greater effect on architectural drift than a centralized IT group would. There is a trend toward apportioning the IT budget to individual business units. This can have an even greater effect. Different people cycle in and out of influential management positions that can affect, negate, and relitigate the decisions that have already been made.

In short, architectural drift is inevitable. It is part of the natural cycle of the organization and the fact that human beings are the major decision-makers. This may appear rather cynical, but this was not the intent. The drift aspect of architectures is recognized. The cyclic (corrective) nature of the ADM is proof of that. Governance is required to reduce drift but not necessarily eliminate it.

The organization will have embarked on the architectural process to fulfill a number of strategic objectives. Depending on the organization, it is likely that cost control was one of them. Other important factors may have been interoperability between systems, security, or more effective customer interfaces. All are valid and, with the architecture delivery, should have been realized. Assuming that the drift factors are inevitable, the effect is a move away from the ideal position—from the desired strategic direction. It is therefore in the best interests of the organization to limit drift wherever possible. This means controlling the factors mentioned in this section.

Architectural compliance is a method of achieving this. It is part of the overall architectural governance process, which in turn forms part of the overall IT governance process. Architectural compliance (and for that matter, governance) relates to the extension of the technical architecture (the output of the ADM) beyond simple environment development and into:

- The mandating of technical standards in the technology selection process
- The structure of commercial relationships
- The incorporation into all aspects of the IT control processes

The objective of architectural compliance is to minimize drift, enable better communication of the architecture and its value proposition, and emphasize the value of aspects such as centralized commercial negotiation.

It is important that the organization have a view of the meaning of architectural compliance and how and what type of IT activities it relates to.

Table 13.2 presents The Open Group definition of the terms conformance and compliance. It is not necessary to use these definitions or terms, but it should be recognized that Table 13.2 provides a full spectrum of classification of IT activities with respect to the architecture.

Table 13.2 adopts the phraseology of an implementation being *in accordance with the architecture*. This is reasonably abstract and needs some definition. There is no hard and fast rule here—much will depend on the artifacts delivered from the architectural process and maintained through the ongoing architectural maintenance phase. The following list provides a number of likely definitions of the term that can be mixed and matched based on the delivered artifacts:

- Supports the stated business and information system strategies and future directions
- Adheres to the stated standards presented in the SIB, including the SIB timeline
- Adheres to the stated architectural principles
- Meets the criteria outlined in the key question list
- Adheres to the requirements stated in the architectural contract
- Uses the functionality delivered by the platform services (as described in the service functionality table) and does not duplicate or circumvent service functionality
- Adheres to relevant technical policy, and policies described within the service policy table
- Provides functionality related to the business system architecture
- Supports the provision of organizational information as defined in the information architecture

Table 13.2. Levels of architectural conformance.

(Architectural Specification) (Implement-ation)	**Irrelevant:** The implementation has no features in common with the architectural specifications. Therefore, the question of conformance does not arise.
(two overlapping circles, left one shaded)	**Consistent:** The implementation has some features in common with the architectural specification, and those features are implemented in accordance with the architecture. Some features of the implementation, however, do not conform with the architecture. Also, the implementation has some features not covered by the architecture.
(shaded circle with smaller white circle inside right portion)	**Compliant:** All features of the implementation are in accordance with the architecture. Some parts of the architecture, however, are not implemented because they do not form part of the implementation.
(shaded circle with larger circle overlapping)	**Conformant:** All features of the architecture are implemented and are in accordance with the architecture. Some features of the implementation are not covered by the architecture.
(single shaded circle)	**Fully Conformant:** There is a one-to-one mapping between the features implemented and the architecture. All features are implemented in accordance with the architecture, and there are no features implemented that are not covered by the architecture.
(two overlapping circles with black square in overlap)	**Nonconformant:** Nonconformant may be used to describe any of the preceding cases (except fully conformant). It occurs when the implemented features do not exist (or are contrary to) the architecture.

Once defined, the compliance criteria can be used to measure and influence all IT initiatives. Each initiative should be assigned a level of architectural compliance. It will depend on the architectural governance structure as to how an initiative is managed with respect to compliance. However, assigning a compliance factor allows the architect to understand the level of drift occurring.

Typically, influence will be exerted on the project activities of the organization because these have the greatest focus and reflect "real" capital investment. The most effective method of influencing the architecture of a solution (and the conformance of the solution to the architecture) is at the early stages of initiation and design. Generally, this will require that architecture compliance influence the cost–benefit analysis, prioritization activities, requirements specifications, tender documents (if there are any), and product selection. The compliance to the architecture is a highly weighted factor in all aspects of selection.

Once past initiation phase, architectural compliance is handed to the project's solution (or application) architect, who is responsible for the detailed solution design in the form of the architectural contract. This person in this role should also be responsible for ensuring ongoing compliance with the technical architecture. To support this, frequent quality-assurance activities are factored into the project's plan to ensure that tactical decisions made during the project are assessed against the architecture. It is important to include sufficient budget (in both time and resources) to enable both the assessment and any rework required. As the project draws closer to implementation, the architectural (and QA) influence becomes less effective. Generally, the cost of change at this point can be excessive and is therefore not encouraged. Furthermore, the effect of architecture compliance during detailed implementation phases is generally less pronounced. In summary, the project should ensure that:

- Architectural compliance is known at an early stage and is tracked throughout the project.
- Architecturally significant components of the project are dealt with earlier rather than later.
- Architectural QA has been factored into the plan and is carried out.
- Communication is maintained between the project and the custodians of the architecture.

13.4 Example

Introduction

During the previous phase of CFL's architectural development, we described the various work packages required to complete the architectural program. They were assessed in terms of costs and benefits. Finally, the individual projects were prioritized and scheduled. In this phase, we take a brief look at aspects of implementation and migration.

Architectural Contract

The architectural contract is a significant artifact for describing the scope of each architectural project. Because the CFL architectural program is not being implemented as a single project, the contract provides the necessary context for the individual project teams. Table 13.3 shows a summarized contract for the EAI integration project.

Maintenance

The change management project incorporates the work packages responsible for establishing the architectural maintenance and governance process. A summary of the direction given to this project (in the architectural contract) is as follows:

- A formal architectural control group will be established.
- An architectural conformance process will be added to the standard project initiation process.
- The reference model and the SIB will be published corporation-wide.
- Architectural control will be assigned a capital and operating budget to manage architectural drift.
- The architectural control body to be assigned responsibility (and budget) for new product versions, new products, and the technical assessment of vendors.
- A full architectural project will be budgeted for at regular intervals, the interval to be aligned with CFL's business strategy planning cycle.
- CFL will enlist an independent organization to benchmark the IT environment at regular intervals. This benchmarking will be used to determine success in meeting architectural objectives.

13.5   Summary

In this chapter, we reviewed the final two stages of the architectural development method: implementation and maintenance. These two phases are responsible for carrying out the architectural program and then ensuring that erosion is kept to a minimum, respectively. In the last

Table 13.3. Example architectural contract.

Category	Contents
Background	The *EAI project* is a key architectural initiative identified as part of the architectural program owned by the CIO and the architectural steering group. It has the following objectives: • To implement the EAI service as defined in the target architecture • To improve intersystem interface quality, reducing error rates • To eliminate customer and supplier complaints regarding interface quality • To reduce the cost of managing current interfaces and the cost of delivering new interfaces • Meet architectural principles
The nature of the agreement	This contract provides the overarching business and technical requirements for the project. The work of the project team will be measured on its implementation and its ability to support the objectives. Final milestone payments for any external vendors involved will be based on this aspect.
Scope	The project's scope is based on the detailed requirements document and the functional service description. A summary of the scope is as follows: • Implementation of the EAI super service as per the functional description • Selection (through tender) of a preferred EAI product that supports the service requirements • Selection (through tender) of a referred message queuing product • Replacement of the current (batch) interfaces with EAI interfaces • Update the architectural artifacts (TRM, SIB, service functions) The scope does not include: • Unification of customer information across systems • Implementation of platform (OS, hardware, etc.)

Table 13.3. Example architectural contract (*continued*).

Category	Contents
Strategic requirements	The key strategic drivers are as follows: • Streamline internal business processes for "best cost"—business strategy. • Interface quality; ensure the quality (both information and reliability) of interfaces between systems—information system strategy.
Criteria measures of effectiveness of projects	Significant criteria for the project include: • Selected product to meet architectural principles and service functionality (including non-functional requirements) • Selected product to meet product selection criteria • Delivery to the SIB (conformance to be assessed) • Interface error reduction of 90% • Customer complaint reduction of 95%
Roles and responsibilities	Key governance responsibility lies with the current architectural steering group, the sponsors of the architectural program. Although this group will be subsumed into the ongoing CFL architectural governance structure, they maintain interim responsibility for the program until this occurs. Key responsibilities of this group include: • Ownership of architectural conformance • Consulting and advice on the EAI service • The EAI project's steering group • Management of the budget for the entire architectural program (including this project)
Roadmap	This project is dependent on: • Security project (security strategy only) • Systems management project (systems management architecture only) • B2B commerce project (message formats only) • Policy project (the software engineering strategy) Other projects that depend on this project: • None

Table 13.3. Example architectural contract (*continued*).

Category	Contents
Conformance requirements	Specific conformance requirements that relate to this project include (note that other architectural projects will be providing further elaboration of specific service requirements): • Interchange: XML, XML-schema, DTD, DOM, IBM's parser • Network: JMS, TCP/IP • Data management: DB/2 (relational) • Software engineering: Java-based • Operating systems: HP-UX, MS NT • Transaction management: XA • Systems management: Tivoli • Security: Systems must be authenticated with the security service before interacting with the EAI service—refer to security project. • Directory: LDAP (Microsoft implementation) • Service qualities: see requirements in EAI service functionality
Target architecture mapping	See the target architecture service instance maps and the EAI service functionality table.
QA milestones	QA responsibility rests with the architectural steering group. The following QA points are required: • Tender review • Product selection • Implementation plan • Solutions architecture • Implementation iterations • Measurement criteria review
References	The following artifacts are important foundation components for this project: • The technical architecture, version 1.0 (including the TRM) • .The SIB • The EAI service functionality table • The EAI cost–benefit analysis Project team members are encouraged to subscribe to eaiQuadrant (www.eaiquadrant.com).

section, on maintenance, we touched on the governance aspects of architectural maintenance. In the last chapter of this book, we look at the people and organizational aspects of the technical architecture, why architectural programs fail, what can be done about this, and how to build an architectural capability in the organization.

CHAPTER 14

A Case for Change

14.1   Introduction

The final chapter of this book is devoted to understanding how architectural initiatives can fail and approaches to mitigate such risks. It is a fact of life in many organizations that enterprise technical architecture initiatives are seen to be ineffective. Criticisms often leveled at architectural projects include their lack of success in meeting stated strategic requirements, that they are difficult to control and maintain, that they do not represent the "real world" of IT, and that they are expensive and have no relevance in the Internet-enabled world. Many of these criticisms are well-founded in experience. The problem is that the architecture is not a project and is not an operational activity. These IT processes are well-understood by both the organization and those who work in the IT group. Architecture, on the other hand, as a discipline must be pervasive throughout the organization. It is not an individual project, a single well-understood process, a policy or guideline, a culture aspect, or a strategic intent; it is all of these and more. It exhibits the same characteristics as quality in an IT sense—a noble objective, but difficult to define, implement, and measure.

Architecture initiatives fail in a number of ways. Not all are catastrophic failures; success of the architecture may be limited but not totally ineffectual. For an organization that is experienced in the architecture process this is the most typical type of failure. Usually, it is influenced by unanticipated events, generally typified by chaos within or external to the organization. The issue of limited success can be dealt with using standard maintenance approaches. Drift can be corrected by reactivating the architectural process or applying control mechanisms already in place.

Architectural stagnation is the most common outcome of an organization's first initiative. Stagnation is a situation that occurs when the cyclic process defined in the architectural development method (ADM) stalls or stops, leaving the architecture either unfinished or unmaintained. Most organizations embark on the architecture program with gusto (although we have had experiences with organizations that are carrying out a "limited" program because a consultant's report said they should) and have high ideals for its success. Many times, this enthusiasm may not be rewarded with the best possible outcome. But architectural programs are complicated and require new skills and greater control over the IT environment. Hence enthusiasm can turn to stagnation. There are varying factors that influence stagnation, some of the main ones being:

- The organization's architects do not have sufficient business, strategic, and technical experience, and therefore the end product may suffer.
- The organization views architectural development as a fixed-term program of work, not a continuous IT discipline.
- People not directly involved in the architecture program can sabotage the program by decrying its lack of practicality, calling it a product of a team from "headquarters" (or even worse, a team of consultants) who have no real understanding of the real way the organization operates.
- The architecture is only stable immediately after release. Significant drift occurs almost immediately due to chaos in other areas.
- There is no embedded process that aids in the continual development of the architecture.
- Corporate buy-in is limited. There is no significant power, or resources, behind the maintenance of the architecture.

Some of the major factors affecting the failure of the architecture are dealt with in sections 14.2–14.4.

14.2   The Ivory Tower Principle

A recurring theme seen in organizations attempting architectural development is that of the *ivory tower principle*. There appears to be a definite philosophical barrier between those who develop the architecture and those whose activities are dictated by it. From the IT group's "shop floor," the architectural team is viewed as a collective of intellectuals producing outputs that has little or no relevance in the real world. Two important points exacerbate this fact:

- The artifacts produced from the process—reference models, service instance diagrams, and standards bases—are not universally accessible to all people of the group; they exude a sense of exclusivity.
- The maintenance process usually requires architectural policies to be adhered to by all those in the group, giving them limited (less than usual) freedom to act.

In short, the architecture is viewed as having been handed down from those who sit high up in the ivory tower.

This is a basic problem of ownership, communications, and change management. As was identified in Chapter 12 when discussing opportunities and solutions, the management of change imposed by the architectural approach is a key undertaking to ensure success. People generally do not like being told what to do; they are cynical and suspicious of grandiose "academic" pronouncements. This does not infer that there is open hostility toward the architecture or intentional attempts to subvert it. However, we have witnessed circumstances where the intent of the architecture is not carried through to the extent necessary. In large, distributed organizations, this can occur simply through ignoring its requirements. In essence, if there is no perceived value in maintaining the architecture, then maintenance is less likely to occur. The task then is to reenforce the value of the architecture and ensure that there is cross-organizational buy-in.

Strategies to employ that limit the effect of the ivory tower barrier include:

- Ensure that there is significant involvement from all parts of the IT group in the development of the architecture. This includes employing members as subject matter experts (even owners) in particular components of the architecture. For instance, contract network support personnel to provide the expert advice on the development of the network service. This approach is most effective during the development of the target architecture and supports effective buy-in from each part of the IT group.
- Ensure that all aspects of the architectural program are communicated to the IT group as a whole. Hold regular briefing sessions and solicit comments and feedback. Ensure that the intent of the architecture is known; validate its business basis with the group. Ensure that the architectural process (the ADM) is understood, at least at a high level. Most importantly, ensure that the documentation of the architecture is accessible. This may require it to be presented in different formats depending on the audience. We have found that using a variety of architectural views can aid this process (see Chapter 8).

- The architect must be sensitive to pragmatism. We have witnessed tensions between the architect and other IT groups created by the architect taking the high ground—"this is what the architect says, this is what you will do, end of story." Such a position is seldom valid and can only harm the cause of the architecture. The architect must remember that the governance structure may give him or her control over the activity of other IT activities. This control should be used wisely, and consideration should be given to the fact that there is always more than one view. Be especially sensitive to project pressures when making architectural prognostications.
- Put in place governance processes that aid, rather than hinder, operational and project activitiees. Remember to align governance styles with organizational culture.

14.3   *Architectural Capability*

As has been seen throughout this text, the ADM is focused on the production of artifacts such as reference models, standards information bases, service functionality documents, and, of course, projects that implement the architecture. A major failing is to consider that the sum total of the architectural approach is these artifacts. Should the emphasis be put solely into these components, the likelihood of the architecture becoming shelfware is high. The key ingredient is people.

The architecture will include policy and guidelines; the TRM and SIB state current and future technology positions. However, regardless of how the organization enforces architectural control, these static paper-based artifacts of the architecture cannot provide their own advocacy. A successful architecture approach is all about the people who developed it, who own it, who maintain it, and who are affected by it. We have experienced successful architectures that are not fully described in written form but rather exist as the organizational knowledge of a few key (and influential) people. There is an advantage to this approach. The architecture is best communicated from person to person (not from paper to person). In this way, the communication style can be changed to reflect the audience. Strong personalities and excellent inter-personnel styles can continue to steer the organization down the correct path, in a way that a policy can not. Furthermore, there will always be the need to interpret the paper-based architecture in a varying degree of circumstances. This can be effectively done by people who both understand the architecture and understand the vision.

An architecture will not be successful without the right people with the right skills. Also remember that there is no such thing as the perfect architecture; there will always be those who do not agree with components or detract from its intent. The advocates of the architecture are key to ensuring that detractors are heard and their views factored in. Also, it is not uncommon for critics to base their opinions on less than the full picture. These views may indeed be valid in the context of their specific area, but tradeoffs are always made when developing an enterprise-wide architecture, and thus these tradeoffs must be communicated. The artifacts alone are not effective at providing this.

Some organizations outsource their architectural capability. In this case, the responsibility for the knowledge and decision-making associated with the architecture is transferred to an external (consultancy) organization, usually because the right skills cannot be found internally. This can be a flawed approach. Although specialist technical, process, or operational skills can be outsourced, strategic capability (including architecture) should not. The ownership of the architecture and its ongoing maintenance should exist within the organization. It is not expected that an external consultant knows more about running the organization's business. The same is true with respect to the architecture. Therefore ensure that key architectural capability is built from internal resources. Consider augmenting from external sources if necessary.

The positions of the architectural advocates within the organization are referenced in the next section, on governance. The other aspect is the skills of these people. The key skills include:

- *Solid experience* in the business domain.
- *Eclectic range of technical skills* and understanding and a desire to constantly keep up-to-date with all technology areas important to the organization. The type of person that suits the role of technical architect is one with wide-ranging but shallow knowledge rather than deep and narrow.
- *Excellent communication skills.* This is a cliché, but the ideal person should be able to communicate well both verbally and in writing and they should be able to communicate effectively with highly technical people and senior executives.
- *Enthusiasm.* There should be a single-minded enthusiasm for the architecture and its success. Enthusiasm begets enthusiasm.
- *Big picture people.* An important trait is the ability to accumulate and process a wide variety of inputs to produce and maintain the enterprise-wide architecture. Many people find it difficult to avoid descending into detail—and in some cases this is necessary (especially with detailed service definition)—but the architectural discipline requires the 30,000 foot view that takes in all influential factors.

Of course, it is usually not possible to obtain all necessary traits in a single individual—it would be a difficult position to recruit for. A single individual in such a role would be a risk as well. Should they move on, the advocacy role stops and the architecture is in danger. It is therefore important that the advocacy role be sustainable through organizational change.

Figure 14.1 portrays the makeup of a conceptual "architectural group" whose role is architectural advocacy. This may, of course, represent the same structure as the team that ran the architectural program. Generally, the team is required to:

- Maintain and advocate the information architecture
- Maintain and advocate the business systems architecture
- Maintain and advocate the technical architecture

This does not imply resource requirements but merely that these skills will be required to support the successful advocacy and maintenance of the architecture. The role of technical advisor is included. This reflects the fact that no matter how eclectic the team may be, there is no possibility that all aspects of technology can be covered by a single skill type. The advisor provides specific (more detailed) skills with respect to numerous technologies, and the role may be fulfilled by a number of different people, depending on the immediate requirement. Such skills can come from external consultant or analyst organizations (such as Gartner Group, Standish Group, and others). Another strategy is to use the specific skills within the organization (the subject matter experts referred to in the ivory tower section) to provide advice. This has a number of benefits:

- A number of people from various operational areas can provide their input into the architecture and its maintenance, thereby facilitating wider ownership.
- Internal representatives can also act as direct advocates for the architecture in their own units.

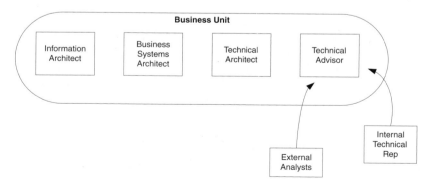

FIGURE 14.1.   Advocacy roles.

14.4 *Governance*

Effective communication and highly skilled people will not be successful in maintaining the architecture alone. Success is heavily reliant on the absorption of architectural processes into the processes of both the IT group and the organization as a whole. The term governance can be defined as:

> A structure of relationships and processes to direct and control the enterprise in order to achieve the enterprise's goals by adding value while balancing risk versus return over IT and its processes.[54]

IT governance relates to all processes and control activities that make up the IT discipline. Governance formalizes these processes, relating them to business processes and objectives. Control activities consist of policies, procedures, organizational structures, practices, and so on. Based on the COBIT framework, the major areas of IT control activities are:

- Monitoring
- Planning and organization
- Acquisition and implementation
- Delivery and support

Development of the technical architecture is a planning and organization control objective. However, the maintenance of the architecture exists in every area. Here there is a similarity between technical architecture and architecture in the physical world in that politics has an important role to play in the acceptance of both forms of architecture. In the real world, it is the dual-focused politics of the environment and commerce, whereas in the world of the technical architecture a consideration of corporate politics is critical.

A technical architecture imposed without appropriate formalized political backing is bound to fail. Therefore, architectural governance consists of incorporating and formalizing architectural control aspects into the numerous IT processes. Figure 14.2 summarizes the major IT activities, as per COBIT, and superimposes areas of architectural control (governance) on the model.

Architectural control processes should be applied to all areas of IT activities, enabling control of drift. Significant architectural governance control areas include:

---

54. COBIT Framework, 3rd edition, IT Governance Institute, July 2000.

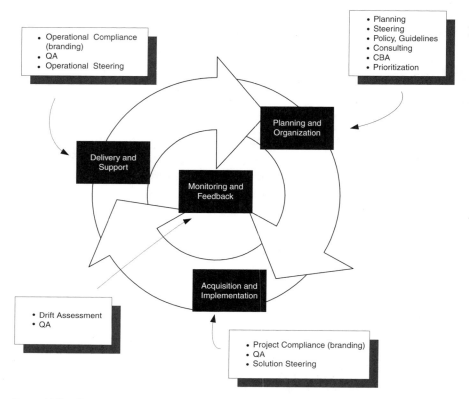

FIGURE 14.2.   Governance structure.

- The actual activities associated with the "architecture team" should be enshrined in process so that roles and responsibilities are well-understood and embedded within the activities of the IT group.
- Architectural compliance is a key criteria for both cost–benefit analysis and the overall prioritization (initiation) process. Control at initiation is critical for the architecture because this is the most effective place to influence solution decisions. Note that using a formal "branding" mechanism (as adopted by some standards organizations) to stamp initiatives as architecturally compliant can provide an interesting communications tool.
- Project-based activities should include significant architectural quality-assurance processes and provide the ability for the architecture to steer the solution. The same approach is used to steer operational activities.
- Monitoring and feedback mechanisms have already been discussed in Chapter 14 and ensure that the architecture does not stagnate and

continues on its maintenance path. Additionally, the measures established for the architecture (for example, cost-effectiveness, cycle time reduction, customer satisfaction, improved security, and so on) must also be tracked.

The implementation of such control objectives requires the necessary resources—both people and financial. The budget of the IT group must ensure that both are provided adequately to support architectural governance.

A vital aspect of architectural governance not shown in Figure 14.2 is that of an architectural governance body. In many organizations, the executive sponsor of the initial architecture effort is the CIO (or other senior executive). However, to gain broad corporate support, a sponsoring body may have more influence. Consider placing the responsibility for the review, maintenance, and steering of the strategic architecture and all of its subarchitectures with an executive-level group. In essence, such a steering group oversees all architectural control activities and operates in the best interest of the architecture. The architecture steering group is typically made responsible, and accountable, for achieving some or all of the following goals:

- Consistency between sub-architectures
- Identifying reusable components
- Flexibility of enterprise architecture
- Meeting changing business needs
- Leveraging new technologies
- Enforcement of architecture compliance
- Improving the maturity level of architecture discipline within the organization

The steering group is the sponsor of the architecture within the enterprise, but the group itself needs an executive sponsor from the highest level of the corporation. This commitment must span the planning process and continue into the maintenance phase of the architecture project. In many companies that fail in an architecture planning effort, there is a notable lack of executive participation and encouragement of the project.

A frequently overlooked source of steering group members is the organization's Board of Directors. These individuals invariably have diverse knowledge about the business and its market. Because they have a significant impact on the business vision and objectives, they may be successful in validating the alignment of IT strategies to business objectives.

After architecture implementation begins and some initial information on the success or failure of the selected technologies is available, the group should conduct reviews at regular intervals to monitor the architecture.

The steering group also works with various groups within the organization to resolve issues, expand the scope of the architecture, review projects, and look for triggers that indicate a necessary change in the architecture, including:

- Project teams
- Advanced development group
- Data administration group
- Strategic planning council

In the ongoing architecture process following the initial architecture effort, the steering group must be rechartered. The executive sponsor will normally review the work of the steering group and evaluate its effectiveness; if necessary, the architecture governance process is updated or changed.

14.5   Example

CFL has completed many of the projects in its architectural program and is beginning to see some of the benefits. The last component they wish to put in place is an architectural governance process. You may remember that the establishment of the governance process was defined as a project within the architectural program.

In this last visit to the CFL example, we are going to concentrate on the establishment of an architectural steering group and the embedding of architectural disciplines within the planning structure of the IT group.

CFL has decided on the establishment of a body to manage and steer the ongoing maintenance of the architecture. To be known as the architecture control service (ACS), it will contain representatives from the following:

- Senior management team
- IT management team
- Regional IT management
- Vendors
- CFL's selected IT consulting organization

The ACS is measured by the success, or otherwise, of the architecture. This will be a centrally funded body that is responsible for ensuring:

- The architectural vision is maintained
- That all IT activities conform to the architecture (a CFL architectural brand has been established as a marketing initiative)
- Funding is available to continue all aspects of the architecture program
- That the architecture is widely communicated and understood by all departments within CFL
- Architectural drift is kept to a minimum
- That quality-assurance activities are included in all projects and that resources are available to carry out QA
- Providing architectural expertise into projects where necessary

The ACS has decided to build a single operational architectural team (known as the business development group), that will carry out day-to-day architectural activities. This team consists of an information and technical architect and is led by a seconded business subject area expert. Technical resources are also seconded (on a part-time basis) from various central and regional IT centers on a rotational basis. The ACS has stipulated that it have control over the IT component of the IT project initiation process. The structure is shown in Figure 14.3.

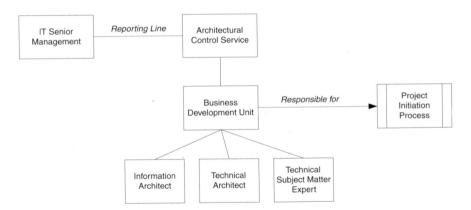

FIGURE 14.3. CFL's architectural control service structure.

14.6 Summary

In the last 14 chapters, we have journeyed through the world of enterprise technical architecture development. We believe that the term *enterprise technical architecture* is underutilized, so most organizations will not have a definitive definition of what this means. Some will assert that protracted architectural approaches to technology in the enterprise have seen their day and that monolithic architectural prognostications make excellent bookends but have no relevance in today's technology environment dominated by the rapid and dynamic Internet world.

This view is only valid when technical architectures are not produced and maintained as they should be. It is not a valid view for the overarching concept of technical architecture. In fact, we assert that the necessity for robust planning of an organization's technical environment is more critical, not less, in the face of Internet time.

Organizations are not expected to take an ad hoc approach to their businesses. Strategic planning is recognized as a key differentiator for success within most sectors. Know what you do, know where you are going, and know how you are going to get there. Yet, why is technology so often managed so tactically?

We stress that it is critical to execute IT to a defined plan that is itself based on the organization's business plan. Taking an architectural approach to technology allows an organization to arrest chaos, control costs, and increase effectiveness of its IT environment. The advent of business-to-business initiatives needs a robust and stable environment—one that can be initiated and maintained through architectural disciplines.

Throughout this book, we have progressed through the life cycle of The Open Group's architectural framework (TOGAF), a method for the development of an organizational technical architecture. We recommend this method because we know that it works. TOGAF tackles the technical, organizational, political, and process issues associated with the development of the architecture. There are other approaches, of course, and we encourage their investigation and comparison with TOGAF. From our perspective, the method is only important as a tool. The objective is the enshrinement of the architectural discipline within all activities of the organization.

Bibliography

2000 Annual Report. Society of Automotive Engineers. December, 2000. <www.sae.org>.

Andrews, K.R. *The Concept of Corporate Strategy*. Irwin, Homewood, IL, 1971.

Ansoff, H.I. *Corporate Strategy*. McGraw-Hill, New York, 1965.

Architecture for Public Key Infrastructure. Document Number G801, ISBN: 1–85912–221–3, The Open Group. March 1999.

Bennis, Warren G., Benne, Kenneth D., and Chin, Robert (Eds). *The Planning of Change (2nd Edition)*. Holt, Rinehart and Winston, New York, 1969.

Beveridge, Tony and Perks, Col. "Messaging is the Medium." *Intelligent Enterprise*, September 29, 2000.

Beveridge, Tony and Perks, Col. "Blueprint for a Flexible Enterprise." *Intelligent Enterprise*. March 1, 2000.

BizTalk Framework v2.0. Biztalk.org. 18 April 2001. <www.biztalk.org/home/framework.asp>.

Boehm, Barry W., Horowitz, Ellis, Madachy, Ray, Reifer, Donald, Clark, Bradford K., Steece, Bert, Brown, A. Winsor, Chulani, Sunita, and Abts, Chris. *Software Cost Estimation with COCOMO*. Prentice-Hall. Englewood, NJ, 2000.

Boeyen, S., Howes, T., and Richard., P. *Internet X.509 Public Key Infrastructure LDAPv2 Schema (RFC 2587)*. IETF. June 1999.

Booch, Rumbaugh, and Jacobson. *The UML Modeling Language User Guide*, Addison-Wesley, Reading, MA, 1999.

Brown, Ray, Baron, Wade, and Chadwick III, William D. *Designing Solutions with COM+ Technologies*. Microsoft Press. Redwood, WA, 2000.

Bray, Tim, Paoli, Jean, Sperberg-McQueen, C. M., and Maler, Eve. *Extensible Markup Language (XML) 1.0 (Second Edition)*. World Wide Web Consortium. October 2000.

Buchholz, Werner Ed. "Comments, Query, and Debate." *IEEE Annals of the History of Computing*. April–May 2000.

C4ISR Architecture [C4ISR], Version 2.0. Federation of American Scientists (FAS). December 1997. <www.fas.org/irp/program/core/c4isr.htm>.

Chadwick, D.W. *Understanding X.500—The Directory*. Information Systems Institute, 1996. <www.isi.salford.ac.uk/staff/dwc/Version.Web/Contents.htm>.

Chandler, A.D. *Strategy and Structure*. MIT Press, Cambridge, MA, 1962.

CORBA/IIOP Specification V 2.4.1. Object Management Group. February 2001. <www.omg.org>.

Cost Benefit Analysis Guide for NIH IT Projects. National Institutes of Health, October 1998. < irm.cit.nih.gov/itmra/cbaguide.html>.

Davenport, Thomas, Eccles, Robert, and Prusak, Laurence. "Information Politics". *Sloan Management Review* (Fall 1992).

Dijkstra, E.W. "The Structure of 'THE' Multiprogramming System." *Communications of the ACM*. Volume 11, number 5, Pages 345–346, 1968.

Distributed TP: The XA+ Specification, Version 2. Document Number S423. ISBN 1–85912–046–6. The Open Group. July 1994.

Dublin Core Metadata Element Set, Version 1.1: Reference Description. Dublin Core Metadata Initiative. August 1999. <dublincore.org/documents>.

Earl, M.J. *Information Management*. Oxford University Press, Oxford, 1996.

ebXML Technical Architecture Specification v1.04. ebXML. February 2001. <www.ebxml.org>.

eCo Architecture for Electronic Commerce Interoperability. Commerce Net. June 1999. <eco.commerce.net>.

Federal Agency Use of Public Key Technology for Digital Signatures and Authentication, NIST Special Publication 800–25, National Institute of Standards and Technology, Gaithersburg, MD, October 2000.

Federal Enterprise Architecture Framework. US General Services Administration (GSA). September 1999. <www.itpolicy.gsa.gov>.

Federated Naming: The XFN Specification. Document Number C403. ISBN 1–85912–052–0. The Open Group. July 1995

Finkelstein, C. *Strategic Systems Development*. Addison-Wesley, Reading, MA, 1992.

Gartner Group. *Advanced Technology Survey: Taking Stock of Technology Management*. Strategic Analysis Report, 7 March, 1996

HL7 Reference Information Model V 1.7c. Health Level 7. March 2001. <www.hl7.org>.

IEEE Architecture Working Group. *Design Specification for IEEE Std 1471 Recommended Practice for Architectural Description*. IEEE, New York, August 1997.

Internet Security Policy: A Technical Guide. NIST Special Publication 800-XX, National Institute of Standards and Technology, Gaithersburg, MD, October 1999.

Information Engineering: An Overview. Centre de Recherche en Informatique (CRI). March 1998. <panoramix.univ-paris1.fr/CRINFO/dmrg/MEE98/misop033>.

IT Governance Institute. *COBIT Framework, 3rd edition*. IT Governance Institute. Rolling Meadows, IL, July 2000.

IT Governance Institute. *COBIT Management Guidelines*, IT Governance Institute. Rolling Meadows, IL, July 2000.

Java 2 Enterprise Edition Specification, v1.2.1. Sun Microsystems. May 2001. <java.sun.com/j2ee>.

Kerberos: The Network Authentication Protocol (RFC1510). Massachusetts Institute of Technology (MIT). September 1993. <web.mit.edu>.

Kazman, Rick, Klein, Mark, and Clements, Paul. *ATAM: A Method for Architecture Evaluation*. Carnegie Mellon Software Engineering Institute. Technical Report CMU/SEI-2000-TR-004. <www.sei.cmu.edu>

McGee, J. and Prusak, L. *Managing Information Strategically*. John Wiley & Sons, New York 1993.

Mills, D. *Simple Network Time Protocol (SNTP) Version 4 for IPv4, IPv6 and OSI (RFC 2030)*. IETF. October 1996.

Single UNIX Specification V 3.0. The Open Group. June 2001.

Myers, J. *SMTP Service Extension for Authentication (RFC 2554)*. IETF. March 1999.

OBI Technical Specifications V 2.1. The Open Buying on the Internet Consortium (OBI). 1999. <www.openbuy.org>.

Perry, P., and Wolfe, A. *SigSoft Software Engineering Notes*. Foundation for the Study of Software Architecture, ACM, Volume 14, Number 4, October 1992.

Porter, M.E. *Competitive Strategy*. Free Press, New York, 1980.

Ramsdell, B. Ed. *S/MIME Version 3 Certificate Handling (RFC 2632)*. IETF. June 1999.

Rational Unified Process 2000. Rational Software Corporation. February 2000 <www.rational.com>.

RosettaNet Implementation Framework V 2.0. RosettaNet. July 2001. <www.rosettanet.org>.

POSC Data Access Specifications V2.0. Petrotechnical Open Software Corporation. December 1997. <www.posc.org>.

Technical Architecture Framework For Information Management (TAFIM) Volumes 1–8, Version 2.0. U.S. Department of Defense, DISA Center for Architecture, 1994. <www.sei.cmu.edu>.

Telecommunications Industry Association. *1999 Standards and Technology Annual Report. 1999.*<www.tiaonline.org>.

Skills and Knowledge of Cost Engineering, 4th Edition. Larew, Richard E. Editor. AACE International, 1999

TOGAF V6.0. The Open Group. December 2000. <www.opengroup.org/architecture>

Specification for the Representation of CIM in XML V 2.0. Distributed Management Taskforce (DMTF). July 2000. <www.dmtf.org>.

The Standish Group. *Chaos Chronicles.* 1994–1999. <www.pm2go.com>.

UDDI Version 2.0 Data Structure Reference: UDDI Open Draft Specification. Uddi.org. June 2001.

Underlying Technical Models for Information Technology Security DRAFT Version 0.2. NIST Special Publication 800-xx. National Institute of Standards and Technology, Gaithersburg, MD, May 15, 2001.

Wahl, M., Howes, T., and Kille, S. *Lightweight Directory Access Protocol (v3) (RFC 2251).* IETF. December 1997.

Workflow Management Coalition. *Workflow Reference Model.* Document Number TC00-I003, Workflow Management Coalition, 1995.

Zachman, J. A. and Sowa, J.F. *Extending and Formalizing the Framework for Information Systems Architecture.* IBM Systems Journal, vol. 31, no. 3, 1992. IBM Publication G321–5488.

Glossary

Architecture
A pragmatic, coherent structuring of a collection of components that through these factors supports the vision of the full "user" in an elegant way.

Architecture, Application
Booch, Rumbaugh, and Jacobson's definition is relevant. They describe an architecture as the set of significant decisions about the organization of a software system, the selection of the structural elements and their interfaces by which the system is composed, together with their behavior as specified in the collaborations among those elements, the composition of these structural and behavioral elements into progressively larger subsystems, and the architectural style that guides this organization.

Architecture, Business Systems
A particular instance of an architecture that collectively relates to the structure and content of all business systems in the organization. The term *business systems architecture* was derived by James Martin from early work in the field of information system engineering. It has been synthesized into a discipline that structures the relationships between information required by the organization and the business systems that manage that information. It provides a policy-based framework to support strategic information system positioning and the overall management of the organization's business system portfolio.

Architecture, Enterprise
The enterprise architecture consists of the family of IT architecture disciplines that supports the successful use of information technology in the achievement of business strategy. In this book, we include information, business, and technical architecture in the enterprise architecture family.

Architecture, Information
A particular instance of an architecture that structures the information required and in use by the organization. Although it is typical that the

information architecture acts on information within IT systems, other information types are also catered to. The information architecture defines both the logical and physical structure of information required for the organization to succeed and includes the interdependences and other relations among information items. A typical information architecture artifact is a corporate data model. The information architecture provides important input into the architecture of the organization's business systems.

Architecture, Technical

Technical architecture is the primary subject of this book. A technical architecture provides and maintains a structured and coherent IT environment for the implementation of information systems that support the information needs of the organization. Unlike application architecture, which deals with the structure of individual applications, the technical architecture describes the makeup of the entire technical environment. It defines the technology standards, policies, and technology vision, and actively maintains that vision. It provides the framework into which individual business systems are delivered. The development of the technical architecture is a factor of strategic and operational principles, financial, organizational, and external constraints, and architectural tradeoffs.

Architectural Continuum

The architectural continuum is a term specific to TOGAF. It describes the logical portion of the enterprise continuum. The architectural continuum provides a generic method of understanding the structure of an organization's technical architecture. It presents a linear (in presentation, although not in usage) roadmap from the very generic to the organizationally specific. The generic end of the continuum denotes reuseable architectural assets for building an individual organization's IT environment. The continuum's specific end evolves the foundation architecture with organization-specific architectural input.

Architectural Constraints

Constraints are essentially propositions that bound the architecture. No architecture is impervious to its surrounding environment—an environment that will impose its own limitations on that which is implemented within it. Understanding the constraints allows the architecture to reflect the practical (and imperfect) world within which it exists. Additionally, the architect is then able to derive and articulate constraint tradeoff decisions.

Architectural Drift

The term is used to describe the movement away from a chosen architectural direction. There are many aspects that enable drift, most have an undesirable effect on the success of the IT environment, and some are unavoidable. Most organizations "plan" for drift and effect realignment through periodic strategic projects. Effective architectural governance and strong management commitment, in essence continual architectural maintenance, aid in the minimization of drift.

Architectural Development Method

The ADM is a specific process defined by TOGAF for the development and maintenance of an organization's technical architecture. The ADM consists of seven major phases: initiation and framework, baseline description, target architecture, opportunities and solutions, migration planning, implementation, and architectural maintenance.

Architectural Framework

An architectural framework, in the context of this book, is a set of tools, methods, processes, and vocabulary that can be used for developing a broad range of different IT architectures. It describes a method for implementing an architecture of multiple types (technical, solution, and application, for instance), and is applicable to many different organizational types. A framework is a reasoned, cohesive, adaptable, vendor-independent, technology-independent, domain-neutral, and scalable conceptual foundation for detailed architecture representation. TOGAF, as an architectural framework, also provides foundation artifacts, such as a list of recommended standards and compliant products that can aid in starting an organization's architectural process.

Architectural Principles

In much the same way that organizations have a set of guiding principles that define the way the organization will behave, effective architectural development also relies on controlling principles. The principles set the high-level vision and goals for the architectural development and the entire IT environment. They are typically derived from organizational business and IT strategic outputs.

Architectural Tradeoff Analysis Method

ATAM, developed by the Software Engineering Institute, defines a structured technique for understanding the tradeoffs inherent in the architectures of software-intensive systems. Primarily, this is a technique used to analyze application architectures, however, it is also useful for performing a similar analysis on solution and technical architectures. ATAM makes considerable use of architectural views (as does TOGAF).

Architectural Views

Views are different slices through an architecture. Each view type embodies a different perspective of the architecture, therefore allowing for a complete architectural analysis. Views are used as a method of cross-checking an architecture to ensure that it meets all aspects of the computational needs that will be imposed on it. Typical views include communications, security, data, computing, user interface, functional, and builders.

Critical Success Factors

A fundamental aspect of the definition of organizational strategy (both technical and business) is the establishment of vision, goals, principles, and objectives. Planning processes can throw up a significant number of these factors. However, the CSFs are a subset of these defined factors that must go well for the organization to succeed. CSFs are actively measured by the organization.

Enterprise Continuum

The TOGAF enterprise continuum collects together the architectural and solutions continua.

Enterprise IT Architecture

The collection of strategic disciplines that encompass the information, business system, and technical architectures.

Foundation Architecture

As part of TOGAF, The Open Group has provided a structurally complete foundation architecture. The foundation architecture contributes a reference model, a service taxonomy, and a list of compliant products and technologies (personified in the standards information base). Although it is a concrete manifestation of the TOGAF framework, its foundation aspects come from its generic composition. It captures a basic structure applicable to many organizations' IT environments and as such can be used as (a) a starting point for the definition of the organization-specific architecture, and (b) an immediate communications and education tool for technical architecture. The TOGAF foundation standards information base is synonymous with the open systems movement.

Gap Analysis

Gap analysis is a general technique for the discovery of gaps that may have resulted during the planning of a transition between an initial state and a target state so that these gaps can be cognitively handled. Gap analysis can use complex mathematics or, as we do in this book, simple matrices to identify gaps.

Governance

Generically, IT governance can be defined as a structure of relationships and processes to direct and control the enterprise to achieve the enterprise's goals by adding value while balancing risk versus return over IT and its processes. Specifically, architectural governance provides the processes, policy, and implementation to reduce the instance of architecture drift, ensuring that the organization continues to support and maintain the architectural vision.

Information Systems Strategic Plan
The ISSP is the organization's strategic plan for IT and the IT group, and hence its subject areas are typical of a general strategic plan. The ISSP will usually be developed at a point in time and will guide the IT organization over a medium- to long-term period. There is overlap between the contents of an ISSP and the enterprise architectures. The enterprise architecture is typically continuously maintained and usually embodies the spirit of the ISSP. The ISSP will set constraints (financial, resource, and political) on the succeeding architectures.

Key Questions List
The KQL is a TOGAF artifact, specifically in the requirements traceability area. The key question list is a set of qualitative and quantitative questions posed at the emerging architecture to test its adherence to requirements.

Open Standards
Whereas a standard can refer to any type of technology that an organization mandates usage of in policy, an *open standard* is commonly used in a wider context. Open standards typically refer to specifications that have been developed in an environment of consensus that are "freely" available for vendors to implement. The degree of openness can be judged by the level of consensus and the availability of the specification. Generically, open standards have the objective of increasing the likelihood of interoperability, portability, and scalability.

Policy
Policies are the nontechnical artifacts that support the governance of the architecture. Policy defines the mandatory rules of the architecture. It sets down necessary guidelines to aid in the interpretation and implementation of the architecture. Policy can be used as an adjunct to a technology service (such as a security policy), as a set of requirements on IT projects (such as platform qualities), or as a process (such as product selection).

Platform, the
The platform is central to the TOGAF concept of architecture. The platform collects all of the key services defined in the architecture so that they are available in the infrastructure for use by individual business

systems. Services that exist in the platform represent technologies that are proven to be both generic and commodity. Generally, technologies begin as application-specific, and as they become increasingly accepted and implemented, they can move into the platform. Once in the platform they are in the realm of the technical architecture (not the application architecture).

Requirements Traceability

Requirements traceability is another central theme of TOGAF. Each stage of TOGAF's ADM stresses the need to review the stage's outputs with the established requirements. Gap analysis is a technique used to support traceability analysis.

Services

A service is a bundle of related functionalities that is provided in some way to a client (in this context, a client refers to a business system or components of a business system). However, a specialization of this concept is the notion of a platform service. Platform services are the crux of the organization's technical architecture and hence technical infrastructure. They define the functions that the IT environment will provide all corporate applications. For functionality bundles to be called a platform service they must;

- Be generic, environment-centered, and usable by cross-domain business applications
- Be accessed through a published and stable interface
- Be replaceable by other implementations, as long as the interface is preserved
- Meet service quality requirements
- Meet an organization's architectural principles
- Not implement organization-specific or domain-specific functionalities

The architectural framework supports the definition of any type of service, provided it adheres to service characteristics. TOGAF provides a set of foundation services grouped into categories; however, an organization may extend, remove, and add whatever services are required for the "platform" to support the organization's requirements. Services need not be implemented in technology but can consist completely of policy elements such as the service-quality service.

Service Portfolio

The service portfolio is the collection of all services, and their implementations, that make up the organization's IT environment (or, in other words, the platform).

Super Services

Super services are a specialization of the TOGAF notion of a service (i.e., they adhere to the characteristics of a service). Super services provide a mechanism for collecting together individual services (or whole service categories) into a service of services. Super services are designed to conceptually represent the way in which contemporary technologies are bundled by vendors into product suites. For instance, modern application servers bundle a number of the foundation services, providing access to the bundle by "simpler" interfaces. In a service hierarchy, super services are close to the application and tend to encapsulate more basic (or the foundation) services.

Solutions Architecture

Solutions architecture is a particular instance of an architecture that deals with the design of multisystem solutions. Typically, a solutions architecture is required to bring together a number of different application architectures to solve a business problem.

Solutions Continuum

The solutions continuum is a component of the enterprise continuum. It represents the physical implementations of the architectures at the corresponding levels of the architectural continuum. At each level, the solutions continuum populates the architecture with purchased products or built components that represent a solution to the organization's business need expressed at that level. A populated solutions continuum can be regarded as a systems inventory or reuse library.

Standards

Standards have both an organizational meaning and a meaning in the wider context of the IT industry. Organizational standards represent those specifications, technologies, and products that are mandated within the IT environment. IT industry standards are commonly accepted (de facto) or open specifications, technologies, and products.

Standards Information Base

The SIB is the collection of the organization's technology standards aligned to the organizational service taxonomy. TOGAF provides an SIB based on the foundation taxonomy. TOGAF does not mandate this SIB; it may be adopted, used as a basis, or discarded altogether.

Technical Reference Model

The TRM simply provides a visual representation of all of the technical functions (or services to use the TOGAF vocabulary) of the "foundation"—in a TOGAF sense—IT environment. TOGAF proposes a simplistic graphic representing the foundation architecture. However, the visual representation of an organization's architecture is not fixed to this graphic. The representation of service graphically can be used also to show the makeup of individual services or services within services (known as subservices). It is a useful communications tool in each sense.

TOGAF Taxonomy

The TOGAF taxonomy defines terminology and provides a coherent description of the components and conceptual structure of an IT environment and its set of services. The aim of the TOGAF taxonomy is to provide a core classification (or vocabulary) that provides a useful, consistent, structured definition of the application platform entity and is widely acceptable. The TOGAF taxonomy is depicted graphically by the technical reference model.

Index

A

A5 interoperability, 180
ADM, 80, 86,
    baseline description phase, 90, 123
    implementation phase, 90, 393
    initiation and framework phase, 89, 95
    maintenance phase, 90, 399
    migration planning phase, 90, 372
    opportunities and solutions phase, 90,
       361
    target architecture phase, 90, 197
Analytical Solution Forum (ASF), 83
Application architecture, 4, 17, 126, 396
Application platform. *see Platform*
Architectural advocates, 422
Architectural building blocks, 309
Architectural capability, 403, 422
Architectural compliance, 406, 411, 426
Architectural constraints, 200, 204
Architectural continuum, 81, 265
Architectural contract, 395
Architectural development method. *See* ADM
Architectural drift, 392, 401
    management-inspired drift, 409
    project-inspired drift, 409
Architectural framework, 9, 77
Architectural governance, 40, 406
Architectural influences, 2
Architectural maintenance, 62
Architectural policy, 370
Architectural principles, 105, 205, 294
Architectural projects, types of, 394
Architectural research, 405
Architectural roadmap, 385
Architectural skills, 425
Architectural stagnation, 420
Architectural statement of work, 156

Architectural tradeoff analysis method,
    154, 403
Architectural views, 151, 166, 211
Architectural work packages, 369
Architecture by,
    checkbook, 8
    integration, 12
    product, 11
    specifications, 9
Architecture principles, 205
Architecture, definition, 1
Asimov's *Foundation* novels, 373
Association for the Advancement of Cost
    Engineering (ACCE), 375

B

B2B, 246
Bennis, Benne, and Chin, 366
BIZTalk Consortium, 331
Booch, Rumbaugh, and Jacobson, 3
Builders view, 151
Building blocks, 125, 129, 199
Business architecture document, 124
Business function clustering, 60
Business process domain view, 169,
Business strategy, 104
Business systems architecture, 4, 16, 25,
    54, 152
Business/strategic drivers, 98

C

C4ISR, 77
CBA, 376
    discounted value, 381
    estimation of benefits, 379
    indirect costs, 379

process, 377
sensitivity analysis, 381
CFL, 66
    Application and infrastructure
        portfolio, 67
    IT goals, 72
    IT strategic plan, 71
    Technical architecture, 74
    The Open Group Architectural
        Framework, 74
Chandler, Ansoff, and Andrews, 43
Change management, 364, 371
Change management, framework, 365
Client/server model, 140, 187
COCOMO, 378
Codd, Edgar, 182
COM, 191, 245, 275, 278
Common off the Shelf, 143
Common systems architecture, 82, 272
Communications view, 191
Computing view, 151, 187
Constraint satisfaction problems, 204
CORBA, 83, 191, 274
Corporate data model, 55
COSMIC-FFP, 378
Cost-benefit analysis. *See* CBA
Critical success factors, 44, 52
Crunchy Frog Ltd. *See* CFL
CSF. *See* Critical success factors

D

Data dictionary, 55, 185
Data intensive systems, 179
Data interchange services, 145
Data management services, 138, 146, 214
Data management view, 182
Data security, 186
Data warehousing, 265
Data Warehousing Institute (DWI), 395
DBMS, 182
Denial of service attacks, 27
Defense Information Systems Agency, 79
Development approaches, 177
Dijkstra, 3
Distributed computing, 271
Distributed Management Task Force, 331
Distributed object model, 190
Distributed security context, 174
DNS, 323

E

Earl, 48
e-business, 27, 35, 36, 37, 63, 126, 219,
    258, 332
e-commerce, 27, 64
EDIFACT, 135
Electronic Industry Association, 282
E-mail viruses, 27
Enterprise application integration, 84, 246
Enterprise continuum, 80, 265
Enterprise information technology
    architecture, 4
Enterprise IT architecture, 12
Erosion. *See* Architectural drift
Example-baseline
    current system assessment, 163
    e-business, 157, 162
    intersystem interfaces, 161
    logistics system, 159
    native views, 157
    network, 157
    plan to capture current system
        information, 156
    regional IT environment, 162
    sales system, 159
Example-current systems in TOGAF format
    assess CFL's systems, 227
    catalogue of services, 231
    gap analysis, 231
    Key question list, 237
    SIB, 231
Example-definition
    B2B Commerce Functionality, 352
    B2B super service, 356
    enterprise application integration
        functionality, 354
    policy initiatives, 355
    selection criteria, 352
    service data interchange SIB, 358
    service instance maps, 355
    SIB, 356
    strategies for realizing services, 351
    TRM, 351
Example-governance
    architecture control service, 428
Example-implementation
    architectural maintenance and
        governance process, 414
    EAI integration project contract, 415

Example-initiation and framework
    architectural principles, 114
    business strategy, 113
    business systems architecture, 113
    information architecture, 115
    ISSP, 113
Example-migration planning
    CBA, 389
    prioritization analysis, 390
    work package clustering, 387
Example-opportunities
    change model, 386
    work packages, 387
Example-service portfolio
    CMA information exchange model, 304
    common systems, 300
    confectionary manufacturers
      association, 301
    CORBA, 302
    EAI (super) service, 303
    foundation service portfolio, 300
    gap analysis, 306
    PKI, 302
    RosettaNet, 301
    systems management service, 302
    TRM, 306, 305
Example-Super Services
    B2B Commerce Service, 251
    B2B functionality, 251
    RossettaNet, 251
eXtreme programming, 396

F

Federated naming API, 323
Finkelstein, 44
Foundation architecture, 81, 136, 144, 269
Function point analysis, 378
Functional decomposition, 57
Functional view, 151, 171
Functionality table, 340

G

Gap analysis, 82, 90, 93, 200, 215, 220, 297,
    348, 368
    Gap Method, 260
    Gap Model, 259
Gartner Group, 30, 80, 424
Godel's theorem, 201

GOSIP, 9
Graphics and imaging services, 146

H

Health Level 7, 282

I

IEEE, 4, 140, 331
IEEE Open System Environment, 263
IEEE P1471, 154
IETF, 11, 331
Industry-specific architecture, 82, 260
Information architecture, 4, 15, 25, 53, 152
Information intensive systems, 179
Information Management Associates
    (IMA), 84
Information systems strategic plan. *see* ISSP
International operation, 270
International operation services, 146
Interoperability, 139, 332
ISO, 4, 331
ISSP, 12, 46, 77, 104, 217, 294
    ISSP methods, 49
IT architecture. *See* Technical architecture
IT governance, 109, 406, 425
    architectural governance model, 425
    architectural governance process, 411
    architecture steering group, 427
    architecture board, 111
    monitoring and feedback, 426
    technical advisor, 424
IT Governance Institute, 110, 407
    COBIT framework, 425
    COBIT Management Guidelines, 407
IT projects, common themes, 38
IT strategic plan. *See* ISSP
Ivory tower principle, 298, 420

J

J2EE, 191, 245, 274,
JMS, 274
JTA, 274

K

Key question list, 223, 298

L

LANs, 192
LDAP, 11, 323
Location and directory services, 146

M

Management view, 151, 175,
MANs, 192
McGee and Prusak, 45

N

Native views, 134
Network services, 146, 214, 324
Non-repudiation, 207

O

Object Management Group, 83, 191, 331
Object-oriented provision of services, 271
OODBMS, 183
OOP, 178
Open Buying on the Internet (OBI), 84
Open Software Foundation. See OSF
Open standards, 315
Open Systems Interconnection. See OSI
Openness scale, 330
Operating system services, 147, 327
Opportunity identification, 363
ORB, 190, 244
Organizational architecture, 84, 214, 285
Organizational strategic planning, 43
OSF, 9, 329
OSI, 191, 193,

P

Petrotechnical Open Software
    Corporation, 282
Platform, 5, 129, 137, 262
Platform drivers, 264
Policy and guidelines, 287, 370
Policy table, 340
Politics of information, 53
Portability, 139, 331
Porter, 63
    Porter forces, 44
    Porter's framework, 44
POSIX.0, 263
Project identification, 367
Project initiation, 373, 374
Project initiation framework, 374
Project management, 373
Project prioritization, 58, 360, 371, 382
Pruzak, Devenport, and Eccles, 53
Public Key Infrastructure architecture, 279

R

Rational Unified Process, 126, 398
Remote Procedure Call, 242
Request for architecture work, 100, 199
Requirements traceability, 92, 215, 223, 259,
    296, 348
RFC, 11

S

Security association, 174
Security context, 173
Security services, 86, 147, 279
Security view, 151, 171
Services
    characteristics, 145
    instance, 313
    instance collections, 320
    instance solution map, 210, 347, 397
    notion of, 313
    portfolio, 125, 226
    portfolio, realization of, 310
    qualities, 149, 170, 269, 339
    taxonomy description, 292
    Super services, 125, 141, 241, 289,
        294, 328
SGML, 282
SIB, 80, 136, 144, 203, 209, 212, 368
    SIB lifecycle, 344
Single UNIX specification, 269, 315
SNMP, 203
Society of Automotive Engineers, 283
Software architecture, 3
Software Engineering Institute (SEI), 3, 395
Software engineering services, 147, 313, 396
Software engineering view, 175
Software portability, 178
Software tiers, 180
Solutions architecture, 127, 396
Solutions continuum, 81, 309
Specifications and products, relationship
    between, 315
Standards information base. See SIB
Standards, definition of, 327
Standish Group, 70, 97, 424
Statement of architecture work, 103, 105,
    199, 324
Sweet-spot service, 336
System and network management
    services, 148

System drift, 24
Systems engineering view *See* Computing
    View

T
TAFIM, 79
TCP/IP, 243
Technical architecture, xi, xii, xvi, 4, 16, 25,
    43, 50
    business advantages, 5
    motherhood statements, 4
Technical architecture document, 199, 220,
    227, 295, 350, 365
Technical reference model, 9, 77
Technology lifecycle, 31, 343
Technology selection criteria, 294, 342
Telecommunications Industry
    Association, 283
Terms of reference. *See* TOR
The Open Group, 101, 111, 268, 331
    Technical reference model, 187
    standards, 269, 313
TOGAF, 78, 126, 167
TOGAF platform. *see Platform*
TOGAF selection criteria, 222
TOGAF taxonomy, 136,
TOGAF terms, 127, 136,
TOGAF vocabulary, 86, 137

TOR, 100, 106, 156
Total cost management framework, 375
Total cost of ownership, 108, 220, 377
Transaction Processing Performance
    Council, 202
Transaction processing services, 147
TRM, 80, 86, 137
    graphic, 291

U
U.S. Department of Defense, 77
UNIX, 268
User interface services, 147
User view, 151, 186

W
WANs, 192
Workflow Management Coalition
    (WfMC), 289

X
X.400, 193
X.500, 10, 193
X/Open, 9, 329
XA Reference Model, 278
XML, 132, 248, 282
XSL, 132